I0888017

The Transformation of Global Trade in a New World

Bartolomé Marco-Lajara
University of Alicante, Spain

Ahu Coşkun Özer
Marmara University, Turkey

Javier Martínez Falcó
University of Alicante, Spain

A volume in the Advances in Business Strategy and Competitive Advantage (ABSCA) Book Series

IGI Global
PUBLISHER of TIMELY KNOWLEDGE

Published in the United States of America by
IGI Global
Business Science Reference (an imprint of IGI Global)
701 E. Chocolate Avenue
Hershey PA, USA 17033
Tel: 717-533-8845
Fax: 717-533-8661
E-mail: cust@igi-global.com
Web site: http://www.igi-global.com

Library of Congress Cataloging-in-Publication Data

Names: Marco Lajara, Bartolomé, editor. | Ozer, Ahu Coskun, DATE- editor. | Martinez Falcó, Javier, 1997- editor.
Title: The transformation of global trade in a new world / Bartolomé Marco-Lajara, Ahu Coskun Ozer, and Javier Martinez Falcó, editors.
Description: Hershey, PA : Business Science Reference, [2023] | Includes bibliographical references. | Summary: "With the asymmetric impact of the coronavirus on international trade and the methods of entry into foreign markets, together with the future prospects of global trade in an era of globalization, this book addresses topics on the field of International business and internationalization"-- Provided by publisher.
Identifiers: LCCN 2022031074 (print) | LCCN 2022031075 (ebook) | ISBN 9781668459508 (hardcover) | ISBN 9781668459546 (paperback) | ISBN 9781668459515 (ebook)
Subjects: LCSH: International trade. | COVID-19 Pandemic, 2020---Economic aspects. | Globalization.
Classification: LCC HF1379 .T744 2023 (print) | LCC HF1379 (ebook) | DDC 382/.3--dc23/eng/20220805
LC record available at https://lccn.loc.gov/2022031074
LC ebook record available at https://lccn.loc.gov/2022031075

This book is published in the IGI Global book series Advances in Business Strategy and Competitive Advantage (ABSCA) (ISSN: 2327-3429; eISSN: 2327-3437)

British Cataloguing in Publication Data
A Cataloguing in Publication record for this book is available from the British Library.

Advances in Business Strategy and Competitive Advantage (ABSCA) Book Series

ISSN:2327-3429
EISSN:2327-3437

Editor-in-Chief: Patricia Ordóñez de Pablos, Universidad de Oviedo, Spain

MISSION

Business entities are constantly seeking new ways through which to gain advantage over their competitors and strengthen their position within the business environment. With competition at an all-time high due to technological advancements allowing for competition on a global scale, firms continue to seek new ways through which to improve and strengthen their business processes, procedures, and profitability.

The **Advances in Business Strategy and Competitive Advantage (ABSCA) Book Series** is a timely series responding to the high demand for state-of-the-art research on how business strategies are created, implemented and re-designed to meet the demands of globalized competitive markets. With a focus on local and global challenges, business opportunities and the needs of society, the **ABSCA** encourages scientific discourse on doing business and managing information technologies for the creation of sustainable competitive advantage.

COVERAGE

- Resource-Based Competition
- Economies of Scale
- Adaptive Enterprise
- Value Creation
- Small and Medium Enterprises
- Cost Leadership Strategy
- Strategic Alliances
- Balanced Scorecard
- Outsourcing
- Strategic Management

IGI Global is currently accepting manuscripts for publication within this series. To submit a proposal for a volume in this series, please contact our Acquisition Editors at Acquisitions@igi-global.com or visit: http://www.igi-global.com/publish/.

The Advances in Business Strategy and Competitive Advantage (ABSCA) Book Series (ISSN 2327-3429) is published by IGI Global, 701 E. Chocolate Avenue, Hershey, PA 17033-1240, USA, www.igi-global.com. This series is composed of titles available for purchase individually; each title is edited to be contextually exclusive from any other title within the series. For pricing and ordering information please visit http://www.igi-global.com/book-series/advances-business-strategy-competitive-advantage/73672. Postmaster: Send all address changes to above address.

Titles in this Series

For a list of additional titles in this series, please visit:
http://www.igi-global.com/book-series/advances-business-strategy-competitive-advantage/73672

Exploring the Economic Opportunities and Impacts of Migrant Entrepreneurship Success Stories and Case Studies
Meena Chavan (Macquarie University, Australia) and Sheba Nandkeolyar (Multiconnexions, Australia)
Business Science Reference • © 2022 • 231pp • H/C (ISBN: 9781668449868) • US $215.00

Analyzing the Relationship Between Corporate Governance, CSR, and Sustainability
Ayberk Soyer (Istanbul Technical University, Turkey) and Umut Asan (Istanbul Technical University, Turkey)
Business Science Reference • © 2022 • 315pp • H/C (ISBN: 9781799842347) • US $215.00

Handbook of Research on Digital Innovation and Networking in Post-COVID-19 Organizations
Ana Pego (Nova University of Lisbon, Portugal)
Business Science Reference • © 2022 • 539pp • H/C (ISBN: 9781668467626) • US $315.00

Antecedents and Outcomes of Employee-Based Brand Equity
Muhammad Waseem Bari (Government College University, Faisalabad, Pakistan) Muhammad Abrar (Government College University, Faisalabad, Pakistan) and Emilia Alaverdov (Tbilisi State University, Georgia)
Business Science Reference • © 2022 • 297pp • H/C (ISBN: 9781668436219) • US $250.00

Cases on Emerging Market Responses to the COVID-19 Pandemic
Raj K. Kovid (Sharda University, India) and Vikas Kumar (Central University of Haryana, India)
Business Science Reference • © 2022 • 332pp • H/C (ISBN: 9781668435045) • US $240.00

Impact of Digital Transformation on the Development of New Business Models and Consumer Experience

For an entire list of titles in this series, please visit:
http://www.igi-global.com/book-series/advances-business-strategy-competitive-advantage/73672

IGI Global
PUBLISHER of TIMELY KNOWLEDGE

701 East Chocolate Avenue, Hershey, PA 17033, USA
Tel: 717-533-8845 x100 • Fax: 717-533-8661
E-Mail: cust@igi-global.com • www.igi-global.com

Editorial Advisory Board

Table of Contents

Detailed Table of Contents

Spain is in a privileged position in the production and marketing of wine, being the world leader in terms of volume of wine exported. It is also the country where exports have grown the most since 1990, as companies have been pushed to increase their foreign exposure by the decline in domestic consumption and more recently by the financial crisis. The present research contributes to the literature on the international wine trade, given that, to the authors' knowledge, no previous research has so recently addressed the export intensity of Spanish wines by autonomous communities, as well as the geographical destinations of these exports. The results show a clear heterogeneity in value and volume between the different Spanish territories when it comes to marketing wine, revealing two competitive models in the Spanish wine industry: cost leadership (focused on volume) and differentiation (focused on quality).

This chapter investigates whether the institutional environment that the firms operate has an impact on their leverage choice. Namely, rule of law is used as an institutional variable. Considering that better implementation of rule of law impacts positively firms' export performance, total exports in each country are also used as the other main explanatory variable. The findings show that both institutional variables and exports negatively and significantly affect the leverage level. This implies that firms in favorable institutional environment tend to borrow less, which results with lower leverage. Moreover, this study finds that the COVID-19 pandemic period as an unprecedented shock to economies pushed the leverage levels higher. Regarding the implications of the findings, firms' capacity to access external finance especially during a significant crisis period depends on the institutional environment. Namely, the effective implementation of rule of law should be first priority for the policy makers.

Governments and corporations with the obstinacy to operate on a global scale can engage in international trade. Even today's global economy relies on the interdependence between nations. The South Asian region's connectivity can only be improved by enhancing intra-regional commerce. The present study is based on the global trade and economic crisis from the perspective of SAARC nations. In the current study, an effort has been made to examine the export, import, economic growth, and links between global trades for SAARC nations from 1990 to 2021. The analysis's findings suggest that the GDP, imports, and exports are growing in a cyclical pattern. The Granger causality result suggests that there are unidirectional and bidirectional causal relationships between world trade and country GDP development as well as within nations in the case of GDP growth. Therefore, the authors draw the conclusion that the key cause of the economic crisis in SAARC nations is global trade.

By the end of May 2022 according to the data, the number of cases increased to 530 million, the number of virus-related deaths increased to 6.3 million, and the CFR decreased to 1.18 with the increase in vaccination. The full vaccination rate increased to 60% at the end of May. It should not be overlooked that vaccination is 18% in Africa and 11.8% in low-income countries. The global output GDP will be 99.4 trillion dollars in 2022 and 147 trillion dollars in 2035. It is also clearly seen that China will surpass the USA in national income at current prices in 2028. It is estimated that global imports will reach 23.5 trillion dollars in 2022 and 36.6 trillion dollars in 2035. It is expected that the chemicals and chemical products industry will be at the top with imports of 6.1 trillion dollars in 2022 and 9.5 trillion dollars in 2035 and is accounted for 25.3% of global imports in 2021. It is estimated that this rate will increase to 28.8% in 2035. Hong Kong is at the top with the Trade Openness Index value of 4.06 in 2022 and 4.5 in 2035.

Considering that approximately 80% of the goods subject to trade are transported by sea, it becomes clear how important the role of maritime transport in the supply chain is. Especially during the COVID-19 pandemic, the delivery of products for basic needs such as food and health to the delivery places has revealed the importance of maritime transportation for combating the pandemic. Among the most important factors of maritime transport are seafarers who play a role in the operation and management of ships. During the COVID-19 pandemic, the closure of the borders of the countries or the quarantine practices created troubles in the embarkation and disembarkation of seafarers. In the study, it was emphasized that seafarers should be considered as "key workers" considering their essential role in the transport of vital goods such as medical supplies and food. In addition, the strategic factors that should be applied to ensure the professional sustainability of seafarers during pandemic periods were also mentioned.

The outbreak of global health and, consequently, the economic crisis caused by the COVID-19 pandemic interrupted five years of positive economic trends in Serbia. To preserve economic stability, the government of Serbia took appropriate measures and provided support to micro, small, and medium enterprises. The chapter aims to evaluate the packages of economic measures introduced to reduce the negative consequences caused by the pandemic. The research covers the period from 2015 to 2022 (i.e., before and during the crisis and after the adopted economic measures). The analysis is based on officially adopted economic measures with a combination of macroeconomic statistical data and forecasts from the Ministry of Finance of the Republic of Serbia and the Fiscal Council of the Republic of Serbia. The results of the research indicate that the crisis caused by the COVID-19 virus did not cause a significant drop in economic activity in the Republic of Serbia, primarily due to the extensive package of aid to the economy, which amounted to 12.5% of GDP.

COVID-19 has reduced international joint ventures. However, most of the organizations across the world have adopted deglobalization, and it has aided in facing the problems of natural disasters and other challenges. Thus, with globalization and internationalization reduced, organizations are focused on the domestic markets for the investment and manufacturing process. This chapter highlights deglobalization. International trade is also one of the expected survivor tools of the current pandemic situation, but due to COVID-19, it has depreciated, and people have started to believe in deglobalization, which has increased the value of domestic markets. Further, this chapter discusses the risk of deglobalization in the world economy and the consequences of deglobalization on international trade post COVID-19.

After three decades of disintegration of the former Union of Soviet Socialist Republics (USSR) and former socialist nations from the Eastern Bloc, the burning issue related to apparent success or failure of globalization and economic transition still persists. This chapter is aimed at formulation of Index of Economic Foundation (IEF) that would help to assess the impact of globalization on a country and how far it has been successful in adapting the model of market economy. In order to serve the purpose, a time series study has been conducted on 10 sample countries spread across Central and Eastern Europe and the independent nation-states that evolved from the disintegration of erstwhile USSR for the time period of 20 years (1996 – 2015) (Base Year = 1995: IEF = 100). The final estimations based on the estimated Present Values (PV) of IEFs' discounted by the values of Gini Coefficient (GIC) on a year-to-year basis for all the sample countries yielded interesting results and findings. The issues of deglobalization and reglobalization were also discussed in reference to year 2020.

Preface

The COVID-19 pandemic has adversely affected global trade. While factories have stopped production worldwide due to COVID-19, global trade has also been adversely affected by the pandemic. The international trade of the world's top exporting countries has begun to decline. Although it is too early to judge the impact of the pandemic on world trade, as the virus has not yet been eradicated, research into the cause-effect relationship between these two phenomena is necessary to understand the magnitude of its impact as well as possible solutions to the problem.

The Transformation of Global Trade in a New World provides relevant theoretical frameworks and the latest findings in the field of international business and internationalization. It addresses the asymmetric impact of the COVID-19 pandemic on international trade and the methods of entry into foreign markets together with the future prospects of global trade in an era of globalization. Covering topics such as economic crisis and its effect on countries' international trade, the effect of global trade on corporate cash policy, the impact of Covid-19 on sustainability, impacts on economic foundations on globalization, and internalization of the wine industry in the world. This premier reference source is an excellent resource for business leaders and executives, economists, logistics professionals, sociologists, students and faculty of higher education, librarians, researchers, and academicians.

Bartolomé Marco-Lajara, Patrocinio Zaragoza-Sáez, Javier Martínez Falcó, and Luis A. Millan-Tudela analyze the wine export intensity of Spain's autonomous communities in the chapter titled 'The Export Intensity of Spain's Autonomous Communities in Terms of the Marketing of Wine and Their Geographical Destinations'. Authors state that "The results show a clear heterogeneity in value and volume between the different Spanish territories when it comes to marketing wine, revealing two competitive models in the Spanish wine industry: cost leadership (focused on volume) and differentiation (focused on quality)."

The chapter titled 'The Internationalization of the Spanish Wine Industry: An Analysis of Trade Flows and Their Degree of Concentration' written by Bartolomé

Marco-Lajara, Patrocinio Zaragoza-Sáez, Javier Martínez Falcó, and Eduardo Sánchez-García evaluates the internalization of Spanish wine industry. Authors state that "The Spanish wine industry is a world leader in terms of wine exports by volume and third in terms of the value of these exports, behind only France and Italy. Spanish wine is therefore present in the world's main wine-consuming markets, contributing to the maintenance and even improvement of the Spain brand on an international scale. Research results show that for the last decade Spain has had a surplus in the wine trade balance of more than 2,000 million euros per year, and more than 80% of the wineries export on a regular basis, with a high concentration of large wineries."

Hasan Tekin, Hidayet Zahid Gürbüz and Saim Kayadibi analyze the influence of geopolitical risk (GPR) and global trade on cash holdings with the existence of the global financial crisis 2008-2009 (GFC) for 11,960 non-financial firms in 18 markets from 2002 to 2017, in the chapter titled 'How Do Geopolitical Risk and Global Trade Shape Corporate Cash Policy? Evidence From the Financial Crisis of 2008-2009'. Authors state that "Findings show that firms in countries with higher GPR and lower trade volume have higher cash balances confirming the predictions of the precautionary motive of cash. Investors should consider countries' financial crises and GPR in specifying where and which firms to invest in."

The chapter titled 'Rule of Law, International Trade, and Corporate Financing Decisions in Europe: Evidence From the COVID-19 Pandemic' written by Ali Yavuz Polat evaluates the institutional environment in which the firms operate has an impact on their leverage choice. According to Polat, better implementation of rule of law impacts positively firms' export performance. Polat states, "Regarding the implications of the findings, firms' capacity to access external finance, especially during significant crisis periods depends on the institutional environment. The effective implementation of rule of law should be the first priority for the policymakers."

The chapter titled 'Global Trade and Economic Crisis: Trade Between South Asian Countries' written by Tanushree Gupta, Disha Sharma and Susobhan Maiti, evaluates the relationship between South Asia Countries' export, import, and world trade. The authors state, "The analysis's findings suggest that the GDP, imports, and exports are growing in a cyclical pattern. Result suggests that there are unidirectional and bidirectional causal relationships between world trade and GDP development of South Asian Countries, so the key cause of the economic crisis in SAARC nations is global trade."

Özlem Özsoy and Metin Gürler evaluate the effect of COVID-19 on global trade in their chapter 'COVID-19 Effect on Global Trade in the Post-Pandemic Period: Forecast Analysis of Global GDP and Trade a Decade After 2025', authors state that "According to the IMF and World bank data, the global output GDP will be 99.4 trillion dollars in 2022 and 147 trillion dollars in 2035. It is also clearly seen that China will surpass the USA in national income at current prices in 2028. It is estimated that global imports will reach 23.5 trillion dollars in 2022 and 36.6 trillion dollars in 2035. It is expected that the 'Chemicals and chemical products industry will be at the top with imports of 6.1 trillion dollars in 2022 and 9.5 trillion dollars in 2035 and is accounted for 25.3% of global imports in 2021, it is estimated that this rate will increase to 28.8% in 2035. Hong Kong is at the top with the "Trade Openness Index" value of 4.06 in 2022 and 4.5 in 2035."

Osman Arslan evaluates the effect of COVID-19 on the maritime labor force in the chapter titled 'The Impact of COVID-19 on the Sustainability of the Maritime Labor Force'. Author states, "Considering that approximately 80% of the goods subject to trade are transported by sea, it becomes clear how important the role of maritime transport in the supply chain is. During the Covid-19 pandemic, the closure of the borders of the countries or the quarantine practices created troubles in the embarkation and disembarkation of seafarers. It is important that seafarers should be considered as 'key workers'."

The chapter titled 'Economic Measures for Mitigation of the Consequences of COVID-19: Evidence From Serbia', written by Darko Marjanović and Ivana Domazet evaluate the economic measures introduced to reduce the negative consequences of the pandemic. The authors state that "The results of the research indicate that the crisis caused by the COVID-19 virus did not cause a significant drop in economic activity in the Republic of Serbia, primarily due to the extensive package of aid to the economy, which amounted to 12.5% of GDP."

Reenu Kumari and Ashwani Sharma evaluate the globalization and deglobalization process in the chapter titled 'The Transformation of Global Trade in a New World: Deglobalization and Its Risk in International Trade Post COVID-19'. Authors state that "International trade is also one of the expected survivor tools of the current epidemic situation but due to the COVID-19 it was depreciated and people started believing in de-globalization which increased the value of domestic markets."

Debasish Roy explains the formulation of the Index of Economic Foundation (IEF) and analyzes the impact of economic foundations on globalization in 10 Central-Eastern Europe countries by using IEF, in the chapter titled 'Impacts on Economic Foundations During Globalization: A Cross-Country Empirical Study'. Roy states, "A summarized view of the results and findings projects the holistic picture that 9 out of 10 sample countries that embraced the transition from planned to market economy failed to mitigate the adverse effects of globalization, especially in the benchmark year of 2020; mainly due to unequal distribution of income and wealth among the poor."

Preface

The scientific production compiled in this book provides an understanding of the transformations of international trade in the new globalized and competitive world. This book is a premier reference source and comprises the original and current researches about issues on international trade.

Bartolomé Marco-Lajara
University of Alicante, Spain

Ahu Coşkun Özer
Marmara University, Turkey

Javier Martínez Falcó
University of Alicante, Spain

Chapter 1
The Export Intensity of Spain's Autonomous Communities in Terms of the Marketing of Wine and Their Geographical Destinations

Bartolomé Marco-Lajara
https://orcid.org/0000-0001-8811-9118
University of Alicante, Spain

Javier Martínez-Falcó
https://orcid.org/0000-0001-9004-5816
University of Alicante, Spain

Patrocinio Zaragoza-Sáez
University of Alicante, Spain

Luis A. Millan-Tudela
https://orcid.org/0000-0003-3669-9960
University of Alicante, Spain

ABSTRACT

Spain is in a privileged position in the production and marketing of wine, being the world leader in terms of volume of wine exported. It is also the country where exports have grown the most since 1990, as companies have been pushed to increase their foreign exposure by the decline in domestic consumption and more recently by the financial crisis. The present research contributes to the literature on the international wine trade, given that, to the authors' knowledge, no previous research has so recently addressed the export intensity of Spanish wines by autonomous communities, as well as the geographical destinations of these exports. The results show a clear heterogeneity in value and volume between the different Spanish territories when it comes to marketing wine, revealing two competitive models in

DOI: 10.4018/978-1-6684-5950-8.ch001

the Spanish wine industry: cost leadership (focused on volume) and differentiation (focused on quality).

INTRODUCTION

Spain is in a privileged position in the production and marketing of wine, being the world leader in terms of volume of wine exported. It is also the country where exports have grown the most since 1990, as companies have been pushed to increase their foreign exposure by the decline in domestic consumption and more recently by the financial crisis. In recent years, Spanish wineries have shown that they know how to take advantage of the opportunities of an increasingly globalized environment to position their products abroad, thus compensating for the weakening of domestic consumption and making exports their main growth driver (AFI, 2020).

Indications of origin, such as Protected Designations of Origin (PDO) or Protected Geographical Indications (PGI), are particularly present in this sector and have been used both to guarantee consumers a more or less constant level of quality and to try to differentiate themselves. In addition, these figures encourage the organization of the production sector and facilitate producers' access to national and international markets. However, in Spain only approximately half of the wine produced belongs to one of these figures, the rest of the wine produced does not have any type of indication of origin.

The winemaking process is a complex process that involves different actors and consists of several stages starting with the harvesting of the grapes in the vineyards. In Spain, this takes place in the months of September and October. Once the grapes are transferred to the wineries, the destemming process begins to separate the grapes from the bunches and the grapes are crushed to extract the must. With the must and the remains of the grapes, the first fermentation and maceration begins for 6-10 days during which the sugar in the must is converted into alcohol, the remains of the grapes are then discarded and the wine is transferred to another tank for a second fermentation for 10-20 days to remove acidity from the wine. Additionally, in some wines, after the racking, clarification and filtration processes (used to clean and improve the quality of the wine), an ageing or maturing process may begin in the barrel for subsequent bottling.

Throughout history, the wealth of the wine-growing areas is reflected in palaces and stately homes, in churches and monasteries, in literature, sculpture and painting, in the architecture of the wineries themselves, and in the development of ancillary trades and businesses such as coopers, tanners, nurseries, etc., as well as in the development of the wine-making trades, sculpture and painting, in the architecture of the wineries themselves, as well as in the development of auxiliary trades and businesses, such as coopers, tanners, nurseries and so on. This fact, adapted to modern times, can still be seen in such phenomena as wineries with unique architecture built by renowned architects, the development of wine museums, the development of ancillary services companies, from those producing bottles or oenological products to those building the tanks, presses and other equipment in the winery, presses and other oenological equipment, or those involved in everything related to vineyards, among many others. Therefore, not only does the wine industry make an important contribution to economic welfare, but it also contributes to the maintenance of the heritage, the environment and the society in which the operations take place (Marco-Lajara et al., 2022a; Marco-Lajara et al., 2022b; Marco-Lajara et al., 2022c; Marco-Lajara et al., 2022d; Marco-Lajara et al., 2022e;Marco-Lajara et al., 2022f; Marco-Lajara et al., 2022g; Marco-Lajara et al., 2022h; Marco-Lajara et al., 2022i; Marco-Lajara et al., 2022j; Marco-Lajara et al., 2022k; Marco-Lajara et al., 2022l; Seva-Larrosa et al., 2022).

What is the export intensity of Spanish territories? To which continents are Spanish wine exports directed? Which are the main importing countries of Spanish wine? These are the questions that the chapter aims to answer, providing new knowledge in the field of the international trade of Spanish wine. This chapter is, therefore, of great relevance, as it allows us to analyze the export intensity of the wineries located in the different autonomous communities, serving as a reference for those academics who wish to analyze the export asymmetry between the different autonomous communities that make up Spain. Moreover, given the novelty of the results, the research serves to analyze the evolution of Spanish wine trade abroad after the impact of COVID-19 on international trade, given that, as pointed out by several scholars, the wine industry was not immune to the impact of the pathogen (Marco-Lajara et al., 2021a; Marco-Lajara et al., 2021b). The study, therefore, also provides insight into the degree of internationalization of Spanish wineries and, therefore, their competitiveness vis-à-vis Old and New World wineries. In addition, the research analyses the destination of Spanish wine exports, both by continent and by country, making it possible to identify Spain's priority trading partners in terms of wine marketing.

The research is therefore motivated by three premises. Firstly, the Spanish wine sector occupies a privileged position in the international wine trade, so it is necessary to periodically analyze its wine exports in order to know how they are evolving. Secondly, given the strategic nature of the wine industry for the Iberian country, this analysis is particularly relevant, as it allows winemakers to have an updated view of the export intensity of the different autonomous communities, as well as to know the priority destinations for Spanish wines. Thirdly, Spanish public institutions can take decisions to reshape the structure of the industry, given that, as explained above, the research allows them to know which are Spain's priority partners in terms of international wine trade, as well as the geographical areas in which Spanish wine exports can be boosted.

The research is structured as follows. After this brief introduction, Section 1 deals with the review of the literature, in which the research that has dealt with the international wine trade in the Spanish context is presented. Section 2 explains the methodology followed to carry out the study. Section 4 presents the main results. Section 5 presents the conclusions derived from the research and, finally, Section 6 explains the main limitations and future lines of research.

BACKGROUND

Research on the international wine trade has taken on its own importance in the last five years. Spain, occupying a predominant position in wine exports, has aroused the interest of different academics, both national and international. Through a study of the research indexed in the Web of Science database on the international trade of Spanish wine, the main active research fronts on international trade in the wine industry are described below.

The research analyzed has been divided into five blocks: (1) the resources and capacities that affect the internationalization of Spanish wine, (2) exports and imports of Spanish wine, (3) sustainability in the marketing of Spanish wine, (3) analysis of bilateral relations between countries in terms of the marketing of Spanish wine and (4) changes in consumption patterns and their effect on the Spanish wine trade.

In the first block of research, Castillo & Cortijo (2014) analyze the factors affecting Spanish wine imports, Garcia-Galan et al. (2014) study the influence of the Denomination of Origin (DO) on the internationalization of wine in the Iberian country, Agostino & Trivieri (2016) study quality studies in the wine industry, as well as its link with the marketing of wines, González & Dans (2018) study the associative movements and export drive, Ferrer (2021), for his part, studies the influence of the organizational capacities of Spanish wineries on internationalization processes and, finally, Fernández-Olmos et al. (2021) study the factors that affect the internationalization processes of Spanish wine.

Secondly, in the second block of research, Gómez-Bezares et al. (2008) analyze, among other aspects, exports of Rioja wine with the aim of quantifying the economic impact of the wine industry in La Rioja, Fischer & Gil-Alana (2009) address the link between tourism and exports of Spanish wine, Gil-Alana & Fischer (2010), for their part, analyze the link between tourism and imports of Spanish wine, Fernández (2012) studies Spain's specialization in the sale of bulk wine in foreign markets, Anon (2015a) studies Spanish wine exports in volume and value, Anon (2015b) studies Spanish wine exports and makes comparisons with other wine-producing countries, Rodriguez-Garcia & Vieira-Rodriguez (2017) study the international marketing of Andalusian wines, Ferrer & López (2018) analyze Spanish exports and the destination countries of these exports and, finally, Anon (2020) investigates the role of the Spanish Tempranillo grape in Spanish wine exports.

Thirdly, in the third block of research, Quintela et al. (2012) investigate the presence of the substance Ochratoxin in Spanish wine exports, Fuentes-García et al. (2015) analyze the potential markets for Spanish organic wine, Ayuda et al. (2020) address the relationship between trade and water footprint, Carrasco et al. (2021) study the carbon footprint generated by Spanish wine exports and, finally, Castillo-Valero et al. (2021) study the carbon footprint generated by Spanish wine exports.

Fourthly, in the fourth block of research, Levi & Folwell (1995) study the import of Spanish wine in the US market, Trujillo-Bolio (2013) analyze the marketing of Spanish wine in the Latin American market, Gundlach (2015) studies the German market for the marketing of Spanish wines, Martínez-Ruiz (2016) analyses the export of Spanish wine to the British market, Suay-Matallana & Guillem-Llobat (2018) study Spanish wine exports to the French market, Yujia (2019) analyses the opportunities for Spanish wine to be marketed in the Chinese market and, finally, Timini (2020) studies wine exports to the Italian market.

Fifth, in the fifth block of research, Pablo-Valenciano & Roman-Sanchez (2011) analyze changes in wine consumption patterns and their effect on international trade and Rebelo et al. (2021) study the effect of COVID-19 on Spanish wine consumption and wine exports.

This research is part of the second block of research, since it aims to analyze the export intensity in volume and value of Spanish wineries, as well as the priority destinations of these exports. The results offered are, therefore, of great relevance, given that, to our knowledge, there is no research that has addressed the export intensity of Spanish wineries by autonomous community, thus making it possible to identify which are the ones that contribute most to wine exports in terms of both volume and value. In this way, the data allow comparisons to be made between the different autonomous communities that make up Spain. Likewise, no previous studies have been found that attempt to analyze the destination of Spanish exports, and this information is of great value for professionals in the sector who are considering their inclusion in foreign markets.

Table 1 shows the paucity of literature on the export intensity of wine companies, as there are only eleven papers indexed in the Web of Science database that have implicitly or explicitly addressed this objective. The table shows the authors, the journal, the title of the article and the research objectives. Furthermore, as can be seen in Table 1, no research has addressed this objective for the Spanish case. This highlights the need to analyze the export intensity of Spanish wine companies, providing new knowledge in the field of international wine trade.

Table 1. Research indexed in the Web of Science database addressing export intensity in the wine industry.

Authors	Journal	Title	Objectives
Amadieu, Maurel & Viviani (2013)	Journal of Wine Economics	Intangibles, export intensity, and company performance in the French wine industry	The article aims to analyze the link between intangible assets and the performance of wine companies, demonstrating a positive and significant effect between the possession of intangibles and wine exports.
Aylward (2005)	Australian and New Zealand Grapegrower and Winemaker	What makes a successful SME exporter within the Australian wine industry.	Characteristics of Australian small/medium wine enterprises which are successful in the export sector are discussed on the basis of a survey and in-depth interviews. Aspects discussed include: export intensity; increasing exports over time; international markets; export-innovation linkages; management attributes and attitudes (case studies); attention to markets; and exporting methods.
Behmiri, Rebelo, Gouveia & António (2019)	International Journal of Wine Business Research.	Firm characteristics and export performance in Portuguese wine firms.	The research aims to identify the organizational characteristics that have a positive impact on the export performance of wineries in the Douro region. The study shows that the larger the size and the younger the age, the higher the export performance of wineries in the region.
Crick, & Crick (2021)	Journal of International Marketing	Internationalizing the coopetition construct: quadratic effects on financial performance under different degrees of export intensity and an export geographical scope	The research focuses on the relationship between coopetition and financial performance in the New Zealand wine context. The study shows that the exporting nature of the organization and the geographical scope positively moderates the relationship.
Crick & Crick (2022)	International Journal of Entrepreneurial Behavior & Research.	Coopetition and international entrepreneurship: the influence of a competitor orientation.	The study aims to contribute to the analysis of the link between coopetition and the performance of internationalized wineries. The research highlights the international orientation of wine managers to achieve such a link.
Echeverría & Gopinath (2008)	Chilean Journal of Agricultural Research	Export behavior in the Chilean agribusiness and food processing industry	The study analyses export decisions and export intensity in the Chilean wine industry. The results show that firms with previous export experience will be more likely to export in the future, as their international performance depends on the stock of prior knowledge they possess.

Continued on following page

Table 1. Continued

Authors	Journal	Title	Objectives
Galati, Crescimanno, Rossi, Farruggia & Tinervia (2014)	International Journal of Globalization and Small Business	The determinants affecting the internationalization of the Italian SMEs producing sparkling wines: an empirical study on the RBV of the firms	The study aims to analyze the factors influencing the export capacity of Italian wineries. The research shows that the degree of innovation and the commercial capacity of the organization are among the main factors driving Italian wine sales.
Köhr, Malorgio, & Aragrande (2017)	International Journal of Wine Business Research.	Exploring determinants of internationalization: the case of late starters.	The research aims to know the factors that influence the export intensity of the wineries. The study shows that distribution partners and organizational resources are the main factors in driving wine exports.
Macedo, Rebelo, & Gouveia (2019)	Bio-based and Applied Economics	Export propensity and intensity in the wine industry: a fractional econometric approach.	The article analyzes the export intensity of wine countries. The study highlights the importance of belonging to the European Union, since it favors the importation of wine between member countries.
Pacheco (2017)	International Journal of Wine Business Research.	Internationalization vs family ownership and management: The case of Portuguese wine firms.	The purpose of this study is to analyze the ownership structure of the wineries and the export performance. The results show that family businesses have a lower export performance than other companies.
Viviani (2009)	International Food and Agribusiness Management Review	Export implicit financial performance: The case of French wine companies	The investigation analyzes how the export performance of the wineries can be measured. To this end, a new method based on portfolio theory is proposed.

Source: own elaboration

METHODOLOGY

The research is carried out using a quantitative approach with a descriptive scope, given that the aim is to describe the export intensity of Spanish wineries by Autonomous Communities, as well as to analyze the destination of these exports. It should be noted that the research is framed within the non-experimental design, given that the context under which the research has been carried out has not been modified (García-Fernández & Cordero-Borjas, 2010). With regard to the sources of information used, secondary sources of information were used, using existing information to create new knowledge (Andrews et al., 2012). In this sense, as Hakim (1982) points out, the review of secondary documentary sources can generate valuable knowledge to contribute to the generation of new scientific knowledge. The study was carried out using information provided by the Spanish Wine Market Observatory (OEMV, by its acronym in Spanish). Specifically, the data relating to the export intensity in volume and value of Spanish wineries was obtained from the annual report *Spanish Wine and Wine Products Exports, Year 2021*. Likewise, the reports published by the OEMV entitled *Profile of the exporting company, Year 2020 and Year 2021*, were used to determine the destination of Spanish wine exports.

RESULTS

The data obtained from the research is shown below in two blocks: (1) intensity of Spanish wine exports by Autonomous Communities and (2) destination of Spanish exports.

Intensity of Spanish Wine Exports

All of Spain's wine-producing autonomous regions send part of their production to the international market, although the export intensity varies from one region to another. This shows the capillarity of the wine industry throughout Spain, as well as the long Spanish tradition of vine cultivation. Table 2 shows the importance of Castilla-La Mancha as the epicenter of Spanish wine exports, both in terms of volume and value. This is related to the surface area of vineyards in this community, given that it has half of the vineyards in the whole country.

There are also substantial differences between exports in value and volume by region (see Figure 1 and 2). Castilla-La Mancha, for example, is the largest exporter in both volume (52.94%) and value (25.93%) in Spain. However, the value generated by its exports is comparatively lower than in other autonomous communities in Spain. Firstly, the case of the Valencian Community stands out, given that although it is the second autonomous community in which wine is exported the most in terms of volume (11.93%), it falls to fourth position if analyzed in terms of value (8.89%). Secondly, the case of Catalonia is striking, given that although it is the third largest exporting region in terms of volume (7.62%), it is the second in terms of exports in value (17.98%). Therefore, contrary to what happens with the Valencian Community, there is a preference for quality wines (bottled) over quantity (bulk wines). This can be seen in the case of La Rioja, Spain's wine region par excellence, given that while it is the sixth largest wine exporting region in terms of volume (4.31%), in terms of value it is the third largest (11.31%). In third place, Gaul is a case worth mentioning, given that although its white wines are recognized and appreciated in the Iberian country, the data show its poorest performance in foreign markets, both in volume (0.62%) and value (1.58%). In fourth and last place, the regions with the

Table 2. Wine export intensity by Spanish regions. Year 2021.

	Exports (Value €)	Exports (Volume l)	Export Share (in Value)	Export Share (in Volume)
Castile-La Mancha	761.393,694	1,399,065,942	25.93%	52.94%
Catalonia	527,983,065	201,302,629	17.98%	7.62%
La Rioja	331,985,603	113,800,903	11.31%	4.31%
Valencian Community	260,911,897	315,267,099	8.89%	11.93%
Basque Country	206,544,804	49,563,679	7.03%	1.88%
Murcia	186,348,777	169,444,260	6.35%	6.41%
Castile and Leon	168,304,251	30,060,603	5.73%	1.14%
Andalusia	102,298,788	44,900,459	3.48%	1.70%
Aragon	96,395,064	45,882,158	3.28%	1.74%
Navarra	93,072,624	46,372,919	3.17%	1.75%
Extremadura	91,237,082	184,704,359	3.11%	6.99%
Madrid	52,394,203	23,621,448	1.78%	0.89%
Galicia	46,501,224	16,380,961	1.58%	0.62%
Balearic Islands	6,432,674	839,985	0.22%	0.03%
Islas Canarias	2,402,379	306,045	0.08%	0.01%
Asturias	1,939,252	1,236,146	0.07%	0.05%
Cantabria	73,845	4,643	0.00%	0.00%
Total	**2,936,219.226**	**2,642,754.238**	**100.00%**	**100.00%**

Source: own elaboration based on OEMV (2021a)

lowest development of international trade in terms of wine exports are Cantabria, Asturias and the two Spanish archipelagos.

Destination of Spanish Exports

With regard to the evolution of Spanish wine exporting companies by continent (see Table 3), Europe is the continent to which most Spanish wine is exported, accounting for 67.67% of total turnover (1,815.7 million euros). The American continent is the next most important destination for Spanish wine exports, with 522 million euros in 2020. This is followed by Asia and Africa with 248.2 and 81.9 million euros in turnover respectively. In last position is Oceania, a continent to which wine was exported to the value of 15.3 million euros, a figure similar to that recorded in 2019. The data offered for 2021 follow the same trend, as Europe was the continent to which most wine was exported, with 1902 million euros exported to that continent.

Figure 1. Export intensity in volume terms of the Spanish Autonomous Communities.
Source: own elaboration based on OEMV (2021a)

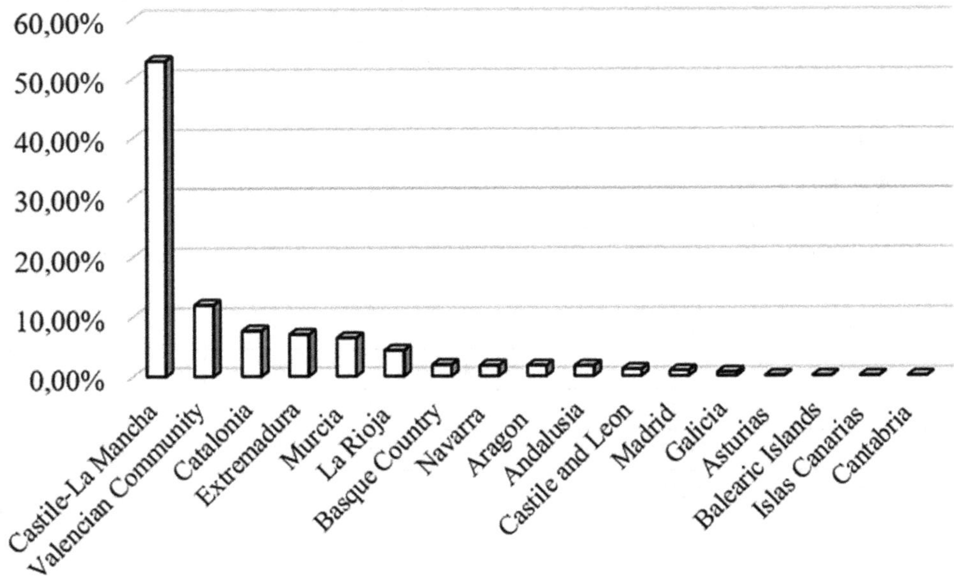

Figure 2. Export intensity by value of the Spanish Autonomous Communities.
Source: own elaboration based on OEMV (2021a)

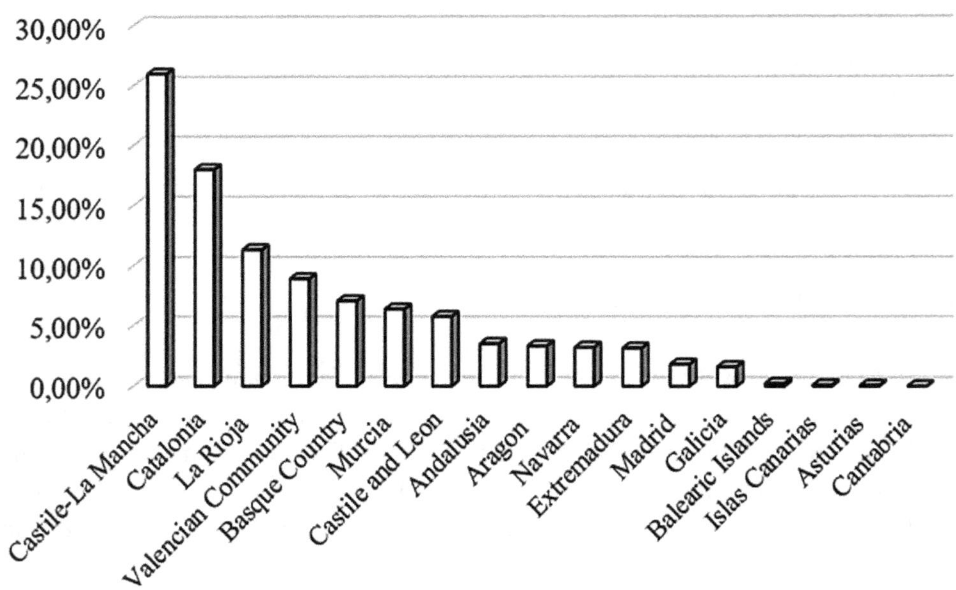

The notable rise of America as the second destination for Spanish wine exports is noteworthy, given that there has been an increase of 21.55%. In fact, in the six years under analysis (2016-2021) a similar figure of exports to this continent had not been recorded. Exports to Asia and Africa also experienced increases in 2021 compared to the previous year. Oceania, on the other hand, experienced a slight decline.

With regard to the evolution of Spanish wine exporting companies by country (see Table 4), Germany is the main destination in value of Spanish wine exports, with 341 million euros in 2020, followed by the United Kingdom, with 336 million euros, the United States, with 283 million euros and France, with 231.3 million euros. These figures highlight the role of the European continent as the driving force behind Spanish wine exports, given that three of the five main destination markets for Spanish wine exports belong to the old continent. In 2021, the role of Germany, the United Kingdom, the United States and China will increase compared to the previous year. The increases, especially in the United Kingdom and the United States, stand out, given that 2021 was the year in which the most wine exports were made to these countries since records began (2017-2021). In aggregate, since 2017 the main countries to which Spanish wine exports have been directed from the top five wine importing countries are Germany (27.47%), the United States (23.66%) and France (20.03%).

This international and diversified presence of Spanish wine products has been promoted by sectoral associations and institutions. In this regard, the Support Programmed for the Spanish Wine Sector (PASVE, by its acronym in Spanish) has a line of support for the promotion abroad of wines with PDO, protected geographical indication, as well as those in which the wine grape varieties are identified. These are measures to publicist the attributes of Spanish wines, with a view to strengthening their international competitive position, with the entry or consolidation of their presence in countries outside the EU.

Table 3. Evolution of the value of wine exports by continent (Mill. €).

	2016	2017	2018	2019	2020	2021
Europe	1.804,60	1.895,20	1.993,00	1.746,00	1.815,70	1.902,00
America	521,90	567,80	573,40	581,90	522,00	634,50
Asia	283,60	335,50	301,30	301,70	248,20	304,50
Africa	77,20	93,50	97,00	94,30	81,90	94,10
Oceania	12,00	14,70	13,60	15,40	15,30	14,60
Total	2.699,30	2.906,70	2.978,30	2.739,30	2.683,10	2.949,70

Source: own elaboration based on OEMV (2020, 2021a)

Table 4. Top-5 destination markets for Spanish wine exports (in terms of value).

	2017	2018	2019	2020	2021	Exports (2017-2021)	% of Total Exports (2017-2021)
Germany	395	400	333	341	355	1,824	27.47%
France	300	335	248	231	216	1,330	20.03%
United States	319	315	314	283	340	1,571	23,66%
United Kingdom	315	312	291	336	351	1,254	18,88%
China	180	147	128	89	118	662	9,97%

Source: own elaboration based on OEMV (2020, 2021a)

CONCLUSION

This research is of great relevance both for wine industry professionals and for academics who study the wine industry, since, to our knowledge, no similar research has been carried out to date.

The results of the study show that Spain's export intensity varies across its autonomous communities. This difference can be seen in the different values observed in export shares, both in volume and value. The asymmetry between autonomous communities is related to the wine production capacity (extension of vineyards) in terms of wine exports in volume and to the commercial capacities of the wineries in terms of wine exports in value. This explains the order of the autonomous communities in the lists shown, given that while Catalonia or La Rioja are internationally renowned for their wines, communities such as Extremadura stand out for their orientation towards wine production in large volumes and, as a consequence, their weight in terms of wine exports in volume is relatively higher.

If we focus on the countries to which exports are destined, it is important to highlight the European continent as the nerve center of Spanish wine exports, especially Germany, the United Kingdom and France. Also important is the role played by the United States as the second largest importer of Spanish wine if we consider imports from 2017 to 2021, as well as the role of China as the main importer of Spanish wine from Asia.

The results of the research point to a number of practical implications. Firstly, the various Spanish state bodies should highlight the strategic nature of the wine sector in their economy, given that, in addition to acting as an engine of employment and economic growth, wine is rooted in the cultural identity of the Iberian country. Secondly, national institutions should make a greater effort to promote exports among small and medium-sized wineries, thereby increasing the volume of their exports. Likewise, the main Spanish wine groups should be identified by the State, since, in the event of the sale or liquidation of these groups, the purchase could be taken over by the State and not by foreign capital, thus maintaining the productive fabric and, consequently, the wine-making tradition in Spain as a whole. Thirdly, the research could be useful for those wineries that are in the process of internationalization and are considering in which countries they should make their first exports, given that the research offers an orientation of the main importing countries of Spanish wine. Fourthly, the study could be used to identify which autonomous communities are excessively focused on exporting wine by volume, in order to move towards a model based on value-based exports, since this exporting favors the positioning of Spanish wines in international markets, improving their reputation and prestige. Fifthly, the research can be useful for those winemakers who are thinking of acquiring or setting up a new winery in the national territory, given that if they want to allocate a phase of their production to export, the study can be useful to see in which communities they can preferably develop their operations. Sixthly, the research can be useful for Spanish institutions in order to strengthen commercial relations with the five main wine exporters, as well as to detect which countries could be penetrated with greater intensity. Finally, seventhly, the research allows winery managers to know the relative variables in terms of exports, thus serving as a guide to understand internationalization in the wine industry and to establish comparisons between the different autonomous communities that make up Spain.

FUTURE RESEARCH DIRECTIONS

Despite the important contributions made in the work, it should be noted that the research suffers from certain limitations. The main limitation is methodological in nature and is related to the use of secondary data for the study. In order to overcome this limitation, as a future line of research, the intention is to carry out a questionnaire to analyze the importance of internationalization through exports, inter-company contracts and subsidiaries in Spanish wineries. Likewise, the aim is to analyze the role played by the degree of internationalization of Spanish wineries in overcoming the crisis caused by COVID-19. In addition, the aim is to delve deeper into the role played by the United States in Spanish wine exports, since, as explained in the research, there has been a notable increase in Spanish wine exports to the United States, with 2021 being the best year since 2017. The aim is therefore to analyze the causes of the notable increase in Spanish wine imports by the United States, delving into the development of bilateral relations between both countries to see if this increase could be encouraged in other wine-consuming countries.

REFERENCES

AFI. (2020). *Importancia económica y social del sector vitivinícola en España* [Economical and Social Importance of the Wine Sector in Spain]. Available at: https://www.interprofesionaldelvino.es/publicaciones/informes-importancia-sector/nacional/

Agostino, M., & Trivieri, F. (2016). European wines exports towards emerging markets. The role of geographical identity. *Journal of Industry, Competition and Trade*, *16*(2), 233–256. doi:10.100710842-015-0210-z

Amadieu, P., Maurel, C., & Viviani, J. L. (2013). Intangibles, export intensity, and company performance in the French wine industry. *Journal of Wine Economics*, *8*(2), 198–224. doi:10.1017/jwe.2013.27

Andrews, L., Higgins, A., Andrews, M., & Lalor, J. (2012). Classic grounded theory to analyse secondary data: Reality and reflections. *The Grounded Theory Review*, *11*(1), 12–26.

Anon, L. (2015a). Wines exports in the ascendancy. *Alimentaria*, *463*, 34–36.

Anon, L. (2015b). Export of bulk and bottled wines. Should Spain follow the Italian example? *Enologos*, *17*(96), 80–81.

Anon, L. (2020). The sky's the limit for Australian Tempranillo. *The Australian & New Zealand Grapegrower & Winemaker*, *676*, 44–48.

Aylward, D. (2005). What makes a successful SME exporter within the Australian wine industry. *The Australian & New Zealand Grapegrower & Winemaker*, *497*, 122–127.

Ayuda, M., Esteban, E., Martín-Retortillo, M., & Pinilla, V. (2020). The blue water footprint of the Spanish wine industry: 1935–2015. *Water (Basel)*, *12*(7), 1872. doi:10.3390/w12071872

Behmiri, N. B., Rebelo, J. F., Gouveia, S., & António, P. (2019). Firm characteristics and export performance in Portuguese wine firms. *International Journal of Wine Business Research*, *31*(3), 419–440. doi:10.1108/IJWBR-07-2018-0032

Carrasco, I., Castillo-Valero, J. S., Córcoles, C., & Carchano, M. (2021). Greening Wine Exports? Changes in the Carbon Footprint of Spanish Wine Exports. *International Journal of Environmental Research and Public Health*, *18*(17), 9035. doi:10.3390/ijerph18179035 PMID:34501620

Castillo, J., & Garcia-Cortijo, M. (2014). Gravity dynamics of Spanish wine exports, 1986-2012. *Historia Agraria, 64*, 1–8.

Castillo-Valero, J. S., Carrasco, I., Carchano, M., & Córcoles, C. (2021). What Is the Environmental Impact of Wine Entering Global Value Chains? Studying the Evolution of CO2 Emissions from the Export of Spanish Denomination of Origin Wines. *Foods, 10*(7), 1664. doi:10.3390/foods10071664 PMID:34359535

Cervera Ferrer, F. J., & Compés López, R. (2018). The performance of Spanish wine exports in international markets. *Economia Agraria y Recursos Naturales, 18*, 23-48.

Crick, J., & Crick, D. (2021). Internationalizing the coopetition construct: Quadratic effects on financial performance under different degrees of export intensity and an export geographical scope. *Journal of International Marketing, 29*(2), 62–80. doi:10.1177/1069031X20988260

Crick, J., & Crick, D. (2022). Coopetition and international entrepreneurship: The influence of a competitor orientation. *International Journal of Entrepreneurial Behaviour & Research, 28*(3), 801–828. doi:10.1108/IJEBR-06-2021-0519

Echeverría, R., & Gopinath, M. (2008). Export behaviour in the Chilean agribusiness and food processing industry. *Chilean Journal of Agricultural Research, 68*(4), 368–379. doi:10.4067/S0718-58392008000400007

Fernandez, E. (2012). Specialising in low quality: Spain and the international market of wine, 1950-1990. *Historia Agraria, 56*, 41–57.

Fernández-Olmos, M., Gargallo-Castel, A., & Malorgio, G. (2021). Do institutional networks affect winery survival? *British Food Journal, 123*(7), 2478–2491. doi:10.1108/BFJ-09-2020-0836

Ferrer, J. R. (2021). Managerial capabilities and generic business strategies in the wineries of the'Cava'protected designation of origin. *Spanish Journal of Agricultural Research, 19*(3), 108–121. doi:10.5424jar/2021193-18018

Fischer, C., & Gil-Alana, L. (2009). The nature of the relationship between international tourism and international trade: The case of German imports of Spanish wine. *Applied Economics, 41*(11), 1345–1359. doi:10.1080/00036840601019349

Galán, M., Moral-Agúndez, A., & Casquet, C. (2014). Valuation and importance of the extrinsic attributes of the product from the firms perspective in a Spanish wine protected designation of origin. *Spanish Journal of Agricultural Research, 3*(3), 568–579. doi:10.5424jar/2014123-6036

Galati, A., Crescimanno, M., Rossi, M., Farruggia, D., & Tinervia, S. (2014). The determinants affecting the internationalisation of the Italian SMEs producing sparkling wines: An empirical study on the RBV of the firms. *International Journal of Globalisation and Small Business*, *6*(2), 100–118. doi:10.1504/IJGSB.2014.066463

García, F., Cosano-Carrillo, A., & Sánchez-Cañizares, S. (2015). Exploratory analysis of foreign markets for Spanish organic wines. *Ciencia e Investigación Agraria: Revista Latinoamericana de Ciencias de la Agricultura*, *42*(2), 139–152.

Garcia-Fernandez, F., & Cordero-Borjas, A. (2010). Proceso de gestion del conocimiento en Carabobo (Venezuela) y Tamaulipas (Mexico). *Pensamiento & Gestión*, *28*, 132–154.

Gil-Alana, L., & Fischer, C. (2010). International travelling and trade: Further evidence for the case of Spanish wine based on fractional vector autoregressive specifications. *Applied Economics*, *42*(19), 2417–2434. doi:10.1080/00036840701858083

González, P., & Dans, E. (2018). The'terroirist'social movement: The reawakening of wine culture in Spain. *Journal of Rural Studies*, *61*, 184–196. doi:10.1016/j.jrurstud.2018.04.014

Gundlach, A. (2015). Brand often more important than región. *Wein+Markt, 10*, 34-37.

Hakim, C. (1982). *Secondary analysis in social research: A guide to data sources and methods with examples*. Allen and Unwin/Unwin Hyman.

Köhr, C. K., Malorgio, G., & Aragrande, M. (2017). Exploring determinants of internationalisation: The case of late starters. *International Journal of Wine Business Research*, *29*(2), 159–177. doi:10.1108/IJWBR-05-2016-0015

Levi, A., & Folwell, R. (1995). US demand for imported wines. *Journal of International Food & Agribusiness Marketing*, *7*(1), 79–91. doi:10.1300/J047v07n01_05

Macedo, A., Rebelo, J., & Gouveia, S. (2019). Export propensity and intensity in the wine industry: A fractional econometric approach. *Bio-Based and Applied Economics*, *8*(3), 261–277.

Marco-Lajara, B., Martínez-Falcó, J., Ruiz-Fernández, L., & Seva-Larrosa, P. (20221). Evolución del pensamiento en la disciplina de dirección estratégica: la visión de la empresa basada en las capacidades dinámicas y en el conocimiento. In *Investigación y transferencia de las ciencias sociales frente a un mundo en crisis* (pp. 1801–1826). Dykinson.

Marco-Lajara, B., Seva-Larrosa, P., Martínez-Falcó, J., & García-Lillo, F. (2022i). Wine clusters and Protected Designations of Origin (PDOs) in Spain: An exploratory analysis. *Journal of Wine Research*, 1–22.

Marco-Lajara, B., Seva-Larrosa, P., Martinez-Falco, J., & Sanchez-Garcia, E. (2021a). How Has COVID- 19 Affected The Spanish Wine Industry? An Exploratory Analysis. *Natural Volatiles & Essential Oils Journal*, *8*(6), 2722–2731.

Marco-Lajara, B., Seva-Larrosa, P., Ruiz-Fernandez, L., & Martinez-Falco, J. (2021b). The Effect of COVID- 19 on the Spanish Wine Industry. In *Impact of Global Issues on International Trade* (pp. 211–232). IGI Global. doi:10.4018/978-1-7998-8314-2.ch012

Marco-Lajara, B., Zaragoza-Saez, P., Martínez-Falcó, J., & Sánchez-García, E. (2022c). COVID-19 and Wine Tourism: A Story of Heartbreak. In Handbook of Research on SDGs for Economic Development, Social Development, and Environmental Protection (pp. 90-112). IGI Global.

Marco-Lajara, B., Zaragoza-Saez, P., & Martínez-Falcó, J. (2022e). Green Innovation: Balancing Economic Efficiency With Environmental Protection. In Frameworks for Sustainable Development Goals to Manage Economic, Social, and Environmental Shocks and Disasters (pp. 239-254). IGI Global.

Marco-Lajara, B., Zaragoza Sáez, P., & Martínez-Falcó, J. (2022j). Does Green Intellectual Capital Affect Green Performance? The Mediation of Green Innovation. *Telematique*, *21*(1), 4594–4602.

Marco-Lajara, B., Zaragoza-Sáez, P., Martínez-Falcó, J., & Millan-Tudela, L. (2022f). Corporate Social Responsibility: A Narrative Literature Review. In Frameworks for Sustainable Development Goals to Manage Economic, Social, and Environmental Shocks and Disasters (pp. 16-34). IGI Global.

Marco-Lajara, B., Zaragoza-Saez, P., Martínez-Falcó, J., & Millan-Tudela, L. A. (2022b). Analysing the Relationship Between Green Intellectual Capital and the Achievement of the Sustainable Development Goals. In *Handbook of Research on Building Inclusive Global Knowledge Societies for Sustainable Development* (pp. 111–129). IGI Global. doi:10.4018/978-1-6684-5109-0.ch005

Marco-Lajara, B., Zaragoza-Sáez, P., Martínez-Falcó, J., & Ruiz-Fernández, L. (2022g). The Effect of Green Intellectual Capital on Green Performance in the Spanish Wine Industry: A Structural Equation Modeling Approach. *Complexity*, *2022*, 1–17.

Marco-Lajara, B., Zaragoza-Sáez, P., Martínez-Falcó, J., & Sánchez-García, E. (2022a). Green Intellectual Capital in the Spanish Wine Industry. In Innovative Economic, Social, and Environmental Practices for Progressing Future Sustainability (pp. 102-120). IGI Global. doi:10.4018/978-1-7998-9590-9.ch006

Marco-Lajara, B., Zaragoza-Sáez, P., Martínez-Falcó, J., & Sánchez-García, E. (2022d). El capital intelectual verde como hoja de ruta para la sostenibilidad: el caso de bodegas Luzón. *GeoGraphos: Revista Digital para Estudiantes de Geografía y Ciencias Sociales*, *13*(147), 137-146.

Marco-Lajara, B., Zaragoza-Sáez, P., Martínez-Falcó, J. M., & Sánchez-García, E. (2022k). Las rutas del vino de España: el impacto económico derivado de las visitas a bodegas y museos. In *Investigación y transferencia de las ciencias sociales frente a un mundo en crisis* (pp. 1774–1800). Dykinson.

Marco-Lajara, B., Zaragoza-Sáez, P. C., Martínez-Falcó, J., & Sánchez-García, E. (2022h). *Does green intellectual capital affect green innovation performance? Evidence from the Spanish wine industry*. British Food Journal, Ahead-of-print.

Martinez-Ruiz, J. (2016). The Spanish wine trade with England in the second half of the seventeenth century: Towards constructing a new annual series and preliminary results. *Historia Agraria*, *70*, 11–24.

OEMV. (2020). *Perfil de la empresa exportadora de vino* [Profile of the Wine Exporting Company]. Available at https://www.oemv.es/perfil-de-la-empresa-exportadora-de-vino-ano-2020

OEMV. (2021a). *Exportaciones españolas de vino y productos vitivinícolas* [Spanish Exports of Wine and Wine Products]. Available at: https://oemv.es/exportaciones-espanolas-de-vino-ano-2021

OEMV. (2021b). *Perfil de la empresa exportadora de vino* [Profile of the Wine Exporting Company]. Available at https://www.oemv.es/perfil-de-la-empresa-exportadora-de-vino-ano-2021

Pablo-Valenciano, J., & Roman-Sanchez, I. (2011). Consumption, merchandising and prospects of Spanish wine market. *Agroalimentaria*, *17*(33), 51–61.

Pacheco, L. M. (2017). Internationalization vs family ownership and management: The case of Portuguese wine firms. *International Journal of Wine Business Research*, *29*(2), 195–209. doi:10.1108/IJWBR-10-2016-0034

Pascual, F., & Díaz, M. (2008). An approach to the valuation of Rioja wine. *Journal of Wine Research, 19*(1), 33–50. doi:10.1080/09571260802164020

Quintela, S., Villarán, M., Armentia, I., & Elejalde, E. (2012). Ochratoxin A in Spanish exportation wine market. *Food Control, 25*(2), 501–504. doi:10.1016/j.foodcont.2011.11.023

Rebelo, J., Compés, R., Faria, S., Gonçalves, T., Pinilla, V., & Simon-Elorz, K. (2021). Covid-19 lockdown and wine consumption frequency in Portugal and Spain. *Spanish Journal of Agricultural Research, 19*(2), 105–121.

Rodríguez García, J., & Vieira Rodríguez, Á. (2017). Análisis del Mercado de los Vinos de Jerez-Xérès-Sherry y Manzanilla de Sanlúcar de Barrameda en el periodo 1982-2012. *Revista de Estudios Andaluces, 34*(1), 155–200.

Seva-Larrosa, P., Martínez-Falcó, J., & Ruiz-Fernández, L. (2022). Analizando las principales variables empresariales en los clusters vinícolas españoles teniendo en cuenta la localización de las empresas y su pertenencia a una marca colectiva. In *Miradas sobre el emprendimiento ante la crisis del coronavirus* (pp. 629–634). Dykinson.

Suarez-Ortega, S. (2003). Export barriers: Insights from small and medium-sized firms. *International Small Business Journal, 21*(4), 403–419. doi:10.1177/02662426030214002

Suay-Matallana, I., & Guillem-Llobat, X. (2018). Poisoned wine: Regulation, chemical analyses, and Spanish-French trade in the 1930s. *Ambix, 65*(2), 99–121. doi:10.1080/00026980.2018.1452838 PMID:29661062

Timini, J. (2020). Staying dry on Spanish wine: The rejection of the 1905 Spanish-Italian trade agreement. *European Journal of Political Economy, 63*, 101892. doi:10.1016/j.ejpoleco.2020.101892

Trujillo-Bolio, M. (2013). Spanish Wine Export to the New Spain Market: Trade networks and circuits, 1790-1810. *America Latina en la Historia Economica, 20*(2), 121–150.

Viviani, J. L. (2009). Export implicit financial performance: The case of French wine companies. *International Food and Agribusiness Management Review, 12*, 23-48.

Yujia, S. (2019). Analysis of the Chinese wine market and sales of Spanish wine to China: The case of Torres China. *Esic Market Economics and Business Journal, 50*(3), 561–579.

ADDITIONAL READING

Bargain, O., Cardebat, J., Chiappini, R., & Laffitte, C. (2018). Long-term prospects of the international wine trade. *Journal of Wine Economics*, *13*(4), 442–450. doi:10.1017/jwe.2018.42

Castillo, J., Villanueva, E., & García-Cortijo, M. (2016). The international wine trade and its new export dynamics (1988–2012): A gravity model approach. *Agribusiness*, *32*(4), 466–481. doi:10.1002/agr.21463

Estreicher, S. (2013). A brief history of wine in Spain. *European Review (Chichester, England)*, *21*(2), 209–239. doi:10.1017/S1062798712000373

Galati, A., Tinervia, S., Crescimanno, M., & Spezia, F. (2017). Changes in the international wine market competitiveness. *International Journal of Globalisation and Small Business*, *9*(4), 277–293. doi:10.1504/IJGSB.2017.089901

Lombardi, P., Dal Bianco, A., Freda, R., Caracciolo, F., & Cembalo, L. (2016). Development and trade competitiveness of the European wine sector: A gravity analysis of intra-EU flows. *Wine Economics and Policy*, *5*(1), 50–59. doi:10.1016/j.wep.2015.12.002

Loose, S., & Pabst, E. (2018). Current state of the German and international wine markets. *German Journal of Agricultural Economics, 67*, 92-101.

Mariani, A., Pomarici, E., & Boatto, V. (2012). The international wine trade: Recent trends and critical issues. *Wine Economics and Policy*, *1*(1), 24–40. doi:10.1016/j.wep.2012.10.001

Meloni, G., & Swinnen, J. (2018). The political economy of regulations and trade: Wine trade 1860–1970. *World Economy*, *41*(6), 1567–1595. doi:10.1111/twec.12655

Pinilla, V., & Ayuda, M. (2007). The International Wine Market, 1850–1938. In Wine, Society, and Globalization (pp. 179-199). Palgrave Macmillan.

KEY TERMS AND DEFINITIONS

Autonomous Community: A unprovincial or pluriprovincial entity with specific territorial limits within Spain, which is endowed with legislative autonomy and executive powers in everything that is not common to the rest of the State.

COVID-19: An infectious disease caused by the SARS-CoV-2 virus.

Exports: Any goods or services shipped outside the national territory.

Imports: Represent the transport of goods and services from abroad, which are purchased by a country for distribution within the country.

Wine: Alcoholic beverage obtained by fermentation of grape juice.

Chapter 2
The Internationalization of the Spanish Wine Industry:
An Analysis of Trade Flows and Their Degree of Concentration

Bartolomé Marco-Lajara
https://orcid.org/0000-0001-8811-9118
University of Alicante, Spain

Javier Martínez-Falcó
https://orcid.org/0000-0001-9004-5816
University of Alicante, Spain

Patrocinio Zaragoza-Sáez
University of Alicante, Spain

Eduardo Sánchez-García
https://orcid.org/0000-0002-8524-4906
University of Alicante, Spain

ABSTRACT

The Spanish wine industry is a world leader in terms of wine exports by volume and third in terms of the value of these exports, behind only France and Italy. Spanish wine is therefore present in the world's main wine consuming markets, contributing to the maintenance and even improvement of the Spain brand on an international scale. Through a descriptive analysis carried out with secondary sources of information, this research aims to analyze wine trade flows as well as the degree of concentration of these flows in order to determine the degree of equality or inequality among Spanish wine exporters. The results show that for the last decade Spain has had a surplus in the wine trade balance of more than 2,000 million euros per year, and more than 80% of the wineries export on a regular basis, with a high concentration of large wineries.

DOI: 10.4018/978-1-6684-5950-8.ch002

INTRODUCTION

The Spanish agri-food industry combines maturity, the predominance of small companies and territorial roots, with a growing process of internationalization, technological innovation and the development of distribution channels (Rodrigo-Alarcón et al., 2014). Within this framework, the core activities of the wine value chain, i.e., viticulture, winemaking and marketing (hereinafter, the wine sector) occupy a prominent place in this industry as a whole, both in terms of the quality and variety of its production (Fuensanta et al., 2015).

The wine industry generates a Gross Value Added (GVA) of more than 23,700 million euros in Spain, equivalent to 2.2% of Spanish GVA, and provides more than 427,700 jobs, representing 2.4% of Spanish employment. Furthermore, wine activity is not only responsible for these contributions in economic and employment terms, but also represents an important source of revenue for the public coffers in terms of taxes and social security contributions. In fact, each year the sector directly contributes more than 3.8 billion euros in tax revenue for the State (AFI, 2020).

Beyond its economic contribution, the link between wine and Spanish culture is inescapable, since the tradition of vine cultivation and winemaking has left a deep imprint on its cultural and heritage legacy, crystallizing in various local festivities and a large number of vineyards in Spain (Marco-Lajara et al., 2022a; Marco-Lajara et al., 2022b; Marco-Lajara et al., 2022c; Marco-Lajara et al., 2022d; Marco-Lajara et al., 2022e;Marco-Lajara et al., 2022f; Marco-Lajara et al., 2022g; Marco-Lajara et al., 2022h; Marco-Lajara et al., 2022i; Marco-Lajara et al., 2022j; Marco-Lajara et al., 2022k; Marco-Lajara et al., 2022l; Seva-Larrosa et al., 2022). In fact, according to the records of the Ministry of Agriculture, Fisheries and Food (MAPA, by its acronym in Spanish) for the year 2020, the presence of vineyards extends throughout all the Spanish autonomous communities.

In order to carry out this research, wine companies (wine production) have been selected as the unit of analysis given their importance for the economic and social development of Spain. Thus, according to the latest data provided by the International Organization of Vine and Wine (OIV), Spain is a world reference in the wine sector, occupying the first place in the world in terms of surface area and export volume, as well as the third in terms of production, which shows the economic weight of the wine industry in the Iberian country. Through this research we contribute to generating useful knowledge for the decision-making process of wineries, which can consider the results of this research as a reference point for the development of the internationalization of their companies.

What is the trade balance of Spanish wine? How many exporting wineries are there in Spain? Are exports concentrated in a few wineries or fragmented among a large number of companies? These are the questions that the chapter aims to answer, providing new knowledge in the field of the international trade of Spanish wine. This chapter is therefore of great relevance, since it allows us to analyze the trade balance of Spanish wine over the last two decades and can serve as a reference for those academics who wish to analyze the impact of the different economic crises on the international wine trade. In particular, given the novelty of the results, the research serves to analyze the impact of COVID-19 on international trade, since, as several academics point out, the wine industry was not immune to the impact of the pathogen (Marco-Lajara et al., 2021a; Marco-Lajara et al., 2021b). The study also provides insight into the degree of internationalization of Spanish wineries and, therefore, their competitiveness vis-à-vis wineries in the Old and New World. In addition, the research analyses the degree of concentration of exports carried out by Spanish wineries through the study of the profile of these companies.

The research, therefore, is motivated by three premises. Firstly, the Spanish wine industry occupies a privileged position in the international wine trade, which is why it is necessary to periodically analyze these trade flows in order to understand how they are evolving. Secondly, given the strategic nature of the wine industry for the Iberian country, this analysis is particularly relevant, since it enables winemakers to have an up-to-date view of wine trade flows and, therefore, to make better decisions. Thirdly, Spanish public institutions can take decisions to reshape the structure of the industry, given that, as explained above, the research provides insight into the degree of concentration of Spanish wine exports.

The research is structured as follows. After this brief introduction, Section 1 deals with the review of the literature, in which the research that has dealt with the international wine trade in the Spanish context is presented. Section 2 explains the methodology followed to carry out the study. Section 4 presents the main results. Section 5 presents the conclusions derived from the research and, finally, Section 6 explains the main limitations and future lines of research.

BACKGROUND

Research on the international wine trade has taken on its own importance in the last five years. Spain, occupying a predominant position in wine exports, has aroused the interest of different academics, both national and international. Table 1 shows the research indexed in the Web of Science database that aims to study the international trade in Spanish wine. Specifically, the table shows the authors, the journal in which the research was published, the title of the article and the objectives pursued in the study.

The research analyzed has been divided into five blocks: (1) the resources and capacities that affect the internationalization of Spanish wine, (2) exports and imports of Spanish wine, (3) sustainability in the marketing of Spanish wine, (3) analysis of bilateral relations between countries in terms of the marketing of Spanish wine and (4) changes in consumption patterns and their effect on the Spanish wine trade.

In the first block of research, Castillo & Cortijo (2014) analyze the factors affecting Spanish wine imports, Garcia-Galan et al. (2014) study the influence of the Denomination of Origin (DO) on the internationalization of wine in the Iberian country, Agostino & Trivieri (2016) study quality studies in the wine industry, as well as its link with the marketing of wines, González & Dans (2018) study the associative movements and export drive, Ferrer (2021), for his part, studies the influence of the organizational capacities of Spanish wineries on internationalization processes and, finally, Fernández-Olmos et al. (2021) study the factors that affect the internationalization processes of Spanish wine.

Secondly, in the second block of research, Gómez-Bezares et al. (2008) analyze, among other aspects, exports of Rioja wine with the aim of quantifying the economic impact of the wine industry in La Rioja, Fischer & Gil-Alana (2009) address the link between tourism and exports of Spanish wine, Gil-Alana & Fischer (2010), for their part, analyze the link between tourism and imports of Spanish wine, Fernández (2012) studies Spain's specialization in the sale of bulk wine in foreign markets, Anon (2015a) studies Spanish wine exports in volume and value, Anon (2015b) studies Spanish wine exports and makes comparisons with other wine-producing countries, Rodriguez-Garcia & Vieira-Rodriguez (2017) study the international marketing of Andalusian wines, Ferrer & López (2018) analyze Spanish exports and the destination countries of these exports and, finally, Anon (2020) investigates the role of the Spanish Tempranillo grape in Spanish wine exports.

Thirdly, in the third block of research, Quintela et al. (2012) investigate the presence of the substance Ochratoxin in Spanish wine exports, Fuentes-García et al. (2015) analyze the potential markets for Spanish organic wine, Ayuda et al. (2020) address the relationship between trade and water footprint, Carrasco et al. (2021) study the carbon footprint generated by Spanish wine exports and, finally, Castillo-Valero et al. (2021) study the carbon footprint generated by Spanish wine exports.

Fourthly, in the fourth block of research, Levi & Folwell (1995) study the import of Spanish wine in the US market, Trujillo-Bolio (2013) analyze the marketing of Spanish wine in the Latin American market, Gundlach (2015) studies the German market for the marketing of Spanish wines, Martínez-Ruiz (2016) analyses the export of Spanish wine to the British market, Suay-Matallana & Guillem-Llobat (2018) study Spanish wine exports to the French market, Yujia (2019) analyses the opportunities for Spanish wine to be marketed in the Chinese market and, finally, Timini (2020) studies wine exports to the Italian market.

Fifth, in the fifth block of research, Pablo-Valenciano & Roman-Sanchez (2011) analyze changes in wine consumption patterns and their effect on international trade and Rebelo et al. (2021) study the effect of COVID-19 on Spanish wine consumption and wine exports.

This research is part of the second block of research, given that it aims to analyze the trade balance of wine in the Spanish context. However, the results offered are extremely relevant, given that, as far as we know, there is no research that has extended the analysis of wine exports and imports up to the year 2021, thus making it possible to see the evolution of wine exports and imports in the pre-pandemic and post-pandemic periods. In this way, the data allow comparisons to be made between the different economic crises experienced in the last two decades in terms of the international marketing of Spanish wine. Likewise, no previous studies have been found that attempt to analyze the profile of wine exporting companies, which is why the present research represents a novel and necessary step in the field of international wine trade.

Table 1. Research indexed in the Web of Science that addresses the study of international trade in Spanish wine.

Authors	Journal	Title	Objectives
Agostino & Trivieri (2016)	Journal of Industry Competition & Trade	European Wines Exports Towards Emerging Markets. The Role of Geographical Identity	The paper provides empirical evidence on the performance of wines with geographical designation and indication in emerging economies, as well as the effect of these labels on the international performance of wines.
Anon (2020)	Australian & New Zealand Grapegrower & Winemaker	The sky's the limit for Australian Tempranillo.	This article analyses the role of the new Spanish grape variety "Tempranillo" in the Australian wine sector, with reference to: the growth of Spanish wine imports; the use of the grape in the production of Australian red wines; the classification of wines according to viticulture and winemaking methods; growth habit, drought tolerance and varietal characteristics.
Anon (2015a)	Alimentaria	Wines exports in the ascendancy	The research analyses Spanish wine exports with reference to: the volumes and value of export sales; the reasons for the recent increase in sales volume; the results by category; and the main Spanish wine exporting companies.

Continued on following page

Table 1. Continued

Authors	Journal	Title	Objectives
Anon (2015b)	Enologos	Export of bulk and bottled wines. Should Spain follow the Italian example?	The study analyses the trends in Spanish wine exports since 2000 and compares them with the evolution of exports in Italy and France.
Ayuda et al. (2020)	Water	The Blue Water Footprint of the Spanish Wine Industry: 1935-2015	This article examines the growth of the Spanish wine industry's blue water footprint and its environmental impact.
Carrasco et al. (2021)	International Journal of Environmental Research and Public	Greening Wine Exports? Changes in the Carbon Footprint of Spanish Wine Exports	The research aims to study to what extent Spanish wine exports made between 2011 and 2016 contributed to the increase of the carbon footprint.
Castillo & Cortijo (2014)	Historia Agraria	Gravity dynamics of Spanish wine exports, 1986-2012	The present research contributes to the analysis of the factors influencing the increase of wine exports in Spain.
Castillo-Valero et al. (2021)	Foods	What Is the Environmental Impact of Wine Entering Global Value Chains? Studying the Evolution of CO2 Emissions from the Export of Spanish Denomination of Origin Wines	The study aims to analyze whether the wines with the longest tradition in Spain are those that most reduced their carbon footprint during the period 2005-5018.
Fernandez (2012)	Historia Agraria	Specializing in low quality: Spain and the international market of wine, 1950-1990	The paper aims to study the scarce investment to produce quality wines in Spain during the middle of the last century up to the present.
Fernandez-Olmos et al. (2021)	British Food Journal	Do institutional networks affect winery survival?	The article aims to analyze the influence of organizational aspects, commercial capacity and online popularity of wineries on the marketing of their wines.

Continued on following page

Table 1. Continued

Authors	Journal	Title	Objectives
Ferrer (2021)	Spanish Journal of Agricultural Research	Managerial capabilities and generic business strategies in the wineries of the 'Cava' protected designation of origin	The research pursues a double objective, given that, on the one hand, we analyze the managerial skills of the wine leaders belonging to the DO Cava and, on the other hand, we intend to analyze how these skills affect the business performance of the wineries.
Ferrer & López (2018)	Economia Agraria y Recursos Naturales	The performance of Spanish wine exports in international markets	The article aims to analyze the evolution of wine exports in Spain through the diversification of wineries, as well as their diversification in international markets.
Fischer & Gil-Alana (2009)	Applied Economics	The nature of the relationship between international tourism and international trade: the case of German imports of Spanish wine	The article analyzes the relationship between international travel and the wine trade, focusing on Spanish wine exports to the German market and German travel to Spain.
Fuentes-Garcia et al. (2015)	Ciencia e Investigacion Agraria	Exploratory analysis of foreign markets for Spanish organic wines	The aim of this work is to study the potential international markets for organic wine exports.
Garcia-Galan et al. (2014)	Spanish Journal of Agricultural Research	Valuation and importance of the extrinsic attributes of the product from the firms' perspective in a Spanish wine protected designation of origin	The study analyses how the brand, price, packaging and ethics affect the performance of the wineries belonging to the DO Ribera del Guadiana.
Gil-Alana & Fischer (2010)	Applied Economics	International travelling and trade: further evidence for the case of Spanish wine based on fractional vector autoregressive specifications	The research addresses the relationship between travelers and wine trade. In particular, it analyses the link between Spanish wine exports to Germany and the arrival of German travelers in Spain.

Continued on following page

Table 1. Continued

Authors	Journal	Title	Objectives
Gómez-Bezares et al. (2008)	Journal of Wine Research	An approach to the valuation of Rioja wine	The study analyses the impact of the wine sector for the Alicante region, as well as its indirect effect on other activities.
Gonzalez & Dans (2018)	Journal of Rural Studies	The 'terroirist' social movement: The reawakening of wine culture in Spain	The article analyses rural and social movements and their effect on the transformation of the Spanish wine landscape.
Gundlach (2015)	Wein+Markt	Brand often more important than region	The study analyses the German market for Spanish wines with reference to: German imports of Spanish wines: best-selling brands; confidence in brand recognition versus region; popularity of wines from the Rioja and Ribera del Duero regions; popularity of white wines from the Rueda region; and prospects for Spanish wines from the 2015 vintage.
Levi & Folwell, (1995)	Journal of International Food & Agribusiness Marketing	U.S. demand for imported wines.	The study analyses US wine imports of French, Italian, Spanish, Portuguese and German wines over the past two decades.
Pablo-Valenciano & Roman-Sanchez (2011)	Agroalimentaria	Consumption, merchandising and prospects of Spanish wine market.	The study addresses the main changes in the wine market in recent years and the trends in world wine consumption in 2000-2007.
Quintela et al. (2012)	Food Control	Ochratoxin A in Spanish exportation wine market	The study analyses the presence of ochratoxin in the DOCa Rioja export wine market.
Rebelo et al. (2021)	Spanish Journal of Agricultural Research	Covid-19 lockdown and wine consumption frequency in Portugal and Spain	The research addresses how COVID-19 affected wine consumption patterns among consumers in the Iberian Peninsula.
Rodriguez-Garcia & Vieira-Rodriguez (2017)	Revista de Estudios Andaluces	Analysis of the Jerez-Xeres-Sherry and Manzanilla de Sanlucar de Barrameda Wines Market in the Period 1982-2012	The research analyses the evolution of sherry wine exports between 1982 and 2012.

Continued on following page

Table 1. Continued

Authors	Journal	Title	Objectives
Martínez-Ruiz (2016)	Historia Agraria	The Spanish wine trade with England in the second half of the seventeenth century: towards constructing a new annual series and preliminary results	Wine became the principal commodity among Spanish exports to England in the 17th century. This article offers a review of current data and a new set of annual data on Spanish wine exports to England from 1664 to 1697, derived from the Port of London and Bristol Books.
Yujia (2019)	Esic Market	Analysis of the Chinese wine market and sales of Spanish wine to China: the case of Torres China	The research studies the opportunities and threats that Spanish wine has to face in the Chinese market, as well as possible practices that could favor its positioning in that market.
Suarez-Ortega (2003)	International Small Business Journal	Export barriers - Insights from small and medium-sized firms	The study aims to analyse the barriers that hinder the export of Spanish wine in foreign markets.
Suay-Matallana y Guillem-Llobat (2018)	Ambix	Poisoned Wine: Regulation, Chemical Analyses, and Spanish-French Trade in the 1930s	The research shows the poisoning caused by the consumption of wine exported from Spain to France in 1932.
Timini (2020)	European Journal of Political Economy	Staying dry on Spanish wine: The rejection of the 1905 Spanish-Italian trade agreement	The research aims to analyze the historical bilateral agreements that have taken place between Spain and Italy for the commercialization of wine.
Trujillo-Bolio (2013)	América Latina en la Historia Económica	The export of Spanish wine to the New Spain market: Commercial networks and circuits, 1790-1810.	The study aims to analyze the trade networks of Spanish beverages and the Mexican market.

Source: own elaboration

METHODOLOGY

The research is carried out under a quantitative approach with a descriptive scope, given that the aim is to describe the trade balance of Spanish wine, as well as the profile of the wineries that carry out exports. It should be noted that the research is framed within the non-experimental design, given that the context under which the research has been carried out has not been modified (García-Fernández & Cordero-Borjas, 2010). With regard to the sources of information used, secondary sources of information were used, using existing information to create new knowledge (Andrews et al., 2012). In this sense, as Hakim (1982) points out, the review of secondary documentary sources can generate valuable knowledge to contribute to the generation of new scientific knowledge. In order to calculate the Spanish wine trade balance, information provided by the Spanish Wine Market Observatory (OEMV, for its acronym in Spanish) was used. In particular, data related to Spanish wine exports were obtained from the annual report Spanish Wine and Wine Products Exports Year 2021. Similarly, the report published by the same organization entitled Wine and Wine Products Imports Year 2021 was used to obtain data on Spanish wine imports. On the other hand, in order to find out how many Spanish wineries were exporting, the directory of exporting companies of the Institute for Foreign Trade (ICEX, for its acronym in Spanish) was used. Finally, to find out the profile of Spanish wine exporting companies, we used the reports published by the OEMV entitled Profile of the Exporting Company for the year 2020 and 2021.

RESULTS

The results are presented in the following three blocks: (1) wine trade flows, (2) exporting wineries and (3) the profile of exporting wineries.

Trade Flows

The volume of Spanish wine exported in 2021 exceeded 2,000 million liters and, although it has been lower than the average annual volume sold abroad during the period 2010-2020, this is above the first decade of the 21st century. As can be seen in Figure 1, the balance of wine products in volume terms is clearly positive, standing at over 2,200 million liters by 2021. It is important to highlight that, since the beginning of the period under study, there has been a clearly positive balance of wine in volume, which reflects the importance of Spanish wine abroad.

The balance of trade of the Spanish wine industry is notoriously positive. In 2021, the trade surplus stood at more than 2.6 billion euros, following foreign sales of wine products worth 2.879 billion euros. Thus, the average annual sales for the last five-year period analyzed (2017-2021) are 9.33% higher than those of the previous five-year period. Likewise, exports in 2021 recorded an increase of 10.28% compared to those of the previous ten years (see Figure 2).

Figure 1. Wine trade flows by volume (million liters).
Source: own elaboration based on data provided by the OEMV (OEMV, 2021a; 2021b)

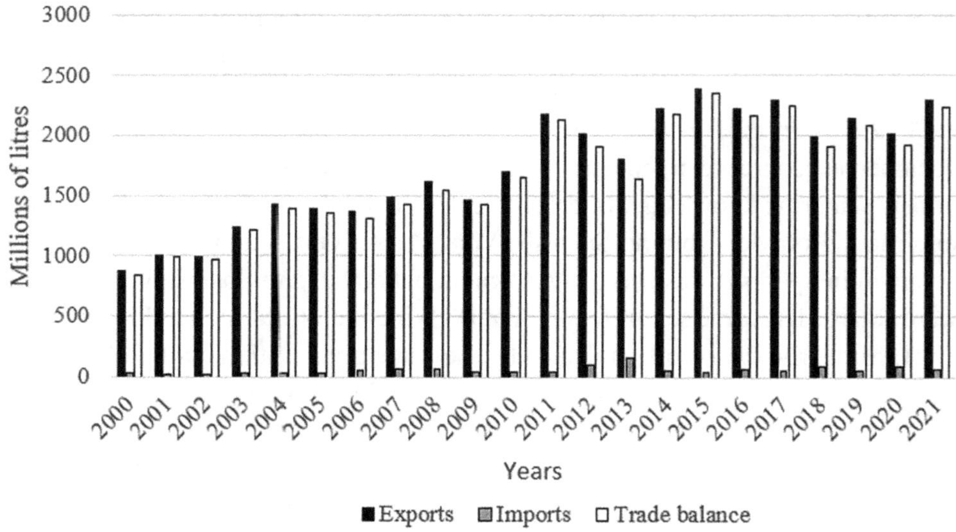

Figure 2. Wine trade flows in value (€ million).
Source: own elaboration based on OEMV (OEMV, 2021a; 2021b)

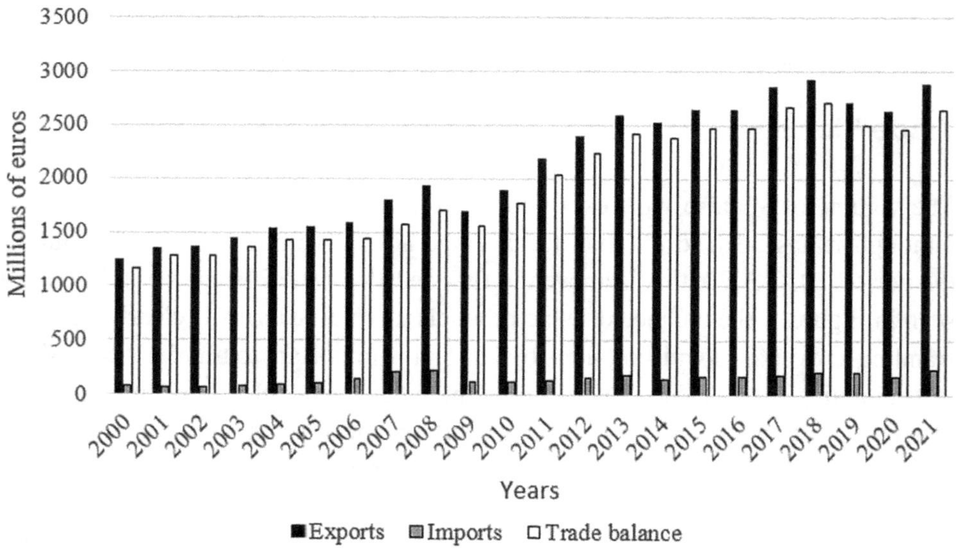

If wine exports and imports are analyzed separately, it is possible to observe how both items have experienced continuous growth over the last two decades. On the one hand, Figure 3 shows the evolution of exports, both in volume and value, over the last twenty years. As can be seen, exports in value increased from 1,244 million euros in 2000 to 2616 million euros in 2021, an increase of 110.29% in the period analyzed. This upward trend has remained largely constant over the period, with the exception of the periods of the 2008 financial crisis and the coronavirus crisis of 2019. Wine exports by volume, meanwhile, follow the same trend as exports by value, experiencing significant growth over the series analyzed. Thus, exports increased from 875 million liters in 2000 to 2,298 million liters in 2020.

Figure 4 shows the evolution of wine imports in both volume and value. As with exports, wine imports show a positive trend over the period analyzed, with sharp declines during the period of the 2008 financial crisis and the current coronavirus crisis. Thus, while imports in volume increased from 32.40 million liters in 2000 to 66.60 million liters in 2020 (105.55%), imports in value grew by 113.25% from 77.70 million euros exported in 2000 to 165.70 million euros in 2020. It is important to highlight that the greater distance between imports in value and volume, compared to exports in value and volume, allows us to demonstrate the greater value of foreign wines on the market compared to Spanish wines, given that Spanish exports are close to parity (one-liter equals one euro).

Figure 3. Evolution of wine exports.
Source: own elaboration based on OEMV (2021a)

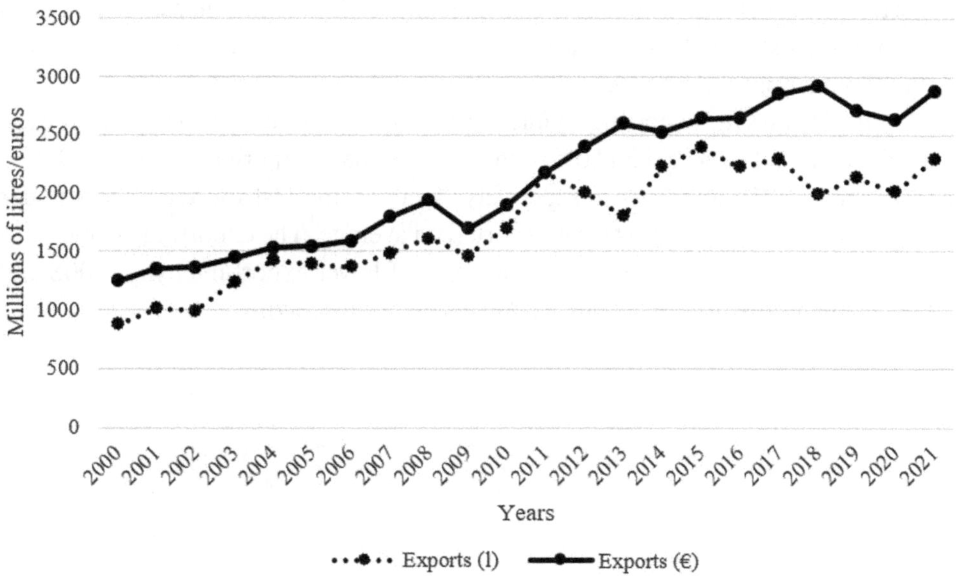

Figure 4. Evolution of wine imports.
Source: own elaboration based on OEMV (2021b)

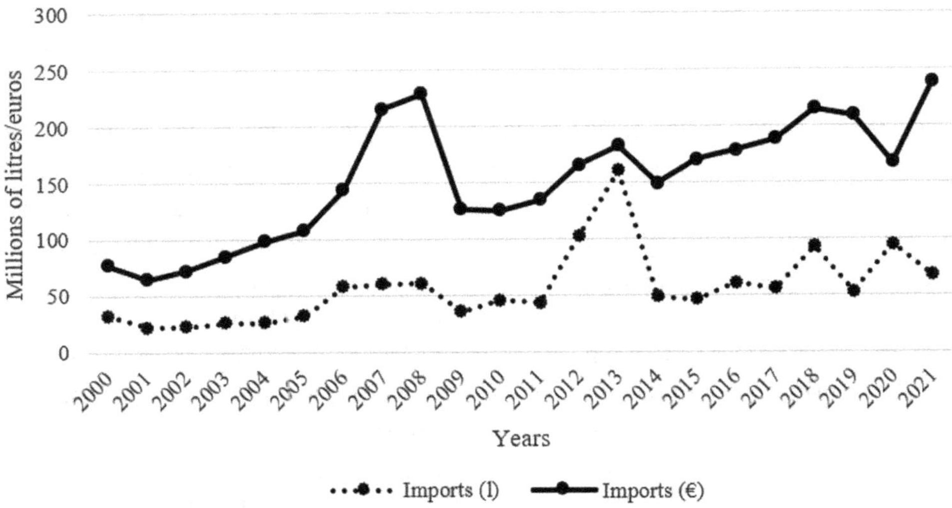

Wineries

Wine is among the main products exported by the Spanish agri-food industry. In fact, in 2021, it was Spain's fourth most exported food item, behind only pork, citrus fruits and olive oil. Likewise, the exporting business network of wineries was made up of 4,071 in 2021 (see Figure 5), of which 3,985 (97.89% of the total), exported wine abroad. Therefore, the majority of Spanish wineries make sales abroad, which shows the existence of a large number of companies in the sector with global competitive capacity.

Figure 6 shows the exporting character of Spanish wineries given that, during the period under study, more than 80% of the wineries have exported, reaching 99.70% or 99.60% in 2010 and 2016 respectively. Thus, in the last fourteen years under study, 93.82% of the wineries have exported on average. The exporting character of Spanish wineries is so strong that in the years of lower export intensity (2008 and 2018) the percentage of 80% of exports was even exceeded.

Figure 5. Wineries and exporting wineries.
Source: Prepared by the authors based on data provided by the ICEX (ICEX, 2021)

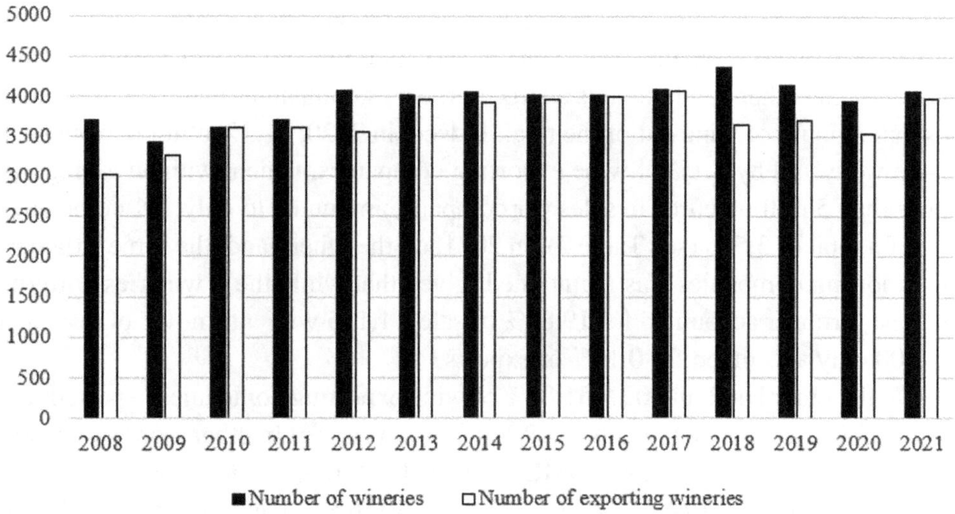

Figure 6. Proportion of exporting wineries.
Source: Prepared by the authors based on data provided by the ICEX (ICEX, 2021)

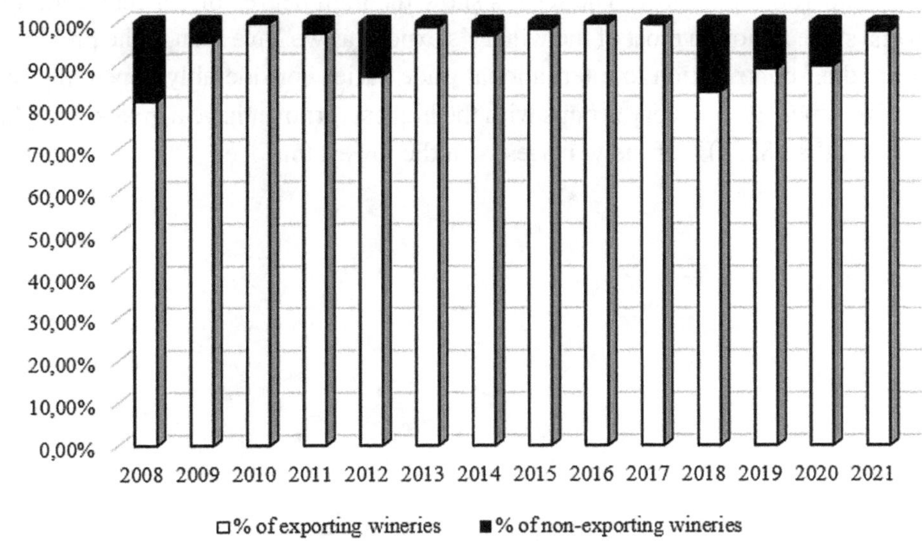

Exporting Wineries Profile

With regard to the degree of concentration/fragmentation of wine exporting companies by sector, it can be seen that a few companies export the majority of Spanish wines, while, on the other hand, there is a large number of companies that together export a small amount of wine out of the total. Indeed, in 2020, 71.3% of total exports by value were sold by 3.1% of wine exporting companies, which, with an average of more than 5 million euros in sales per company, amounted to only 111 companies out of a total of 3,536 (see Table 2). In 2021, on the other hand, the same structure of exporting companies was maintained, given that while the 6 wineries with the highest turnover accounted for 19.80% of sales, 1,185 with a turnover of less than €5,000 only accounted for 0.10% of exports.

On the other hand, in 2021, 51.80% of wine exporting companies exported less than €25,000 each, reaching only 0.50% of total turnover. In other words, there are many companies, most of them SMEs, engaged in foreign trade. However, exports are concentrated in very few companies. Thus, the top 50 wineries exporting wine, in terms of value, account for 52.20% of total exports by value, and the top 1,000, 97.50%. These percentages of concentration relative to exports have remained relatively stable in recent years. According to Table 3, which shows the accumulated export percentages of the different companies, the top 25 companies account for 38.60% of wine export turnover, the top 50 companies account for 52.20% of total turnover and the top 100 for 66.30%. The results show the high degree of concentration of exports, since although most of the winery's export, as we have seen in the previous section, their contribution to international trade varies considerably depending on their size, since the 6 winery groups with the highest turnover have a greater weight in exports than 85.70% of the wineries with the lowest turnover.

Table 2. Profile of the Spanish wine exporting company. Year 2020 and 2021.

Turnover Brackets	Number of Companies	Exports (Millions €)	Number of Companies (%)	Exports (%)
Year 2020				
< 5.000€	962	1,65	27,20%	0,10%
From 5.000€ to 25.000€	902	11,30	25,50%	0,40%
From 25.000€ to 50.000€	344	12,45	9,70%	0,50%
From 50.000€ to 500.000€	819	137,50	23,20%	5,10%
From 500.000€ to 5 Mill. €	398	607,20	11,30%	22,60%
From 5 Mill€ to 50 Mill. €	106	1.352,76	3,00%	50,30%
> 50 Mill €	5	564,58	0,10%	21,00%
Total	3,536	2.687,43	100,00%	100,00%
Year 2021				
< 5.000€	1185	1,80	29,70%	0,10%
From 5.000€ to 25.000€	882	11,10	22,10%	0,40%
From 25.000€ to 50.000€	404	14,55	10,10%	0,50%
From 50.000€ to 500.000€	948	162,77	23,80%	5,50%
From 500.000€ to 5 Mill. €	449	711,9	11,30%	24,10%
From 5 Mill€ to 50 Mill. €	111	1467,84	2,80%	49,70%
> 50 Mill €	6	586,22	0,20%	19,80%
Total	3,985	2956,12	100,00%	100,00%

Source: own elaboration based on OEMV (2020; 2021c)

Table 3. Cumulative percentage of exports by number of companies.

	2014	2015	2016	2017	2018	2019	2020	2021
5 First wineries	21,40%	21,90%	21,60%	21,30%	21,90%	20,10%	21,00%	18,00%
10 First wineries	28,50%	29,90%	29,5%	28,50%	29,40%	26,50%	27,60%	24,90%
25 First wineries	41,00%	42,80%	42,20%	42,00%	43,00%	39,80%	40,80%	38,60%
50 First wineries	54,30%	56,40%	55,50%	55,40%	56,70%	53,10%	54,80%	52,20%
100 First wineries	68,80%	69,60%	69,20%	69,00%	70,60%	67,80%	69,20%	66,30%
500 First wineries	92,90%	92,90%	92,70%	92,50%	93,40%	92,60%	93,80%	92,30%
1.000 First wineries	98,00%	97,80%	97,80%	97,70%	97,90%	97,70%	98,20%	97,50%
Total	100,00%	100,00%	100,00%	100,00%	100,00%	100,00%	100,00%	100,00%

Source: own elaboration based on OEMV (2021c)

CONCLUSION

This research is of great relevance both for wine industry professionals and for academics who study the wine industry, since, to our knowledge, no similar research has been carried out to date.

The results of the study show that the wine trade balance has been in surplus in both volume and value for more than two decades, amounting to more than 2 billion euros over the last decade. This may be due to the long tradition of vine cultivation and marketing in the Iberian country, given that, together with France and Italy, it is the largest wine producer in the Old World. The wine sector is therefore a strategic sector for the Spanish economy, being one of the flagships of the Spanish agri-food industry.

The research also highlights the marked exporting character of the wineries that make up the Spanish wine industry, given that in the last fourteen years, 93.82% of the wineries have exported their wines abroad on average. This shows that Spanish wineries, in addition to marketing their products through the traditional channels of Horeca and home consumption, have worked on marketing their products in foreign markets, increasing their competitiveness against foreign wineries.

However, if we analyze the structure of exporting wineries, we can see that a small proportion of wineries make the majority of exports abroad. Specifically, in 2021, while the 6 winery groups accounted for 16.80% of exports, 3,419 wineries only exported 6.50%. This concentration of exports represents a problem for the survival of the wine industry in Spain, given that the wealth generated by the income obtained from sales abroad is located mainly in the wineries with the highest turnover. Such is the concentration of international trade that the 100 wineries with the highest turnover account for 66.30% of exports.

The results of the research allow us to point out a series of practical implications. Firstly, Spain's various state bodies should highlight the strategic nature of the wine industry in its economy, given that, as well as acting as an engine of employment and economic growth, wine is rooted in the cultural identity of the Iberian country. Secondly, national institutions should do more to promote exports among small and medium-sized wineries, thereby increasing the volume of their exports. Likewise, the main Spanish winemaking groups should be identified by the state, given that, in the event of the sale or liquidation of these groups, the purchase could be taken over by the state and not by foreign capital, thus maintaining the productive fabric and, as a consequence, the wine-making tradition in Spain as a whole. Thirdly, the research can be useful for those wineries that are in the process of making acquisitions and/or mergers, given that, based on the turnover brackets, it is possible to find out what the export performance is and, therefore, whether or not it is advisable to carry out the operation. Finally, fourthly, the research allows the managers of the wineries to know the relative variables in terms of wine exports and imports, thus serving as a guide to understand internationalization in the wine industry and to establish comparisons between the company's variables and the average for the sector.

FUTURE RESEARCH DIRECTIONS

Despite the important contributions made in the work, it should be noted that the research suffers from certain limitations. The main limitation is methodological in nature and relates to the use of secondary data for the study. In order to overcome this limitation, as a future line of research, the aim is to carry out a questionnaire to analyze the importance of internationalization carried out through exports, inter-company contracts and subsidiaries in Spanish wineries. Likewise, the aim is to analyze the role played by the degree of internationalization of Spanish wineries in overcoming the crisis caused by COVID-19.

REFERENCES

AFI. (2020). *Importancia económica y social del sector vitivinícola en España* [Economic and Social Importance of the Wine Sector in Spain]. Available at: https://www.interprofesionaldelvino.es/publicaciones/informes-importancia-sector/nacional/

Agostino, M., & Trivieri, F. (2016). European wines exports towards emerging markets. The role of geographical identity. *Journal of Industry, Competition and Trade*, *16*(2), 233–256. doi:10.100710842-015-0210-z

Andrews, L., Higgins, A., Andrews, M., & Lalor, J. (2012). Classic grounded theory to analyse secondary data: Reality and reflections. *The Grounded Theory Review*, *11*(1), 12–26.

Anon, L. (2015a). Wines exports in the ascendancy. *Alimentaria*, *463*, 34–36.

Anon, L. (2015b). Export of bulk and bottled wines. Should Spain follow the Italian example? *Enologos*, *17*(96), 80–81.

Anon, L. (2020). The sky's the limit for Australian Tempranillo. *The Australian & New Zealand Grapegrower & Winemaker*, *676*, 44–48.

Ayuda, M., Esteban, E., Martín-Retortillo, M., & Pinilla, V. (2020). The blue water footprint of the Spanish wine industry: 1935–2015. *Water (Basel)*, *12*(7), 1872. doi:10.3390/w12071872

Carrasco, I., Castillo-Valero, J. S., Córcoles, C., & Carchano, M. (2021). Greening Wine Exports? Changes in the Carbon Footprint of Spanish Wine Exports. *International Journal of Environmental Research and Public Health*, *18*(17), 9035. doi:10.3390/ijerph18179035 PMID:34501620

Castillo, J., & Garcia-Cortijo, M. (2014). Gravity dynamics of Spanish wine exports, 1986-2012. *Historia Agraria*, *64*, 1–8.

Castillo-Valero, J. S., Carrasco, I., Carchano, M., & Córcoles, C. (2021). What Is the Environmental Impact of Wine Entering Global Value Chains? Studying the Evolution of CO2 Emissions from the Export of Spanish Denomination of Origin Wines. *Foods*, *10*(7), 1664. doi:10.3390/foods10071664 PMID:34359535

Cervera Ferrer, F. J., & Compés López, R. (2018). The performance of Spanish wine exports in international markets. *Economia Agraria y Recursos Naturales*, *18*, 23-48.

Fernandez, E. (2012). Specialising in low quality: Spain and the international market of wine, 1950-1990. *Historia Agraria*, *56*, 41–57.

Fernández-Olmos, M., Gargallo-Castel, A., & Malorgio, G. (2021). Do institutional networks affect winery survival? *British Food Journal, 123*(7), 2478–2491. doi:10.1108/BFJ-09-2020-0836

Ferrer, J. R. (2021). Managerial capabilities and generic business strategies in the wineries of the'Cava'protected designation of origin. *Spanish Journal of Agricultural Research, 19*(3), 108–121. doi:10.5424jar/2021193-18018

Fischer, C., & Gil-Alana, L. (2009). The nature of the relationship between international tourism and international trade: The case of German imports of Spanish wine. *Applied Economics, 41*(11), 1345–1359. doi:10.1080/00036840601019349

Fuensanta, M., Sancho, F., & Marco, V. (2015). In vino veritas: Factores competitivos en distritos industriales productores de vino. *Journal of Regional Research*, (32), 149–164.

Galán, M., Moral-Agúndez, A., & Casquet, C. (2014). Valuation and importance of the extrinsic attributes of the product from the firms perspective in a Spanish wine protected designation of origin. *Spanish Journal of Agricultural Research, 3*(3), 568–579. doi:10.5424jar/2014123-6036

García, F., Cosano-Carrillo, A., & Sánchez-Cañizares, S. (2015). Exploratory analysis of foreign markets for Spanish organic wines. *Ciencia e Investigación Agraria: Revista Latinoamericana de Ciencias de la Agricultura, 42*(2), 139–152.

Garcia-Fernandez, F., & Cordero-Borjas, A. (2010). Proceso de gestion del conocimiento en Carabobo (Venezuela) y Tamaulipas (Mexico). *Pensamiento & Gestión, 28*, 132–154.

Gil-Alana, L., & Fischer, C. (2010). International travelling and trade: Further evidence for the case of Spanish wine based on fractional vector autoregressive specifications. *Applied Economics, 42*(19), 2417–2434. doi:10.1080/00036840701858083

González, P., & Dans, E. (2018). The'terroirist'social movement: The reawakening of wine culture in Spain. *Journal of Rural Studies, 61*, 184–196. doi:10.1016/j.jrurstud.2018.04.014

Gundlach, A. (2015). Brand often more important than región. *Wein+Markt, 10*, 34-37.

Hakim, C. (1982). *Secondary analysis in social research: A guide to data sources and methods with examples*. Allen and Unwin/Unwin Hyman.

ICEX. (2021). *Directorios de exportadores españoles*. Available at: https://www.icex.es/icex/es/navegacion-principal/nuevos-exportadores/empresas-asociaciones-organismos/directorios-de-exportadores-espanyoles/index.html?idSector=120

Levi, A., & Folwell, R. (1995). US demand for imported wines. *Journal of International Food & Agribusiness Marketing*, *7*(1), 79–91. doi:10.1300/J047v07n01_05

Marco-Lajara, B., Martínez-Falcó, J., Ruiz-Fernández, L., & Seva-Larrosa, P. (2022l). Evolución del pensamiento en la disciplina de dirección estratégica: la visión de la empresa basada en las capacidades dinámicas y en el conocimiento. In *Investigación y transferencia de las ciencias sociales frente a un mundo en crisis* (pp. 1801–1826). Dykinson.

Marco-Lajara, B., Seva-Larrosa, P., Martínez-Falcó, J., & García-Lillo, F. (2022i). Wine clusters and Protected Designations of Origin (PDOs) in Spain: An exploratory analysis. *Journal of Wine Research*, 1–22.

Marco-Lajara, B., Seva-Larrosa, P., Martinez-Falco, J., & Sanchez-Garcia, E. (2021a). How Has COVID- 19 Affected The Spanish Wine Industry? An Exploratory Analysis. *Natural Volatiles & Essential Oils Journal*, *8*(6), 2722–2731.

Marco-Lajara, B., Seva-Larrosa, P., Ruiz-Fernandez, L., & Martinez-Falco, J. (2021b). The Effect of COVID- 19 on the Spanish Wine Industry. In *Impact of Global Issues on International Trade* (pp. 211–232). IGI Global. doi:10.4018/978-1-7998-8314-2.ch012

Marco-Lajara, B., Zaragoza-Saez, P., Martínez-Falcó, J., & Sánchez-García, E. (2022c). COVID-19 and Wine Tourism: A Story of Heartbreak. In Handbook of Research on SDGs for Economic Development, Social Development, and Environmental Protection (pp. 90-112). IGI Global.

Marco-Lajara, B., Zaragoza-Saez, P., & Martínez-Falcó, J. (2022e). Green Innovation: Balancing Economic Efficiency With Environmental Protection. In Frameworks for Sustainable Development Goals to Manage Economic, Social, and Environmental Shocks and Disasters (pp. 239-254). IGI Global.

Marco-Lajara, B., Zaragoza Sáez, P., & Martínez-Falcó, J. (2022j). Does Green Intellectual Capital Affect Green Performance? The Mediation of Green Innovation. *Telematique*, *21*(1), 4594–4602.

Marco-Lajara, B., Zaragoza-Sáez, P., Martínez-Falcó, J., & Millan-Tudela, L. (2022f). Corporate Social Responsibility: A Narrative Literature Review. In Frameworks for Sustainable Development Goals to Manage Economic, Social, and Environmental Shocks and Disasters (pp. 16-34). IGI Global.

Marco-Lajara, B., Zaragoza-Saez, P., Martínez-Falcó, J., & Millan-Tudela, L. A. (2022b). Analysing the Relationship Between Green Intellectual Capital and the Achievement of the Sustainable Development Goals. In *Handbook of Research on Building Inclusive Global Knowledge Societies for Sustainable Development* (pp. 111–129). IGI Global. doi:10.4018/978-1-6684-5109-0.ch005

Marco-Lajara, B., Zaragoza-Sáez, P., Martínez-Falcó, J., & Ruiz-Fernández, L. (2022g). The Effect of Green Intellectual Capital on Green Performance in the Spanish Wine Industry: A Structural Equation Modeling Approach. *Complexity, 2022*, 1–17.

Marco-Lajara, B., Zaragoza-Sáez, P., Martínez-Falcó, J., & Sánchez-García, E. (2022a). Green Intellectual Capital in the Spanish Wine Industry. In Innovative Economic, Social, and Environmental Practices for Progressing Future Sustainability (pp. 102-120). IGI Global. doi:10.4018/978-1-7998-9590-9.ch006

Marco-Lajara, B., Zaragoza-Sáez, P., Martínez-Falcó, J., & Sánchez-García, E. (2022d). El capital intelectual verde como hoja de ruta para la sostenibilidad: El caso de bodegas Luzón. *GeoGraphos: Revista Digital para Estudiantes de Geografía y Ciencias Sociales*, *13*(147), 137–146.

Marco-Lajara, B., Zaragoza-Sáez, P., Martínez-Falcó, J. M., & Sánchez-García, E. (2022k). Las rutas del vino de España: el impacto económico derivado de las visitas a bodegas y museos. In *Investigación y transferencia de las ciencias sociales frente a un mundo en crisis* (pp. 1774–1800). Dykinson.

Marco-Lajara, B., Zaragoza-Sáez, P. C., Martínez-Falcó, J., & Sánchez-García, E. (2022h). *Does green intellectual capital affect green innovation performance? Evidence from the Spanish wine industry*. British Food Journal, Ahead-of-print.

Martinez-Ruiz, J. (2016). The Spanish wine trade with England in the second half of the seventeenth century: Towards constructing a new annual series and preliminary results. *Historia Agraria, 70*, 11–24.

OEMV. (2020). *Perfil de la empresa exportadora de vino* [Profile of the Wine Exporting Company]. Available at https://www.oemv.es/perfil-de-la-empresa-exportadora-de-vino-ano-2020

OEMV. (2021a). *Exportaciones españolas de vino y productos vitivinícolas* [Spanish Exports of Wine and Wine Products]. Available at: https://oemv.es/exportaciones-espanolas-de-vino-ano-2021

OEMV. (2021b). *Importaciones españolas de vino y productos vitivinícolas*. Available at: https://www.oemv.es/importaciones-espanolas-de-vino-ano-2021

OEMV. (2021c). *Perfil de la empresa exportadora de vino* [Profile of the Wine Exporting Company]. Available at https://www.oemv.es/perfil-de-la-empresa-exportadora-de-vino-ano-2021

Pablo-Valenciano, J., & Roman-Sanchez, I. (2011). Consumption, merchandising and prospects of Spanish wine market. *Agroalimentaria, 17*(33), 51–61.

Pascual, F., & Díaz, M. (2008). An approach to the valuation of Rioja wine. *Journal of Wine Research, 19*(1), 33–50. doi:10.1080/09571260802164020

Quintela, S., Villarán, M., Armentia, I., & Elejalde, E. (2012). Ochratoxin A in Spanish exportation wine market. *Food Control, 25*(2), 501–504. doi:10.1016/j.foodcont.2011.11.023

Rebelo, J., Compés, R., Faria, S., Gonçalves, T., Pinilla, V., & Simon-Elorz, K. (2021). Covid-19 lockdown and wine consumption frequency in Portugal and Spain. *Spanish Journal of Agricultural Research, 19*(2), 105–121.

Rodrigo-Alarcón, J., Parra-Requena, G., & García-Villaverde, P. M. (2014). Efectividad de la orientación emprendedora: El papel del capital social y las capacidades. *Investigaciones Europeas de Dirección y Economía de la Empresa, 20*(3), 131–139. doi:10.1016/j.iedee.2013.09.002

Rodríguez García, J., & Vieira Rodríguez, Á. (2017). Análisis del Mercado de los Vinos de Jerez-Xérès-Sherry y Manzanilla de Sanlúcar de Barrameda en el periodo 1982-2012. *Revista de Estudios Andaluces, 34*(1), 155–200.

Seva-Larrosa, P., Martínez-Falcó, J., & Ruiz-Fernández, L. (2022). Analizando las principales variables empresariales en los clusters vinícolas españoles teniendo en cuenta la localización de las empresas y su pertenencia a una marca colectiva. In *Miradas sobre el emprendimiento ante la crisis del coronavirus* (pp. 629–634). Dykinson.

Suarez-Ortega, S. (2003). Export barriers: Insights from small and medium-sized firms. *International Small Business Journal, 21*(4), 403–419. doi:10.1177/02662426030214002

Suay-Matallana, I., & Guillem-Llobat, X. (2018). Poisoned wine: Regulation, chemical analyses, and Spanish-French trade in the 1930s. *Ambix, 65*(2), 99–121. doi:10.1080/00026980.2018.1452838 PMID:29661062

Timini, J. (2020). Staying dry on Spanish wine: The rejection of the 1905 Spanish-Italian trade agreement. *European Journal of Political Economy, 63*, 101892. doi:10.1016/j.ejpoleco.2020.101892

Trujillo-Bolio, M. (2013). Spanish Wine Export to the New Spain Market: Trade networks and circuits, 1790-1810. *America Latina en la Historia Economica*, *20*(2), 121–150.

Yujia, S. (2019). Analysis of the Chinese wine market and sales of Spanish wine to China: The case of Torres China. *Esic Market Economics and Business Journal*, *50*(3), 561–579.

ADDITIONAL READING

Bargain, O., Cardebat, J., Chiappini, R., & Laffitte, C. (2018). Long-term prospects of the international wine trade. *Journal of Wine Economics*, *13*(4), 442–450. doi:10.1017/jwe.2018.42

Castillo, J., Villanueva, E., & García-Cortijo, M. (2016). The international wine trade and its new export dynamics (1988–2012): A gravity model approach. *Agribusiness*, *32*(4), 466–481. doi:10.1002/agr.21463

Estreicher, S. (2013). A brief history of wine in Spain. *European Review (Chichester, England)*, *21*(2), 209–239. doi:10.1017/S1062798712000373

Galati, A., Tinervia, S., Crescimanno, M., & Spezia, F. (2017). Changes in the international wine market competitiveness. *International Journal of Globalisation and Small Business*, *9*(4), 277–293. doi:10.1504/IJGSB.2017.089901

Lombardi, P., Dal Bianco, A., Freda, R., Caracciolo, F., & Cembalo, L. (2016). Development and trade competitiveness of the European wine sector: A gravity analysis of intra-EU flows. *Wine Economics and Policy*, *5*(1), 50–59. doi:10.1016/j.wep.2015.12.002

Loose, S., & Pabst, E. (2018). Current state of the German and international wine markets. *German Journal of Agricultural Economics*, *67*, 92-101.

Mariani, A., Pomarici, E., & Boatto, V. (2012). The international wine trade: Recent trends and critical issues. *Wine Economics and Policy*, *1*(1), 24–40. doi:10.1016/j.wep.2012.10.001

Meloni, G., & Swinnen, J. (2018). The political economy of regulations and trade: Wine trade 1860–1970. *World Economy*, *41*(6), 1567–1595. doi:10.1111/twec.12655

Pinilla, V., & Ayuda, M. (2007). The International Wine Market, 1850–1938. In Wine, Society, and Globalization (pp. 179-199). Palgrave Macmillan.

KEY TERMS AND DEFINITIONS

Balance of Trade: The balance of trade is a record of a country's imports and exports in a given period.

COVID-19: An infectious disease caused by the SARS-CoV-2 virus.

Exports: Any goods or services shipped outside the national territory.

Horeca: An acronym for HOtels, REstaurants and CAterings, used to refer to the food service sector.

Imports: Represent the transport of goods and services from abroad, which are purchased by a country for distribution within the country.

Chapter 3
How Do Geopolitical Risk and Global Trade Shape Corporate Cash Policy?
Evidence From the Financial Crisis of 2008-2009

Hasan Tekin
https://orcid.org/0000-0003-2855-215X
Karabuk University, Turkey

Hidayet Zahid Gürbüz
Karabuk University, Turkey

Saim Kayadibi
Karabuk University, Turkey

ABSTRACT

This chapter investigates the influence of geopolitical risk (GPR) and global trade on cash holdings with the existence of the global financial crisis 2008-2009 (GFC) for 11,960 non-financial firms in 18 markets from 2002 to 2017. Findings show that firms in countries with higher GPR and lower trade volume have higher cash balances confirming the predictions of the precautionary motive of cash. The implications of the findings are manifold. Managers should shape their cash policies considering the uncertainties, GPR, and trade level. Investors should consider countries' financial crises and GPR in specifying where and which firms to invest in. Policymakers can reshape the regulations and policies related to holding cash rather than paying dividends not to hurt firms in times of turbulence like the pandemic. Researchers and practitioners should count the macro-specific factors and market turmoil and their influence on cash holding in risky countries. The implications are particularly relevant to the post-pandemic era when exogenous shocks and uncertainties are further expected.

DOI: 10.4018/978-1-6684-5950-8.ch003

INTRODUCTION

Firms may understand the importance of cash retention during the exogenous shocks when the accessing finance becomes costly (Duchin et al., 2010). However, financial market turmoils are not only factors affecting the corporate cash policy, but geopolitical risk (GPR) is also another factor. Therefore, this chapter answers the question of how GPR impacts cash holding before, during and after the global financial crisis 2008-2009 as well as questioning the possible impact of international trade.

Geopolitical risks may be defined as *the risks associated with wars, terrorist acts, and tensions between states that affect the normal and peaceful course of international relations* (Caldara & Iacoviello, 2022: 1195). Geopolitical incidents such as military attacks, terrorist acts or diplomatic tension are sources of great concern to business, public media and policy makers. For instance, when the trade wars happened between the United States and China, the economy of China suffered a terrific loss (Jiang et al., 2020). Moreover, geopolitical risk is also seen as an important matter influencing decision-making in multinational firms (Kotcharin & Maneenop, 2020). Also, geopolitical risks are essential factors of investment policies for especially corporate managers and policy makers (Demiralay & Kilincarslan, 2019).

International trade is one of the most noticeable issues in economic development. Also, according to Foley & Manova (2015), global trade has an impression on financial policies of firms. Research about international trade usually concentrates on the effect of productivity of trade and cross-country differences in predicting the gains from trade. One of the most important roles of firms' export possibility and capacity is the internal finance ensured by cash holdings or profit (Huang & Liu, 2017).

While the importance of geopolitical risk and global trade on corporate decisions grows over time, limited research analyzes their effect on corporate cash policies (Demir et al., 2019; Kotcharin & Maneenop, 2020; Lee & Wang, 2021; Tekin, 2021b; Wang et al., 2021). The contribution of this research to previous research by analyzing the consequences of geopolitical risk and international trade on cash retention in times of the recession.

Employing 127,775 firm-years from 18 economies empirical findings show that GPR has a positive effect, but global trade has a negative effect on cash hoardings. The positive influence of GPR on cash holdings increases during the GFC and does not differ in the post-GFC. Moreover, the impact of international trade on cash retention does not change in time of the GFC and its aftermath.

This chapter first proposes a theoretical framework and empirical studies related to the GPR, trade, the GFC, and cash holdings. Next, this study empirically evaluates the question of how the GPR, as well as trade, impacts cash policy across countries in the GFC context.

CONTROVERSIES IN THE LITERATURE

Theoretical Framework

This chapter focuses on three theories that explain the characteristics of the firm that affect its cash holding decisions. These theories have different perspectives on firm's cash holding dynamics.

Trade-off Theory

Trade-off theory claims that companies arrange their optimal cash holdings by considering the balance between the marginal benefits and the marginal costs related with holding such liquid assets (Al-Najjar & Belghitar, 2011). According to Ferreira & Vilela (2004), there are multiple benefits relevant to holding cash. First, cash holdings reduce the probability of financial trouble. As an example, it is a safety reserve to overcome unexpected losses. Then, cash holdings allow the continuation of the convenient investment policy for firms even when faced with financial constraints. Next, cash holdings make contribution to reduce the liquidation costs or costs of external funds (Ferreira & Vilela, 2004). On the other hand, previous research revealed that the advantages of holding cash are relying on two motives which are transaction costs and precautionary motives (Dittmar et al., 2003). Transaction costs can broadly be defined as firms hold cash reserves in consequence of the costs based on external financing (Ozkan & Ozkan, 2004). Precautionary motive refers that investments can be reduced by the reason of investment costs (Ozkan & Ozkan, 2004).

Pecking Order Theory

Previous studies mostly defined this theory as firms have a tendency to rely on firstly internal sources of funds then secondly external funds. In compliance with this theory, when cash flows are inadequate, the firm cut down on dividends, cash holdings and, finally, issues debt (Ferreira & Vilela, 2004). In other words, this theory argues that firms encountered with an excess cash, use the revenues to pay off debt, as for that while those encountered with a cash shortage raise capital to meet the deficiency (D'Mello et al., 2008).

Free Cash Flow Theory

The free cash flow theory relies on disagreements of agency interests among shareholders and managers (Al-Najjar & Belghitar, 2011). Managers have desire to save cash to increase the amount of assets under their control. The manager who has cash for investment, does not need to external funds and to provide information about the investment projects. Consequently, managers could take in charge on investments that have an unfavorable impact on shareholders (Ferreira & Vilela, 2004). According to Lee & Suh, (2011), surplus cash held by firms should be allocate to shareholders instead of unprofitable projects.

Impact of the Financial Crisis on Corporate Cash Policy

Previous research demonstrates financial crises profoundly affect financial markets and corporate financial choices (Duchin et al., 2010; Sun & Wang, 2015; Chang et al., 2017; Alves, 2018; Chen et al., 2018; Polat, 2020a, b; Tekin, 2020a, b, d; Tekin & Polat, 2020c; Muğaloğlu et al., 2021a, b; Polat, 2021a, b; Polat et al., 2021).

The Global Financial Crisis which is defined as a shock to the supply of credit to all firms, affected some firms more than others (Chang et al., 2017; Polat, 2018;). According to Duchin et al. (2010), the financial crisis encouraged financially constrained firms to rely more on their cash holdings for investments. Moreover, during a crisis, when debt financing is more costly and difficult to access, the use of cash holdings would be more sensible choice (Chang et al., 2017).

Also, cash holding is a strategic decision, especially in situations where access to external financing is limited. Cash assets become very important for the survival of companies, especially during financial crises (Tekin, 2021a, b, c; Tekin & Polat, 2021a, b, c, d; Tekin et al., 2021a, b; Tekin, 2022a, b, c).

In the literature, there are different results for the relationship between a financial crisis and a corporate cash policy. For example, Chen et al. (2018) researched the role of cash holding behavior in helping financially limited firms during the 2000 dot-com crash and the 2008 financial crisis. And findings show that when they have pre-saved more cash, financially constrained firms tend to raise their investments during serious economic downturns.

Sun & Wang (2015) show that US firms cannot save cash because of the restriction on loan supply in 2007 but hold more cash due to an increase in loan demand. Moreover, Alves (2018) found a negative relationship between cash hoardings and financial crisis for firms in 32 economies as a piece of international evidence in his research.

Impact of Geopolitical Risk on Corporate Cash Policy

As more recent scientometric analyze, Aysan et al. (2022) mention geopolitical risk becomes crucial day by day throughout the world, especially in financial markets.

Geopolitical uncertainty and economic conditions which have volatility could sensitize financial behavior (Kotcharin & Maneenop, 2020).

In the literature, there are several research examined the geopolitical risk and corporate cash policy together. One of them was examined by Kotcharin & Maneenop (2020), using a sample data period of 1987–2017 to analyze the cash retention behavior of some shipping firms giving response to GPR measures.

Lee & Wang (2021) examine whether geopolitical risk affects firms' cash holding decisions. They found a considerably positive link between cash holdings and geopolitical risk. Moreover, their findings show that the relationship changes in firms under various financial circumstances. Another research use data of years between 2013 and 2017 on firms from China. The paper has researched the determinants of corporate financing behavior of firms, including geopolitical risk.

Further, there is research that analyzed the relation between corporate cash holdings and geopolitical risks using data from more than a hundred hospitality firms from emerging countries for the years of 2008 to 2017, by Demir et al. (2019). Then the findings include that the hospitality industries are negatively impacted by geopolitical risk.

The next study includes empirical research that focuses on financial data of firms from Asian countries from 1995 to 2018 by Le & Tran (2021). As a result of this study, there is an inverse association between geopolitical risks and the investment opportunities. GPR in China and Russia have a major effect on investing decisions, vice versa in Turkiye and India.

Wang et al. (2021) assess corporate cash holdings and GPR for Chinese firms in oil industry. Their sample includes the period of 2002-2019. Their results show that GPR has a directive influence on the oil industry to reserve more cash.

Impact of Global Trade on Corporate Cash Policy

This topic is exemplified in the work undertaken by Huang and Liu in 2017. Firm-level data for the period of 2005–2009 are used in this study. Also, this study involves firms' financial behavior including cash holdings in case of international trade. As this study concludes that firms who have no restricted financial condition are more likely to ply an international trade.

By employing firms in 82 countries for the period 2002-2016, Tekin (2021b) analyzes the link between corporate financial policies and global trade including cash policy in the financial crisis context. He finds a negative and weak link between global trade and cash holdings. Namely, firms in lower trade volume countries hold more cash.

RESEARCH QUESTION

The literature assesses in detail the effect of exogenous shocks on cash holdings (Chen et al., 2018; Tekin, 2020b; Tekin & Polat, 2020b). Surprisingly, while there is a crucial and growing effect of geopolitical risk on financial markets, very little research has addressed the question of how GPR influences cash retention (Demir et al., 2019; Kotcharin & Maneenop, 2020; Lee & Wang, 2021; Wang et al., 2021). Also, there has been very little research directly investigating the association between global trade and cash holdings (Tekin, 2021b). So far, however, the role of geopolitical risk and global trade on cash holdings has still not been empirically investigated in the 2008-2009 global financial crisis context.

METHODOLOGY AND DATA

Methodology

When the numbers of firms and years are higher and lower, respectively, the literature employ fixed effect panel method by checking whether fixed effect is preferable to random effects (Tekin & Polat, 2021c). The base-line model includes geopolitical risk (GPR), global trade (TRA) and the 2008-2009 global financial crisis (GFC) as explanatory variables and control variables.

$$\begin{aligned} CH_{ij,t} &= \beta_0 + \beta_1 GPR_{j,t} + \beta_2 TRA_{j,t} + \beta_3 SIZE_{i,t} + \beta_4 MBR_{i,t} + \beta_5 INV_{i,t} \\ &+ \beta_6 LEV_{i,t} + \beta_7 NWC_{i,t} + \beta_8 CFA_{i,t} + \beta_8 R\&D_{i,t} + \alpha_i F_i + \alpha_t Y_t + \varepsilon_{i,t} \end{aligned} \tag{1}$$

where, $CH_{i,t}$ is cash holdings for firm i at time t, $GPR_{j,t}$ is Geopolitical risk for country j at time t, $TRA_{j,t}$ is global trade for country j at time t, $SIZE_{i,t}$ is firm size for firm i at time t, $MBR_{i,t}$ is market-to-book ratio for firm i at time t, $INV_{i,t}$ is investment for firm i at time t, $LEV_{i,t}$ is leverage for firm i at time t, $NWC_{i,t}$ is net working capital for firm i at time t, $CFA_{i,t}$ is cash flow for firm i at time t, $R\&D_{i,t}$ is research and development dummy for firm i at time t, αi is firm fixed effect, αt $_i$s year fixed effect and εi,t $_{is}$ the error term.

To analyze the effect of the GFC on CH, the dummy variable of GFC and the interaction terms of GFC x GPR and GFC x TRA to explore the joint effect of the trade and GPR with GFC on cash are presented by the model as follows:

$$CH_{ij,t} = \beta_0 + \beta_1 GPR_{j,t} + \beta_2 TRA_{j,t} + \beta_3 GFC_t + \beta_4 \left(GFC_t xGPR_{j,t}\right) + \beta_5 \left(GFC_t xTRA_{j,t}\right) + \beta_6 SIZE_{i,t} + \beta_7 MBR_{i,t} + \beta_8 INV_{i,t} + \beta_9 LEV_{i,t} + \beta_{10} NWC_{i,t} + \beta_{11} CFA_{i,t} + \beta_{12} R\&D_{i,t} + \alpha_i F_i + \varepsilon_{i,t} \quad (2)$$

where, GFC_t is the period dummy for the Global financial crisis 2008-2009, $GFC_t \times GPR_{j,t}$ is the interaction term of GFC and GPR; $GFC_t \times TRA_{j,t}$ is the interaction term of GFC and TRA.

$$CH_{ij,t} = \beta_0 + \beta_1 GPR_{j,t} + \beta_2 TRA_{j,t} + \beta_3 POST_t + \beta_4 \left(POST_t xGPR_{j,t}\right) + \beta_5 \left(POST_t xTRA_{j,t}\right) + \beta_6 SIZE_{i,t} + \beta_7 MBR_{i,t} + \beta_8 INV_{i,t} + \beta_9 LEV_{i,t} + \beta_{10} NWC_{i,t} + \beta_{11} CFA_{i,t} + \beta_{12} R\&D_{i,t} + \alpha_i F_i + \varepsilon_{i,t} \quad (3)$$

where, $POST_t$ is the period dummy for the post-GFC, $POST_t \times GPR_{j,t}$ is the interaction term of POST and GPR; $POST_t \times TRA_{j,t}$ is the interaction term of POST and TRA.

Data

The data is retrieved from Worldscope in Datastream International. Since the differences in their accounting systems, financial and utility firms are excluded from the sample. Hence, the final sample includes 11,960 non-financial firms and 127,775 firm-years for 18 countries (Brazil, China, Colombia, Hong Kong, India, Indonesia, Israel, Malaysia, Mexico, Philippines, Russia, Saudi Arabia, South Africa, South Korea, Thailand, Turkiye, Ukraine, and Venezuela) over the period 2002-2017. Table 1 presents the structure of the sample across the country and year. GPR and trade as country-level factors are taken from Caldara & Iacoviello (2022) and World Bank, respectively.

Table 1. Sample construction.

Country	Observation	Year	Observation
Brazil	2,751	2002	4,162
China	28,673	2003	4,671
Colombia	298	2004	5,092
Hong Kong	14,870	2005	6,781
India	22,413	2006	7,363
Indonesia	4,304	2007	7,840
Israel	2,149	2008	8,303
Malaysia	10,374	2009	8,844
Mexico	1,334	2010	9,272
Philippines	1,807	2011	9,516
Russia	3,183	2012	9,582
Saudi Arabia	1,183	2013	9,952
South Africa	3,000	2014	10,281
South Korea	21,297	2015	10,501
Thailand	6,572	2016	10,585
Turkiye	3,328	2017	5,030
Ukraine	90		
Venezuela	149		

Source: Worldscope

Variable Definitions

This chapter analyzes the impact of geopolitical risk and global trade on cash holdings. Dependent variable is cash holdings, which are measured as cash and short-term investments to total assets. The main explanatory variables are geopolitical risk – GPR and international trade – TRA. First, GPR has been developed by Caldara & Iacoviello (2022) and utilized by previous research (Wang et al., 2021). Next, TRA is the total import and export in the country (Tekin, 2021b). As firm-level control variables, this study includes firm size (SIZE), research and development expenses (R&D), cash flows (CFA), net working capital (NWC), investment (INV), and market-to-book ratio (MBR) as the literature do (Ozkan & Ozkan, 2004). This work also contains two-period dummies: GFC (2008-2009) and POST-GFC (2010-2017). Table 2 shows the variable definitions.

Summary Statistics

Summary statistics for the whole period (2002-2017), PRE-GFC (2002-2007), GFC (2008-2009) and POST-GFC (2010-2017) are presented in Table 3. Means of cash holdings rise in time. Also, the means of GPR and trade decrease and increase during and after the GFC, respectively.

Table 2. Definitions of variables.

Variables	Definitions
CH	Cash and short–term investments / Total assets
GPR	The log of geopolitical risk index is developed by Caldara & Iacoviello for each country
TRA	The log of import and export for each country
SIZE	The log of total assets
MBR	[Total assets – Book value of equity + Market value of equity] / Total assets
INV	Capital expenditures / Total assets
LEV	Total debt / Total assets
NWC	[Current assets – Current liabilities – Cash and short-term investments] / Total assets
CFA	[Total taxable income + Depreciation] / Total assets
R&D	Equals one for the R&D investing firms in current year, otherwise zero
GFC	Equals one for years 2008-2009, otherwise zero
POST-GFC	Equals one for years 2010-2017, otherwise zero

Source: Worldscope

Table 3. Summary statistics.

		CH	GPR	TRA	SIZE	MBR	INV	LEV	NWC	CFA	R&D
2002-2017	Mean	0.157	96.951	107.005	15.160	0.604	0.005	0.246	0.023	0.014	0.312
	SD	0.165	21.621	107.094	2.805	0.964	0.037	0.218	0.224	0.159	0.463
	Minimum	0.000	48.999	22.106	4.762	0.088	0.000	0.000	-0.649	-0.823	0.000
	Median	0.105	92.246	59.506	14.691	0.507	0.000	0.211	0.029	0.021	0.000
	Maximum	0.940	261.257	442.620	26.427	20.876	0.477	1.000	0.863	0.933	1.000
2002-2007	Mean	0.143	96.200	105.868	14.792	0.629	0.005	0.253	0.016	0.017	0.225
	SD	0.151	18.049	94.023	2.750	1.007	0.034	0.214	0.222	0.162	0.418
	Minimum	0.000	73.619	25.293	4.762	0.088	0.000	0.000	-0.649	-0.823	0.000
	Median	0.094	88.916	62.208	14.346	0.531	0.000	0.226	0.023	0.025	0.000
	Maximum	0.940	156.362	362.150	25.256	20.876	0.477	1.000	0.863	0.933	1.000
2008-2009	Mean	0.152	96.030	103.389	15.006	0.612	0.006	0.254	0.019	0.010	0.245
	SD	0.162	12.079	96.217	2.774	0.991	0.039	0.221	0.226	0.166	0.430
	Minimum	0.000	71.811	22.106	4.762	0.088	0.000	0.000	-0.649	-0.823	0.000
	Median	0.101	94.527	57.613	14.557	0.523	0.000	0.221	0.025	0.018	0.000
	Maximum	0.940	148.304	376.657	25.511	20.876	0.477	1.000	0.863	0.933	1.000
2010-2017	Mean	0.165	97.490	108.297	15.361	0.590	0.005	0.241	0.027	0.012	0.365
	SD	0.171	24.498	114.606	2.817	0.937	0.038	0.219	0.224	0.156	0.481
	Minimum	0.000	48.999	22.772	4.762	0.088	0.000	0.000	-0.649	-0.823	0.000
	Median	0.111	92.534	55.794	14.880	0.491	0.000	0.203	0.032	0.020	0.000
	Maximum	0.940	261.257	442.620	26.427	20.876	0.477	1.000	0.863	0.933	1.000

Source: Worldscope

Correlation Matrix

To understand whether the sample suffer from multicollinearity issue, previous research uses the variance inflation factor (VIF) (Tekin & Polat, 2021c). Reported VIF values across the whole- and sub-samples, which shown in Table 4 are smaller than five. Consequently, the whole- and sub-samples do not face with the multicollinearity problem.

Table 4. Correlation matrix.

		CH	GPR	TRA	SIZE	MBR	INV	LEV	NWC	CFA	VIF
	GPR	0.031									1.06
	TRA	0.194	-0.083								1.07
	SIZE	-0.089	0.113	-0.191							1.20
	MBR	-0.099	0.010	-0.039	-0.108						1.24
2002-2017	INV	0.026	0.072	-0.055	-0.115	0.177					1.06
	LEV	-0.356	-0.044	-0.100	0.102	0.335	0.029				1.40
	NWC	-0.018	-0.019	-0.016	-0.100	-0.283	0.025	-0.415			1.30
	CFA	0.160	-0.039	-0.081	0.072	-0.221	0.019	-0.312	0.284		1.19
	R&D	0.106	0.181	-0.072	0.267	-0.061	0.014	-0.082	0.061	0.037	1.12
	GPR	0.018									1.01
	TRA	0.213	0.002								1.14
	SIZE	-0.083	0.002	-0.297							1.26
	MBR	-0.086	0.005	-0.041	-0.114						1.21
2002-2007	INV	0.022	0.044	-0.062	-0.112	0.186					1.08
	LEV	-0.330	-0.027	-0.133	0.073	0.301	-0.016				1.34
	NWC	-0.045	-0.041	0.018	-0.056	-0.261	0.042	-0.405			1.29
	CFA	0.125	-0.060	-0.085	0.095	-0.206	0.039	-0.284	0.295		1.19
	R&D	0.052	0.015	-0.039	0.274	-0.029	0.047	-0.069	0.074	0.016	1.11
	GPR	-0.019									1.03
	TRA	0.196	0.122								1.10
	SIZE	-0.084	0.038	-0.173							1.19
	MBR	-0.071	-0.007	-0.015	-0.095						1.23
2008-2009	INV	0.069	-0.062	-0.049	-0.099	0.067					1.03
	LEV	-0.335	-0.001	-0.126	0.101	0.338	0.047				1.35
	NWC	-0.071	0.007	-0.027	-0.099	-0.299	0.014	-0.369			1.26
	CFA	0.171	-0.012	-0.097	0.048	-0.245	0.030	-0.308	0.262		1.18
	R&D	0.050	-0.046	0.028	0.270	-0.036	0.032	-0.048	0.044	0.019	1.11
	GPR	0.038									1.12
	TRA	0.187	-0.130								1.07
	SIZE	-0.104	0.159	-0.157							1.20
	MBR	-0.111	0.015	-0.043	-0.107						1.27
2010-2017	INV	0.016	0.103	-0.055	-0.121	0.204					1.08
	LEV	-0.371	-0.054	-0.082	0.123	0.352	0.044				1.45
	NWC	0.004	-0.016	-0.027	-0.127	-0.290	0.021	-0.430			1.33
	CFA	0.178	-0.035	-0.077	0.073	-0.224	0.007	-0.329	0.285		1.20
	R&D	0.129	0.254	-0.104	0.244	-0.078	-0.003	-0.088	0.056	0.058	1.14

Source: Worldscope

Note. This table shows correlation matrices and variance inflation factors (VIF) across the entire period (2002-2017), pre-GFC (2002-2007), GFC (2008-2009) and post-GFC (2010-2017). VIF demonstrates whether the sample deal with multicollinearity issue in the last column. All VIF values smaller than five that is why there is no multicollinearity problem in the whole sample and subsamples.

EMPIRICAL FINDINGS

Univariate Analyses

Table 5 shows how cash holdings differ from pre- to post-GFC across countries and the geopolitical risk and trade level. The sample is divided into the above and below mean of geopolitical risk and trade across countries and years. Cash levels of firms increase in all countries, excluding Colombia, Saudi Arabia, South Africa, and Ukraine. Besides, firms in risky and with higher trade volume countries have higher cash. Last, all firms raise their cash level in the post-GFC period.

Table 5. Comparison of mean of cash across countries, geopolitical risk and trade.

Countries	Pre	Post	Post – Pre	Countries	Pre	Post	Post – Pre
Brazil	11.94%	13.40%	1.46%***	Philippines	13.58%	17.29%	3.71%***
China	17.20%	21.34%	4.14%***	Russia	8.62%	10.12%	1.50%***
Colombia	7.34%	6.05%	-1.29%*	Saudi Arabia	12.78%	9.49%	-3.29%***
Hong Kong	23.00%	24.92%	1.92%***	South Africa	15.05%	12.77%	-2.28%***
India	7.22%	7.94%	0.72%***	South Korea	16.31%	17.45%	1.14%***
Indonesia	10.83%	12.21%	1.38%***	Thailand	9.79%	13.05%	3.26%***
Israel	20.23%	26.20%	5.97%***	Turkiye	9.13%	9.63%	0.50%
Malaysia	13.28%	16.26%	2.98%***	Ukraine	11.60%	5.72%	-5.88%***
Mexico	8.62%	10.45%	1.83%***	Venezuela	9.29%	10.37%	1.08%
Geopolitical risk				*Global trade*			
Higher risk	15.43%	17.43%	2.00%***	Higher volume	16.53%	18.40%	1.87%***
Lower risk	13.39%	15.80%	2.41%***	Lower volume	12.24%	14.91%	2.67%***
Higher-Lower	2.04%***	1.63%***		Higher-Lower	4.29%***	3.49%***	

Source: Worldscope

Note. This table compares the mean of cash across pre-GFC (2002-2007) and post-GFC (2010-2017) by considering the above and below mean across country and year of geopolitical risk and international trade. *p<0.10, ***p<0.01.

Multivariate Analyses

Table 6 presents the response to how geopolitical risk and trade affect corporate cash policy during and after the global financial crisis. Regarding the proper model, the results of the null hypothesis *"Difference in coefficients not systematic"* and Hausman tests show that the fixed effect is superior to the random effect.

In column 1, the roles of GPR and TRA on CH have been investigated by adding year dummies. GPR is positive and significant (the coefficient of GPR is 0.009 at 1%), but TRA is negative and significant (the coefficient of TRA is 0.009 at 5%). In other words, firms with higher risk and lower trade volume have to hold more cash which is in line with the literature (Kotcharin & Maneenop, 2020; Tekin, 2021b).

In column 2, the impact of the GFC and its interaction with the GPR and TRA on corporate cash holdings has been analyzed. During the GFC, while firms in the sample drop their cash level (the coefficient of GFC is –0.123 at 1%), firms in higher GPR countries hoard more cash (the coefficient of GFC x GPR is 0.028 at 1%). However, the influence of trade on cash retention does not change in turbulence.

In column 3, firms do not change their cash holding in the post-GFC. Also, the effects of GPR and trade on cash policy do not differ.

Table 6. Geopolitical risk, trade and cash holdings during and after the global financial crisis

	Dependent Variable: CH		
	(1)	(2)	(3)
GPR	0.009***	–0.005**	–0.006*
	(0.003)	(0.002)	(0.000)
TRA	–0.009**	0.000	–0.002
	(0.005)	(0.003)	(0.000)
GFC		–0.123***	
		(0.028)	
GFC x GPR		0.028***	
		(0.006)	
GFC x TRA		–0.002	
		(0.002)	
POST			–0.018
			(0.020)
POST x GPR			0.005
			(0.004)
POST x TRA			0.003
			(0.002)
Controls			
SIZE	–0.015***	–0.010***	–0.015***
	(0.001)	(0.001)	(0.001)
MBR	–0.004**	–0.003*	–0.004**
	(0.002)	(0.002)	(0.002)
INV	0.492***	0.508***	0.493***
	(0.060)	(0.061)	(0.060)
LEV	–0.169***	–0.176***	–0.170***
	(0.006)	(0.006)	(0.006)
NWC	–0.128***	–0.130***	–0.128***
	(0.005)	(0.005)	(0.005)
CFA	0.088***	0.086***	0.091***
	(0.005)	(0.005)	(0.005)
R&D	–0.008***	–0.007***	–0.009***
	(0.002)	(0.002)	(0.002)

Continued on following page

Table 6. Continued

	Dependent Variable: CH		
	(1)	(2)	(3)
Constant	0.414***	0.350***	0.431***
	(0.021)	(0.017)	(0.020)
Firm FE	YES	YES	YES
Year FE	YES	NO	NO
Hausman test	2420.62***	2473.33***	2762.18***
Firms	11,960	11,960	11,960
Observations	127,775	127,775	127,775

Note. This table shows how geopolitical risk-GPR and trade-TRA influence cash holdings over the period 2002-2017. In columns 2 and 3, interaction effects of GFC with GPR and TRA (2); and POST with GPR and TRA (3) on cash analyzed. Variables definitions are presented in Table 2. Hausman test results confirm that Fixed effect is preferable than Random effect. *p<0.10, **p<0.05, ***p<0.01.

FUTURE RESEARCH DIRECTIONS

This research evaluates how the GFC impacts cash holdings by considering the GPR and trade. Further research may include the effects of COVID-19 on corporate cash policy in the GPR context.

CONCLUSION

Since growing importance of GPR and trade, this chapter examines the influence of GPR and trade on cash holdings in a financial crisis context. Employing 127,775 firm-years for the period 2002-2017, firms in countries with higher GPR and trade have higher cash. Also, firms in countries with both higher and lower GPR and trade increase their cash holdings after the GFC. Hence, the GFC has substantial influence on cash retention with GPR and trade.

Considering the multivariate analyses, using fixed-effects model, empirical results mention that geopolitical risk has positive effect, but global trade has negative influence on cash hoarding. Namely, firms in countries with higher geopolitical risk and lower trade volume have higher cash balances. These results are aligned with the predictions of precautionary motive of cash.

The contributions of this chapter are manifold. First, this research investigates the impact of GPR and trade on corporate cash policy across 18 countries in the GFC era. The empirical findings have several implications. First, managers should shape their cash retention policies taking into account the exogenous shocks, GPR and trade level in their country of residence. Investors should count the market turmoils and GPR of countries in determining where and which firms to invest in. Policymakers may restructure the policies and regulations associated with cash hoarding rather than dividend payouts not to hurt firms during exogenous shocks like COVID-19. Practitioners and researchers should consider the macro-specific factors and the uncertainty periods and their impact on cash retention in risky countries. These results are particularly relevant to the post-COVID-19 world where unexpected shocks are even more expected.

ACKNOWLEDGMENT

This research received no specific grant from any funding agency in the public, commercial, or not-for-profit sectors.

REFERENCES

Al-Najjar, B., & Belghitar, Y. (2011). Corporate cash holdings and dividend payments: Evidence from simultaneous analysis. *Managerial and Decision Economics*, *32*(4), 231–241. doi:10.1002/mde.1529

Alves, P. (2018). Cash holdings around the world: Financial crisis, culture and shareholder rights. *MPRA Paper*, 100159.

Aysan, A. F., Polat, A. Y., Tekin, H., & Tunalı, A. S. (2022). The ascent of geopolitics: Scientometric analysis and ramifications of geopolitical risk. *Defence and Peace Economics*, 1–19. doi:10.1080/10242694.2022.2062981

Caldara, D., & Iacoviello, M. (2022). Measuring geopolitical risk. *The American Economic Review*, *112*(4), 1194–1225. doi:10.1257/aer.20191823

Chang, Y., Benson, K., & Faff, R. (2017). Are excess cash holdings more valuable to firms in times of crisis? Financial constraints and governance matters. *Pacific-Basin Finance Journal*, *45*, 157–173. doi:10.1016/j.pacfin.2016.05.007

Chen, H. C., Chou, R. K., & Lu, C. L. (2018). Saving for a rainy day: Evidence from the 2000 dot-com crash and the 2008 credit crisis. *Journal of Corporate Finance*, *48*, 680–699. doi:10.1016/j.jcorpfin.2017.12.025

D'Mello, R., Krishnaswami, S., & Larkin, P. J. (2008). Determinants of corporate cash holdings: Evidence from spin-offs. *Journal of Banking & Finance*, *32*(7), 1209–1220. doi:10.1016/j.jbankfin.2007.10.005

Demir, E., Díez-Esteban, J. M., & García-Gómez, C. D. (2019). The impact of geopolitical risks on cash holdings of hospitality companies: Evidence from emerging countries. *Journal of Hospitality and Tourism Management*, *39*, 166–174. doi:10.1016/j.jhtm.2019.04.004

Demiralay, S., & Kilincarslan, E. (2019). The impact of geopolitical risks on travel and leisure stocks. *Tourism Management*, *75*, 460–476. doi:10.1016/j.tourman.2019.06.013

Dittmar, A., Mahrt-Smith, J., & Servaes, H. (2003). International Corporate Governance and Corporate Cash Holdings. *Journal of Financial and Quantitative Analysis*, *38*(1), 111. doi:10.2307/4126766

Duchin, R., Ozbas, O., & Sensoy, B. A. (2010). Costly external finance, corporate investment, and the subprime mortgage credit crisis. *Journal of Financial Economics*, *97*(3), 418–435. doi:10.1016/j.jfineco.2009.12.008

Ferreira, M. A., & Vilela, A. S. (2004). Why do firms hold cash? Evidence from EMU countries. *European Financial Management*, *10*(2), 295–319. doi:10.1111/j.1354-7798.2004.00251.x

Foley, C. F., & Manova, K. (2015). *International trade, multinational activity, and corporate finance.* NBER Working Paper Series, No: 20634.

Huang, X., & Liu, X. (2017). How do firms finance their exports?–evidence from China. *The Journal of International Trade & Economic Development*, *26*(2), 154–173. doi:10.1080/09638199.2016.1227869

Jiang, Y., Tian, G., Wu, Y., & Mo, B. (2020). Impacts of geopolitical risks and economic policy uncertainty on Chinese tourism-listed company stock. *International Journal of Finance & Economics*, *27*(1), 320–333. doi:10.1002/ijfe.2155

Kotcharin, S., & Maneenop, S. (2020). Geopolitical risk and corporate cash holdings in the shipping industry. *Transportation Research Part E, Logistics and Transportation Review*, *136*(January), 101862. doi:10.1016/j.tre.2020.101862

Kotcharin, S., & Maneenop, S. (2020). Geopolitical risk and shipping firms' capital structure decisions in belt and road initiative countries. *International Journal of Logistics Research and Applications*, *23*(6), 544–560. doi:10.1080/13675567.2020.1766003

Le, A. T., & Tran, T. P. (2021). Does geopolitical risk matter for corporate investment? Evidence from emerging countries in Asia. *Journal of Multinational Financial Management*, *62*, 100703. doi:10.1016/j.mulfin.2021.100703

Lee, B. S., & Suh, J. (2011). Cash holdings and share repurchases: International evidence. *Journal of Corporate Finance*, *17*(5), 1306–1329. doi:10.1016/j.jcorpfin.2011.06.006

Lee, C. C., & Wang, C. W. (2021). Firms' cash reserve, financial constraint, and geopolitical risk. *Pacific-Basin Finance Journal*, *65*, 101480. doi:10.1016/j.pacfin.2020.101480

Muğaloğlu, E., Polat, A. Y., Tekin, H., & Dogan, A. (2021a). Oil price shocks during the COVID-19 pandemic: Evidence from United Kingdom energy stocks. *Energy Research Letters*, *2*(1). Advance online publication. doi:10.46557/001c.24253

Muğaloğlu, E., Polat, A. Y., Tekin, H., & Kılıç, E. (2021b). Assessing the impact of Covid-19 pandemic in Turkey with a novel economic uncertainty index. *Journal of Economic Studies (Glasgow, Scotland)*. Advance online publication. doi:10.1108/JES-02-2021-0081

Ozkan, A., & Ozkan, N. (2004). Corporate cash holdings: An empirical investigation of UK companies. *Journal of Banking & Finance*, *28*(9), 2103–2134. doi:10.1016/j.jbankfin.2003.08.003

Polat, A. Y. (2018). Subprime mortgages and lending bubbles. *Bulletin of Monetary Economics and Banking*, *21*(2), 191–216.

Polat, A. Y. (2020a). Borç vadesi ve finansal kriz: Türkiye örneği. *Journal of Erciyes University Faculty of Economics and Administrative Sciences*, (1), 118-130.

Polat, A. Y. (2020b). Davranışsal iktisat ve kamu politikaları. In *Ekonomi ve İşletmede Güncel Yaklaşımlar* [Behavioral economics and public policy. In Economics and Current Approaches in Business] (pp. 101–133). Gazi Kitabevi.

Polat, A. Y. (2021). *Davranışsal finans teorisi ve kripto paralar* [Behavioral Finance Theory and Cryptocurrencies]. Efe Akademi Yayınları.

Polat, A. Y., Aysan, A. F., Tekin, H., & Tunali, A. S. (2021). Bitcoin-specific fear sentiment matters in the COVID-19 outbreak. *Studies in Economics and Finance*, *39*(1), 98–110. doi:10.1108/SEF-02-2021-0080

Sun, Z., & Wang, Y. (2015). Corporate precautionary savings: Evidence from the recent financial crisis. *The Quarterly Review of Economics and Finance*, *56*, 175–186. doi:10.1016/j.qref.2014.09.006

Tekin, H. (2020a). Firm size and dividend policy of European firms: Evidence from financial crises. *Marmara Journal of European Studies*, *28*(1), 109–121. doi:10.29228/mjes.11

Tekin, H. (2020b). Firma riski ve COVID-19: *Birleşik Krallıktaki havayolu yolcu taşımacılığı örneği* [Example of Air Passenger Transport in the UK]. 7. Uluslararası Muhasebe ve Finans Araştırmaları Kongresi.

Tekin, H. (2020c). How optimal cash changed by the global financial crisis? A multi-country analysis. *Economics and Business Letters, 9*(2), 114–123. doi:10.17811/ebl.9.2.2020.114-123

Tekin, H. (2020d). Optimal leverage of travel and leisure firms in Europe. *Marmara Conference on European Studies (MCES) 2020,* 387-394. http://katalog.marmara.edu.tr/muyayinevi/YN875.pdf

Tekin, H. (2021a). Avrupa'da kâr payı dağıtımı, pay geri alımları ve finansal krizler [Dividend distribution, share buybacks and financial crises in Europe]. In *5. Uluslararası Ekonomi ve Finans Konferansı Gelisim-UWE 2021.* http://acikerisim.gelisim.edu.tr/xmlui/handle/11363/2893

Tekin, H. (2021b). How the global financial crisis and international trade affected corporate decisions?: International evidence. In *Impact of Global Issues on International Trade* (pp. 137–157). IGI Global. doi:10.4018/978-1-7998-8314-2.ch008

Tekin, H. (2021c). Market differences and adjustment speed of debt, equity, and debt maturity. *Australian Journal of Management, 46*(4), 629–651. doi:10.1177/0312896220968266

Tekin, H. (2022a). Does corruption matter on corporate payouts in the Covid era? Evidence from Muslim countries. *FICCOMS FEMFEST International Conference on Economics, Management and Business 2022.*

Tekin, H. (2022b). *Gelişen ekonomilerde sermaye yapısı* [Capital Structure in Emerging Economies]. Genişletilmiş 2. Baskı, Efe Akademi Yayınları.

Tekin, H. (2022c). How do financial constraints and financial crises matter in cash management?: Evidence from developing Asian economies. In *Handbook of Research on Current Trends in Asian Economics, Business, and Administration* (pp. 228–248). IGI Global. doi:10.4018/978-1-7998-8486-6.ch012

Tekin, H., & Polat, A. Y. (2020a). Agency theory: A review in finance. *Anemon: Journal of Social Sciences of Mus Alparslan University, 8*(4), 1323–1329.

Tekin, H., & Polat, A. Y. (2020b). Is saving vital? Evidence from the financial crisis. *Economics and Business Letters, 9*(2), 124–134. doi:10.17811/ebl.9.2.2020.124-134

Tekin, H., & Polat, A. Y. (2020c). The global financial crisis and capital structure decisions of Turkish SMEs: A review. *International Journal of Management Economics and Business*, *16*(3), 513–535. doi:10.17130/ijmeb.798509

Tekin, H., & Polat, A. Y. (2021a). Adjustment speed of debt maturity: Evidence from financial crises in East Asia. *Bulletin of Monetary Economics and Banking*, *24*(1), 71–92. doi:10.21098/bemp.v24i1.1287

Tekin, H., & Polat, A. Y. (2021b). Do market differences matter on dividend policy? *Borsa Istanbul Review*, *24*(2), 197–208. doi:10.1016/j.bir.2020.10.009

Tekin, H., & Polat, A. Y. (2021c). *Is leverage a substitute or outcome for governance? Evidence from financial crises*. International Journal of Emerging Markets. doi:10.1108/IJOEM-03-2020-0297

Tekin, H., & Polat, A. Y. (2021d). Küresel finansal krizin araştırma-geliştirme harcamaları ayarlama hızı üzerindeki etkisi [The effect of the global financial crisis on the rate of adjustment of research and development expenditures]. *Verimlilik Dergisi*, *21*(4), 119–131. doi:10.51551/verimlilik.829028

Tekin, H., Polat, A. Y., Aysan, A. F., & Muğaloğlu, E. (2021a). Cash management, governance, and the global financial crisis: Evidence from developing Asia. *Asian Economics Letters*, *2*(4), 27135. doi:10.46557/001c.27135

Tekin, H., Polat, A. Y., & Muğaloğlu, E. (2021b). Küresel finansal kriz ve nakit tutma ayarlama hızı [The Global Financial Crisis and the Pace of Cash Holding Adjustment]. *Anemon Muş Alparslan Üniversitesi Sosyal Bilimler Dergisi*, *9*(4), 1099–1110. doi:10.18506/anemon.888504

Wang, K. H., Xiong, D. P., Mirza, N., Shao, X. F., & Yue, X. G. (2021). Does geopolitical risk uncertainty strengthen or depress cash holdings of oil enterprises? Evidence from China. *Pacific-Basin Finance Journal*, *66*, 101516. doi:10.1016/j.pacfin.2021.101516

ADDITIONAL READING

Bates, T. W., Kahle, K. M., & Stulz, R. M. (2009). Why do US firms hold so much more cash than they used to? *The Journal of Finance*, *64*(5), 1985–2021. doi:10.1111/j.1540-6261.2009.01492.x

Campello, M., Graham, J. R., & Harvey, C. R. (2010). The real effects of financial constraints: Evidence from a financial crisis. *Journal of Financial Economics*, *97*(3), 470–487. doi:10.1016/j.jfineco.2010.02.009

Keynes, J. M. (1936). *The general theory of employment, interest and money.* Macmillan Cambridge University Press.

Opler, T., Pinkowitz, L., Stulz, R., & Williamson, R. (1999). The determinants and implications of corporate cash holdings. *Journal of Financial Economics*, *52*(1), 3–46. doi:10.1016/S0304-405X(99)00003-3

KEY TERMS AND DEFINITIONS

Corporate Cash Holdings: The ratio of cash and cash equivalent divided by total assets.

Financial Crisis of 2008-2009: The crisis of banking and financial system collapse and situation of financial strait at the beginning that started in 2008.

Geopolitical Risk: The threat, realization, and escalation of adverse events.

Global Trade: The import and export of goods and services across international boundaries.

APPENDIX

Table 7 represents the means of cash holdings (CH), geopolitical risk (GPR), and trade (TRA) for each country in the sample. While firms in Israel and Hong Kong have the highest cash level, those in Colombia and Ukraine have the lowest cash level. Ukraine has the highest GPR, and Indonesia is at the bottom of the list. Regarding the trade volume, Malaysia follows Hong Kong, which is at the top of the list by a considerable margin.

Table 7. Means of cash holdings, geopolitical risk, and trade by country.

Country	CH	GPR	TRA	Country	CH	GPR	TRA
Brazil	0.129	100.056	25.639	Philippines	0.159	110.135	68.283
China	0.202	96.675	48.649	Russia	0.098	104.097	49.952
Colombia	0.063	80.458	37.298	Saudi Arabia	0.105	108.637	80.048
Hong Kong	0.243	90.436	379.901	South Africa	0.138	87.766	59.883
India	0.076	82.608	47.510	South Korea	0.171	113.347	84.115
Indonesia	0.117	75.043	49.683	Thailand	0.118	104.127	128.711
Israel	0.245	89.277	68.997	Turkiye	0.094	124.650	50.190
Malaysia	0.150	98.197	164.430	Ukraine	0.062	134.145	99.805
Mexico	0.097	107.573	61.420	Venezuela	0.099	104.839	51.732

Source: Worldscope

Chapter 4
Rule of Law, International Trade, and Corporate Financing Decisions in Europe:
Evidence From the COVID-19 Pandemic

Ali Yavuz Polat
Abdullah Gül University, Turkey

ABSTRACT

This chapter investigates whether the institutional environment that the firms operate has an impact on their leverage choice. Namely, rule of law is used as an institutional variable. Considering that better implementation of rule of law impacts positively firms' export performance, total exports in each country are also used as the other main explanatory variable. The findings show that both institutional variables and exports negatively and significantly affect the leverage level. This implies that firms in favorable institutional environment tend to borrow less, which results with lower leverage. Moreover, this study finds that the COVID-19 pandemic period as an unprecedented shock to economies pushed the leverage levels higher. Regarding the implications of the findings, firms' capacity to access external finance especially during a significant crisis period depends on the institutional environment. Namely, the effective implementation of rule of law should be first priority for the policy makers.

DOI: 10.4018/978-1-6684-5950-8.ch004

INTRODUCTION

Corporate finance has focused on the effects of imperfections on capital structure considering the "idealistic" assumptions of Modigliani and Miller (1958). One of the deviations from the ideal Modigliani-Miller world is the existence of agency conflicts between the shareholders and managers (Jensen, 1986). Firms may have different strategies to overcome agency problems. Besides, the institutional environment that the firms operate may affect firms' agency costs. Thus, the strength of legal environment and institutional quality, as a tool to minimize agency problems, impacts the leverage choice of the firms. The institutional literature confirms the positive effect of high-quality institutions on increasing firm performance and accordingly facilitating economic growth (North, 1993; Acemoglu et al., 2003). However, what is interesting and overlooked in the literature is the joint effect of country governance quality and international trade on leverage choice of the firms. This is because high quality institutional setting in a country may create more favorable environment impacting positively firms' performance (LiPuma et al., 2013) As a complementary argument, the firms who benefit interaction with outside world may also have advantages in overcoming conflicts within the firms. Therefore, it is interesting and timely to analyze the impact of both institutional environment and trade performance on firms' corporate financing decisions.

This chapter aims to empirically analyze how country governance impact on leverage of European firms considering international trade as well. A comprehensive firm-level data is utilized from 25 European countries retrieved from Datastream. This chapter considers *rule of law* as the proxy for institutional quality collected from WGI database. This variable reflect the institutional environment that firms operate in, which has an impact on corporate financing decisions (Tekin, 2022a, 2022b; Tekin and Polat, 2020c, 2021a; Tekin et al. 2021a). Namely, firms tend to use leverage as a tool to mitigate agency conflict and to discipline the managers if institutional environment is not good enough to deal with agency problems (Tekin and Polat, 2020a; 2021c). Though there are studies focusing on the relationship between international trade and the capital structure separately, there are no studies examining the effect of country governance and trade on the choice of financial leverage in Europe. For trade variable total value of exports of a country is used as a proxy, since there is an important relationship between institutional quality and export performance (Francois and Manchin, 2006; 2013).

This study focuses on European evidence in order to understand the changing dynamic due to the Covid-19 pandemic (Mugaloglu et al., 2021a, 2021b; Polat, 2020a,b; Polat, 2021; Polat et al. 2021) which significantly affects all European countries. Considering the effect of the pandemic on world trade and supply chain it will be insightful to analyze the pandemic in terms of its global impacts. Crisis periods such as the Covid-19 pandemic provides a natural experiment opportunity as an external shock to investigate the role of country governance during turbulence periods (Tekin, 2020a, 2020b, 2021a, 2021b, 2021c, 2022c; Tekin and Polat 2021d; Tekin et al. 2021b). More specifically, the chapter focuses on how rule of law, together with exports interact in impacting corporate capital structure decisions during the pandemic.

Our findings show that both institutional variables and exports negatively and significantly affect the leverage level. This implies that firms in favorable institutional environment tend to borrow less which results in lower leverage. Moreover, this study finds that the COVID-19 pandemic period as an unprecedented shock to economies pushed the leverage levels higher. Regarding the implications of the findings, firms' capacity to access external finance, especially during a significant crisis period depends on the institutional environment. Namely, the effective implementation of rule of law should be the first priority for the policymakers.

The contribution of this chapter is manifold. First, the influence of international trade on the leverage choice of firms is investigated considering the difference in the institutional environment that the firms operate. This is important since institutional quality (such as rule of law) impacts firms' financing decisions. Second, the date covers also the COVID-19 pandemic period, which helps us to infer insights about the impact of the pandemic.

BRIEF LITERATURE

Earlier studies in the literature mention that macroeconomic conditions impact capital structure decisions (Demirguc-Kunt *et al.*, 2020). Especially during downturns, the credit supply squeezes so that there are less available funds for firms (Deyoung *et al.*, 2015; Thakor, 2015). Being caught in a financial downturn with high leverage level creates extra problems, since the financial crisis puts more pressure to the firms operating in a poor government environment. Moreover, even though there are studies focusing on the dynamics of leverage choice during financial crises, there are very limited studies examining the combined effect of governance and international trade on the firm's debt choice. Considering that the COVID-19 pandemic also caused a significant economic crisis, one should expect an effect on firms capital structure choice. This study fills this gap in the literature by including the pandemic period into the analysis.

Institutional environment is expected to impact on the leverage level. Depending on whether firms operate in a high- or low-quality institutional setting may affect the role of leverage as a tool to mitigate agency problems (Tekin 2020a, Tekin and Polat, 2020b, 2021b). Firms may choose their leverage level strategically in order to limit managers discretionary power and avoid their inefficient use of firm's resources, since with higher leverage managers are left with less cash flow (La Porta et al., 2000; Tekin and Polat, 2021c). On the other hand, high leverage during a financial crisis may put stress on firms' capital structure (Polat, 2018; Aysan et al. 2016). Therefore, it is insightful to analyze the changing dynamics of firms' leverage choice considering a significant crisis due to the pandemic. During a crisis such as the pandemic, information asymmetry will widen so that firms may face bigger problems. Therefore, firms in poorly governed countries tend to have a higher borrowing level to limit managerial discretion.

The institutional environment of a country is also expected to impact the propensity to export for firms since higher exports imply a bigger competitive power for these firms (Francois and Manchin, 2006; 2013). Thus, one expects a positive relationship between high quality institutions and export, especially for small firms. Ranjan et al. (2005) build a theoretical argument that enforcement of contracts is important for trade patterns. Their result is consistent with our findings that the rule of law and regulatory quality matter for firms' capital structure choices. The findings in the literature provide evidence that institutional quality is a significant determinant for trade (Levchenko, 2007) and matters for bilateral trade as well (Anderson and Marcouiller, 2002).

DATA

For governance variables, country-level governance (Worldwide Governance Indicators) data is utilized from Kaufmann et al. (2011). Namely, *rule of law* is used as a proxy for intuitional quality. Firm-level variables-leverage and control variables-describe firm characteristics. Leverage is our variable of interest so leverage is the dependent variable. Leverage is measured as the Total Book Leverage (BLEV) which is the ratio of total debt to total assets (Van Hoang et al., 2018).

Firm-specific variables are gathered from Worldscope data provided by Datastream spanning from 2013 to 2020 covering 25 European countries; Austria, Belgium, Bosnia Herzegovina, Bulgaria, Switzerland, Cyprus, Czechia, Denmark, Germany Spain, Croatia, Finland, France, Greece, United Kingdom, Hungary, Ireland, Italy, Netherlands, Norway, Poland, Portugal, Sweden and Turkey.

We obtain governance data called as Worldwide Governance Indicators (WGI) from Kaufmann et al. (2011). WGI is formed of six different indicators: Rule of law, control of corruption, government effectiveness, politic stability, regulatory quality, and voice and accountability. This study specifically focuses on "rule of law". Trade data is gathered from UN Comtrade Database. Each countries' total exports in USD value is considered as the second important explanatory variable.

For firm characteristics, only non-financial firms are included and the utility firms are excluded as well. This choice is due to financial and utility firms' having quite different accounting structure (Bates et al. 2018).

Table 1. Variable definitions.

Variables	Symbols	Definitions
Leverage	LEV	Total debt (WC03255) / Total assets (WC02999)
Rule of Law	RL	Rule of law score for a country which varies from -2.5 to 2.5 (high)
Exports	EXP	Logarithm of Total exports in USD value
Cash holdings	CASH	Cash and short–term investments (WC02001) / Total assets (WC02999)
Firm size	SIZE	The log of total assets (WC02999)
Market-to-book ratio	MBR	[Total assets (WC02999) – Book value of equity (WC03501) + Market value of equity (WC08001)] / Total assets (WC02999)
Profitability	PROF	Earnings before interest and tax (EBIT, WC18191)/Total assets (WC02999)]
Tangibility	TAN	Net tangible assets (NTA) / Total assets (WC02999)
Covid-19 Pandemic Crisis	COVID	Dummy variable equals one for the year 2020, otherwise zero

Source: Worldscope and UN Comtrade

Descriptive Statistics

Table 2 provides descriptive statistics.

Table 2. Descriptive statistics

Variable	Obs	Mean	Std. Dev.	Min	Max
LEV	30680	0.222	0.227	0	1
RL	31329	1.297	0.703	-0.359	2.130
SIZE	31477	11.939	2.757	3.784	22.410
MBR	28287	2.410	3.344	0.076	20.198
PROF	30550	-0.019	0.289	-0.989	1
TAN	30509	0.252	0.267	0	1
CASH	31170	0.189	0.224	0	1
EXP	32066	26.230	1.152	21.482	28.077

Note. This table presents the mean, standard deviation (SD), minimum and maximum values of the variables

Table 3 presents the correlation between the variables.

Table 3. Correlation matrix

	LEV	RL	EXP	SİZE	MBR	PROF	TAN	CASH
LEV	1							
RL	-0.116	1						
EXP	-0.062	0.352	1					
SİZE	0.103	0.183	-0.012	1				
MBR	0.020	0.016	0.029	-0.284	1			
PROF	0.031	-0.193	-0.021	0.225	-0.091	1		
TAN	0.309	-0.223	-0.227	0.141	-0.092	0.158	1	
CASH	-0.203	0.079	0.091	-0.287	0.372	-0.147	-0.246	1

Note. This table presents the correlation values between variables.

METHODOLOGY

The literature mainly employs panel data (Rajan & Zingales, 1995; Frank & Goyal, 2009). There are different estimation methods for panel data. Since the nature of panel data includes both time and group effects, there are mainly two methods utilized in the literature: Fixed Effect (FE) and Random Effect model (RE) models. Also, as group sizes are larger than the time periods, Fixed Effects model is usually preferred over Random Effects model (Fan et al., 2012; Oztekin, 2015; Tekin & Polat, 2020).

$$LEV_{i,j,t} = \beta_0 + \beta_1 RL_{j,t} + \beta_2 EXP_{J,t} + \beta_3 SIZE_{i,t} + \beta_4 MBR_{i,t} + \beta_5 PROF_{i,t} + \beta_6 TAN_{i,t} + \beta_7 CASH_{i,t} + \alpha_i F_i + \varepsilon_{ij,t} \quad (1)$$

$$LEV_{ij,t} = \beta_0 + \beta_1 RL_{j,t} + \beta_2 COVID_t + \beta_3 RL_{j,t} \times COVID_t + \beta_4 EXP_{J,t} + \beta_5 SIZE_{i,t} + \beta_6 MBR_{i,t} + \beta_7 PROF_{i,t} + \beta_8 TAN_{i,t} + \beta_9 CASH_{i,t} + \alpha_i F_i + \varepsilon_{ij,t} \quad (2)$$

$$LEV_{ij,t} = \beta_0 + \beta_1 RL_{j,t} + \beta_2 EXP_{J,t} + \beta_3 COVID_t + \beta_4 EXP_{J,t} \times COVID_t + \beta_5 SIZE_{i,t} + \beta_6 MBR_{i,t} + \beta_7 PROF_{i,t} + \beta_8 TAN_{i,t} + \beta_9 CASH_{i,t} + \alpha_i F_i + \varepsilon_{ij,t} \quad (3)$$

where, $LEV_{i,t}$ is the leverage defined as the ratio of total debt to total assets for firm i in country j at time t, $RL_{j,t}$ is the rule of law measure as our governance indicator, $EXP_{j,t}$ is total exports to world in USD, $SIZE_{i,t}$ is the firm size defined, $MBR_{i,t}$ is the market-to-book ratio, $TAN_{i,t}$ is tangibility, $PROF_{i,t}$ is the profitability, $CASH_{i,t}$ cash and short-term investments to total assets, $COVID_t$ is dummy variable equals 1 for the Covid-19 pandemic period. F_i is the firm fixed effects and $\varepsilon_{ij,t}$ is the error term.

This chapter investigates the impact of RL and EXP on leverage via three empirical models. Model (1) tests the hypothesis for the entire period, whereas models (2) and (3) include COVID dummies and their interaction with RL and EXP respectively. In that sense, we aim to understand whether the pandemic has a specific impact on firms' leverage choices.

RESULTS

The impact of rule of law (RL) and exports (EXP) on firms' leverage choice is analyzed in Table 4 below for the period between 2013 to 2020. Considering that our period spans the COVID-19 pandemic, COVID dummy and interaction terms are exploited in order to understand the impact of the pandemic.

In model 1, both rule of law (RL) and exports (EXP) are negatively and significantly associated with leverage (LEV). This implies that firms operating in countries with efficient rule of law borrow less. In other words, firms in poorly governed countries tend to borrow more to limit agency problems with their managers. This is in line with the substitute view of debt (La Porta et al., 2000). Considering the negative impact of EXP, firms with a higher propensity to export tend to have smaller debt. Regarding the control variables, all of them are significant and their signs are in line with theoretical predictions.

Table 4. Rule of Law, Exports and Leverage

Dependent Variable: Leverage (LEV)			
MODEL	**(1)**	**(2)**	**(3)**
RL	-0.092*** (0.012)	-0.055*** (0.012)	-0.052*** (0.012)
EXP	-0.024*** (0.009)	-0.005 (0.009)	-0.004 (0.009)
COVID		0.028*** (0.006)	-0.116** (0.053)
RL x COVID		0.002 (0.004)	
EXP x COVID			0.006*** (0.002)
Controls			
SIZE	0.022*** (0.004)	0.019*** (0.004)	0.019*** (0.004)
MBR	0.006*** (0.001)	0.005*** (0.001)	0.005*** (0.001)
PROF	-0.141*** (0.011)	-0.138*** (0.011)	-0.138*** (0.011)
TAN	0.303*** (0.024)	0.295*** (0.024)	0.295*** (0.024)
CASH	-0.081*** (0.014)	-0.089*** (0.014)	-0.090*** (0.014)
Constant	0.635*** (0.236)	0.123 (0.236)	0.094 (0.239)
Firm FE	INCLUDED	INCLUDED	INCLUDED
R-squared	0.804	0.806	0.806
Hausman test	339.98***	265.46***	261.74***
Firms	4045	4045	4045
Observations	25222	25222	25222

Note. This table presents how *rule of law* (RL) and *exports* (EXP) affect leverage. The definitions of variables are presented in Table 1. Hausman test results confirm that Fixed effect should be preferred rather than Random effect. Robust standard errors are presented in parentheses (.). *p<0.10, **p<0.05, ***p<0.01.

Regarding model 2, where the joint impact of COVID and RL is considered, COVID has a positive and significant effect on LEV implying that during the pandemic period firms borrowed more. This is an expected result, since the pandemic created a huge economic crisis where firms had to spent their cash holdings and increase their leverage in order to survive this unprecedented times. The joint impact of RLxCOVID is insignificant implying that the impact of the COVID-19 period is robust.

Considering model 3, the firms which are in a country where exports are higher tend to borrow more during the pandemic period. This result can be accounted for better terms for the firms in these countries so that they may access external finance easier during the pandemic. Regarding the control variables, all of them are significant in all three models and their signs are also the same, in line with theoretical predictions.

ROBUSTNESS ANALYSIS

Kaufmann et al. (2009) provides six different measures as proxies for a country's institutional quality. Among them "regulatory quality" is also considered in this chapter as a robustness check. Moreover, there is a vast literature on the impact of corruption on institutions. Thus we also consider "control of corruption" variable of Kaufmann et al. (2009) and rerun our main analysis. The results are provided in Table 5 below.

Regarding the "regulatory quality" variable, the main analysis is qualitatively similar. The firms operating in a better institutional environment (higher regulatory quality) tend to have smaller leverage levels. This result is in line with the substitute view of leverage (La Porta et al., 2000). Regarding the variable "control of corruption (CC)" we have qualitatively similar results. Moreover, when we repeat the analysis in model 2 and 3 for CC, we still get similar results that of "rule of law (RL)" estimations. Table 5 provides the analysis where "regulatory quality" is used as the institutional (governance) variable. The results are qualitatively similar to that of model (1) but only EXP variable loses its significance in the model (4) where *regulatory quality* (RQ) is used.

Table 5. Regulatory Quality, Exports and Leverage

Dependent Variable: Leverage (LEV)		
MODEL	**(4)**	**(5)**
RQ	-0.045*** (0.010)	
CC		-0.044*** (0.013)
EXP	-0.013 (0.009)	-0.022** (0.009)
Controls		
SIZE	0.026*** (0.004)	0.026*** (0.004)
MBR	0.006*** (0.001)	0.006*** (0.001)
PROF	-0.144*** (0.011)	-0.145*** (0.011)
TAN	0.306*** (0.024)	0.307*** (0.024)
CASH	-0.081*** (0.014)	-0.080*** (0.014)
Constant	0.230 (0.233)	0.460* (0.239)
Firm FE	INCLUDED	INCLUDED
R-squared	0.803	0.803
Hausman test	303.25***	337.74***
Firms	4045	4045
Observations	25222	25222

Note. This table presents how *regulatory quality* (RL) / *control of corruption* (CC) and *exports* (EXP) affect leverage. The definitions of variables are presented in Table 1. Robust standard errors are presented in parentheses (.). *p<0.10, **p<0.05, ***p<0.01.

CONCLUSION

This chapter aims to find out whether the institutional environment in which firms operate has an impact on their leverage choice. Namely, rule of law is used as an institutional variable. Considering that better implementation of rule of law impacts positively firms' export performance, total exports in each country are also used as the other main explanatory variable. Our findings show that both institutional variables-rule of law, regulatory quality and control of corruption-and exports negatively and significantly affect the leverage level. This implies that firms in favorable institutional environment tend to borrow less which results in lower leverage. Moreover, this study finds that the COVID-19 pandemic period as an unprecedented shock to economies pushed the leverage levels higher.

This study contributes to the literature in multiple ways. First, there is no earlier study focusing on the impact of rule of law and exports on the leverage choice of firms. Second, the date covers also the COVID-19 pandemic period, which helps us to infer insights about the impact of the pandemic.

The results also have implications for both policymakers and managers. Firms' capacity to access external finance, especially during a significant crisis period depends on the institutional environment. Namely, the effective implementation of rule of law should be the priority for the policymakers. Considering managers, they should be also careful about their policies depending on the environment that they operate in.

ACKNOWLEDGMENT

This study received no funding.

REFERENCES

Acemoglu, D., Johnson, S., Robinson, J. A., & Thaicharoen, Y. (2003). Institutional causes, macroeconomics symptoms: Volatility, crises, and growth. *Journal of Monetary Economics*, *50*(1), 49–122. doi:10.1016/S0304-3932(02)00208-8

Anderson, J. E., & Marcouiller, D. (2002). Insecurity and the pattern of trade: An empirical investigation. *The Review of Economics and Statistics*, *84*(2), 342–352. doi:10.1162/003465302317411587

Aysan, A. F., Ozturk, H., Polat, A. Y., & Saltoğlu, B. (2016). Macroeconomic drivers of loan quality in Turkey. *Emerging Markets Finance & Trade*, *52*(1), 98–109. doi:10.1080/1540496X.2016.1105688

Bates, T. W., Chang, C. H., & Chi, J. D. (2018). Why has the value of cash increased over time? *Journal of Financial and Quantitative Analysis*, *53*(2), 749–787. doi:10.1017/S002210901700117X

Claessens, S., Djankov, S., & Xu, L. C. (2000). Corporate performance in the East Asian financial crisis. *The World Bank Research Observer*, *15*(1), 23–46. doi:10.1093/wbro/15.1.23

Demirguc-Kunt, A., Peria, M. S. M., & Tressel, T. (2020). The global financial crisis and the capital structure of firms: Was the impact more severe among SMEs and non-listed firms? *Journal of Corporate Finance*, *60*, 101514. doi:10.1016/j.jcorpfin.2019.101514

Deyoung, R., Gron, A., Torna, G., & Winton, A. (2015). Risk overhang and loan portfolio decisions: Small business loan supply before and during the financial crisis. *The Journal of Finance*, *70*(6), 2451–2488. doi:10.1111/jofi.12356

Francois, J., & Manchin, M. (2006). *Institutional quality, infrastructure, and the propensity to export*. Working Paper.

Francois, J., & Manchin, M. (2013). Institutions, infrastructure, and trade. *World Development*, *46*, 165–175. doi:10.1016/j.worlddev.2013.02.009

Frank, M. Z., & Goyal, V. K. (2009). Capital structure decisions: Which factors are reliably important? *Financial Management*, *38*(1), 1–37. doi:10.1111/j.1755-053X.2009.01026.x

Jensen, M. C. (1986). Agency cost of free cash flow, corporate finance and takeovers. *The American Economic Review*, *76*(2), 323–329.

Kaufmann, D., Kraay, A., & Mastruzzi, M. (2011). The worldwide governance indicators: Methodology and analytical issues. *Hague Journal on the Rule of Law*, *3*(2), 220–246. doi:10.1017/S1876404511200046

La Porta, R., Lopez-de-Silanes, F., Shleifer, A., & Vishny, R. W. (2000). Agency problems and dividend policies around the world. *The Journal of Finance*, *55*(1), 1–33. doi:10.1111/0022-1082.00199

Levchenko, A. (2007). Institutional quality and international trade. *The Review of Economic Studies*, *74*(3), 791–819. doi:10.1111/j.1467-937X.2007.00435.x

LiPuma, J. A., Newbert, S. L., & Doh, J. P. (2013). The effect of institutional quality on firm export performance in emerging economies: A contingency model of firm age and size. *Small Business Economics*, *40*(4), 817–841. doi:10.100711187-011-9395-7

Modigliani, F., & Miller, M. H. (1958). The cost of capital, corporate finance and theory of investment. *The American Economic Review*, *48*(4), 261–297.

Muğaloğlu, E., Polat, A. Y., Tekin, H., & Dogan, A. (2021a). Oil price shocks during the COVID-19 pandemic: Evidence from United Kingdom energy stocks. *Energy Research Letters*, *2*(1). Advance online publication. doi:10.46557/001c.24253

Muğaloğlu, E., Polat, A. Y., Tekin, H., & Kılıç, E. (2021b). Assessing the impact of Covid-19 pandemic in Turkey with a novel economic uncertainty index. *Journal of Economic Studies (Glasgow, Scotland)*. Advance online publication. doi:10.1108/JES-02-2021-0081

North, D. C. (1993). Institutions and credible commitment. *Journal of Institutional and Theoretical Economics*, *149*, 11–23.

Polat, A. Y. (2018). Subprime mortgages and lending bubbles. *Bulletin of Monetary Economics and Banking*, *21*(2), 191–216.

Polat, A. Y. (2020a). Borç vadesi ve finansal kriz: Türkiye örneği [Debt Maturity and Financial Crisis: The case of Turkey]. *Erciyes Üniversitesi İktisadi ve İdari Bilimler Fakültesi Dergisi*, (1), 118–130. doi:10.18070/erciyesiibd.846318

Polat, A. Y. (2020b). Davranışsal iktisat ve kamu politikaları [Behavioral Economics and Public Policy]. In *Ekonomi ve İşletmede Güncel Yaklaşımlar* (pp. 101-133). Gazi Kitabevi.

Polat, A. Y. (2021). *Davranışsal finans teorisi ve kripto paralar* [Behavioral Finance Theory and Crypticurrencies]. Efe Akademi Yayınları.

Polat, A. Y., Aysan, A. F., Tekin, H., & Tunali, A. S. (2021). Bitcoin-specific fear sentiment matters in the COVID-19 outbreak. *Studies in Economics and Finance*, *39*(1), 98–110. doi:10.1108/SEF-02-2021-0080

Rajan, P., & Lee, J. Y. (2003). *Contract enforcement and the volume of international trade in different types of goods*. Working Paper.

Rajan, R. G., & Zingales, L. (1995). What do we know about capital structure? Some evidence from international data. *The Journal of Finance*, *50*(5), 1421–1460. doi:10.1111/j.1540-6261.1995.tb05184.x

Tekin, H. (2020a). Firm size and dividend policy of European firms: Evidence from financial crises. *Marmara Journal of European Studies*, *28*(1), 109–121. doi:10.29228/mjes.11

Tekin, H. (2020b). How optimal cash changed by the global financial crisis? A multi-country analysis. *Economics and Business Letters*, *9*(2), 114–123. doi:10.17811/ebl.9.2.2020.114-123

Tekin, H. (2021a). Avrupa'da kâr payı dağıtımı, pay geri alımları ve finansal krizler [Dividend distribution, share buybacks and financial crises in Europe]. *5. Uluslararası Ekonomi ve Finans Konferansı Gelisim-UWE 2021*. http://acikerisim.gelisim.edu.tr/xmlui/handle/11363/2893

Tekin, H. (2021b). How the global financial crisis and international trade affected corporate decisions?: International evidence. In *Impact of Global Issues on International Trade* (pp. 137–157). IGI Global. doi:10.4018/978-1-7998-8314-2.ch008

Tekin, H. (2021c). Market differences and adjustment speed of debt, equity, and debt maturity. *Australian Journal of Management*, *46*(4), 629–651. doi:10.1177/0312896220968266

Tekin, H. (2022a). Does corruption matter on corporate payouts in the Covid era? Evidence from Muslim countries. *FICCOMS FEMFEST International Conference on Economics, Management and Business 2022.*

Tekin, H. (2022b). *Gelişen ekonomilerde sermaye yapısı. Genişletilmiş 2* [Capital Structure in Emergin Economies. Extended 2]. Efe Akademi Yayınları.

Tekin, H. (2022c). How do financial constraints and financial crises matter in cash management?: Evidence from developing Asian economies. In *Handbook of Research on Current Trends in Asian Economics, Business, and Administration* (pp. 228–248). IGI Global. doi:10.4018/978-1-7998-8486-6.ch012

Tekin, H., & Polat, A. Y. (2020a). Agency theory: A review in finance. *Anemon: Journal of Social Sciences of Mus Alparslan University*, *8*(4), 1323–1329.

Tekin, H., & Polat, A. Y. (2020b). Is saving vital? Evidence from the financial crisis. *Economics and Business Letters*, *9*(2), 124–134. doi:10.17811/ebl.9.2.2020.124-134

Tekin, H., & Polat, A. Y. (2020c). The global financial crisis and capital structure decisions of Turkish SMEs: A review. *International Journal of Management Economics and Business*, *16*(3), 513–535. doi:10.17130/ijmeb.798509

Tekin, H., & Polat, A. Y. (2021a). Adjustment speed of debt maturity: Evidence from financial crises in East Asia. *Bulletin of Monetary Economics and Banking*, *24*(1), 71–92. doi:10.21098/bemp.v24i1.1287

Tekin, H., & Polat, A. Y. (2021b). Do market differences matter on dividend policy? *Borsa Istanbul Review*, *24*(2), 197–208. doi:10.1016/j.bir.2020.10.009

Tekin, H., & Polat, A. Y. (2021c). *Is leverage a substitute or outcome for governance? Evidence from financial crises.* International Journal of Emerging Markets. doi:10.1108/IJOEM-03-2020-0297

Tekin, H., & Polat, A. Y. (2021d). Küresel finansal krizin araştırma-geliştirme harcamaları ayarlama hızı üzerindeki etkisi [The effect of the global financial crisis on the rate of adjustment of research and development expenditures]. *Verimlilik Dergisi*, *21*(4), 119–131. doi:10.51551/verimlilik.829028

Tekin, H., Polat, A. Y., Aysan, A. F., & Muğaloğlu, E. (2021a). Cash management, governance, and the global financial crisis: Evidence from developing Asia. *Asian Economics Letters*, *2*(4), 27135. doi:10.46557/001c.27135

Tekin, H., Polat, A. Y., & Muğaloğlu, E. (2021b). Küresel finansal kriz ve nakit tutma ayarlama hızı [The global financial crisis and the pace of cash holding adjustment]. *Anemon Muş Alparslan Üniversitesi Sosyal Bilimler Dergisi*, *9*(4), 1099–1110. doi:10.18506/anemon.888504

Thakor, A. (2015). Lending booms, smart bankers, and financial crises. *The American Economic Review*, *105*(5), 305–309. doi:10.1257/aer.p20151090

Van Hoang, T. H., Gurau, C., Lahiani, A., & Seran, T. L. (2018). Do crises impact capital structure? A chapter of French micro-enterprises. *Small Business Economics*, *50*(1), 181–199. doi:10.100711187-017-9899-x

KEY TERMS AND DEFINITIONS

Agency Costs: Especially for large firms, the owners are usually not the managers, thus there is a basic principal-agent relationship which brings agency costs.

COVID-19 Pandemic: At the beginning of 2020, the SARS-CoV-2 virus spread to all the world creating one the most significant health crisis in modern times. Thus, the health crisis also results in a catastrophic economic crisis.

Leverage: The ratio of the total debt of a firm to its total assets.

Rule of Law: A numeric proxy for the efficient implementation of rule of law in a country. It includes both formal and informal institutions. The higher the value the better the implementation.

APPENDIX

Table 6. Descriptive statistics for main variables according to each country

Country		LEV	RL	EXP	Country		LEV	RL	EXP
Austria	Mean	0.279	1.861	25.809	**Hungary**	Mean	0.181	0.518	25.449
	Median	0.275	1.843	25.812		Median	0.133	0.527	25.454
	S.D.	0.181	0.046	0.070		S.D.	0.203	0.062	0.074
	Min	0.000	1.800	25.698		Min	0.000	0.407	25.331
	Max	1.000	1.943	25.899		Max	1.000	0.588	25.543
Belgium	Mean	0.253	1.424	26.419	**Ireland**	Mean	0.205	1.557	25.689
	Median	0.221	1.377	26.417		Median	0.163	1.499	25.651
	S.D.	0.230	0.065	0.081		S.D.	0.230	0.149	0.159
	Min	0.000	1.358	26.258		Min	0.000	1.383	25.498
	Max	1.000	1.552	26.501		Max	1.000	1.765	25.939
Bosnia	Mean	0.137	-0.227	22.513	**Italy**	Mean	0.273	0.332	26.953
	Median	0.074	-0.217	22.497		Median	0.258	0.314	26.953
	S.D.	0.180	0.046	0.106		S.D.	0.179	0.066	0.064
	Min	0.000	-0.306	22.352		Min	0.000	0.241	26.848
	Max	0.872	-0.152	22.695		Max	1.000	0.441	27.033
Bulgaria	Mean	0.166	-0.086	24.129	**Netherlands**	Mean	0.255	1.845	27.013
	Median	0.057	-0.088	24.176		Median	0.214	1.801	27.078
	S.D.	0.225	0.036	0.094		S.D.	0.210	0.076	0.089
	Min	0.000	-0.130	23.973		Min	0.000	1.760	26.865
	Max	1.000	-0.006	24.243		Max	1.000	1.978	27.100
Croatia	Mean	0.290	0.320	23.427	**Norway**	Mean	0.291	2.000	25.403
	Median	0.275	0.353	23.479		Median	0.245	1.985	25.366
	S.D.	0.219	0.064	0.122		S.D.	0.255	0.025	0.196
	Min	0.000	0.187	23.268		Min	0.000	1.966	25.139
	Max	1.000	0.395	23.569		Max	1.000	2.037	25.769
Cyprus	Mean	0.252	0.843	21.928	**Poland**	Mean	0.176	0.594	26.137
	Median	0.261	0.760	21.935		Median	0.136	0.540	26.123
	S.D.	0.210	0.166	0.220		S.D.	0.178	0.160	0.114
	Min	0.000	0.581	21.482		Min	0.000	0.420	25.994
	Max	1.000	1.077	22.346		Max	1.000	0.820	26.291

Continued on following page

Table 6. Continued

Country		LEV	RL	EXP	Country		LEV	RL	EXP
Czechia	Mean	0.239	1.073	25.928	**Portugal**	Mean	0.358	1.122	24.858
	Median	0.189	1.055	25.929		Median	0.351	1.132	24.863
	S.D.	0.245	0.042	0.093		S.D.	0.211	0.040	0.091
	Min	0.000	1.020	25.781		Min	0.000	1.045	24.731
	Max	1.000	1.141	26.034		Max	1.000	1.183	25.029
Denmark	Mean	0.212	1.917	25.374	**Spain**	Mean	0.330	0.990	26.467
	Median	0.146	1.877	25.410		Median	0.316	1.013	26.467
	S.D.	0.229	0.094	0.062		S.D.	0.216	0.053	0.072
	Min	0.000	1.815	25.273		Min	0.000	0.902	26.347
	Max	1.000	2.106	25.431		Max	1.000	1.059	26.570
Finland	Mean	0.262	2.066	24.944	**Sweden**	Mean	0.162	1.900	25.767
	Median	0.245	2.079	24.932		Median	0.100	1.862	25.766
	S.D.	0.188	0.041	0.098		S.D.	0.189	0.083	0.066
	Min	0.000	1.965	24.772		Min	0.000	1.806	25.661
	Max	1.000	2.130	25.044		Max	1.000	2.026	25.844
France	Mean	0.235	1.408	26.998	**Switzerland**	Mean	0.205	1.912	26.466
	Median	0.201	1.410	26.984		Median	0.177	1.931	26.463
	S.D.	0.197	0.036	0.066		S.D.	0.190	0.059	0.058
	Min	0.000	1.327	26.915		Min	0.000	1.805	26.392
	Max	1.000	1.457	27.066		Max	1.000	1.995	26.604
Germany	Mean	0.198	1.669	27.994	**Turkey**	Mean	0.347	-0.183	25.827
	Median	0.155	1.622	28.003		Median	0.005	-0.232	25.832
	S.D.	0.198	0.094	0.054		S.D.	0.457	0.145	0.064
	Min	0.000	1.558	27.915		Min	0.000	-0.359	25.729
	Max	1.000	1.855	28.077		Max	1.000	0.067	25.921
Greece	Mean	0.385	0.247	24.245	**United Kingdom**	Mean	0.191	1.687	26.864
	Median	0.334	0.184	24.300		Median	0.123	1.678	26.872
	S.D.	0.266	0.128	0.122		S.D.	0.226	0.107	0.099
	Min	0.000	0.075	24.049		Min	0.000	1.497	26.704
	Max	1.000	0.472	24.399		Max	1.000	1.879	27.030

Chapter 5
Global Trade and Economic Crisis:
In Context to South Asian Countries

Tanushree Gupta
https://orcid.org/0000-0002-3738-1690
Sandip University, Nashik, India

Disha Sharma
https://orcid.org/0000-0003-2124-0970
Amity University, Raipur, India

Susobhan Maiti
https://orcid.org/0000-0002-5725-9844
JAIN University (Deemed), Bangalore, India

ABSTRACT

Governments and corporations with the obstinacy to operate on a global scale can engage in international trade. Even today's global economy relies on the interdependence between nations. The South Asian region's connectivity can only be improved by enhancing intra-regional commerce. The present study is based on the global trade and economic crisis from the perspective of SAARC nations. In the current study, an effort has been made to examine the export, import, economic growth, and links between global trades for SAARC nations from 1990 to 2021. The analysis's findings suggest that the GDP, imports, and exports are growing in a cyclical pattern. The Granger causality result suggests that there are unidirectional and bidirectional causal relationships between world trade and country GDP development as well as within nations in the case of GDP growth. Therefore, the authors draw the conclusion that the key cause of the economic crisis in SAARC nations is global trade.

DOI: 10.4018/978-1-6684-5950-8.ch005

INTRODUCTION

The single counterintuitive idea about trade deals is that they are not all about trade. The modern era of free trade started about 1944 when all the bright minds of liberal economics has get to gather at 'Bretton Woods', New Hampshire. At that time the world was a pretty dim place and people were not yet overcome with World War I and World War II was raging across the Atlantic. And at that time the only thing at the top of everyone's mind is to maintain world peace. Thus, the creation of such an economy is much needed that fosters and necessitates world peace (Bhandari & Mohite, 2022). This idea emerges and seized out as economic independence, this involves the basic idea that if nation-states were dependent on each other for supply chain, and hence they couldn't go to war with each other. This is all the idea behind the 'Bretton Woods Conference' which later became General Agreement on Tariffs and Trade (GATT). GATT created the world we know today for trade, it created outsourcing, it created globalisation, it basically created the Multi-National Corporations (MNCs) we are looking at today, the structure we are looking at today (Upender, 2007) .

Trade is the engine of the global economy, more people, more goods, and more services are crossing borders today than ever before. But the scenario in trade has changed dramatically in the 21st century. Throughout much of history, a good produced in the country is largely made a part source there today products are composed the parts from all over the world. In order to fully understand trade, we have to measure the value-added at each point in the process, which outlines that the standard trade data do not reflect the accessory part considered in the production of the final product (Siriwardana, 2007). This brings out the need of developing the system for tracing the value that is added by all countries involved that produced the accessories of that product.

The Organization for Economic Co-operation and Development (OECD) - World Trade Organization (WTO) trade, and value-added initiatives aim for people to understand that traditional trade data is telling incomplete stories. Standard data shows that China has high surfaces with the United States and the European Union and a large deficit with Japan looked at in value-added terms, China surpluses and deficit decrease as Chinese exports have a high foreign content (Abdin, 2015). Japan is another country that runs high trade surfaces with the United States and more recently with China value-added data reveals smaller surfaces with China and larger surfaces with the United States. This analysis is able to illustrate the beneficiary who actually benefits from the trade and the quantified value in terms of both income and jobs. Trade improves competitiveness, cheaper imports of parts, and cheaper access to services bring benefits to consumers and companies alike. To realize the full potential we need seamless border crossings, simpler customer procedures, more trade liberalization, and decent logistics, especially in services (Gunawardhana & Damayanthi, 2020).

The Bretton woods brought GAAT on the period of extreme disruption, and convulsion of prosperity. From the time the GAAT was first signed, till late of 70s, the global GDP grew exponentially by seven percent per year (Anita et al., 2022). This trend soon came to vane and this phenomenon declined in late 70s and early 80s when the economist had another Bretton woods round and called as Uruguay Round. This eight year long discussion has changed the scenario and it can be seen that they are inspired with the idea of global efficiency instead of economic interdependence and peace. This basically talks about boosting our global economy. Though at the time of 80s the tariffs are already low and they ultimately they sized on the idea of non-tariffs barriers. From here and now this begins the era of modern trade and tariffs and to compete at an uneven playing field. In 1990s our trade was governed with this philosophy and in 1995 we get rid of GATT and replaced it with WTO. During this time parallel there were many other bilateral powerful trade agreements were taking place like North American Free Trade Agreement (NAFTA), Central America-Dominican Republic Free Trade Agreement (CAFTA) etc. These all are governed with the same philosophy of non-trade barriers which incidentally asks the countries to align their national trade policies, national trade laws with that global sense of efficiencies (Doshi et al., 2019; Siriwardana, 2007). This reflects the contradictory approach as they are in favour of free trade but are against the Trans-Pacific partnership.

Better Understanding of Trade Flows of South Asian Countries

The South Asian countries have attempted several ways in enhancing the trade patterns between the countries. Many South Asian nations boast some very ultimate stories. For our chapter, we have selected eight countries which are Afghanistan, Bangladesh, Bhutan, India, Maldives, Nepal, Pakistan, and Sri Lanka (arranged in lexical order). For the last many financial years, the infrastructure of most of the South Asian countries shares strong economic ties around the globe (Taneja & Bimal, 2020). As per a World Bank report, only 5 percent of the total trade of South Asia accounts for Intraregional trade as compared to ASEAN countries which amount to almost 25 percent. Thus, the severe scope of recovering the trade and its position among various Asian nations (Jain & Singh, 2009).

The additional factors for the restrictions with the South Asian nations are the availability of inadequate channels of transportation of such as road, marine, and air transportation. Another broader challenge is the trading of South Asian nations with non-South Asian nations (Al-Swidi et al., 2014; Muhammad et al., 2011) constraints contain perceived non-tariff barriers, protective tariffs, and entry or trade restrictions.

Thus, to support these pitfalls the nations themselves along with multiple global bodies, among all main contributors is World Bank (Paudel & Shrestha, 2022). World Bank has introduced multiple schemes to uplift the trade amongst South Asian countries, some of the schemes are; Afghanistan Digital Casa Project; Bangladesh Regional Connectivity Project 1; Khyber Pass Economic Corridor (Pakistan); West Bengal Transport and Logistics Improvement (India); Nepal-India Regional Trade and Transport Project, etc.

In our present chapter, **Firstly,** to find out the growth of export, import and economic growth which is measured by growth of GDP of south Asian countries and critically analyse their movement. Side by side to find out the linkage between trades related variables, proxy of economic growth and world trade. **Secondly**, to find out unidirectional or bidirectional causality of export, import and proxy of economic growth between the south Asian countries.

BACKGROUND

What Trade Deals Are Really About?

Trade is good in this ever-transforming world. Trade is something that is a contract agreed upon by the parties on the same terms and identification. Economists have quantified the benefits of trade and converted it into a model called Production Possibilities Frontier PPF) (Paudel & Shrestha, 2022). Basically, on any given day we are limited by the number of skills, time, resources, etc. This model simplifies the agenda of trade that has the elementary working culture of working together, a system of interdependence, and conditions of mutual benefits. International trade is the blood of the global economy, which includes goods as well as services (Nasir et al., 2018).

While considering the fundamentals a nation is very much concerned about the available opportunities in the wider market. Afghanistan has a surplus and hence their main export is Rugs, Dried Fruits, and Medicinal Plants mainly to the native Asian nations. In the context of main export partners, it includes United Arab Emirates (UAE) and Pakistan followed by India, the US, and China. As per the reports, Afghanistan stands at 105th in the largest good trading partner. Whereas Bangladesh stands as the 46th largest goods trading partner (Kappa, 2022). The major exports contain apparel, textile articles, footwear, vegetable fibres, etc. India is one of the prime countries amongst all Asian nations, say in terms of economic contribution, maintaining peace, largest skilled population, and decent terms with neighbouring nations. In the context of economies, India and Bangladesh are the two largest growing economies. In recent times the Government of India (GOI) has been taking various steps order to boost the economy by adopting and equating the terms of trade with the other nation's trade policies. The Maldives reportedly has not been able to increase the trade by less than 10 Percent since 2015 and the Non-fillet frozen fish has led the most recent export (Hossain et al., 2018).

Nepal has the top export product as soybean oil, knotted carpets, and non-retail synthetic fibres. Though the country has announced liberal trade policies and modern trade policies in the year 1992 and 2014 respectively, instead due to high production cost is considered a problem with trading with Nepal (Erum et al., 2016; Hossain et al., 2018). Bhutan by exporting electricity to India, the main trade exports (approx. 50 percent of total trade) is considered electricity export followed by metals, chemical products, food, water, etc. In Bhutan on the other hand, there is also not enough availability of infrastructure and a comparatively small economy. Pakistan continues to dominate the export more than that manpower supply. Cotton textiles and apparel are among the top exported goods and petroleum, chemicals and fertilizers stand amongst the most imported goods. United States (US) followed by China and United Kingdom (UK) is the top trading partner of Pakistan. Sri Lanka ranked at 83rd position in exporter's list of 2020. Sri Lanka leads in the exporting garments and textiles including other spices (Doshi et al., 2019) (Mcinnes et al., 2022).

Ease of Doing Business: Measuring and Comparing

The trade between South Asian countries amounts to $ 20-25 billion trade. The lacuna in these nations is the trade frequency between these countries can be three-time of the way it is now, which is only 5 percent of whole intraregional trade (The world bank, 2019). It can be said that there is a large gap between the reality and the actual potential carried by these nations (Doshi et al., 2019). The South Asian have not realized the benefits of proximity due to connectivity restrictions and multiple trade barriers. Along with it, there are certain historical and political tensions that reflect a lack of trust and indicate disparities. Prime hindrance is the high-tariffs which ultimately end up making goods and services expensive to customers. Duties imposed on the imported products make the domestic products cheaper and apparently more available to the consumers. The tariffs charged by the South Asian countries are almost double the world or nation's quotas (Siriwardana, 2007).

Most of the products are under the category of perishable goods and count under the sensitive lists. Surprisingly these products do not include in the category of South Asian Free Trade Agreements (SAFTA). The countries included in South Asia are members of South Asian Association for Regional Cooperation (SAARC) constituted in 1985, in 2007 it included Afghanistan as one of the South Asian countries. In SAFTA the para-tariffs are kept out of the scope and eventually it leads to artificial higher tariffs. The result can be seen in the para-tariff prices of geographically trivial nations. Non-tariff barriers (NTBs) in the form of labour, sanitary, etc. are unusually high resulting in a change in the inflation impact (Jain & Singh, 2009; Taneja & Bimal, 2020)

Financial Capability and Debt

As per TechRound Report, the deficiency of border infrastructure and the delay due to procedural activities is the purpose of the inefficient and slow trade among SAARC nations. The presence of inefficient customs and border procedures makes the process dawdling and expensive and increases the cost of a trade. Apart from that poor regional connectivity in the medium of Air, Water, and Land transportation is hugely restricted and reflects the unfriendly relations between the SAARC nations (Doshi et al., 2019; Siriwardana, 2007)

The lack of normal trade and complex relationships between India and Pakistan have impacted the South Asian trade. These countries are operating at the level of only 0.054 percent of actual potential. Additionally, the security dilemma is the prime issue in the South Asian region this could be due to geographical conditions and area distribution. This fear and insecurity give rise to mistrust which is prolonged further by the absence of people-to-people interaction and partnerships (Gunawardhana & Damayanthi, 2020).

The Effervesce of FDI

The role played by Foreign Direct Investment (FDI) in any economic empowerment is a vital and substantial interest. The significant pattern of channelling the resources and total capital inflow of the developing nations. In recent times South Asians have seen massive growth in context to rise in MNCs, global capital market liberalization, and economic globalisation of the developing nations (Abdin, 2015). Despite many factors, the determinants that impact the FDI are the nation's intrinsic as well as extrinsic factors as well like, exchange rates, wage rates, infrastructure, labour, tax rates, political instability, and governmental policies (Nasir et al., 2018).

Maldives is the country attracted growth in FDI in recent times followed by Bhutan, India, and Bangladesh. The product of the export basket of SAARC countries is of a similar type and trying to get attention by keeping the equation the same. This is the reflection of sub-conscious competition instead of supplementing each other. Moreover, nations can vouch for FDI in the context of tourism by attracting foreigners say India, Nepal, Bhutan, Bangladesh, Pakistan, and Afghanistan can consider hills as pull. On the other hand, Maldives can promote the beaches to attract tourists (Bhandari & Mohite, 2022).

Major FDI receiving in Afghanistan is in the chronology of agriculture, construction, telecommunication, transportation, and power. In Bangladesh, it is textiles, finance, electricity, transportation, and chemical and chemical products. Bhutan holds maximum FDI in Hotels followed by Agro and Food, Financial Services, IT, and Ferro Alloys and Power. India leads in unspecified secondary resources, hotels, finance, electricity, and construction in gaining FDI. The Maldives excels in tourism, followed by fisheries, transportation, telecom, and power. In Nepal major revenue in FDI is generated through hydroelectricity, tourism, health, education, and ICT. Petroleum, Finance, chemicals, motor vehicles, and electricity and gas are the top five determining factors of Pakistan. In Sri Lanka, it leads in Chemical products, food beverages, metal and metal products, textile, clothing, and leather (Anita et al., 2022).

Evincing Import – Export: Connexion and Long-run Relationship

SAARC is a group of eight South Asian nations constituted in the year 1985. Under the aegis of SAARC many bilateral or multilateral free or preferential trade agreements are constituted for smoothening the trade relations between the South Asian nations such as SAPTA, SAARC Preferential Trading Agreement (SAPTA), Asia Pacific Trade Agreements (APTA), and Free Trade Warehousing Zones (FTWZs), etc. The concept of economic liberalisation can be implemented and benefit from by open trade regime. Among all the Free Trade Agreements (FTAs) the major are between the South Asian nations and instead of keeping it countries specific the majority of the agreements are framed to keep product specific. Apart from that the FTAs also vouch for mutual relaxation followed by mutual benefits (Paudel & Shrestha, 2022).

Exports are very important as we grow, the basic fundamental fact behind export is to maintain the proportionate balance between imports and export. As these transactions directly impact the financial flows of a nation and are able to maintain the current account deficit. All the past economic theories have supported the balance of imports and export keeping the bottom line is the presence of a deficit will lead a nation to borrow more money or sell things to arrange the money (Saleem et al., 2022). This cannot be considered as the position of power and running of the smooth economy of that nation. Thus, in order to keep the agenda, open nations must maintain the import-export proportion and target the holistic approach for improvement. Including the upliftment of the whole of the South Asian nations will eventually end up strengthening each nation's economy (Anita et al., 2022).

Data and Variables

In the present paper, four variables i.e., Export of goods and services, Import of goods and services, Economic Growth, and World Trade have been used. The study is based on time-series data from the period 1990 to 2021 for seven south Asian countries (Bangladesh, Bhutan, India, Maldives, Nepal, Pakistan, and Sri Lanka) except Afghanistan collected from World Development Indicators (WDI) published by the World Bank. Real GDP is used as the proxy for economic growth.

Export of Bangladesh, Bhutan, India, Maldives, Nepal, Pakistan, Sri Lanka and World are represented by BANX, BHUX, INDX, MALX, NEPX, PAKX, SRIX and WX respectively. Import of Bangladesh, Bhutan, India, Maldives, Nepal, Pakistan, Sri Lanka and World are represented by BANM, BHUM, INDM, MALM, NEPM, PAKM, SRIM and WM respectively. GDP of Bangladesh, Bhutan, India, Maldives, Nepal, Pakistan, and Sri Lanka are represented by BANG, BHUG, INDG, MALG, NEPG, PAKG, and SRIG respectively and Global trade by WT.

Methodology

To understand the linkage between variables, two methods have been used which are as under:

1. Karl Pearson's correlation coefficient and
2. Granger Causality Test

The Pearson product-moment correlation coefficient, generally denoted by *r* is a measure of the correlation i.e., linear dependence between two variables *X* and *Y*. The formula for *r* is:

$$r = \frac{\sum_{i=1}^{n}(X_i - \bar{X})(Y_i - \bar{Y})}{\sqrt{\sum_{i=1}^{n}(X_i - \bar{X})^2}\sqrt{\sum_{i=1}^{n}(Y_i - \bar{Y})^2}}$$

Where n is the sample size.

A common practice prior to handling time series data and for performing a co-integration test is to determine the stationarity of the series or its degree of integration, *I*(d) (Maiti, 2016). For this Augmented-Dickey-Fuller (ADF) Unit Root Test (Dickey & Fuller, 1979) has been used. It is essential to keep in mind that these tests presuppose the absence of any structural breaks.

The econometric methodology first examines the stationarity properties of each time series of consideration. The present study uses ADF unit root test to examine the stationarity of the data series. It consists of running a regression of first difference of the series against the series lagged once, a constant and a time trend. This can be expressed as follows:

$$\Delta Y_t = \alpha_0 + \alpha_1 t + \alpha_2 Y_{t-1} + \sum_{j=1}^{p} \alpha_j \Delta Y_{t-j} + \varepsilon_t$$

The extra lagged phrases are added to confirm that the errors are unrelated. The test for a unit root is performed on the coefficient of Yt-1 in the regression in this ADF process. If the coefficient deviates considerably from zero, the hypothesis that Yt has a unit root is rejected. Stationarity is implied by rejecting the null hypothesis (Dickey & Fuller, 1979).

H_0: $\alpha_2=0$ i.e., Y_t is a non-stationary series
H_1: $\alpha_2<0$ i.e., Y_t is a stationary series.

The null hypothesis, H0, is accepted and the series is considered nonstationary or not integrated of order zero, I, if the estimated value of the ADF statistic is greater than McKinnon's critical values (0) (Engle & Granger, 1991). Alternately, if the rejection of the null hypothesis is not successful, this indicates that the data is not stationary. In the event that the null hypothesis is not rejected, the test on the difference of the series must be carried out. If this fails, more differencing must be carried out until stationarity is obtained and the null hypothesis is rejected (Azolibe, 2020).

To determine whether or not one time period can be helpful in forecasting another, a statistical hypothesis test that can be called the Granger causality test is performed. In general, regressions just show "mere" correlations, but this test indicates something interesting about the causation involved.

It is claimed that a time series X is a Granger cause of another time series Y if it can be shown that the values of the time series X convey statistically significant information about the values of Y in the future (Chakraborty & Jana, 2021). The examination is carried out in the following way:

Let *y* and *x* be stationary time series.

The null hypothesis is H_0: X does not Granger-cause Y,

The following regression should be used to determine the correct value to use for Y after it has been lagged:

This is the limited model that must be purchased in order to receive SSRR.

The next step is to strengthen the autoregression by including the lag values of x, as shown in the following equation:

$$y_t = \alpha_0 + \alpha_1 y_{t-1} + \alpha_2 y_{t-2} + \ldots \alpha_m y_{t-m} + b_p x_{t-p} + \ldots + b_q x_{t-q} + residual_t$$

This is the model that does not have any restrictions for obtaining Sum square residual unrestricted (SSRUR).

The following serves as the test statistic in order to put the hypothesis to the test:

$$F = ((SSR_R - SSR_{UR})/c) \, / \, SSR_{UR}/(n - 1)$$

Where c represents the number of lagging terms that were taken, n represents the sample size, and l is the number of parameters that were estimated using the unconstrained equation.

If there are no lagged values of x that are kept in the regression, then one may accept the null hypothesis that x does not Granger-cause y. This is the only condition under which this hypothesis can be accepted (Chakraborty & Jana, 2021).

Analysis of Result

There is a fluctuating pattern in the growth of South Asian countries' GDP, imports, and exports. Table A1 examines GDP, imports, and exports year-over-year from 1990 through 2021. Since the COVID-19 epidemic broke out, the world's economy has taken a serious hit. The World Trade Organization (WTO) predicted that global trade will contract by 12.9% in 2020. And it has had a devastating impact on countries across the globe, including those in the South Asian region (Wei et al., 2021). Analyzing the growth tendency between 2020 and 2021 is critical in this context. Nevertheless, the COVID-19 pandemic resulted in a decline in export, import, and GDP growth.

Further, relationship between imports of south Asian countries; export of south Asian countries and GDP of south Asian countries have analyzed with the help of coefficient of correlation. As a result, the Pearson correlation coefficient was used to investigate the relationship between the growth of exports from one South Asian country to another in Table 1; the growth of imports from one South Asian country to another in Table 2; and the growth of GDP from South Asian countries and World Trade in Table 3.

Table 1 shows the results of the export growth correlation between the countries in South Asia (Bangladesh, Bhutan, India, Nepal, Pakistan, and Sri Lanka). There is also a high association between the countries' export growth, which is significant at the 0.01 level of significance (Patrick, 2018). Table 1 shows that there is a positive and significant correlation between the south Asian countries because their p values are less than the threshold limit (0.05). In addition, Table 1 examines the relationship between world export and south Asian countries. There's also a strong and positive correlation that's significant at the 0.001 level of confidence.

Table 1. Pearson Correlation Coefficient for growth of Export.

Variables	BANX	BHUX	INDX	MALX	NEPX	PAKX	SRIX	WX
BANX	1							
BHUX	.955**	1						
INDX	.979**	.987**	1					
MALX	.898**	.797**	.836**	1				
NEPX	.947**	.856**	.892**	.857**	1			
PAKX	.967**	.978**	.988**	.817**	.889**	1		
SRIX	.990**	.941**	.969**	.904**	.957**	.961**	1	
WX	.977**	.989**	.998**	.828**	.899**	.990**	.970**	1

Source: Author's calculation

**Correlation is significant at the 0.01 level (2-tailed).

In addition, Table 2 presents how there is a positive correlation of growth of import of one country on another country. Such as: the correlation of growth of import of Bhutan on the growth of import of Bangladesh; growth of import of India on the growth of import of Bangladesh and Bhutan and so on. As per the result there is a positive correlation between South Asian countries. Because their p values is less than the threshold of 0.05. . Consequently, the world's trade and the economies of South Asia are positively correlated. In other words, if global trade expands, so will the import of goods from South Asian countries.

Table 2. Pearson Correlation Coefficient for growth of import.

Variables	BANM	BHUM	INDM	MALM	NEPM	PAKM	SRIM	WM
BANM	1							
BHUM	.966**	1						
INDM	.971**	.995**	1					
MALM	.924**	.848**	.844**	1				
NEPM	.993**	.948**	.955**	.935**	1			
PAKM	.968**	.959**	.970**	.865**	.965**	1		
SRIM	.981**	.970**	.976**	.894**	.974**	.965**	1	
WM	.971**	.991**	.997**	.848**	.956**	.973**	.981**	1

Source: Author's calculation
**Correlation is significant at the 0.01 level (2-tailed).

Despite, The trade balance is one of the most important parts of a country's gross domestic product. GDP rises when there is a trade surplus, and vice versa (*World Trade Report 2021*, 2021). As a result, Table 3 in this study examines the correlation coefficient between GDP growth and world trade. To begin, Table 3 depicts the relationship between one country's GDP growth and that of another. The second is the correlation between a country's GDP growth and world trade. With r values of 0.932 between world trade and Bangladesh, 0.985 between world trade and Bhutan, 0.981 between world trade and India, 0.984 between world trade and Maldives, 0.961 between world trade and Nepal, 0.986 between world trade and Pakistan, and 0.977 between world trade and Sri Lanka, Table 3 reflects the positive and strong correlation between GDP growth and world trade. At the 0.01 level of significance, the correlation is significant.

With r-value of 0.932 between world trade and Bangladesh, 0.985 between world trade and Bhutan, 0.981 between world trade and India, 0.984 between world trade and Maldives, 0.961 between world trade and Nepal, 0.986 between world trade and Pakistan, and 0.977 between world trade and Sri Lanka, Table 3 reflects the positive and strong correlation between GDP growth and world trade and it is significant on 0.01 level of significance. Other than that, the correlation between world trade and the South Asian countries has also analyzed in Table 3. As per the result, there is a positive and significant correlation between world trade and GDP of South Asian countries.

Table 3. Pearson Correlation Coefficient between the growth of GDP and World Trade.

Variables	BANG	BHUG	INDG	MALG	NEPG	PAKG	SRIG	WT
BANG	1							
BHUG	.967**	1						
INDG	.977**	.997**	1					
MALG	.962**	.989**	.986**	1				
NEPG	.986**	.985**	.991**	.973**	1			
PAKG	.967**	.991**	.992**	.992**	.984**	1		
SRIG	.973**	.986**	.991**	.981**	.990**	.990**	1	
WT	.932**	.985**	.981**	.984**	.961**	.986**	.977**	1

Source: Author's calculation

**Correlation is significant at the 0.01 level (2-tailed)

Table 4. ADF Unit Root Test of Export.

Variables	In Levels	Result	In First Difference	Result	Conclusion
BANX	-1.637	Do not reject H_0	-4.971***	Reject H_0	I (1)
BHUX	-1.277	Do not reject H_0	-3.181**	Reject H_0	I (1)
INDX	-1.368	Do not reject H_0	-3.363**	Reject H_0	I (1)
MALX	-1.036	Do not reject H_0	-5.077***	Reject H_0	I (1)
NEPX	-2.718	Do not reject H_0	-3.574**	Reject H_0	I (1)
PAKX	-1.974	Do not reject H_0	-4.830***	Reject H_0	I (1)
SRIX	-2.190	Do not reject H_0	-5.921***	Reject H_0	I (1)
WX	-1.434	Do not reject H_0	-4.610***	Reject H_0	I (1)

Source: Author's calculation

***, **, * represents statistical significance of 1%, 5% and 10% respectively

Table 5. ADF Unit Root Test of Import.

Variables	In Levels	Result	In First Difference	Result	Conclusion
BANM	-0.309	Do not reject H_0	-5.631***	Reject H_0	I (1)
BHUM	-1.348	Do not reject H_0	-4.853***	Reject H_0	I (1)
INDM	-1.929	Do not reject H_0	-3.562**	Reject H_0	I (1)
MALM	-0.801	Do not reject H_0	-4.626***	Reject H_0	I (1)
NEPM	-0.577	Do not reject H_0	-4.213***	Reject H_0	I (1)
PAKM	-0.967	Do not reject H_0	-4.265***	Reject H_0	I (1)
SRIM	-1.886	Do not reject H_0	-4.709***	Reject H_0	I (1)
WM	-1.434	Do not reject H_0	-4.610***	Reject H_0	I (1)

Source: Author's calculation
***, **, * represents statistical significance of 1%, 5% and 10% respectively

Table 6. ADF Unit Root Test of GDP and World Trade.

Variables	In Levels	Result	In First Difference	Result	Conclusion
BANG	0.964	Do not reject H_0	-3.641**	Reject H_0	I (1)
BHUG	-0.100	Do not reject H_0	-4.902***	Reject H_0	I (1)
INDG	0.093	Do not reject H_0	-5.401***	Reject H_0	I (1)
MALG	-1.913	Do not reject H_0	-3.707***	Reject H_0	I (1)
NEPG	0.522	Do not reject H_0	-4.496***	Reject H_0	I (1)
PAKG	-1.344	Do not reject H_0	-4.557***	Reject H_0	I (1)
SRIG	-1.245	Do not reject H_0	-9.785***	Reject H_0	I (1)
WT	-1.434	Do not reject H_0	-4.610***	Reject H_0	I (1)

Source: Author's calculation
***, **, * represents statistical significance of 1%, 5% and 10% respectively

The regression was run with intercept and trend for GDP, Export and Import series of seven countries in level and for the first difference with intercept. For the ADF test, the optimum lag is selected based on Schwartz Information Criterion (0 to 4 lags). It is found that the null hypotheses of unit roots cannot be rejected at conventional significance levels, and therefore it can be concluded that all the series are non-stationary in level, but are stationary in first difference (Maiti, 2016). Therefore, all the series are integrated in first difference. The result of ADF Unit root test for three series are presented in Table 4, 5 and 6 respectively.

Generally, Granger causality test has been undertaken to assess the causal relationship between two variables. It assists in examining the patterns of correlation by using the empirical database (Leamer, 1985). Here in the present study, Granger causality is employed to verify whether there is any causal relationship between the export of South Asian countries or not Table 7, Table 7 offers the Granger causal relationship in the import of South Asian countries and Table 7 presents the Granger causal relationship on GDP. Table 7 depicts the Granger causality test for export. We can divide the result into three parts, first where there is a unidirectional Granger causality relationship. Second when there is a bidirectional Granger causality relationship and third when there is no Granger cause between the two variables.

Bhutan and Bangladesh have unidirectional Granger causality relations. Because Bhutan has Granger cause Bangladesh ($p<0.05$), while Bangladesh does not have Granger cause Bhutan ($p<0.05$). In comparison to Bangladesh Bhutan has a GDP of 3.00 M US $ and Bangladesh has GDP of 1.96 M US $. Most importantly there is a huge difference in exports also. Bangladesh has export of 0.30 M US$ while Bhutan has 1.02 M US $. That would be the biggest reason behind the unidirectional casual relation between Bangladesh and Bhutan.

India and Bangladesh have also unidirectional Granger causality relationship from India to Bangladesh. The biggest reason behind this that in compare to Bangladesh India is a huge economy with a remarkable difference in GDP and exports (World data info, 2021). Since gaining its independence, India's economy has performed better than Bangladesh's in both of these categories. Bangladesh's economy has often been over 10 times larger than India's in terms of absolute GDP and GDP growth rates, and it has expanded more quickly each year. India exported $7.91 billion to Bangladesh in 2020. India's exports to Bangladesh have increased over the past 25 years at a yearly rate of 8.46 percent, from $1.04 in 1995 to $7.91 in 2020 (OEC WORLD, 2020).

Pakistan and Bangladesh have a unidirectional Granger causality relationship. Because Pakistan has Granger cause Bangladesh, while Bangladesh does not Granger cause Pakistan. The main cause of this unidirectional Granger cause is Pakistan's greater wealth compared to Bangladesh. Bangladesh is the 33rd largest economy in the world, with a GDP of $411 billion, behind only Pakistan's $347 billion. Most significantly, over the past 25 years, Pakistan's exports to Bangladesh have grown at a yearly rate of 4.23 percent (OEC WORLD, 2020).

Sri Lanka has a Granger cause Bangladesh, which is a unidirectional Granger cause, while Bangladesh does not Granger have cause Sri Lanka. Sri Lanka and Bangladesh both have shared the export and import. But the exports of Sri Lanka to Bangladesh have increased by 14.2 percent in 2020 while the exports of Bangladesh to Sri Lanka have increased by 5% only in 2020. With this it is clear that Sri Lanka export to Bangladesh will impact more. Other than that, Pakistan and India; Sri

Lanka and India; Sri Lank and Nepal; Bhutan and Bangladesh; India and Bangladesh; Pakistan and Bangladesh; Sri Lanka and Bangladesh; Pakistan and India; Sri Lanka and India and Sri Lanka and Nepal have unidirectional Granger cause relationship. Because Granger causality runs one way in these South Asian countries. Apart from this, there is no bidirectional Granger causal relationship found there in the South Asian countries. While there are some countries are there where there is no Granger causal relationship. Such as: Maldives and Bangladesh; Nepal and Bangladesh; India and Bhutan; Maldives and Bhutan; Nepal and Bhutan; Pakistan and Bhutan; Sri Lanka and Bhutan; Maldives and India; Nepal and India and so on.

Table 7 also illustrates the Granger cause link between world trade and South Asian countries to find out whether there is any long-term association between world trade and South Asian countries. Firstly, World trade has a unidirectional Granger cause on Bangladesh. i.e., there is a one-way Granger cause of world trade to Bangladesh ($p<0.05$). However, there is two-way Granger causal relation of world trade to India. This means world trade has Granger cause India ($p<0.05$) and as well as India has Granger cause world trade ($p<0.05$) which known as bidirectional Granger cause. India's share of global merchandise exports was 1.7%, according to WTO data published in April 2019. India contributed 3.5 percent of the world's service exports in 2018. Therefore, it is clear that India's exports are having a positive impact on world trade. While world trade combines the export and import of several nations. Additionally, India had trade links with more than 22 nations. Therefore, it is evident that there is a two-way or bidirectional cause between global trade and Indian export (Ministry of commerce & industry, 2019). Apart from this world trade has no Granger cause on the remainder of South Asian countries (Table 7).

Table 7. Result of Granger Causality Test for Export, Import and GDP.

Null Hypothesis	Country/ World	Export (X)		Import (M)		GDP (G)	
		F-Statistic	Prob.	F-Statistic	Prob.	F-Statistic	Prob.
BAN does not Granger Cause	BHU	1.234	0.309	1.267	0.300	0.844	0.442
	IND	2.940	0.072	3.301	0.054	0.773	0.473
	MAL	2.498	0.103	2.422	0.110	2.288	0.123
	NEP	3.863	0.035	2.327	0.119	1.560	0.231
	PAK	3.101	0.063	0.226	0.799	1.196	0.320
	SRI	4.070	0.030	0.229	0.797	1.332	0.283
	W/WT	1.484	0.247	1.380	0.271	0.588	0.563
BHU does not Granger Cause	BAN	8.773	0.001	5.786	0.009	1.552	0.232
	IND	0.666	0.523	0.417	0.664	5.175	0.014
	MAL	1.535	0.236	1.702	0.204	1.525	0.238
	NEP	2.776	0.082	3.505	0.046	9.292	0.001
	PAK	1.181	0.324	7.667	0.003	8.222	0.002
	SRI	1.164	0.329	5.963	0.008	2.268	0.125
	W/WT	3.835	0.036	2.535	0.100	3.063	0.065
IND does not Granger Cause	BAN	12.542	0.000	18.496	0.000	2.328	0.119
	BHU	4.246	0.026	1.572	0.228	3.967	0.033
	MAL	2.003	0.157	2.495	0.104	0.313	0.734
	NEP	3.346	0.052	3.590	0.043	25.709	0.000
	PAK	9.348	0.001	8.338	0.002	6.773	0.005
	SRI	2.615	0.094	4.978	0.016	3.793	0.037
	W/WT	27.631	0.000	15.250	0.000	5.349	0.012
MAL does not Granger Cause	BAN	0.593	0.561	0.186	0.831	1.516	0.240
	BHU	0.004	0.997	0.510	0.607	3.062	0.065
	IND	1.434	0.258	1.068	0.360	3.529	0.045
	NEP	0.971	0.393	0.040	0.960	7.195	0.004
	PAK	0.400	0.675	0.006	0.994	2.773	0.083
	SRI	0.596	0.559	0.377	0.690	2.354	0.117
	W/WT	1.293	0.293	1.227	0.311	0.715	0.499
NEP does not Granger Cause	BAN	1.864	0.177	2.364	0.116	3.111	0.063
	BHU	3.700	0.040	0.964	0.396	2.810	0.080
	IND	5.244	0.013	1.776	0.191	2.304	0.122
	MAL	1.087	0.353	1.793	0.188	0.788	0.466
	PAK	0.666	0.523	0.021	0.980	0.616	0.548
	SRI	1.795	0.188	0.018	0.982	0.429	0.656
	W/WT	4.202	0.027	0.738	0.489	0.653	0.529

Continued on following page

Table 7. Continued

Null Hypothesis	Country/ World	Export (X)		Import (M)		GDP (G)	
		F-Statistic	Prob.	F-Statistic	Prob.	F-Statistic	Prob.
PAK does not Granger Cause	BAN	7.625	0.003	1.439	0.257	2.881	0.076
	BHU	1.237	0.308	0.800	0.461	0.548	0.585
	IND	0.511	0.606	1.220	0.313	3.769	0.038
	MAL	2.072	0.148	1.512	0.241	6.231	0.007
	NEP	3.815	0.036	4.179	0.028	8.123	0.002
	SRI	3.153	0.061	0.628	0.542	3.199	0.059
	W/WT	0.538	0.591	0.710	0.502	0.077	0.926
SRI does not Granger Cause	BAN	7.049	0.004	8.780	0.001	2.472	0.106
	BHU	0.453	0.641	1.152	0.333	0.252	0.779
	IND	8.758	0.001	3.942	0.033	0.656	0.528
	MAL	2.628	0.093	2.559	0.098	1.455	0.253
	NEP	8.515	0.002	3.063	0.065	6.039	0.008
	PAK	0.099	0.906	1.174	0.326	1.963	0.162
	W/WT	0.536	0.592	1.250	0.304	0.675	0.518
W/WT does not Granger Cause	BAN	11.350	0.000	11.705	0.000	1.332	0.283
	BHU	1.791	0.188	0.693	0.510	2.065	0.149
	IND	15.324	0.000	4.252	0.026	2.277	0.124
	MAL	1.801	0.187	1.593	0.224	1.632	0.217
	NEP	4.120	0.029	2.510	0.102	3.175	0.060
	PAK	1.677	0.208	4.669	0.019	1.440	0.257
	SRI	1.942	0.165	2.110	0.143	8.193	0.002

Source: Author's calculation

Table 7 represents the Granger causality test for Import to find out the correlation patterns (Leamer, 1985). Table 7 depicts the Granger causality test for import. We can divide the result into three parts, first where there is a unidirectional Granger causality relationship second when there is a bidirectional Granger causality relationship, and third when there is no Granger cause between the two variables. Firstly, there is a one-way Granger cause relation between Bhutan to Bangladesh. While Bangladesh does not Granger because Bhutan this is also known as the unidirectional Granger cause relationship (Leamer, 1985). Secondly, India has Granger cause on Bangladesh while Bangladesh does not Granger cause India. India and Bangladesh have a bilateral trading relationship. Even yet, Bangladesh imported $5.88 billion worth of Indian goods. Bangladesh's exports to India totalled $1.76

billion in 2021 (Trade economics, 2022). The import of Bangladesh from India is huge in comparison to from India Bangladesh. So on the basis of this ground we, can say that India has one way Granger cause Bangladesh (OEC WORLD, 2020). Thirdly, Sri Lanka Granger causes Bangladesh while Bangladesh does not Granger cause Sri Lanka. At last, there is no Granger cause relationship between the imports and rest of the South Asian countries.

Besides Granger causality test was also performed on world trade and import of South Asian countries. World trade Granger cause Bangladesh this is unidirectional Granger cause. Because Bangladesh does not Granger cause world trade (Table 7). World trade also Granger cause India but India does not Granger cause world trade. This means this is also a unidirectional Granger cause. Apart from this there is no Granger cause between the world trade and other South Asian countries such as: Bhutan, Maldives, Nepal, and Pakistan (Table 7).

Table 7 shows the result of Granger causality for GDP of South Asian countries. Results can be divided in two parts i.e., first when there is unidirectional Granger cause, second when there is no Granger cause relationship. So, Bhutan GDP has unidirectional Granger cause Nepal GDP; Bhutan GDP has unidirectional Granger cause Pakistan GDP; India GDP has unidirectional Granger cause Nepal GDP; India GDP has unidirectional Granger cause Pakistan GDP; Maldives GDP has unidirectional Granger cause Nepal GDP; Pakistan GDP has unidirectional Granger cause Nepal GDP.

Despite this, the Granger cause relationship between global trade and the GDP of South Asian countries is also shown in Table 7. India's GDP has a unidirectional Granger cause in world trade, while the latter has no Granger cause in world trade, according to the findings. On the other hand, Sri Lanka's GDP does not have a direct impact on world trade. While global trade causes Sri Lanka's GDP to grow (Table 7). Because world trade has a unidirectional Granger cause Sri Lanka's GDP. In addition, there is no Granger causality between the world trade and the rest of South Asian countries (Bangladesh, Bhutan, Nepal, Pakistan and Maldives).

CONCLUSION AND POLICY SUGGESTION

In the current study, an effort has been made to examine the export, import, economic growth, and links between global trades for South Asian countries from 1990 to 2021. The analysis's findings suggest that the GDP, imports, and exports of South Asian countries are growing in a cyclical pattern. In this regard, it is crucial to analyse the growth trend between 2020 and 2021. However, the COVID-19 epidemic slowed down GDP growth as well as export and import growth. Additionally, the relationship between South Asian imports, exports, and GDP of South Asian countries have been examined with the use of correlation coefficients. Significant correlations exist between countries export and global export, countries import and global imports, as well as countries GDP and global trade. Comparing the South Asian countries export, import, and GDP, we also discovered a considerable degree of connection. According to the Granger causality conclusion, there are unidirectional and bidirectional causal linkages between world trade-related factors and country trade related variables as well as within countries for trade-related variables. The Granger causality result also implies that there are unidirectional and bidirectional causal relationships between world trade and country GDP development as well as within nations in the case of GDP growth. We can therefore draw the conclusion that one of the key causes of the economic crisis in South Asian countries is global trade. So, South Asian countries should give more focus on bilateral trade as well as participate in global trade.

Limitations

The existing research does have its share of caveats and restrictions. Because the research was conducted exclusively in nations located in Southern Asia (Bangladesh, Bhutan, India, Maldives, Nepal, Pakistan, and Sri Lanka), the findings may not be applicable to countries located in other parts of the world. Second, Afghanistan has not joined the rest of the South Asian countries since there is a dearth of information regarding the global development indices. Third, the analysis takes into consideration exports and imports, as well as economic growth and international trade. On the other hand, the research might have taken into account any number of other factors.

REFERENCES

Abdin, M. J. (2015). Foreign Direct Investment (FDI) in SAARC Countries. *Global Journal of Management and Business Research. C Finance*, *15*(8), 13–20. doi:10.2139srn.2660625

Al-Swidi, A., Huque, S. M. R., Hafeez, M. H., & Shariff, M. N. M. (2014). The role of subjective norms in theory of planned behavior in the context of organic food consumption. *British Food Journal*, *116*(10), 1561–1580. doi:10.1108/BFJ-05-2013-0105

Anita, S. S., Tasnova, N., & Nawar, N. (2022). Are non-performing loans sensitive to macroeconomic determinants? an empirical evidence from banking sector of SAARC countries. *Future Business Journal*, *8*(1), 1–16. doi:10.118643093-022-00117-9

Azolibe, C. B. (2020). Banking Sector Intermediation Development and Growth of a Developing Economy: An Empirical Investigation of Nigeria. Research Square, 1–18. doi:10.21203/rs.3.rs-95127/v1

Bhandari, V., & Mohite, V. (2022). Entrepreneurship Ecosystem: An Appraisal for Sultanate of Oman Using the Ease of Doing Business Index. Research Square, 1–16. doi:10.21203/rs.3.rs-1203598/v1

Chakraborty, C., & Jana, A. (2021). Economic Growth and Trade-related Variables: An Empirical Study Using Indian Data. In Global Tariff War: Economic, Political and Social Implications (pp. 141–152). Emerald Publishing Limited. doi:10.1108/978-1-80071-314-720211011

Dickey, D. A., & Fuller, W. A. (1979). Distribution of the Estimators for Autoregressive Time Series with a Unit Root. *Journal of the American Statistical Association, 74*(366a), 427–431. doi:10.1080/01621459.1979.10482531

Doshi, R., Kelley, J. G., & Simmons, B. A. (2019). The Power of Ranking: The Ease of Doing Business Indicator and Global Regulatory Behavior. *International Organization*, *73*(3), 611–643. doi:10.1017/S0020818319000158

Engle, R., & Granger, C. (1991). *Long-run economic relationships: Readings in cointegration.* Oxford University Press. https://econpapers.repec.org/bookchap/oxpobooks/9780198283393.htm

Erum, N., Hussain, S., & Yousaf, A. (2016). Foreign Direct Investment and Economic Growth in SAARC Countries. *The Journal of Asian Finance. Economics and Business*, *3*(4), 57–66. doi:10.13106/jafeb.2016.vol3.no4.57

Gunawardhana, C. S., & Damayanthi, N. M. M. (2020). Determinants of Foreign Direct Investment and its impact on Economic Growth: Evidence from South Asian Association for Regional Corporation (SAARC) Countries. *Kelaniya Journal of Management*, *8*(2), 91. doi:10.4038/kjm.v8i2.7605

Hossain, M. T., Hassan, Z., Shafiq, S., & Basit, A. (2018). Ease of doing business and its impact on inward FDI. *Indonesian Journal of Management and Business Economics*, *1*(1), 52–65. doi:10.32455/ijmbe.v1i1.52

Jain, R., & Singh, J. B. (2009). Trade Pattern in SAARC Countries: Emerging Trends and Issues. *Reserve Banks of India Occasional Papers, 30*(3), 72–116.

Kappa, K. (2022). Do the vegetable exports lead to economic growth? An empirical evidence in selected SAARC economies. *Journal of Public Affairs*, *22*(2), 1–11. doi:10.1002/pa.2484

Leamer, E. E. (1985). Sensitivity analyses would help. *The American Economic Review*, *75*(3), 308–313. https://www.jstor.org/stable/1814801

Maiti, S. (2016). Export and Economic Growth in India: An Econometric Analysis. *Look East*, *6*(1), 68–78.

Mcinnes, A., Colombage, S., Grose, R., Imam, T., & Grose, R. (2022). Opportunities and Barriers for FinTech in SAARC and ASEAN Countries. *Journal of Risk and Financial Management, 15*(2), 2–37. doi:10.3390/jrfm15020077

Ministry of Commerce & Industry. (2019). *Indian global trade share*. https://pib.gov.in/PressReleasePage.aspx?PRID=1593704

Muhammad, A., Shahid, M., Syed, S. H., Muhammad, F., & Hassan, M. A. (2011). Empirical Analysis of Determinants of Economic Growth: Evidence from SAARC Countries. *Journal of Economics and Behavioral Studies*, *3*(2), 115–121. doi:10.22610/jebs.v3i2.261

Nasir, A., Arshah, R., & Ab Hamid, M. (2018). The significance of main constructs of theory of planned behavior in recent information security policy compliance behavior study: a comparison among top. *International Journal of Engineering and Technology, 7*(2), 737–741.

OEC World. (2020). *India (IND) and Bangladesh (BGD) Trade*. https://oec.world/en/profile/bilateral-country/ind/partner/bgd

Patrick, S. (2018). Correlation coefficients: Appropriate use and interpretation. *Anesthesia and Analgesia, 126*(5), 1763–1768. doi:10.1213/ANE.0000000000002864 PMID:29481436

Paudel, Y., & Shrestha, S. (2022). Agroforestry Practices Prevailing in SAARC Countries: A Review. *Indonesian Journal of Social and Environmental Issues*, *3*(1), 10–18. doi:10.47540/ijsei.v3i1.390

Saleem, R., Nasreen, S., & Azam, S. (2022). Role of financial inclusion and export diversification in determining green growth: Evidence from SAARC economies. *Environmental Science and Pollution Research International*, *29*(40), 1–14. doi:10.100711356-022-20096-2 PMID:35420339

Siriwardana, M. (2007). *Looking beyond SAARC: some trade liberalisation options for Sri Lanka.* doi:10.1080/10357820108713321

Taneja, N., & Bimal, S. (2020). *Informal Trade in the SAARC Region.* Springer. doi:10.1007/978-981-15-3932-9_14

Trade Economics. (2022). *India Imports from Bangladesh - 2022 Data 2023 Forecast 1988-2021 Historical*. https://tradingeconomics.com/india/imports/bangladesh

Upender, M. (2007). Long Run Equilibrium between Indias's Exports and Imports During 1949-50 - 2004-05. *Applied Econometrics and International Development, 7*(1), 186–196. https://papers.ssrn.com/sol3/papers.cfm?abstract_id=1249742

Wei, P., Jin, C., & Xu, C. (2021). The Influence of the COVID-19 Pandemic on the Imports and Exports in China, Japan, and South Korea. *Frontiers in Public Health*, *9*, 682693. Advance online publication. doi:10.3389/fpubh.2021.682693 PMID:34368056

World Bank. (2019). *Why# one south asia?* https://www.worldbank.org/en/programs/south-asia-regional-integration/trade

World Data Info. (2021). *Country comparison Bangladesh : Bhutan*. https://www.worlddata.info/country-comparison.php?country1=BGD&country2=BTN

World trade report 2021. (2021). https://www.wto.org/english/res_e/booksp_e/wtr21_e/00_wtr21_e.pdf

APPENDIX

Table 8. Year to Year Growth Rate

Year	Ban	Bhu	Ind	Mal	Nep	Pak	Sri
Year to Year Growth Rate of GDP							
1990							
1991	-2.03	-16.46	-15.85	13.65	8.10	14.03	12.05
1992	2.43	-0.04	6.70	16.56	-13.27	7.14	7.81
1993	4.60	-5.92	-3.09	13.18	7.61	5.98	6.55
1994	1.82	14.60	17.18	10.42	11.11	0.93	13.34
1995	12.35	12.15	10.09	12.07	8.22	15.95	11.20
1996	22.40	4.47	9.05	12.88	2.74	4.43	6.66
1997	3.89	16.09	5.85	12.84	8.78	-1.40	8.59
1998	3.61	3.18	1.32	6.27	-1.27	-0.39	4.66
1999	2.57	9.85	8.89	9.10	3.65	1.26	-0.88
2000	4.09	6.31	2.09	5.96	9.15	30.24	4.31
2001	1.16	8.71	3.64	39.35	9.33	-3.09	-3.56
2002	1.36	12.87	6.08	3.10	0.73	0.53	5.00
2003	9.93	15.97	18.01	17.29	4.62	14.84	14.18
2004	8.23	12.99	16.69	16.61	14.90	17.44	9.43
2005	6.66	16.76	15.69	-5.17	11.77	11.41	18.12
2006	3.42	9.79	14.61	35.40	11.24	14.33	15.87
2007	10.85	33.52	29.40	18.61	14.17	11.02	14.39
2008	15.10	5.09	-1.47	21.58	21.50	11.61	25.85
2009	11.84	0.51	11.93	3.24	2.47	-1.13	3.32
2010	12.49	25.44	24.87	10.36	24.49	5.36	34.85
2011	11.59	14.80	8.80	7.19	35.11	20.56	15.10
2012	3.67	0.24	0.25	4.03	0.38	5.05	4.81
2013	12.47	-1.41	1.59	14.17	2.12	3.05	8.60
2014	15.26	8.59	9.82	12.21	2.57	5.68	6.78
2015	12.84	5.06	3.16	11.15	7.17	10.72	1.57
2016	13.50	7.75	9.09	6.56	0.67	2.99	2.23
2017	12.78	13.50	15.54	8.56	18.14	9.30	6.10
2018	9.74	-0.14	1.87	11.50	14.29	3.28	0.61
2019	10.41	3.63	6.27	5.79	3.25	-11.29	-4.52
2020	6.77	-8.68	-7.32	-33.26	-1.55	-5.89	-3.95

Continued on following page

Table 8. Continued

Year	Ban	Bhu	Ind	Mal	Nep	Pak	Sri
2021	-24.04	5.93	-0.70	26.75	-10.58	14.61	-4.11
Year to Year Growth Rate of Export							
1990							
1991	10.48	-0.03	1.34	2.31	18.00	30.56	6.70
1992	16.63	-0.24	11.08	18.22	20.47	9.28	19.17
1993	24.32	-7.43	7.77	-2.63	24.29	-0.57	13.36
1994	1.64	7.68	17.82	27.87	14.49	0.66	13.38
1995	35.61	43.14	20.73	1.81	42.29	19.91	17.07
1996	9.35	-1.89	4.44	7.61	-6.13	5.63	4.79
1997	12.60	17.02	8.96	7.07	25.52	-6.19	13.45
1998	15.79	-5.04	4.42	6.60	-14.42	2.11	3.82
1999	2.58	4.50	13.18	6.19	3.77	-5.69	-2.96
2000	9.28	-1.05	15.86	5.83	11.23	2.81	14.69
2001	9.71	-2.94	0.14	5.51	5.94	6.64	-7.72
2002	-6.04	2.38	20.49	5.22	-20.81	3.84	-1.80
2003	1.26	23.86	23.67	4.96	-7.40	26.44	13.33
2004	5.53	37.30	39.42	4.73	22.10	10.29	11.57
2005	37.72	43.66	27.00	4.52	-2.29	11.92	8.11
2006	17.51	55.98	24.33	4.32	2.56	12.92	7.96
2007	15.20	34.58	26.56	4.14	9.16	3.80	10.55
2008	19.59	-6.62	14.16	3.98	20.74	4.58	7.38
2009	7.29	-7.91	-5.24	3.83	-0.39	-1.02	-11.29
2010	6.41	19.05	37.11	3.68	-3.95	14.88	23.62
2011	38.73	11.43	19.19	3.55	9.82	24.58	23.02
2012	4.91	-5.84	0.23	3.43	12.77	-6.75	-0.61
2013	8.99	3.03	5.30	3.32	8.47	10.37	11.36
2014	12.03	-1.84	-0.81	405.55	11.72	-2.55	10.82
2015	3.01	-3.40	-11.01	-4.61	8.13	-4.10	1.21
2016	9.00	-7.32	5.48	-2.11	-19.39	-11.17	3.01
2017	1.85	15.28	13.33	9.06	12.83	-1.32	9.40
2018	8.03	2.30	8.10	8.12	14.34	12.22	6.17
2019	14.31	14.12	-1.79	4.78	2.77	-0.25	-4.14
2020	-16.46	-19.85	-6.15	-52.45	-14.45	-6.43	-31.13
2021	-19.70	-24.77	-6.55	-110.32	-16.90	-6.87	-45.20
Year to Year Growth Rate of Import							

Continued on following page

Table 8. Continued

Year	Ban	Bhu	Ind	Mal	Nep	Pak	Sri
1990							
1991	-8.26	6.80	-15.45	13.97	15.70	4.13	14.38
1992	3.43	37.23	20.48	17.19	-3.72	18.37	13.85
1993	19.48	-26.02	-0.80	8.31	20.24	15.71	12.56
1994	0.08	2.93	21.63	9.71	21.47	-14.45	19.28
1995	40.56	21.00	29.89	10.02	18.82	19.16	12.22
1996	15.52	11.85	4.71	8.48	6.08	15.20	1.71
1997	0.31	16.79	9.37	7.82	15.09	-4.42	7.85
1998	5.69	10.38	7.71	7.25	-11.27	-15.94	1.42
1999	5.80	14.05	14.75	6.76	-9.10	-1.98	1.51
2000	6.27	-0.19	6.21	6.33	19.10	1.67	19.62
2001	11.50	7.26	0.14	5.96	12.07	4.59	-15.32
2002	-10.31	16.47	20.36	5.62	-13.65	-2.54	-0.18
2003	7.74	19.34	21.11	5.32	4.82	21.23	12.14
2004	4.79	38.16	46.53	5.05	18.59	6.81	18.76
2005	35.80	20.82	31.89	4.81	11.83	49.42	10.40
2006	12.49	0.67	25.16	4.59	18.16	38.06	15.50
2007	16.91	29.00	31.68	4.39	15.66	1.89	9.83
2008	25.20	6.42	15.89	4.20	27.38	31.00	22.78
2009	3.73	7.87	-1.07	4.03	6.78	-16.19	-25.39
2010	5.82	42.54	29.61	3.88	30.74	3.63	29.96
2011	40.90	14.41	25.93	3.73	5.51	18.19	46.34
2012	5.37	-10.39	0.82	3.60	3.00	13.00	-2.61
2013	7.68	-2.58	-7.66	3.47	14.01	1.27	-0.79
2014	9.95	0.25	0.32	252.23	12.92	-1.68	7.61
2015	9.41	13.22	-12.12	5.91	8.94	1.18	-0.57
2016	-2.30	-8.64	3.24	15.41	-6.28	-2.38	1.93
2017	7.29	7.87	21.21	11.64	28.21	19.00	8.31
2018	26.94	4.24	9.79	17.78	26.09	17.82	5.51
2019	0.96	-6.43	-5.86	-0.87	5.37	-10.46	-8.33
2020	-7.71	-11.98	-15.06	-41.79	-19.55	-18.95	-24.68
2021	-6.67	30.10	25.21	16.62	-5.00	22.63	39.48

Chapter 6
COVID-19's Effect on Global Trade in the Post-Pandemic Period:
Forecast Analysis of Global GDP and Trade a Decade After 2025

Özlem Özsoy
https://orcid.org/0000-0003-4438-5734
EKOL Hospital, Turkey

Metin Gürler
https://orcid.org/0000-0002-9263-0258
Istanbul Medipol University, Turkey

ABSTRACT

By the end of May 2022 according to the data, the number of cases increased to 530 million, the number of virus-related deaths increased to 6.3 million, and the CFR decreased to 1.18 with the increase in vaccination. The full vaccination rate increased to 60% at the end of May. It should not be overlooked that vaccination is 18% in Africa and 11.8% in low-income countries. The global output GDP will be 99.4 trillion dollars in 2022 and 147 trillion dollars in 2035. It is also clearly seen that China will surpass the USA in national income at current prices in 2028. It is estimated that global imports will reach 23.5 trillion dollars in 2022 and 36.6 trillion dollars in 2035. It is expected that the chemicals and chemical products industry will be at the top with imports of 6.1 trillion dollars in 2022 and 9.5 trillion dollars in 2035 and is accounted for 25.3% of global imports in 2021. It is estimated that this rate will increase to 28.8% in 2035. Hong Kong is at the top with the Trade Openness Index value of 4.06 in 2022 and 4.5 in 2035.

DOI: 10.4018/978-1-6684-5950-8.ch006

INTRODUCTION

After meeting the 2022 year with 288.9 million COVID-19 cases, 5.4 million deaths and a case fatality rate (CFR) of 1.88 worldwide, with from the first months of 2022 new variants of the virus became as a new problem. By the end of May 2022, the number of cases increased to 530 million, the number of virus-related deaths increased to 6.3 million and the CFR decreased to 1.18 with the increase in vaccination. Although the full vaccination rate, which was 49.40% at the beginning of 2022, increased to 58.03% at the end of March, and 60 percent at the end of May, it is seen that there is still a substantial unvaccinated population in the world. It should not be overlooked that vaccination is 18% in Africa and 11.8% in low-income countries.

Although the pandemic has deeply affected the global economy in 2020, the countries and international organizations have started to take rapid measures and responses against the pandemic. Many firms, sectors and vulnerable parts of the societies have been supported to increase their resistance against the negative effects of the pandemic. All these efforts started to yield positive results and with the base effect of 2021, economies around the world started to recover. All these positive developments were overshadowed by the global inflation that skyrocketed as a result of rising commodity prices especially the energy related products and the regional conflicts between Russia and Ukraine.

As a result of the forecast analysis, it is estimated that the global output (Gross Domestic Product, GDP) will be 99.4 trillion dollars in 2022, 111 trillion dollars in 2025, 127.6 trillion dollars in 2030 and 147 trillion dollars in 2035. It is also clearly seen that China will surpass the USA in national income at current prices in 2028. It is predicted that China will have a GDP of 19.7 trillion dollars in 2022, a national income of 24.3 trillion dollars in 2025, a national income of 28.3 trillion dollars in 2030 and a national income of 33.8 trillion dollars in 2015. It is predicted that the USA will have a GDP of 22.8 trillion dollars in 2022, a national income of 24.9 trillion dollars in 2025, a national income of 27.9 trillion dollars in 2030 and a national income of 30.9 trillion dollars in 2015.

It is estimated that global imports will reach 23.5 trillion dollars in 2022, 26.2 trillion dollars in 2025, 31.1 trillion dollars in 2030 and 36.6 trillion dollars in 2035. It is expected that China will be at the top with imports of 2.93 trillion dollars in 2022, 3.33 trillion dollars in 2025, 4 trillion dollars in 2030 and 4.7 trillion dollars in 2035. It is seen that China will surpass the USA in global imports in 2027. The USA will follow China with 3.2 trillion dollars in 2022, 3.43 trillion dollars in 2025, 3.82 trillion dollars in 2030 and 4.2 trillion dollars in 2035.

It is seen that China will again be at the top in global exports, as in global imports in 2035. It is expected that China will have the highest export value with

3.9 trillion dollars in 2022, 4.4 trillion dollars in 2025, 5.4 trillion dollars in 2030 and 6.3 trillion dollars in 2035. China will be followed by the USA with exports of 1.94 trillion dollars in 2022, 2.1 trillion dollars in 2025, 2.4 trillion dollars in 2030 and 2.7 trillion dollars in 2035.

When the global imports are analysed by sectoral breakdown, it is expected that the "Chemicals and chemical products" industry will be at the top with imports of 6.1 trillion dollars in 2022, 6.7 trillion dollars in 2025, 8 trillion dollars in 2030 and 9.5 trillion dollars in 2035. While this sector alone accounted for 25.3% of global imports in 2021, it is estimated that this rate will increase to 28.8% in 2035. It is expected that this sector will be followed by the "Electric & Electronic" sector with 4.8 trillion dollars in 2022, 5.5 trillion dollars in 2025, 6.4 trillion dollars in 2030 and 7.6 trillion dollars in 2035. While this sector alone accounted for 21.4 percent of global imports in 2021, it is estimated that this rate will decrease to 20.6 percent in 2035.

It is seen that nineteen countries among the first twenty countries in global imports are also in the first twenty in global exports. It is seen that Poland, which is among the first twenty countries in global imports, ranks 22nd in global export rankings after 2022, while Russia, which is among the first twenty countries in global exports, ranks 21st in global imports.

When the "Trade Openness Index" values are examined, Hong Kong is at the top with the index value of 4.06 in 2022, 4.3 in 2025, 4.4 in 2030 and 4.5 in 3025. Hong Kong is followed by Singapore with an index value of 2.18 in 2022, 2.29 in 2025, 2.23 in 2030 and 2.25 in 2035.

While full vaccination has not yet been completed and the negative effects of the pandemic have not been fully overcome worldwide, the war between Ukraine and Russia at the end of February 2022 has caused disruptions in the supply chain of energy and other products, especially food safety. The foreign trade caused the recovery in the global economy in 2021. However, disruption risk of foreign trade in 2022, caused the positive expectations about the future global economic growth to be revised downwards, and many countries faced the risk of recession and even stagflation as a result of rising prices and unemployment.

Human capital in very important in economic growth according to modern growth theories. The pandemic negatively affected the human capital and economies. By prioritizing investment in human capital a creative generation should be achieved, the innovation competence of the private sector should be encouraged, and if there is a lack of firms' entrepreneurship in R&D the public should lead the private sector in R&D in order to become a technology producing country rather than a technology importer and user (Gürler 2016, Gürler 2021). Investments, production, foreign trade and employment declined, and global supply and value chains disrupted. Traditional attitudes and methods in social life and education changed, so that individualism and digitalism gained speed. Lost in working hours reduced the productivity and total output, so that real incomes diminished. Developing a resilient supply chain strategy can help the Micro Small and Medium Enterprises (MSMEs) which plays a crucial role contributing to GDP and foreign trade of the countries can handle any kind of disruption such as pandemic (Mukherjee, S., Baral, M. M., and Venkataiah, C. 2022).

Not only the economic growth but also the distribution of income in a country is also important. The inequality of income distribution within the country and between countries may cause chaos and conflict inside the country and in international trade. The pandemic affected especially the fragile parts of the population, such as the elder population. The pandemic showed that COVID-19 related deaths are higher among the elderly population who are more in need of care and have chronic diseases. Public health is a main goal of social states. The government aims to ensure an equal health system for the society, so that everybody can access to the health services, especially the elderly population who need support and care. Facing lower physical and mental capacity otherwise causes older people to live more negatively in additional life years (Özsoy and Gürler 2021a).

In this study, post-pandemic global income and global foreign trade were analysed for the 2022-2035 era. Global income, global imports and exports are estimated by country breakdown for the aforementioned period. In addition, after analysing global imports by sectoral breakdown, trade openness index, which is one of the important indicators of the internationalization of the countries that play a leading role in global trade, have been estimated over the same period.

In the study global COVID-19 related indicators such as cases, deaths, Case Fatality Rate (CFR), vaccination, and global export data were analysed for regional and the World Bank's income classification by tables and graphs. For the analysis of the health system capacity, data for number of nurses and medical doctors were researched. The effect of COVID-19 on global export was also taken into consideration by correlation matrix.

Milestone of Pandemic (Covid-19)

Total COVID-19 related cases reached to 529 million, total COVID-19 related deaths reached to 6.3 million total CFR reached to 1.18, which means that nearly 1.2 of each hundred COVID-19 related cases ended with death, in the world at the end of May 2022. As May 31, fully vaccinated people ratio has exceeded 60 percent (people fully vaccinated per hundred people) in the world and reached 4.74 billion people. Cases and deaths per 100,000 people by the end of May 2022 is 6,645 and 78.6 respectively (**Table 1**).

Table 1 (a). COVID-19 related health indicators.

Month	Cases	Deaths	Fully Vaccinated People	Cases (Cumulative)	Deaths (Cumulative)
2020.01	9,370	196		9,370	196
2020.02	76,098	2,730		85,468	2,926
2020.03	783,513	41,730		868,981	44,656
2020.04	2,441,826	195,908		3,310,807	240,564
2020.05	2,907,005	152,131		6,217,812	392,695
2020.06	4,315,908	143,833		10,533,720	536,528
2020.07	7,117,676	175,216		17,651,396	711,744
2020.08	7,943,984	183,352		25,595,380	895,096
2020.09	8,503,729	164,650		34,099,109	1,059,746
2020.10	12,108,542	181,597		46,207,651	1,241,343
2020.11	17,291,638	277,234		63,499,289	1,518,577
2020.12	19,542,628	356,107	43,648	83,041,917	1,874,684
2021.01	19,556,544	418,041	12,851,304	102,598,461	2,292,725
2021.02	11,257,969	310,034	45,188,642	113,856,430	2,602,759
2021.03	14,851,118	300,091	84,942,437	128,707,548	2,902,850
2021.04	22,547,286	379,286	143,664,958	151,254,834	3,282,136
2021.05	19,703,404	379,298	160,458,224	170,958,238	3,661,434
2021.06	11,477,569	271,560	199,902,851	182,435,807	3,932,994
2021.07	15,737,472	261,526	281,727,296	198,173,279	4,194,520
2021.08	19,887,010	301,084	1,217,066,959	218,060,289	4,495,604
2021.09	15,937,697	266,243	519,338,335	233,997,986	4,761,847
2021.10	13,098,924	217,271	384,726,667	247,096,910	4,979,118
2021.11	15,641,164	216,058	361,584,778	262,738,074	5,195,176
2021.12	25,604,120	219,370	477,378,055	288,342,194	5,414,546
2022.01	89,415,376	238,762	276,491,937	377,757,570	5,653,308
2022.02	58,122,669	278,871	218,092,469	435,880,239	5,932,179
2022.03	51,442,636	177,822	186,581,266	487,322,875	6,110,001
2022.04	25,003,161	87,742	90,685,752	512,326,036	6,197,743
2022.05	16,192,103	53,008	78,958,991	528,518,139	6,250,751

Source: Our World in Data (OWID 2022), UNDESA (2022a)

Table 1 (b). COVID-19 related health indicators.

CFR (Monthly Cumulative)	Fully Vaccinated People (Cumulative)	Cases per 100,000 People (Cumulative)	Deaths per 100,000 People (Cumulative)	Fully Vaccinated People per Hundred People (Cumulative)
2.09		0	0.0	
3.42		1	0.0	
5.14		11	0.6	
7.27		43	3.1	
6.32		80	5.1	
5.09		136	6.9	
4.03		227	9.2	
3.50		330	11.5	
3.11		439	13.7	
2.69		595	16.0	
2.39		818	19.6	
2.26	43,648	1,070	24.1	0.0
2.23	12,894,952	1,303	29.1	0.2
2.29	58,083,594	1,446	33.1	0.7
2.26	143,026,031	1,634	36.9	1.8
2.17	286,690,989	1,921	41.7	3.6
2.14	447,149,213	2,171	46.5	5.7
2.16	647,052,064	2,317	49.9	8.2
2.12	928,779,360	2,516	53.3	11.8
2.06	2,145,846,319	2,769	57.1	27.2
2.03	2,665,184,654	2,971	60.5	33.8
2.02	3,049,911,321	3,138	63.2	38.7
1.98	3,411,496,099	3,336	66.0	43.3
1.88	3,888,874,154	3,662	68.8	49.4
1.50	4,165,366,091	4,749	71.1	52.4
1.36	4,383,458,560	5,480	74.6	55.1
1.25	4,570,039,826	6,127	76.8	57.5
1.21	4,660,725,578	6,441	77.9	58.6
1.18	4,739,684,569	6,645	78.6	59.6

Source: Our World in Data (OWID 2022), UNDESA (2022a)

"COVID-19 related cases per hundred people" has maximum value in January

2022 as 1,124. The cumulative data for "COVID-19 related cases per hundred people" indicator is 6,645 at the end of May 2022 (**Figure 1**). It seems monthly "COVID-19 related cases per hundred people" data is reached its maximum value and then started to decrease and follow constant ratio whereas cumulative ""COVID-19 related cases per hundred people" data seems to reach the maximum level and will start to decline in a couple months.

Figure 1. Covid-19 related cases per hundred people.
Source: Our World in Data (OWID 2022), UNDESA (2022a)

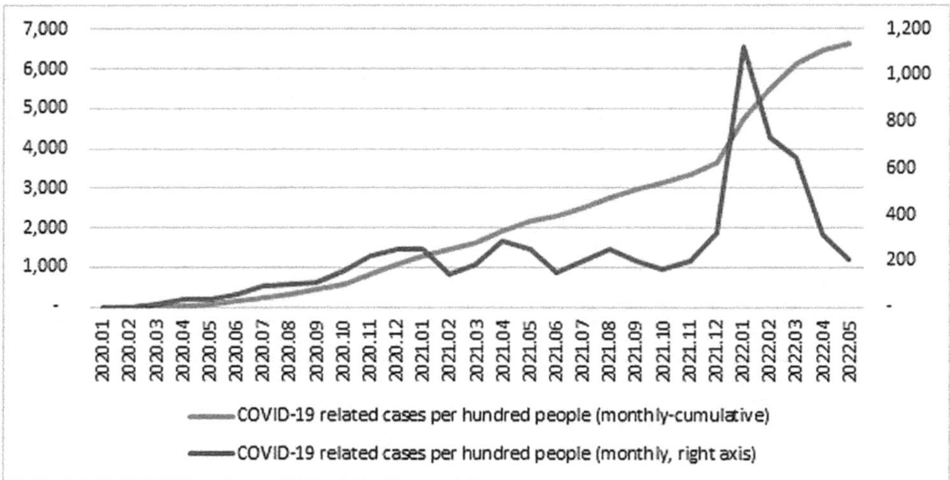

"COVID-19 related deaths per hundred people" has maximum value in January 2021 as 5.31. The cumulative data for "COVID-19 related deaths per hundred people" indicator is 78.6 at the end of May 2022 (**Figure 2**). It seems monthly "COVID-19 related deaths per hundred people" data is reached its maximum value and then started to decrease and follow constant ratio whereas cumulative "COVID-19 related deaths per hundred people" data seems to reach the maximum level in May 2022 and will start to decline in a couple months.

Figure 2. Covid-19 related deaths per hundred people.
Source: Our World in Data (OWID 2022), UNDESA (2022a)

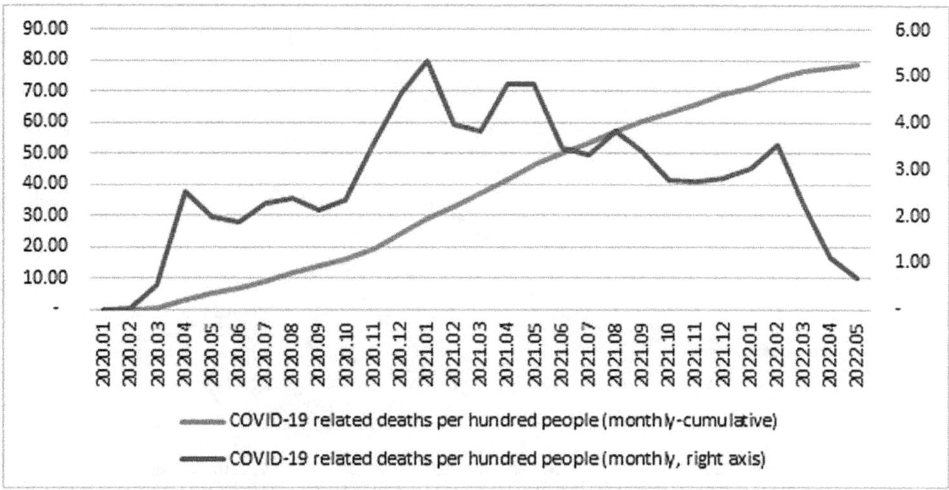

Total fully vaccinated people per hundred in the world reached the highest value on August 2021 as 1.22 billion. The fully vaccination curve looks like a normal (bell shaped) curve. (**Figure 3**). Cumulative monthly people fully vaccinated per hundred population reached 60 percent as the end of May 2022. It seems monthly "fully vaccinated people per hundred" data is reached its maximum value as 15.5 percent on August 2021 and then started to decrease and follow constant ratio whereas cumulative "fully vaccinated people per hundred" data seems to reach the maximum level in May 2022 and will start to decline in a couple months.

Figure 3. Global fully vaccinated people per hundred population (monthly, December 2020-May 2022).
Source: Our World in Data (OWID 2022)

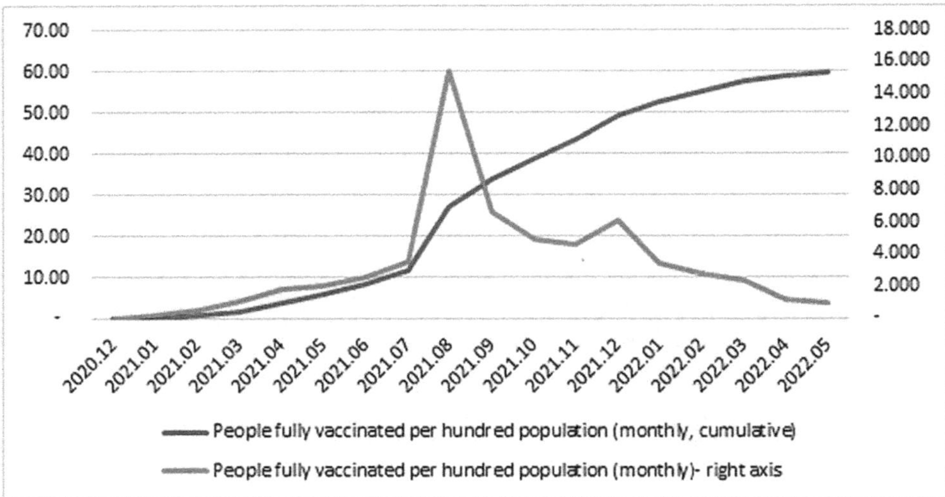

COVID-19 RELATED HEALTH INDICATORS

With COVID-19, for fighting with the pandemic, the health system and health personnel play crucial role. The need for a strong health system and healthcare workforce especially for the medical doctors and nurses emerged. Medical technology is not sufficient itself, so that health staff will take place to use it in favour of the people. There is unequal distribution in health personnel around the world for a resilience health system. Lack of health personnel was very important before the pandemic and became more evident by the pandemic (Özsoy 2021).

The COVID-19 pandemic is not a country's individual problem anymore; it is a global problem even for the human development and a collaborated partnership is needed (Özsoy and Gürler 2021b). Apart from limited capacity of the health system in the countries, skilled health personnel has very crucial importance. Health workforce including nurses is the other main input of the health system in the countries (Özsoy 2021). Abi-Rached (2021), in his five-book review study, has not only argued that after the pandemic, everything should be rediscovered and that we need a more "flexible" health system, but also stated that human health has a priority over profits, and that more investment should do be done in prevention and preparedness against epidemics.

A skilled health workforce and good working conditions are indispensable to have a strong health system in a country. The healthcare personnel including medical doctors and nurses are responsible for both daily healthcare needs and emergencies. By 2030, according to the Sustainable Development Goal 3c (SDG 3c), mostly in low-income countries and lower-middle income countries, the world needs 18 million more healthcare staff and nine million of them are the nurses and midwives (WHO 2020a, WHO 2020b).

According to WHO (2020a), 59 percent of the global health professions are nursing workforce. There are 27.9 million nurses and 19.3 million of them are professional nurses. The associate professional nurses are 22 percent of total nurses as 6.0 million. There was a global shortage of nurses before the pandemic and need for them has increased during pandemic.

The human resources in health care are not distributes equally in the world. The capacity and competence of the health systems and the skills of the health personnel in the countries play a very crucial role to fight with the pandemic. While the countries that have sufficient health system, health personnel and vaccination have achieved success in the fight against the pandemic. The pandemic also showed that countries should review their policies regarding the education and training of health personnel, their continuing professional development and the equal geographical distribution of personnel in the country. It has become clear that countries need to plan how they will meet the future demand for health professionals and how they will manage the supply of health professionals. Countries should encourage healthcare professionals to follow the technological developments and innovations in the field of health in the world and ensure that they meet these technologies as soon as possible and have innovative devices and methods (Özsoy and Gürler 2021b).

Health Personnel

There are totally 28.9 million nurses and 12.7 million medical doctors in the world in 2022 and most recent year (World Health Organization "WHO" 2022). Asia has more than 12 million nurses and the highest share in nurses as 41.8 percent. America has nearly 8.2 million nurses and the share in global nurses as 28.4 percent. North America has more than 6.1 million nurses and the share in global nurses as 21.2 percent. Europe has more than 6.7 million nurses and the share in global nurses as 23.3 percent. European Union has more than 4.2 million nurses and the share in global nurses as 14.7 percent. Oceania is the region with the least nurse share as 1.3 percent and more than 375 thousand nurses.

Asia has nearly 6.4 million medical doctors and the highest share in medical doctors as 50.4 percent. America has nearly 2.5 million medical doctors and the share in global medical doctors as 19.7 percent. North America has nearly 1.5 million medical doctors and the share in global medical doctors as 11.7 percent. Europe has nearly 3.2 million medical doctors and the share in global medical doctors as

25.2 percent. European Union has nearly 1.9 million medical doctors and the share in global medical doctors as 14.9 percent. Oceania is the region with the minimum medical doctor share as 1 percent and more than 124 thousand medical doctors.

Global average number of nurses and medical doctors per thousand population are 3.7 and 1.6 respectively. Number of nurses per thousand population in Africa, America, Asia, Europe and Oceania regions are 1.10, 7.94, 2.57, 9.00 and 8.68 respectively. Number of medical doctors per thousand population in Africa, America, Asia, Europe and Oceania regions are 0.34, 2.42, 1.36, 4.26 and 2.89 respectively (**Table 2**).

Table 2. The number of nurses and medical doctors by region.

Region	Population (2021)	Number of Nurses	Number of Medical Doctors	Region's Share in Nurses	Region's Share in Medical Doctors	Number of Nurses per Thousand Population	Number of Medical Doctors per Thousand Population
Africa	1,373,486,000	1,514,698	473,462	5.2%	3.7%	1.10	0.34
America	1,030,852,137	8,185,938	2,493,452	28.4%	19.7%	7.94	2.42
-North America	596,592,000	6,130,740	1,474,291	21.2%	11.7%	10.28	2.47
-South America	434,260,137	2,055,198	1,019,161	7.1%	8.1%	4.73	2.35
Asia	4,679,661,000	12,047,365	6,373,908	41.8%	50.4%	2.57	1.36
Europe	747,747,000	6,732,603	3,188,054	23.3%	25.2%	9.00	4.26
-European Union	447,207,489	4,231,907	1,884,212	14.7%	14.9%	9.46	4.21
Oceania	43,219,954	375,105	124,813	1.3%	1.0%	8.68	2.89
World	7,874,966,091	28,855,709	12,653,688	100.0%	100.0%	3.66	1.61

Source: WHO (2022), UNDESA (2022a), Eurostat (2022a)

According to income group, high-income country group has more than 13.2 million nurses and the highest share in nurses as 45.9 percent. Upper-middle income country group has more than 9.4 million nurses and the share in nurses as 32.7 percent. Lower-middle income country group has more than 5.6 million nurses and the share in nurses as 19.5 percent. Low-income country group has more than 534 thousand nurses and the share in nurses as 1.9 percent.

High-income country group has more than 3.8 million medical doctors and the share in medical doctors as 30.5 percent. Upper-middle income country group has nearly 6 million medical doctors and the highest share in medical doctors as 47.4 percent. Lower-middle income country group has more than 2.5 million medical doctors and the share in medical doctors as 20.3 percent. Low-income country group has more than 231 thousand medical doctors and the share in medical doctors as 1.8 percent.

Number of nurses per thousand population in high-income, upper-middle income, lower-middle income and low-income countries are 10.45, 11.85, 1.80 and 0.20 respectively. Number of medical doctors per thousand population in high-income, upper-middle income, lower-middle income and low-income countries are 3.05, 7.53, 0.82 and 0.09 respectively (**Table 3**).

Table 3. The number of nurses and medical doctors by income group countries.

Income Group	Population (2021)	Number of Nurses	Number of Medical Doctors	Income Group's Share in Nurses	Income Group's Share in Medical Doctors	Number of Nurses per Thousand Population	Number of Medical Doctors per Thousand Population
H	1,267,675,000	13,252,301	3,863,647	45.9%	30.5%	10.45	3.05
L	2,669,551,000	534,520	231,869	1.9%	1.8%	0.20	0.09
LM	3,138,572,000	5,636,592	2,564,408	19.5%	20.3%	1.80	0.82
UM	796,190,000	9,432,296	5,993,765	32.7%	47.4%	11.85	7.53
	7,871,988,000	28,855,709	12,653,688	100.0%	100.0%	3.67	1.61

Source: WHO (2022), UNDESA (2022a), Eurostat (2022a), the World Bank (2022b)

COVID-19 Related Indicators (Cases, Deaths, Case Fatality Rate "CFR", Vaccination)

As May 31, total COVID-19 related cases reached to 529 million in the world. Europe region has the highest cases, America and Asia regions follow Europe at the end of May 2022. Africa region has 2.2 percent of total COVID-19 related cases as 11.9 million, America region has 20.7 percent of total infected people as 157.1 million, and Asia region has 28.9 percent of total cases as 152.5 million. On the other hand, Europe has 37.5 percent of total cases as 198.2 million whereas 143.1 million of them are in European Union, and Oceania region has 1.7 percent of total COVID-19 related cases as 8.8 million.

Total COVID-19 related deaths reached to 6.3 million in the world at the end of May 2022. America region has the highest death numbers, Europe and Asia regions follow America. Africa region has 4.1 percent of total COVID-19 related deaths reached to 254 thousand, America region has 43.4 percent of total deaths as 2.72 million, and Asia region has 22.9 percent of total deaths as 1.43 million. On the other hand, Europe has 29.4 percent of total deaths as 1.84 million whereas 1.1

million of them are in European Union, and Oceania region has 0.2 percent of total COVID-19 related deaths as 12.4 thousand. North America has the 23.1 percent of total deaths in the world as 1.44 million deaths and South America has the 20.4 percent as 1.27 million deaths.

Case Fatality Rate is the ratio of total COVID-19 related deaths to total COVID-19 related cases in the population; hence, it is the death ratio of cases in hundred population. Total CFR reached to 1.18 in the world at the end of May 2022, which means that nearly 1.2 of each hundred COVID-19 related cases ended with death. Africa region has the highest CFR value, America, Asia and Europe regions follow Africa. Africa region has 2.14 CFR value, America region has 1.73, and Asia region has 0.94 CFR value. On the other hand, Europe has 0.93 CFR value whereas it is 0.77 in European Union, and Oceania region has 0.14 CFR value. North America has a CFR as 1.45 and South America has 2.21 CFR value.

As May 31, fully vaccinated people ratio has exceeded 60 percent (people fully vaccinated per hundred people) in the world and reached 4.74 billion people. South America region has the highest ratio with 74.9 whereas Asia region with 69.8 percent and Europe region with 65.9 percent (in European Union 73.4 percent of the population was fully vaccinated) followed South America. Africa region has 5.2 percent of total fully vaccinated people as 247.4 million, America region has 14.9 percent of total fully vaccinated people as 704.4 million, and Asia region has 68.9 percent of total fully vaccinated people as 3.3 billion. On the other hand, Europe has 10.4 percent of total fully vaccinated people as 492.9 million whereas 328.4 million of them are in European Union, and Oceania region has 0.6 percent of total fully vaccinated people as 43.2 million (**Table 4**).

Table 4. COVIS-19 related indicators by region.

Region	Total Cases	Total Deaths	Case Fatality Rate (CFR)	People Fully Vaccinated	Cases per Hundred Thousand Population	Deaths per Hundred Thousand Population	People Fully Vaccinated per Hundred Population	Population (2021)
Africa	11,867,790	253,869.00	2.14%	247,392,437.00	864.1	18.5	18.0	1,373,486,000
America	157,132,847	2,715,595.00	1.73%	704,431,535.00	15,243.0	263.4	68.3	1,030,852,137
-North America	99,554,662	1,441,198.00	1.45%	379,012,231.00	16,687.2	241.6	63.5	596,592,000
-South America	57,578,185	1,274,397.00	2.21%	325,419,304.00	13,258.9	293.5	74.9	434,260,137
Asia	152,491,031	1,428,766.00	0.94%	3,267,386,091.00	3,258.6	30.5	69.8	4,679,661,000
Europe	198,201,682	1,840,094.00	0.93%	492,853,641.00	26,506.5	246.1	65.9	747,747,000
-European Union	143,133,302	1,095,396.00	0.77%	328,390,658.00	32,006.0	244.9	73.4	447,207,489
Oceania	8,824,068	12,412.00	0.14%	27,620,865.00	20,416.7	28.7	63.9	43,219,954
World	528,517,418	6,250,736	1.18%	4,739,684,569	6,711.4	79.4	60.2	7,874,966,091

Source: Our World in Data (OWID 2022), UNDESA (2022a), Eurostat (2022a)

High-income country group has the highest COVID-19 related cases, upper-middle income and lower-middle income groups follow high-income. High-income group has 58.2 percent of total COVID-19 related cases as 307.4 million, upper-middle income has 24.3 percent of total infected people as 128.4 million, and lower-middle income group has 17.2 percent of total cases as 90.8 million. On the other hand, low-income countries has 0.3 percent of total cases as 1.83 million. It seems that as economic mobility and income per capita increases the spread speed and transmission risk of the virus from people to people increase.

Upper-middle income country group has the highest COVID-19 related deaths, high-income and lower-middle income groups follow high-income. Upper-middle income has 40 percent of total COVID-19 related deaths as 2.5 million, high-income group has 38.4 percent of total infected people as 2.4 million, and lower-middle income group has 20.9 percent of total deaths as 1.3 million. On the other hand, low-income countries have 0.7 percent of total deaths as 43.2 thousand. It seems that the high-income countries use the early access to vaccine to prevent from deathful effect of the pandemic due to the purchasing power of the high-income per capita and R&D ability to invent vaccine.

Low-income country group has the highest CFR value, upper-middle income and lower-middle income groups are second and third respectively. High-income country group region has 0.78 CFR value, upper-middle income group has 1.95, and lower-middle income group has 1.44 CFR value. On the other hand, low-income country group has highest CFR value as 2.36. Accessing to vaccine prevents the people in high-income countries from death.

Low-income countries have 2 percent of total fully vaccinated people as 94.1 million, lower-middle countries have 37.6 percent of total fully vaccinated people as 1.78 billion, upper-middle income countries have 41.2 percent of total fully vaccinated people as 1.95 billion and high-income countries have 19.2 percent of total fully vaccinated people as 908 million.

The number of fully vaccinated people per hundred population was 11.8 in low-income countries, 56.8 in lower-middle income countries, 73.2 in upper-middle income countries and 71.7 in high-income countries. It is clear that the vaccination rate against COVID-19 is quite high in upper-middle income and high-income countries. It seems that as income increases vaccination rate increases too. More than half of the population were vaccinated in lower-middle, upper-middle and high income countries. Low-income countries have difficulties to access to vaccine. The global supply chains connect the countries with each other so that lack of vaccination will cause negative effects on global trade because of the internationalization (**Table 5**).

Table 5. COVIS-19 related indicators by income group countries.

Income Group	Total Cases	Total Deaths	Case Fatality Rate (CFR)	People Fully Vaccinated	Cases per Hundred Thousand Population	Deaths per Hundred Thousand Population	People Fully Vaccinated per Hundred Population
High-income countries	307,410,626	2,402,564	0.78%	908,530,425	24,250.0	189.5	71.7
Upper-middle-income countries	128,416,648	2,501,391	1.95%	1,954,276,842	4,810.4	93.7	73.2
Lower-middle-income countries	90,834,480	1,303,531	1.44%	1,782,748,444	2,894.1	41.5	56.8
Low-income countries	1,830,789	43,187	2.36%	94,128,858	229.9	5.4	11.8

Source: Our World in Data (OWID 2022), UNDESA (2022a), Eurostat (2022a), the World Bank (2022b)

CORRELATION BETWEEN COVID-19 AND GLOBAL TRADE

In the study, COVID-19 related cases, deaths, Case Fatality Rate (CFR) and fully vaccinated people data were taken into consideration as COVID-19 related indicators and global export as an indicator of global foreign trade. The effect of the pandemic on global trade was analysed by correlation matrix. Tables and figures were used to investigate the relationships, flow, and changes in time series between the data. Higher number of health workforce is a good estimator to fight with the pandemic so that these indicators and COVID-19 related data are analysed in the study. To see the effect of pandemic on global trade, correlation between global exports and COVID-19 related indicators were also analysed in the study.

Normality of the Data

Determining the normality of the data is important whether to use non-parametric or parametric correlation tests to use for investigating the relationship between the indicators. If the data is normally distributed, then Pearson correlation test as a parametric test should be applied and if the data is not normally distributed then Spearman's Rho correlation test as a parametric test should be applied.

H_0: Data is normally distributed.
H_1: Data is not normally distributed.

For testing the normality of the data set, Kolmogorov-Smirnov and Shapiro-Wilk normality tests were applied to the COVID-19 related indicators and global export. Since the test statistics for "Fully vaccination per hundred population" and "Case Fatality Rate (CFR" are not statistically significant (all p values are smaller than the critical value 0.05) so that the null hypothesis will be rejected, and these data are not normally distributed. Test statistics for "Cumulative cases per 100,000 people", "Global exports" and "Cumulative deaths per 100,000 people" data are statistically significant (all p values are greater than the critical value 0.05) so that the null hypothesis cannot be rejected and these data are normally distributed (**Table 6**).

Table 6. Normality tests of COVID-19 related indicators and global export

	Kolmogorov-Smirnov			Shapiro-Wilk		
	Statistic	**df**	**Sig.**	**Statistic**	**df**	**Sig.**
Global export	.092	16	.200	.957	16	.614
Fully vaccinated people	.212	16	.053	.852	16	.015
COVID-19 related cases	.138	16	.200	.920	16	.166
COVID-19 related deaths	.104	16	.200	.954	16	.560
Case Fatality Rate (CFR)	.248	16	.010	.800	16	.003

Source: OWID (2022), UNDESA (2022a), WTO (2022), IBM-SPSS (2022)

Correlation Between COVID-19 Indicators and Global Export

Since the test statistics for "Fully vaccination per hundred population" and "Case Fatality Rate (CFR" are not statistically significant (all p values are smaller than the critical value 0.05) so that the null hypothesis can be rejected and these data are not normally distributed. For these two indicators Spearman's Rho correlation test can be used. Due to the vaccination started in December 2020, the correlation between COVID-19 indicators and global export are analysed for the period December 2200- March 2022 (16 months). The latest available data for global export belongs to March 2022.

Test statistics for "Cumulative cases per 100,000 people", "Global exports" and "Cumulative deaths per 100,000 people" data are statistically significant (all p values are greater than the critical value 0.05) so that the null hypothesis cannot be rejected and these data are normally distributed. For these three indicators Pearson correlation test should be used.

Global export is positively correlated with "Fully vaccination per hundred population", "Cumulative cases per 100,000 people" and "Cumulative deaths per 100,000 people" and negatively correlated with CFR. As CFR increases global export decreases. Growth in cases is greater than growth in deaths so that CFR is negatively correlated with both cases and deaths. "Cumulative deaths per 100,000 people" is positively correlated with "Cumulative cases per 100,000 people" and "Fully vaccination per hundred population". As cases increase in the world deaths and to prevent deaths vaccination increase too (**Table 7**).

Table 7. Correlation between COVID-19 indicators and global export.

	Global Exports	Fully Vaccination per Hundred Population	Cumulative Cases per 100,000 People	Cumulative Deaths per 100,000 People	CFR
Global exports	1.000	0.656	0.563	0.722	-0.614
Fully vaccination per hundred population	0.656	1.000	1.000	1.000	-0.979
Cumulative cases per 100,000 people	0.563	1.000	1.000	0.925	-0.979
Cumulative deaths per 100,000 people	0.722	1.000	0.925	1.000	-0.979
CFR	-0.614	-0.979	-0.979	-0.979	-0.979

Source: OWID (2022), UNDESA (2022a), WTO (2022), IBM-SPSS (2022)

FORECAST ANALYSIS OF GROSS DOMESTIC PRODUCT (GDP) IN 2022-2035 PERIOD

Due to the pandemic, the global economy shrank by 3.1 percent in 2020 according to IMF (2022a) and 3.3 percent according to World Bank (2022a). In 2021, that is, in the post-pandemic period, there is a 6.1 percent recovery according to the IMF (2022a) and 5.7 percent according to the World Bank (2022a). This positive picture and expectations were adversely affected by the war that broke out suddenly between the Russian Federation and Ukraine in February 2022.

The IMF (2022a) predicts that the global economy will grow by 3.59 percent in 2022, 3.55 percent in 2023, 3.4 percent in 2024, 3.38 percent in 2025, 3.32 percent in 2026 and 3.26 percent in 2027. The World Bank (2022a), on the other hand, predicts that the global economy will grow by 2.9 percent in 2022, 3 percent in 2023 and 3 percent in 2024. The OECD (2022a) also predicts that the global economy will grow by 3.02 percent in 2022 and 2.77 percent in 2023.

Of course, the decrease in global production has caused a decline in both the budget revenues of governments and the income per capita of the countries. Closures, lockdowns and restrictions preventing mobility and foreign trade have adversely affected both the total production (supply side) and total consumption (demand side) of the economies. Decreases in both domestic and foreign demand also accelerated the decline in national income. The decrease in national incomes has been seen more in countries, which are integrated into the global supply chain; hence have higher trade openness indices.

By vaccination against COVID-19, which was started at the end of 2020, many countries started to reduce restrictions, remove flight bans and made the transition to the "new normal". Although all these positive developments were interrupted by the emergence of new variants of the virus, they also affected the global economy positively, and a "V"-shaped recovery was seen throughout the world in 2021.

It is observed that this recovery is more in developing countries with 6.8 percent than in developed countries with 5.2 percent (IMF 2022a). Undoubtedly, the share of the 26 percent increase in global trade according to UNCTAD (2022) data is quite high in this positive development. Due to this positive relationship between global imports and national income, hence marginal propensity to import, the change in the national incomes and per capita incomes of the target market countries is one of the most important indicators that should be followed carefully by exporting countries.

Despite these positive developments in the world economy, it seems that countries will continue to grapple with important problems for a while. Some of these problems are:

- Increase in total gross debt, external debt and public debt due to the aid, transfer payments and domestic and foreign credits used in pandemic period (e.g. China's macro leverage ratio, the ratio of total debt to GDP, increased to 281.7 percent in the first quarter of 2022, of which 62.1 percent is mortgage credits, according to NIFD (2022),
- Destructive effect of the war between Russian Federation and Ukraine on global supply chain, especially on food and energy,
- Disruption of global supply and value chains due to challenges in global production,
- According to the International Labour Organization data (ILO 2022a), global unemployment increased from 5.35% in 2019 pre-pandemic period to 6.57 percent in 2020 pandemic period and estimated to be 6.17 percent in 2021 post-pandemic period (this decrease was more common in middle-income countries, such as 5.97 percent, 6.74 percent, 6.75 percent in 2019, 2020 and 2021 respectively),
- Decrease in per capita income as a result of increased unemployment and loss of working hours[1] due to the closures despite the aids,
- All commodity prices increased 52.8 percent (inflation) due to rising raw material and energy prices,
- Energy prices increased 101.8 percent whereas oil price increased by 63.85 percent, natural gas prices increased 262.6 percent and coal prices increased 110.8 percent in 2021,
- Industrial raw materials increased 40.1 percent and agricultural raw materials increased 15.8 percent,

- Increase in inputs already increased the global Consumer Price Index (CPI) raised by 4.7 percent on average; CPI increased 3.1 percent in developed countries and 5.7 percent in emerging and developing countries (IMF 2022b),
- Container crisis and rising logistics costs,
- The slowdown in global foreign direct investment (FDI) flows, which conducive to close the capital and technology gap in developing countries, increased by 64 percent in 2021 from the extraordinarily low level of 998.9 billion dollars in 2020 to 1.58 trillion dollars, surpassing the pre-pandemic level. The FDI share of developed economies was 33.1 percent in 2020, raised to 47.1 percent in 2021 whereas the FDI share of developing economies was 66.9 percent in 2020, and diminished to 52.9 percent in 2021.

The countries should manage the above-mentioned problems with an "agile" management approach and turn the crisis into an opportunity. Since the global import of countries is directly proportional to their national income, it is very important to follow closely the future projected values of the national income of the countries.

The IMF (2022a) predicts that the national income of the USA will increase to 31 trillion dollars, China's national income to 29.1 trillion dollars, Germany's national income to 5.4 trillion dollars and Japan's national income to 6.26 trillion dollars in 2027.

Table 8 shows the GDP projections of the top first twenty countries in the GDP ranking for the years 2022-2035 by authors' own calculation using international organizations' data. Global production is 95.2 trillion dollars in 2021, it is predicted that it will reach 110.9 trillion dollars in 2025, 127.6 trillion dollars in 2030, and 147 trillion dollars in 2035.

According to our own calculation, China will surpass the USA in in the national income ranking 2028 with the current growth trend. While the USA has a national income of 23 trillion dollars in 2021, it is predicted that its national income will increase to 24.9 trillion dollars in 2025, to 27.9 trillion dollars in 2030 and to 30.9 trillion dollars in 2035. While the USA realized 24.2 percent of global production in 2021, it is expected to realize 21 percent in 2031. The annual average GDP growth rate of USA will be 2.5 percent in 2021-2025 period with current prices. China has a national income of 17.7 trillion dollars in 2021, its national income is expected to increase to 24.3 trillion dollars in 2025, to 28.3 trillion dollars in 2030 and to 33.8 trillion dollars in 2035. While China realized 18.6 percent of global production in 2021, it is expected to realize 23 percent in 2035. The annual average GDP growth rate of USA will be 6.5 percent in 2021-2025 period. It is seen that Japan will leave its third place to Germany. While Japan has a national income of 4.9 trillion dollars in 2021, it will reach 5.1 trillion dollars in 2025, 5.3 trillion dollars in 2030 and 5.4 trillion dollars in 2035. While Germany has a GDP of 4.2 trillion dollars in 2021, its national income is expected to increase to 4.6 trillion dollars in 2025, to 5.2 trillion dollars in 2030 and to 5.7 trillion dollars in 2035. It is clear that with vaccination, the global economy has improved and surpassed the pre-pandemic level. The annual average GDP growth rate of Japan and Germany will be 0.7 and 2.5 percent respectively for 2021-2035 period.

The top twenty big economies produced 81.5 percent of the total global output in 2021 and the share is predicted to be 78.3 percent in 2035. Concentration in production will decrease which means the other countries which are not listed at the table will increase their contribution to global output.

Table 8 (a). GDP projections (2022-2035, trillion dollars)

Country	2021	2022	2025	2030	2035	Share in Global GDP (2021, %)
China	17.7	19.7	24.3	28.3	33.8	18.6%
United States	23.0	22.8	24.9	27.9	30.9	24.2%
Germany	4.2	4.4	4.6	5.2	5.7	4.4%
Japan	4.9	5.0	5.1	5.3	5.4	5.2%
India	3.1	3.0	3.7	4.3	4.8	3.3%
United Kingdom	3.2	3.5	3.4	3.9	4.2	3.3%
France	2.9	3.0	3.1	3.3	3.5	3.1%
Canada	2.1	2.2	2.3	2.7	3.0	2.2%
Russia	1.8	2.0	2.1	2.5	2.9	1.9%
Italy	2.1	2.2	2.3	2.5	2.7	2.2%
Korea	1.8	1.9	2.0	2.3	2.6	1.9%
Australia	1.6	1.8	1.9	2.2	2.6	1.7%
Brazil	1.6	1.7	1.9	2.2	2.5	1.7%
Indonesia	1.2	1.2	1.4	1.7	1.9	1.2%
Spain	1.4	1.5	1.5	1.6	1.6	1.5%
Mexico	1.3	1.3	1.4	1.5	1.6	1.4%
Iran	0.9	0.9	1.0	1.2	1.4	0.9%
Netherlands	1.0	1.0	1.1	1.2	1.3	1.1%
Saudi Arabia	0.8	0.9	1.0	1.1	1.3	0.9%
Türkiye	0.8	0.8	0.9	1.1	1.2	0.8%
Other countries	17.6	18.6	20.8	25.8	31.9	18.5%
Global import	95.2	99.4	110.9	127.6	147.0	100.0%

Source: Authors' own calculation by IMF (2022b), Eurostat (2022b), OECD (2022b), and the World Bank (2022b) data

Table 8 (b). GDP projections (2022-2035, trillion dollars)

Share in Global GDP (2035, %)	Average Annual Change in Global Export (2021-2035, %)	2021	2022	2025	2030	2035
23.0%	6.5%	2	2	2	1	1
21.0%	2.5%	1	1	1	2	2
3.9%	2.5%	4	4	4	4	3
3.7%	0.7%	3	3	3	3	4
3.3%	3.8%	6	7	5	5	5
2.9%	2.3%	5	5	6	6	6
2.4%	1.4%	7	6	7	7	7
2.0%	3.2%	9	9	8	8	8
2.0%	4.5%	11	10	10	10	9
1.9%	2.2%	8	8	9	9	10
1.8%	3.3%	10	11	11	11	11
1.7%	4.1%	12	12	12	12	12
1.7%	3.9%	13	13	13	13	13
1.3%	4.4%	16	16	15	14	14
1.1%	1.1%	14	14	14	15	15
1.1%	1.9%	15	15	16	16	16
1.0%	4.2%	18	18	18	17	17
0.9%	2.0%	17	17	17	18	18
0.9%	4.0%	19	19	19	19	19
0.8%	3.8%	21	21	21	20	20
21.7%	5.8%					
100.0%	3.9%					

Source: Authors' own calculation by IMF (2022b), Eurostat (2022b), OECD (2022b), and the World Bank (2022b) data

According to World Economic League Table 2022 report announced by the British Centre for Economics and Business Research (CEBR 2021), China will surpass the USA in in the national income ranking 2030 with the current growth trend. While the USA has a national income of 22.9 trillion dollars in 2021, it is predicted that its national income will increase to 29 trillion dollars in 2026, to 35.4 trillion dollars in 2031 and to 43.3 trillion dollars in 2036. While the USA realized 24.2 percent of global production in 2021, it is expected to realize 22.4 percent in 2036. China has a national income of 16.8 trillion dollars in 2021, its national income is expected to increase to 24.9 trillion dollars in 2026, to 37.6 trillion dollars in 2031 and to 55.1 trillion dollars in 2036. While China realized 17.8 percent of global production in 2021, it is expected to realize 28.5 percent in 2036. It is seen that Germany will leave its third place to India. While India has a national income of 2.9 trillion dollars in 2021, it will reach 4.3 trillion dollars in 2026 and 6.8 trillion dollars in 2031. While Germany has a GDP of 4.2 trillion dollars in 2021, its national income is expected to increase to 5.4 trillion dollars in 2026, to 5.3 trillion dollars in 2031 and to 7.4 trillion dollars in 2036. It is clear that with vaccination, the global economy has improved and surpassed the pre-pandemic level. The top twenty big economies produced 80 percent of the total global output in 2021 and the share is predicted to be 88.5 percent in 2036.

According to the report, Bangladesh, Indonesia, India and Vietnam appear as surprise countries. Vietnam has the highest GDP growth rate with an annual average growth rate of 13.9 percent in the 2021-2036 period. Bangladesh with a growth rate of 11.5 percent, India with 11.1 percent, Indonesia with 10.6 percent and China with 9.1 percent follows Vietnam.

While India realized 3.1 percent of global production in 2021, it is expected to realize 5.6 percent in 2036. Bangladesh realized 0.38 percent of global production in 2021, it is expected to realize 0.69 percent in 2036. Indonesia realized 1.2 percent of global production in 2021; it is expected to realize 2.1 percent in 2036. Vietnam realized 0.4 percent of global production in 2021; it is expected to realize 0.8 percent in 2036. In the same report, it is predicted that China will rise to the class of high-income country in 2024.

As stated above, China is expected to surpass the US economy in 2030, and it is expected to be at the top in the following years. The USA is expected to take the second place after China in 2031 and 2036. India, on the other hand, is expected to maintain its rank in 2036, after rising to the third rank in 2031, from the seventh rank in 2021. Japan is expected to rank third in the 2022-2026 period; it is expected to rank fourth in 2031 and fifth in 2035. As Japan Germany is expected to maintain its rank in the fourth place in the 2022-2026 period, and it is expected to rank fifth in 2031 and fourth again in 2036.

In the table, the highest jump in the GDP ranking in the 2021-2036 period is seen in Vietnam, which is expected to rise 21 places, followed by Indonesia, which is expected to rise eight places, and India, which is expected to rise 4 places.

FORECAST ANALYSIS OF GLOBAL TRADE IN 2022-2035 PERIOD

According to UNCTAD (2022) data, there was a 7.15 percent decrease in 2020 and 26 percent increase in 2021 in total global merchandise import value. The volume of global goods imports decreased 5.5 percent in 2020 and increased by 9.8 percent in 2021. The increase in the import unit price is clearly moderate in 2021. The global service imports decreased 17.7 percent in 2020 and increased 15 percent in 2021.

The IMF (2022) predicts that the global import volume will increase in 2022 even the growth rate will be less than 2021 value. The global import volume will increase 4.88 percent in 2022, 3.86 percent in 2023, 3.48 percent in 2024, 3.69 percent in 2025, 3.58 percent in 2026 and 3.55 percent in 2027.

Total Imports by Country in 2022-2035 Period

As mentioned above, global goods imports declined 7.5 percent in pandemic period, increased 26 percent in 2021, which is more than 16.6 percent comparing with pre-pandemic value, and reached to 22.5 trillion dollars. Africa is the region whose imports mostly contacted due to the COVID-19 with 13.7 percent in 2021. America region has the highest decrease in import with 9.3 percent. The Europe region was the least affected region by the pandemic with a 6.4 percent contraction in imports.

Asia region has the highest import share in the world with 8.5 trillion dollars import value and 37.7 percent share and Europe has the second highest importin region in the world with 8.38 trillion dollars import value and 37.2 percent in 2021. America's import was 4.7 trillion dollars with 20.9 percent in global import. The pandemic has caused a decrease in import share of Europe and America and an increase in Asia region (**Table 9**).

Table 9. Global imports (CIF) by region.

Region	Import (Billion $, 2019)	Import (Billion $, 2020)	Import (Billion $, 2021)	Change (2019-2020; %)	Change (2020-2021; %)	Share of the Region (%, 2019)	Share of the Region (%, 2020)	Share of the Region (%, 2021)
Africa	585.408	505.181	628.580	-13,70	24,43	3,03	2,83	2,79
America	4.126.778	3.742.516	4.704.886	-9,31	25,71	21,36	20,94	20,89
Asia	7.049.454	6.554.274	8.478.404	-7,02	29,36	36,49	36,67	37,65
Europe	7.274.432	6.807.736	8.381.799	-6,42	23,12	37,66	38,09	37,22
Oceania	280.619	262.284	325.119	-6,53	23,96	1,45	1,47	1,44
World	19.316.692	17.871.990	22.518.788	-7,48	26,00			
Memo item								
Middle East	769.769	672.523	819.372	-12,63	21,84	3,98	3,76	3,64
European Union	5.544.301	5.154.615	6.456.884	-7,03	25,26	28,70	28,84	28,67
Euro Area (19)	4.560.034	4.203.938	5.260.854	-7,81	25,14	23,61	23,52	23,36
North American Free Trade Agreement (USMCA)	3.498.799	3.215.020	3.958.818	-8,11	23,14	18,11	17,99	17,58
South and Central America and the Caribbean	623.506	523.461	741.551	-16,05	41,66	3,23	2,93	3,29
Africa, CIS and Middle East	1.755.352	1.547.482	1.908.297	-11,84	23,32	9,09	8,66	8,47
Association of Southeast Asian Nations (ASEAN)	1.388.343	1.268.698	1.620.848	-8,62	27,76	7,19	7,10	7,20
BRICS members	3.119.023	2.929.205	3.912.656	-6,09	33,57	16,15	16,39	17,38
G-7 (Group of Seven)	6.812.150	6.275.397	7.583.769	-7,88	20,85	35,27	35,11	33,68
G-20	14.887.998	13.793.496	17.353.745	-7,35	25,81	77,07	77,18	77,06

Source: WTO (2022), UN (2022)

By income group analysis, the highest decrease in imports was in lower-middle income group due to the COVID-19 with 13.8 percent. The upper-middle income group has least negative effect of pandemic on imports with a 6.4 percent decrease. The lower income group is another group who has less negative effect of pandemic on imports with a 7.1 percent decrease. After pandemic lower-middle income group increased their import by 36.8 percent, whereas upper-middle income, high-income and low-income groups increased by 30.2 percent, 23.3 percent and 10 percent respectively.

High-income countries made most of the import with 14.9 trillion dollars import value and 66.1 percent share, upper-middle income group has followed this group with 5.5 trillion dollars import value, and 24.3 percent share in 2021. The pandemic has caused a decrease in imports share of high-income country and low-income groups and an increase in upper-middle and lower-middle income group's share (**Table 10**).

Table 10. Global imports by income group.

Income Group	Export (Billion $, 2019)	Export (Billion $, 2020)	Export (Billion $, 2021)	Change (2019-2020; %)	Change (2020-2021; %)	Share of the Group (%, 2019)	Share of the Group (%, 2020)	Share of the Group (%, 2021)
H	12.969.949	12.061.597	14.876.911	-7,00	23,34	67,14	67,49	66,06
L	110.241	102.401	112.685	-7,11	10,04	0,57	0,57	0,50
LM	1.754.574	1.512.460	2.068.374	-13,80	36,76	9,08	8,46	9,19
UM	4.481.928	4.195.533	5.460.818	-6,39	30,16	23,20	23,48	24,25
World	19.316.692	17.871.990	22.518.788	-7,48	26,00			

Source: WTO (2022), the World Bank (2022c)

Table 11 shows the global goods import and ranking projections for the 2022-2035 period, by the top twenty importing countries breakdown by years using EViews (2022) forecasting software. According to the analysis, global imports are expected to reach 31.1 trillion dollars in 2030 and 36.6 trillion dollars in 2035. Global imports are expected to increase approximately 89.5 percent in 2035 compared to 2019 and 104.8 percent compared to 2020, when the pandemic was felt most severely. Global imports are expected to increase by about 4.5 percent annually in average in the 2021-2035 period.

While China is expected to import 2.93 trillion dollars in 2022, country's import is expected to increase to 3.33 trillion dollars in 2025, 4 trillion dollars in 2030, and 4.67 trillion dollars in 2035. For USA, global good import is expected to be 3.2 trillion dollars in 2022, 3.4 trillion dollars in 2025, 3.8 trillion dollars in 2030 and 4.2 trillion dollars in 2035. Germany is expected to import 1.55 trillion dollars in 2022, 1.68 trillion dollars in 2025, to 1.86 trillion dollars in 2030 and to 2.05 trillion dollars in 2035.

China's share in global imports, which was approximately 11.9% in 2021, will increase to 12.8% in 2035. The share of the USA will decrease from 13 percent to 11.5 percent in 2035, whereas Germany's global import share will contract from 6.3 percent to 5.6 percent in 2035. Vietnam's global goods import share will increase from 1.5 percent in 2021 to 1.7 percent in 2035. India's import share will increase from 2.5 percent to 3.1 percent in 2035. While the first three countries accounted for 31.3 percent of global imports in 2021, it is expected to make 32.7 percent in 2022, 32.2 percent in 2025, 31.1 percent in 2030 and 29.8 percent in 2035. It is observed that the country concentration in imports has decreased over time and the global import shares of other countries will increase.

While China is expected to be the second largest importing country in 2025, it is predicted that it will surpass the USA in 2027 to become the largest importer country. While the USA lost the leadership to China in 2027, the country will always follow China in global imports after 2027. It is seen that Germany, which is the third largest importing country in the world, will maintain its third place in 2025, 2030 and 2035.

Turkey, on the other hand, is the twenty-second largest importing country in 2021 and is expected to rank in this rank until 2035. It is predicted that Turkey's imports will be 446.2 billion dollars in 2030 and 511.2 billion dollars in 2035. Turkey's share in global imports, which was 1.21 percent in 2021, is expected to increase to 1.40 percent in 2035.

Among the countries in the table, India, which is expected to rise four steps, will have the highest improvement in global import in the period of 2022-2035 with an annual average change in global import as 6.8 percent. Belgium and Canada, which are expected to rise three steps, take the second place.

Spain's, Belgium's and Singapore's imports are expected to increase by approximately 6.5 percent annually on average in the 2021-2035 period, whereas Vietnam has 6.4 percent, Switzerland and Taiwan have 6.2 percent, Poland has 6.1 percent and Canada with an increase of 5.8 percent.

Since countries where an increase in global imports is expected will be possible target markets for global exporters, it is beneficial to conduct studies and analysis on these markets.

Table 11 (a). Global import projection (2022-2035).

Country	2021	2022	2025	2030	2035	Share of the Country in Global Import (2021, %)
China	2,687.5	2,929.8	3,334.5	4,000.8	4,667.3	11.9%
USA	2,937.3	3,198.0	3,426.6	3,815.1	4,203.5	13.0%
Germany	1,419.5	1,546.0	1,675.5	1,864.7	2,053.8	6.3%
Netherlands	757.7	876.2	963.2	1,108.2	1,253.2	3.4%
Hong Kong	712.4	825.8	921.9	1,080.8	1,239.8	3.2%
India	573.7	679.9	762.3	924.1	1,118.0	2.5%
Korea, Rep.	615.1	746.5	831.5	970.6	1,109.8	2.7%
Japan	769.0	880.4	924.0	1,011.2	1,098.4	3.4%
France	714.2	785.5	843.5	929.8	1,016.3	3.2%
Belgium	510.2	590.5	662.0	804.1	974.2	2.3%
Canada	503.7	550.5	619.1	752.6	912.6	2.2%
United Kingdom (UK)	695.4	746.9	772.7	814.7	856.7	3.1%
Mexico	522.5	587.0	646.2	745.1	844.1	2.3%
Spain	418.2	479.4	539.0	656.7	797.7	1.9%
Singapore	406.2	465.0	523.2	637.8	775.1	1.8%
Italy	550.6	615.0	652.9	710.0	767.2	2.4%
Taiwan	382.1	424.2	479.3	585.2	712.0	1.7%
Viet Nam	331.6	373.7	421.8	516.3	629.5	1.5%
Poland	338.3	373.1	421.5	516.0	629.1	1.5%
Switzerland	322.6	357.6	403.4	494.2	603.1	1.4%
Other countries	6,351.0	5,418.5	6,364.6	8,184.6	10,340.5	28.2%
Global import	22,518.8	23,449.3	26,188.7	31,122.8	36,601.9	100.0%

Source: WTO (2022), EViews (2022)

Table 11 (b). Global import projection (2022-2035).

Share of the Country in Global Import (2035, %)	Annual Average Change in Global Import (2021-2035, %)	2021	2022	2025	2030	2035
12.8%	5.3%	2	2	2	1	1
11.5%	3.1%	1	1	1	2	2
5.6%	3.2%	3	3	3	3	3
3.4%	4.7%	5	5	4	4	4
3.4%	5.3%	7	6	6	5	5
3.1%	6.8%	10	10	10	9	6
3.0%	5.7%	9	9	8	7	7
3.0%	3.1%	4	4	5	6	8
2.8%	3.0%	6	7	7	8	9
2.7%	6.5%	13	12	11	11	10
2.5%	5.8%	14	14	14	12	11
2.3%	1.7%	8	8	9	10	12
2.3%	4.4%	12	13	13	13	13
2.2%	6.5%	15	15	15	15	14
2.1%	6.5%	16	16	16	16	15
2.1%	2.8%	11	11	12	14	16
1.9%	6.2%	17	17	17	17	17
1.7%	6.4%	19	18	18	18	18
1.7%	6.1%	18	19	19	19	19
1.6%	6.2%	20	20	20	20	20
28.3%	4.5%					
100.0%	4.5%					

Total Exports by Country in 2022-2035 Period

Global exports declined 7.15 percent in pandemic period, increased 26.3 percent in 2021, and reached to 22.2 trillion dollars, which is more than pre-pandemic value. Africa is the region whose exports mostly contacted due to the COVID-19 with 17.5 percent in 2021. The Asian region was the least affected region by the pandemic with a 4.5 percent contraction in exports. Asia region has the highest export in the world with 9.3 trillion dollars export value and 41.8 percent share and Europe has the second highest export share in the world with 8.55 trillion dollars export value and 38.4 percent in 2021. America has 3.5 trillion dollars export value and

15.6 percent. The pandemic has caused a decrease in exports share of Europe and America and an increase in Asian countries' share (**Table 12**).

Table 12. Global exports (FOB) by region.

Region	Export (Billion $, 2019)	Export (Billion $, 2020)	Export (Billion $, 2021)	Change (2019-2020; %)	Change (2020-2021; %)	Share of the Region (%, 2019)	Share of the Region (%, 2020)	Share of the Region (%, 2021)
Africa	476.505	393.053	545.176	-17,51	38,70	2,51	2,23	2,45
America	3.142.041	2.771.028	3.471.695	-11,81	25,29	16,53	15,70	15,58
Asia	7.591.318	7.247.562	9.308.538	-4,53	28,44	39,94	41,07	41,77
Europe	7.468.661	6.930.675	8.554.917	-7,20	23,44	39,30	39,28	38,39
Oceania	326.031	302.862	403.492	-7,11	33,23	1,72	1,72	1,81
World	19.004.555	17.645.180	22.283.819	-7,15	26,29			
Memo item								
Middle East	1.069.286	805.511	1.131.789	-24,67	40,51	5,63	4,57	5,08
European Union	5.825.354	5.475.445	6.625.560	-6,01	21,00	30,65	31,03	29,73
Euro Area (19)	4.836.769	4.505.246	5.454.198	-6,85	21,06	25,45	25,53	24,48
North American Free Trade Agreement (USMCA)	2.549.925	2.232.888	2.752.175	-12,43	23,26	13,42	12,65	12,35
South and Central America and the Caribbean	590.525	536.742	717.918	-9,11	33,75	3,11	3,04	3,22
Africa, CIS and Middle East	2.113.364	1.653.915	2.331.305	-21,74	40,96	11,12	9,37	10,46
Association of Southeast Asian Nations (ASEAN)	1.423.179	1.385.241	1.720.051	-2,67	24,17	7,49	7,85	7,72
BRICS members	3.554.660	3.494.750	4.657.779	-1,69	33,28	18,70	19,81	20,90
G-7 (Group of Seven)	5.852.991	5.227.698	6.309.176	-10,68	20,69	30,80	29,63	28,31
G-20	14.584.002	13.568.934	17.039.070	-6,96	25,57	76,74	76,90	76,46

Source: WTO (2022), UN (2022)

By income group analysis, lower-middle income group is mostly affected due to the COVID-19 with 9.6 percent. The low-income group is the only group who gained by pandemic with a 10.7 percent increase in exports. This may be because of less connectivity to the international markets. After pandemic lower-middle income group increased their export by 31.8 percent, whereas upper-middle income, high-income and low-income groups increased by 30.5 percent, 23.9 percent and 23.5 percent respectively.

High-income countries made most of the export with 14.25 trillion dollars export value and 63.9 percent share, upper-middle income group has followed this group with 6.3 trillion dollars export value, and 28.2 percent share in 2021. The pandemic has caused a decrease in exports share of high-income country group and an increase in upper-middle income group's share (**Table 13**).

Table 13. Global exports by income group.

Income Group	Export (Billion $, 2019)	Export (Billion $, 2020)	Export (Billion $, 2021)	Change (2019-2020; %)	Change (2020-2021; %)	Share of the Group (%, 2019)	Share of the Group (%, 2020)	Share of the Group (%, 2021)
H	12.506.645	11.496.485	14.245.842	-8,08	23,91	65,81	65,15	63,93
L	54.499	60.338	74.504	10,71	23,48	0,29	0,34	0,33
LM	1.408.043	1.273.028	1.678.067	-9,59	31,82	7,41	7,21	7,53
UM	5.035.368	4.815.329	6.285.406	-4,37	30,53	26,50	27,29	28,21
World	19.004.555	17.645.180	22.283.819	-7,15	26,29			

Source: WTO (2022), the World Bank (2022)

As a result of the analysis in **Table 14**, it is predicted that global exports will reach 23.1 trillion dollars in 2022, 25.8 trillion dollars in 2025, 30.6 trillion dollars in 2030 and 36 trillion dollars in 2035. Global exports are expected to increase by approximately 4.5 percent annually in the 2021-2035 period.

It is seen that China, as the most exporting country, will not leave the top to anyone. China's export is expected to reach 3.9 trillion dollars in 2022, 4.45 trillion dollars in 2025, to 5.36 trillion dollars in 2030, and to 6.27 trillion dollars in 2035. USA, as the second highest exporting country, is expected to export 1.94 trillion dollars in 2022, 2.11 trillion dollars 2025, 2.40 trillion dollars in 2030 and 2.68 trillion dollars in 2035. Comparing **Table 11** and **Table 14**, it means that the foreign trade deficit of the USA will increase every year, it is predicted that USA will import 4.2 trillion dollars against 2.68 trillion dollars of exports and the foreign trade deficit will be 1.5 trillion dollars in 2035. This may be a sign that the USA may take new measures to reduce its foreign trade deficit hence will deepen trade war. is expected to lose its place to Germany in 2031.

It is predicted that Germany, which is the third largest exporting country in 2021, will export 1.66 trillion dollars in 2022, and its exports will increase to 1.75 trillion dollars in 2025, 1.91 trillion dollars in 2030 and 2.07 trillion dollars in 2035.

China's share in global exports, which was approximately 15.2 percent in 2021, will increase to 17.4 percent in 2035, whereas the share of the USA will decrease from 7.9 percent to 7.5 percent in 2035, and Germany's share will decrease from 7.4 percent to 5.7 percent in 2035. In contrast, Vietnam's share is expected to increase from 1.5 percent to 1.8 percent in 2035, and India's share from 1.8 percent to 2 percent. While the top three countries made 30.5 percent of global exports in 2021, it is expected to account for 32.5 percent in 2022, 32.3 percent in 2025, 31.6 percent in 2030 and 30.6 percent in 2035. As in imports, it is seen that the country concentration in exports has decreased over time and the shares of other countries in global exports will increase after 2022.

It is predicted that Vietnam, which is expected to rise seven steps in the 2021-2035 period, will make the highest jump in the export ranking, while Taiwan, which is expected to rise four steps, and India, which is expected to rise three places have good exporting performance too. The highest annual average increase in export will be 6.9 percent in Vietnam, 6.2 percent in China, 5.7 percent in India, 5.3 percent in Hong Kong, 4.8 percent in Taiwan, 4.4 percent in Korea Republic and 4.3 percent in Mexico respectively.

Although the countries whose global exports are expected to increase will compete with each other, it is obvious that their global imports from other countries will increase in order to realize their exports due to the fact that these countries are connected to the global supply chain. For the global value chain, it is useful to follow both the export and import trends of these countries over the years.

Table 14 (a). Global export projection (2022-2035).

Country	2021	2022	2025	2030	2035	Share of the Country in Global Export (2021, %)
China	3,364.0	3,897.7	4,449.2	5,361.5	6,273.8	15.2%
USA	1,754.5	1,944.8	2,112.4	2,397.1	2,681.8	7.9%
Germany	1,631.7	1,658.3	1,753.3	1,910.1	2,066.9	7.4%
Netherlands	836.3	928.7	1,021.0	1,167.8	1,314.6	3.8%
Hong Kong	669.9	778.5	868.6	1,018.0	1,167.4	3.0%
Korea, Rep.	644.4	727.6	800.8	922.8	1,044.7	2.9%
Japan	756.0	802.4	832.8	884.4	935.9	3.4%
Italy	610.3	646.8	695.3	776.5	857.8	2.8%
Belgium	545.3	608.8	656.5	731.0	805.6	2.5%
Mexico	494.2	554.2	610.1	702.3	794.6	2.2%
Russian Fed.	494.0	623.9	653.5	702.3	751.1	2.2%
Taiwan	447.7	503.2	559.9	654.6	749.3	2.0%
France	584.9	617.0	643.4	685.7	728.1	2.6%
India	395.5	449.0	509.8	611.6	713.4	1.8%
Viet Nam	335.9	383.1	446.4	553.1	659.9	1.5%
Canada	507.5	540.4	567.1	612.8	658.4	2.3%
Singapore	457.4	503.4	533.1	581.9	630.6	2.1%
UK	468.4	530.2	539.1	553.8	568.5	2.1%
Spain	384.5	407.1	436.4	485.1	533.9	1.7%
Switzerland	379.9	390.7	420.8	469.6	518.4	1.7%
Other countries	6,382.1	5,563.6	6,644.0	8,823.2	11,538.3	28.8%
Global export	22,144.3	23,059.4	25,753.3	30,605.3	35,993.2	100.0%

Source: WTO (2022), EViews (2022)

Table 14 (b). Global export projection (2022-2035).

Share of the Country in Global Export (2035, %)	Annual Average Change in Global Export (2021-2035, %)	2021	2022	2025	2030	2035
17.4%	6.2%	1	1	1	1	1
7.5%	3.8%	2	2	2	2	2
5.7%	1.9%	3	3	3	3	3
3.7%	4.1%	4	4	4	4	4
3.2%	5.3%	6	6	5	5	5
2.9%	4.4%	7	7	7	6	6
2.6%	1.7%	5	5	6	7	7
2.4%	2.9%	8	8	8	8	8
2.2%	3.4%	10	11	9	9	9
2.2%	4.3%	12	12	12	10	10
2.1%	3.7%	13	9	10	11	11
2.1%	4.8%	16	16	14	13	12
2.0%	1.7%	9	10	11	12	13
2.0%	5.7%	17	17	17	15	14
1.8%	6.9%	22	20	18	18	15
1.8%	2.1%	11	13	13	14	16
1.8%	2.7%	15	15	16	16	17
1.6%	1.5%	14	14	15	17	18
1.5%	2.8%	18	18	19	19	19
1.4%	2.6%	19	19	20	20	20
32.1%	5.8%					
100.0%	4.5%					

Total Imports by Sectors in 2022-2035 Period

Table 15 shows the global import projection by sectoral breakdown by years. According to the analysis, "Chemicals and Products" will be the most importing sector with 6.1 trillion dollars in 2022, 6.7 trillion dollars in 2025, 8 trillion dollars in 2030 and 9.5 trillion dollars in 2035. The import in "Electric and Electronic" sector is expected to be 4.8 trillion dollars in 2022, 5.5 trillion dollars in 2025, 6.4 trillion dollars in 2030 and 7.6 trillion dollars in 2035 whereas the import in the "Automotive Industry" sector will be 2.2 trillion dollars in 2022, 2.4 trillion dollars in 2025, 2.8 trillion dollars in 2030 and 3.3 trillion dollars in 2035. The "Hazelnuts and Products" sector will import 16.8 billion dollars, the "Olive and Olive Oil" sector will import 19.9 billion dollars, and the "Carpet" will import 24.25 billion dollars in 2035.

While the global import in the "Chemicals and Products" sector is expected to constitute 25.3 percent of the total global imports, the "Electric and Electronic" sector accounts for 21.4 percent, the "Automotive Industry" sector 9 percent, the "Machinery and Accessories" sector will constitute 4.9 percent, and the "Jewellery" sector will constitute 3.8 percent of the total global imports in 2021. "Chemicals and Products" sector is expected to constitute 25.8 percent of the total global imports, the "Electric and Electronic" sector accounts for 20.6 percent, the "Automotive Industry" sector 8.9 percent, the "Machinery and Accessories" sector will constitute 4.9 percent, and the "Jewellery" sector will constitute 4.3 percent of the total global imports in 2035. The first three sectors are expected to constitute 56.1 percent of the total global imports in 2022, 55.6 percent in 2025, 55.5 percent in 2030 and 55.4 percent in 2035.

In the sectoral breakdown, the "Jewellery" sector is expected to have the highest increase in imports in the 2021-2035 period with an annual increase of 5.8 percent. "Chemicals and Products" and "Cereals, Pulses, Oil Seeds and Products" sectors are expected to have with an annual increase of 4.7 percent. The "Mining Products" with an annual average increase of 4.6 percent, "Automotive industry" and "Machinery and Machinery Accessories" sectors will have 4.3 percent increase in imports.

Table 15. Global demand (import) projection by sectors (billion dollars, 2025-2035).

Sector	2021	2022	2025	2030	2035	Share of the Sector in Global Import (2021, %)	Share of the Sector in Global Import (2035, %)	Annual Average Change in Global Import (2021-2035, %)
Chemicals and chemical products	5.7	6.1	6.7	8.0	9.5	25.3%	25.8%	4.7%
Electric & Electronic	4.8	4.8	5.5	6.4	7.6	21.4%	20.6%	4.0%
Automotive industry	2.0	2.2	2.4	2.8	3.3	9.0%	8.9%	4.3%
Machinery and Machinery Accessories	1.1	1.2	1.3	1.5	1.8	4.9%	4.9%	4.3%
Jewellery	0.9	0.9	1.0	1.3	1.6	3.8%	4.3%	5.8%
Cereals, Pulses, Oil Seeds and Products	0.9	0.9	1.0	1.3	1.5	4.0%	4.1%	4.7%
Ferrous and Non-Ferrous Metals	0.9	0.9	1.0	1.2	1.4	3.9%	3.8%	4.2%
Mining Products	0.7	0.7	0.8	1.0	1.2	3.2%	3.3%	4.6%
Steel industry	0.7	0.7	0.8	1.0	1.1	3.3%	3.1%	3.7%
Furniture, Paper and Forestry Products	0.7	0.7	0.8	0.8	1.0	2.9%	2.6%	3.2%
Other sectors	4.1	4.2	4.8	5.8	6.8	18.2%	18.7%	4.8%
Total import	22.5	23.4	26.2	31.1	36.6	100.0%	100.0%	4.5%

Source: Authors' own calculation by WTO (2022) data

According to the **Table 16**, the projection of the global import ranking by the sectoral breakdown by years, "Chemicals and Chemical Products", "Electric and Electronics" and "Automotive Industry" sectors are expected to take the first three places among the sectors with the highest imports in the 2022-2035 period. "Jewellery" sector is expected to have the highest rise in the ranking, which is the seventh importing sector in 2021, and will be the fifth in 2035. This sector is followed by the "Air Conditioning Industry, HVAC-R" "Mining Products", "Aqua and Animal Products", "Leather and Leather products", "Fruit and Vegetables", "Fresh Fruit and Vegetables" and "Ornamental Plants and Products" sectors, which are expected to rise one step during the period. "Textiles and Raw Materials" is expected to decrease three steps; "Ready-to-wear and Apparel" will decrease two steps during the period. "Cereals, Pulses, Oil Seeds and Products", "Ferrous and

Non-Ferrous Metals", "Steel" and "Dried Fruit" sectors are expected to decrease one step. It is foreseen that other sectors will maintain their place in the ranking.

Table 16. Global demand (import) ranking by sectors (2022-2035).

Sector	2021	2022	2025	2030	2035
Chemicals and chemical products	1	1	1	1	1
Electric & Electronic	2	2	2	2	2
Automotive industry	3	3	3	3	3
Machinery and Machinery Accessories	4	4	4	4	4
Jewellery	7	6	5	5	5
Cereals, Pulses, Oil Seeds and Products	5	7	6	6	6
Ferrous and Non-Ferrous Metals	6	5	7	7	7
Mining Products	9	9	8	8	8
Steel industry	8	8	9	9	9
Furniture, Paper and Forestry Products	10	10	10	10	10

Source: Authors' own calculation by WTO (2022) data

Best Performances in Trade Openness Index in 2022-2035 Period

Trade Openness Index is calculated by the division of country's total foreign trade (imports and export of merchandise products) by its GDP. Hong Kong with a 4.54 index value, which means total foreign trade is 4.5 times greater than total GDP of the country, is at the top of the list in 2035. Hong Kong's Trade Openness Index value was 3.76 in 2021 and is predicted to be 4.06 in 2022, 4.28 in 2025, and 4.42 in 2030.

Singapore with a 2.25 index value, which means total foreign trade is 2.3 times greater than total GDP of the country, will follow Hong Kong in 2035. Singapore's Trade Openness Index value was 2.18 in 2021 and is predicted to be 2.18 in 2022, 2.30 in 2025, and 2.23 in 2030. Belgium with a 2.13 index value, which means total foreign trade is 2.1 times greater than total GDP of the country, will be ranked third in 2035. Belgium's Trade Openness Index value was 1.76 in 2021 and is predicted to be 1.90 in 2022, 1.99 in 2025, and 2.05 in 2030 (**Table 17**).

The countries, which have higher Trade Openness Index values, mean that these countries take more place in global supply chain and more internationalized.

Table 17. Best performances in Trade Openness Index in 2022-2035 period.

Country	2021	2022	2025	2030	2035
Hong Kong	3.755	4.058	4.279	4.416	4.544
Singapore	2.176	2.176	2.295	2.228	2.250
Belgium	1.760	1.902	1.993	2.053	2.134
Netherlands	1.566	1.729	1.787	1.896	1.969
Viet Nam	1.841	2.210	1.762	2.192	1.648
Taiwan	1.068	1.149	1.237	1.298	1.370
Poland	1.003	1.032	1.050	1.071	1.104
Mexico	0.787	0.846	0.907	0.962	1.002
Switzerland	0.864	0.894	0.862	0.904	0.945
Korea, Rep.	0.702	0.777	0.798	0.814	0.818
Spain	0.563	0.600	0.643	0.734	0.814
Germany	0.722	0.733	0.741	0.732	0.723
Italy	0.553	0.572	0.588	0.590	0.593
Canada	0.488	0.496	0.511	0.513	0.524
France	0.442	0.466	0.474	0.491	0.495
Russian Federation	0.450	0.498	0.495	0.474	0.466
India	0.309	0.377	0.344	0.359	0.380
Japan	0.309	0.340	0.346	0.361	0.374
United Kingdom	0.365	0.368	0.381	0.355	0.337
China	0.341	0.347	0.320	0.331	0.324
United States of America	0.204	0.226	0.222	0.223	0.223

Source: Authors' own calculation by WTO (2022), IMF (2022b), Eurostat (2022b), OECD (2022b), and the World Bank (2022b) data

CONCLUSION

Due to the COVID-19, most of us lost our relatives and the pandemic has left some negative effects on our body. Besides the health, pandemic has altered global supply and value chains. Expansionary monetary and fiscal policies ended up with high inflation and budget deficits. Increasing costs and decreasing profits also decreased the employment. While full vaccination has not yet been completed and the negative effects of the pandemic have not been fully overcome worldwide, the war between Ukraine and Russia at the end of February 2022 has caused disruptions in the supply chain of energy and other products, especially food safety. Disruption risk of foreign trade in 2022, caused the positive expectations about the future global economic growth to be revised downwards, and many countries faced the risk of recession and even stagflation as a result of rising prices and unemployment. The challenges in economic life, social life and foreign trade and new variants of the virus, which the known vaccines may not effect, still cause risks. After the pandemic, it seems that nothing will be the same and the new normal will change the known attitudes.

Health and food sectors played crucial role due to the pandemic. Not only the food security but also the capacity of the health system and the skilled and agile health workforce in a country is important role in fighting with the pandemic as well. Many governments and international institutions took rapid responses to the pandemic prevent the vulnerable population and firms (Özsoy and Gürler 2021a). The pandemic showed that as financial crises, it is not the problem of a single country, and the world must move together against the global challenges and problems. A new global social contract consisting of structural reform, new technology and reintegration that began at the national level is the solution to the post-pandemic recovery (Song and Zhou 2020).

Highlights

- As May 31, total COVID-19 related cases reached to 529 million in the world at the end of May 2022. Europe region has the highest cases, America and Asia regions follow Europe.
- Total COVID-19 related deaths reached to 6.3 million in the world at the end of May 2022. America region has the highest death numbers, Europe and Asia regions follow America.
- Case Fatality Rate is the ratio of total COVID-19 related deaths to total COVID-19 related cases in the population; hence, it is the death ratio of cases in hundred population. Total CFR reached to 1.18 in the world at the end of May 2022, which means that nearly 1.2 of each hundred COVID-19 related cases ended with death. Africa region has the highest CFR value, America, Asia and Europe regions follow Africa.
- As May 31, fully vaccinated people ratio has exceeded 60 percent (people fully vaccinated per hundred people) in the world and reached 4.74 billion people.
- South America region has the highest ratio with 74.9 whereas Asia region with 69.8 percent and Europe region with 65.9 percent (in European Union 73.4 percent of the population was fully vaccinated) followed South America.
- "COVID-19 related cases per hundred people" has maximum value in January 2022 as 1,124. The cumulative data for "COVID-19 related cases per hundred people" indicator is 6,645 at the end of May 2022. It seems monthly "COVID-19 related cases per hundred people" data is reached its

maximum value and then started to decrease and follow constant ratio whereas cumulative ""COVID-19 related cases per hundred people" data seems to reach the maximum level and will start to decline in a couple months.

- "COVID-19 related deaths per hundred people" has maximum value in January 2021 as 5.31. The cumulative data for "COVID-19 related deaths per hundred people" indicator is 78.6 at the end of May 2022. It seems monthly "COVID-19 related deaths per hundred people" data is reached its maximum value and then started to decrease and follow constant ratio whereas cumulative "COVID-19 related deaths per hundred people" data seems to reach the maximum level in May 2022 and will start to decline in a couple months.
- It seems monthly "fully vaccinated people per hundred" data is reached its maximum value as 15.5 percent on August 2021 and then started to decrease and follow constant ratio whereas cumulative "fully vaccinated people per hundred" data seems to reach the maximum level in May 2022 and will start to decline in a couple months.
- Accessing to vaccine prevents the people in high-income countries from death.
- Global average number of nurses and medical doctors per thousand population are 3.7 and 1.6 respectively.
- Number of nurses per thousand population in Africa, America, Asia, Europe and Oceania regions are 1.10, 7.94, 2.57, 9.00 and 8.68 respectively. Number of medical doctors per thousand population in Africa, America, Asia, Europe and Oceania regions are 0.34, 2.42, 1.36, 4.26 and 2.89 respectively.
- Number of nurses per thousand population in high-income, upper-middle income, lower-middle income and low-income countries are 10.45, 11.85, 1.80 and 0.20 respectively. Number of medical doctors per thousand population in high-income, upper-middle income, lower-middle income and low-income countries are 3.05, 7.53, 0.82 and 0.09 respectively.
- Due to the pandemic, the global economy shrank by 3.1 percent in 2020 according to IMF (2022a) and 3.3 percent according to World Bank (2022a). In 2021, that is, in the post-pandemic period, there is a 6.1 percent recovery according to the IMF (2022a) and 5.7 percent according to the World Bank (2022a). This positive picture and expectations were adversely affected by the war that broke out suddenly between the Russian Federation and Ukraine in February 2022.
- According to UNCTAD (2022) data, there was a 7.15 percent decrease in 2020 and 26 percent increase in 2021 in total global merchandise import value. The volume of global goods imports decreased 5.5 percent in 2020 and increased by 9.8 percent in 2021. The increase in the import unit price is

clearly moderate in 2021. The global service imports decreased 17.7 percent in 2020 and increased 15 percent in 2021.

- By vaccination against COVID-19, which was started at the end of 2020, many countries started to reduce restrictions, remove flight bans and made the transition to the "new normal". Although all these positive developments were interrupted by the emergence of new variants of the virus, they also affected the global economy positively, and a "V"-shaped recovery was seen throughout the world in 2021.
- The risk of new variants of the COVID-19 which vaccination will not be effective still exist.
- Increasing unemployment rate and price levels (inflation), which are primary indicators of "stagflation", logistic costs, total gross debt and decreasing income per capita and economic growths are possible challenges in the future.
- Global export is positively correlated with "Fully vaccination per hundred population", "Cumulative cases per 100,000 people" and "Cumulative deaths per 100,000 people" and negatively correlated with CFR. As CFR increases global export decreases.
- "Cumulative deaths per 100,000 people" is positively correlated with "Cumulative cases per 100,000 people" and "Fully vaccination per hundred population". As cases increase in the world deaths and to prevent deaths vaccination increase too
- Our analysis shows that global production is 95.2 trillion dollars in 2021, it is predicted that it will reach 110.9 trillion dollars in 2025, 127.6 trillion dollars in 2030, and 147 trillion dollars in 2035.
- According to the analysis, global imports are expected to reach 31.1 trillion dollars in 2030 and 36.6 trillion dollars in 2035. Global imports are expected to increase approximately 89.5 percent in 2035 compared to 2019 and 104.8 percent compared to 2020, when the pandemic was felt most severely. Global imports are expected to increase by about 4.5 percent annually in average in the 2021-2035 period.
- While China is expected to be the second largest importing country in 2025, it is predicted that it will surpass the USA in 2027 to become the largest importer country.
- India, which is expected to rise four steps, will have the highest improvement in global import in the period of 2022-2035 with an annual average change in global import as 6.8 percent. Belgium and Canada, which are expected to rise three steps, take the second place.
- It is predicted that global exports will reach 23.1 trillion dollars in 2022, 25.8 trillion dollars in 2025, 30.6 trillion dollars in 2030 and 36 trillion dollars in

2035. Global exports are expected to increase by approximately 4.5 percent annually in the 2021-2035 period.

- While China is expected to import 2.93 trillion dollars in 2022, country's import is expected to increase to 3.33 trillion dollars in 2025, 4 trillion dollars in 2030, and 4.67 trillion dollars in 2035. For USA, global good import is expected to be 3.2 trillion dollars in 2022, 3.4 trillion dollars in 2025, 3.8 trillion dollars in 2030 and 4.2 trillion dollars in 2035. Germany is expected to import 1.55 trillion dollars in 2022, 1.68 trillion dollars in 2025, to 1.86 trillion dollars in 2030 and to 2.05 trillion dollars in 2035.
- It is seen that China, as the most exporting country, will not leave the top to anyone. China's export is expected to reach 3.9 trillion dollars in 2022, 4.45 trillion dollars in 2025, to 5.36 trillion dollars in 2030, and to 6.27 trillion dollars in 2035. USA, as the second highest exporting country, is expected to export 1.94 trillion dollars in 2022, 2.11 trillion dollars 2025, 2.40 trillion dollars in 2030 and 2.68 trillion dollars in 2035.
- It is predicted that Vietnam, which is expected to rise seven steps in the 2021-2035 period, will make the highest jump in the export ranking, while Taiwan, which is expected to rise four steps, and India, which is expected to rise three places have good exporting performance too. The highest annual average increase in export will be 6.9 percent in Vietnam, 6.2 percent in China, 5.7 percent in India, 5.3 percent in Hong Kong, 4.8 percent in Taiwan, 4.4 percent in Korea Republic and 4.3 percent in Mexico respectively.
- According to the analysis, "Chemicals and Products" will be the most importing sector with 6.1 trillion dollars in 2022, 6.7 trillion dollars in 2025, 8 trillion dollars in 2030 and 9.5 trillion dollars in 2035. The import in "Electric and Electronic" sector is expected to be 4.8 trillion dollars in 2022, 5.5 trillion dollars in 2025, 6.4 trillion dollars in 2030 and 7.6 trillion dollars in 2035 whereas the import in the "Automotive Industry" sector will be 2.2 trillion dollars in 2022, 2.4 trillion dollars in 2025, 2.8 trillion dollars in 2030 and 3.3 trillion dollars in 2035. The "Hazelnuts and Products" sector will import 16.8 billion dollars, the "Olive and Olive Oil" sector will import 19.9 billion dollars, and the "Carpet" will import 24.25 billion dollars in 2035.

FUTURE RESEARCH DIRECTIONS

The future studies can be done with new health related data and macroeconomic data about GDP and foreign trade. This study covers the current data about GDP and foreign trade for most recent year as 2021. However, the Russian federation-Ukraine war and new variants of COVID-19 caused new risks on global supply chains, value chains and foreign trade briefly global economy, the new forecast can be done in future.

Like global trade and national account data, data for health related indicators such as health infrastructure, health workforce and health technology can be collected worldwide under WHO.

REFERENCES

Abi-Rached, J. M. (2021). The Covid-19 caesura and the post-pandemic future. *Biosocieties*, *16*(1), 142–156. doi:10.105741292-020-00212-6

Eurostat. (2022a). *All data/ Population and social conditions/ Demography, population stock and balance/ Population (national level).* Retrieved from: https://ec.europa.eu/eurostat/databrowser/view/demo_pjan/default/table?lang=en

Eurostat. (2022b). *National accounts/Data/Main tables.* Retrieved from: https://ec.europa.eu/eurostat/web/national-accounts/data/main-tables

Eviews. (2022). *Innovative Solutions for econometric analysis, forecasting & simulation.* Retrieved from: https://www.eviews.com/home.html

Gürler, M. (2016). *Rekabetçiliğin Orta Gelir Tuzağından Çıkıştaki Etkisi: Türkiye Analizi* [The Effect of Competitiveness on Getting Out of the Middle Income Trap: Analysis of Turkey] [PhD Thesis]. Marmara University Institute of Social Sciences. Retrieved from https://tez.yok.gov.tr/UlusalTezMerkezi/TezGoster?key=Br_XTptK8CZ70f0JGX9xElMxSRn6vvzfG2ieGoPn1cC86ezAG3-IOuIswc7Uvmww

Gürler, M. (2021). The effect of the researchers, research and development expenditure as innovation inputs on patent grants and high-tech exports as innovation outputs in OECD and emerging countries especially in BRIICS. *European Journal of Science and Technology*, (32), 1140–1149. doi:10.31590/ejosat.1051899

IBM-SPSS. (2022). *IBM SPSS Statistics.* https://www.ibm.com/products/spss-statistics

International Labour Organization (ILO). (2022a). *ILOSTAT explorer: Unemployment rate by sex and age.* Retrieved from: https://www.ilo.org/shinyapps/bulkexplorer49/?lang=en&segment=indicator&id=UNE_2EAP_SEX_AGE_RT_A

International Labour Organization (ILO). (2022b). *ILOSTAT explorer: Working hours lost due to the COVID-19 crisis, by sex.* Retrieved from: https://www.ilo.org/shinyapps/bulkexplorer6/?lang=en&segment=indicator&id=HOW_2LSS_SEX_RT_A

Mukherjee, S., Baral, M. M., Venkataiah, C., Pal, S. K., & Nagariya, R. (2021). Service robots are an option for contactless services due to the COVID-19 pandemic in the hotels. *Decision (Washington, D.C.)*, *48*(4), 445–460. doi:10.100740622-021-00300-x

National Institution for Finance and Development (NIFD). (2022). *Data: China's macro leverage ratio.* Retrieved from: http://114.115.232.154:8080/

Organisation for Economic Co-operation and Development (OECD). (2022a). *Economic Outlook No 111-June 2022*. Retrieved from: https://stats.oecd.org/Index.aspx?DataSetCode=EO

Organisation for Economic Co-operation and Development (OECD). (2022b). *National accounts*. Retrieved from: https://stats.oecd.org/Index.aspx?DataSetCode=SNA_TABLE1

Our World in Data. (2022a). *Dataset: Home/Coronavirus/Vaccinations*. Retrieved from: https://ourworldindata.org/coronavirus

Özsoy, Ö. (2021). Dilemma in Health during Pandemic in OECD Countries: Increasing Health Expenditures for Preventing against the Pandemic Will Cause a Crowding-out in Increasing the Employment in Nursing Service or not? *European Journal of Science and Technology*, (32), 1094–1102.

Özsoy, Ö., & Gürler, M. (2021a). *Poverty and social exclusion of older people in ageing European Union and Turkey. J Public Health.* doi:10.100710389-021-01525-x

Özsoy, Ö., & Gürler, M. (2021b). The Negative Effects of COVID-19 on the Sustainable Development Goals, Economic Growth, Foreign Trade, and Social Life. *Advances in Human Services and Public Health*, 105–155. doi:10.4018/978-1-7998-8202-2.ch007

Song, L., & Zhou, Y. (2020). The COVID-19 pandemic and its impact on the global economy: What does it take to turn crisis into opportunity? *China & World Economy*, *28*(4), 1–25. doi:10.1111/cwe.12349

The British Centre for Economics and Business Research (CEBR). (2021). *World Economic League Table 2022*. Retrieved from: https://cebr.com/wp-content/uploads/2022/01/WELT-2022.pdf

The International Monetary Fund (IMF). (2022a). *World Economic Outlook, April 2022: War Sets Back The Global Recovery*. Retrieved from: https://www.imf.org/external/datamapper/PCPIPCH@WEO/OEMDC/ADVEC/WEOWORLD

The International Monetary Fund (IMF). (2022b). *IMF Datamapper. World Economic Outlook, April 2022 Database: Inflation rate, average consumer prices*. Retrieved from: https://www.imf.org/-/media/Files/Publications/WEO/2022/April/English/text.ashx

The World Bank. (2022a). *Global Economic Prospects, June 2022*. Retrieved from: https://openknowledge.worldbank.org/bitstream/handle/10986/37224/9781464818431.pdf?sequence=5&isAllowed=y

The World Bank. (2022b). *Data: World Bank Country and Lending Groups/Country Classification*. Retrieved from: https://databank.worldbank.org/data/download/site-content/OGHIST.xlsx

TradeMap. (2022). *Trade statistics for international business development*. Retrieved from: https://www.trademap.org/Product_SelProduct_TS.aspx?nvpm=1%7c%7c%7c%7c%7c%7cTOTAL%7c%7c%7c2%7c1%7c1%7c1%7c2%7c1%7c1%7c1%7c1%7c1

UN Department of Economic and Social Affairs (UNDESA). (2022a). *Population Dynamics/World Population Prospects 2019*. Retrieved from: https://population.un.org/wpp/DataQuery/

UNCTAD. (2022). *UNCTAD Statistics*. Retrieved from: https://unctadstat.unctad.org/wds/ReportFolders/reportFolders.aspx

UNDESA. (2022b). *Statistic Division: Methodology/Standard country or area codes for statistical use*. Retrieved from: https://unstats.un.org/unsd/methodology/m49/overview/

World Health Organization (WHO). (2020a). *State of the world's nursing 2020: investing in education, jobs and leadership*. Retrieved from: https://apps.who.int/iris/rest/bitstreams/1274201/retrieve

World Health Organization (WHO). (2020b). *Home/Newsroom/Fact sheets/Detail/Nursing and midwifery/Key facts*. Retrieved from: https://www.who.int/news-room/fact-sheets/detail/nursing-and-midwifery

World Health Organization (WHO). (2022). *World health statistics 2022: monitoring health for the SDGs, sustainable development goals/Country, WHO region and global statistics*. Retrieved from: https://www.who.int/data/gho/publications/world-health-statistics

World Trade Organization (WTO). (2022). *Merchandise exports by product group*. Retrieved from: https://stats.wto.org/

ENDNOTE

1 According to ILO (2022b) data, global working time losses increased from 8.63 percent in 2020 and is predicted to be 3.90 percent in 2021.

Chapter 7
The Impact of COVID-19 on the Sustainability of the Maritime Labour Force

Osman Arslan
https://orcid.org/0000-0003-4384-3510
Maritime Faculty, Kocaeli University, Turkey

ABSTRACT

Considering that approximately 80% of the goods subject to trade are transported by sea, it becomes clear how important the role of maritime transport in the supply chain is. Especially during the COVID-19 pandemic, the delivery of products for basic needs such as food and health to the delivery places has revealed the importance of maritime transportation for combating the pandemic. Among the most important factors of maritime transport are seafarers who play a role in the operation and management of ships. During the COVID-19 pandemic, the closure of the borders of the countries or the quarantine practices created troubles in the embarkation and disembarkation of seafarers. In the study, it was emphasized that seafarers should be considered as "key workers" considering their essential role in the transport of vital goods such as medical supplies and food. In addition, the strategic factors that should be applied to ensure the professional sustainability of seafarers during pandemic periods were also mentioned.

DOI: 10.4018/978-1-6684-5950-8.ch007

INTRODUCTION

The new type of coronavirus has spread rapidly to many countries of the world since December 2019. The World Health Organization declared Covid-19 as a "pandemic" on 11.03.2020, and then worldwide precautions were commenced to be taken in the fight against the pandemic. The effects of the Covid-19 pandemic on public health, the speed and severity of its spread have put a great deal of pressure on national health systems. This was followed by socio-economic problems arising in the fields of production, supply chain and employment. It is understood that the COVID-19 pandemic has also deeply affected the maritime sector on a globally. Sustainability of maritime transport, which is at a key point, is important in order to ensure the continuity of commercial activities and the transportation of needed basic products, raw materials and medical products. However, the Covid-19 pandemic has adversely affected the maritime sector as well as all sectors.

Maritime transport is very important for the sustainability of international trade. Considering that approximately 80% of world trade on volume basis and more than 70% on value basis is transported by sea (UNCTAD, 2020), it is possible for ship operators to protect their assets with a sustainable maritime labour force. However, when both the literature and the reports obtained from the maritime sector are examined, it is seen that there is a constant supply shortfall especially in the officers and the lack of seafarers is emphasized. According to the "Man Power Report" published by Baltic International Maritime Council (BIMCO, 2015), it is expected that the global demand for the maritime labour force will increase until 2025. It is also seen that the BIMCO/ICS (2021) report emphasizes the seafarers' shortage until 2026. When the difficulties inherent in maritime nature and the difficulties of working conditions are added to the difficulties caused by the Covid-19 pandemic, it becomes clear that seafarers need to be supported much more to do their jobs. The longevity of the human factor, which is at the center of sustainability, has become an important issue for the maritime industry. For this reason, the International Maritime Organization (IMO) has made multiple calls, in collaboration with a wide range of relevant shipping associations, to designate seafarers as 'key workers' who will exempt them from travel restrictions and allow seafarer changeovers (IMO, 2020a; ILO, 2021). Despite this, many seafarers all over the world have faced the uncertainties brought on by the pandemic.

Public health strategies to prevent the Covid-19 pandemic have included the closure of national borders and the cancellation of international flights, which have affected crew changeovers. The measures taken led to the long stay of seafarers on vessel or at home, who should be considered "key workers" in terms of their main role in maintaining the flow of vital commodities such as food, medical equipments and fuel (Slišković, 2020).

In the study, after an introduction to the subject was made, the subject was explained in the background and supported by a literature review. Sustainability and its dimensions, which are among the basic concepts of the study, were explained, and especially the social dimension in which the human factor was included was emphasized. In the next part, an overview of maritime transport in the Covid-19 pandemic was made. In the next section, the working conditions were mentioned by defining the seafarer, which is one of the main factors of maritime transport. In particular, the difficulty of the maritime profession due to its nature was explained and the shortage of seafarer was emphasized. It was told about the difficulties experienced by maritime labour force during the Covid-19 pandemic of seafaring, which is usually a difficult profession. The increasing number of problems experienced during the pandemic has pushed the maritime labour force further away from being a sustainable profession. The MLC 2006 contract, which includes seafarers' employment contracts and the obligations of maritime companies on these contracts, working hours, health and safety, living spaces and seafarers' welfare, was included in the study as it is closely related to the subject and the applicability of the MLC 2006 contract during the pandemic was mentioned. In the next part, strategic factors were put forward and solutions and recommendations were made for the continuity of maritime transport and the sustainability of the maritime workforce, which ensures the operation of ships, in order not to disrupt international trade in cases such as the Covid-19 pandemic. Finally, the conclusion was reached by including other future studies related to the study.

BACKGROUND

The Covid-19 (Coronavirus) pandemic, which initial appeared in China, and has recently extendet all over the world, has caused a serious concern with its pressure in international markets and death rates and high case numbers in all countries. The fact that the pandemic caused economic instability around the world caused countries to take urgent measures. Curfews, cities, regions and international travel restrictions stand out among the international measures taken and the practices put into effect to prevent the spread of Covid-19.

Taking the measures against the Covid-19 virus late has left the world economy facing a great threat. With the effect of Covid-19 in the world, the global trade started to decline and there was a great reduce in world external trade. Thence, countries have become incapable to import and export (Kaya, 2020). It is vague what the greatness of the economic impact of the covid-19 pandemic will be. Before the emergence of Covid-19, the world economy was on the way to recovery, but as this pandemic spread, the world economy was deeply wounded (Tosunoğlu & Kasal, 2020).

Countries with the highest number of cases of Covid-19 include United States, United Kingdom, China, Germany, Japan and France. These countries account for 57% of the World's Gross Domestic Product, 63% of its production and 38% of its exports (Çatuk & Aydın, 2021). Demand shocks and supply detriorations experienced in these countries have caused global reactions. The shrinkage in demand in six countries has significantly slowed down world trade. Since global giants are at the center of the global supply chain, they ensure significant inputs to third countries and to each other. The coronavirus pandemic, which severely impress global supply chains, has adversely affected the economies of the countries in many ways due to the disruptions it caused in the supply chains (Çatuk & Aydın, 2021). The disruptions in manufacturing owing to the pandemic has compelled plants to close in most of the world's production centers; in less affected areas, it has broken the supply chain on the supply side because it has not been able to provide the necessary inputs. Viewed by demand, while demand for basic commoduties such as food, medical equipment and health supplies was high, there were a decline in total demand as consumers remain at home to prevent further spread of the disease. The service sector has been severely affected since the first days of the pandemic, starting with accommodation, tourism and travel; The situation has worsened due to increased quarantines and limitations and growing unemployment. Quickly changing developments every week have also made economic predictions more difficult (Şanlı, 2020).

From the date of its outbreak, the new coronavirus has shown its effect in many fields, particularly in economic, logistics and transportation. It is impossible to assess the effect of the new coronavirus on the logistics and transport sectors separately from the economy. Therefore, the effects of Covid-19 should be evaluated as a whole. As a result of the new coronavirus pandemic, cargo and passenger motions have been more and more interrupted in the world, and all transportation modes have been affected. The effects of Covid-19 began to be felt in maritime transport. Nearly 50% of vessels trading between Europe and Asia were canceled in the first quarter of 2020. Due to Covid-19 that emerged in China, problems such as the late departure of the vessels bringing raw materials to China from the harbours, their late discharge or disability to discharge the goods, and the late arrival of the cargoes imported from China caused the freight to increase. This situation has caused disruptions in the export of countries (Akçacı & Çınaroğlu, 2020).

According to the directives of the WHO, a red alert has been issued for this virus that has affected the entire world. It turned out that international travels were effective in the spread of this pandemic in the world. Therefore, governments have decided to take several journey measures to interrupt the spread of the virus (Wilson & Chen, 2020). Travel restrictions and quarantine measures taken by countries to prevent the spread of the pandemic have also deeply affected maritime transport. Considering the incubation periods of the corona virus by the WHO, in the first place, the ships were kept at anchor for 14 days as a precaution before they approached the port. Many of the cruise ships were not even taken into the ports. At the same time, border closure and quarantine applications have been implemented in some countries. All these practices led to the inability to change crews and the inability to return the seafarers who left the ship to their countries. In addition, the inability to conduct training related to the certification of seafarers and the inability to make the necessary replenishments so as not to compromise the quality of life on board have put great pressure on seafarers. This situation has caused seafarers, who play an important role in the transportation of goods subject to global trade, to stay on the ship for longer periods. The fact that seafarers are away from social life and their families has turned the maritime profession into a much more difficult profession during the pandemic period.

SUSTAINABILITY

The word "Sustainability" comes from the Latin "*sustinere", and means to "maintain", "sustain", "support", "endure", and* "*to restrain*" (Caradonna, 2014; Katunian, 2019; Pal & Hazra, 2015). The term of sustainability was first appeared in forestry, where it means never harvesting more than what the forest yields in new growth (Wiersum, 1995).

The adoption of the concept of sustainability in the report Our Common Future of the UN World Commission on Environment and Development in 1987 was welcomed. With the Burunland report, the concept has become a popular concept today. The Brundtland Report explains sustainability as "development that meets the needs of the present without compromising the ability of future generations to meet their own needs" (WCED, 1987). Since the publication of the Brundtland report, the principle of sustainable development has gained general acceptance. The organizing standard for sustainability is sustainable development, which includes the four areas: ecology, economics, culture, and politics (Pal & Hazra, 2015). In this report, sustainability refers to the capability to sustain three fundamental dimensions of a human system over time, namely, economic development, conservation of the environment and social inclusion (Roca-Puig, 2019).

Economic sustainability should be able to consistently manufacture commodity and services, protect grades of state outer debt, and avoid excessive industrial unbalances that harm industrial or agricultural manufacture (Harris, 2000).

Environmental dimension; it is a concept related to reducing the damages caused to nature by human beings, primarily industrial activities and protecting the environment and ecosystem (Akkoyun, 2016).

Social dimension refers to fairly, respectful, safe, liberal, contributing to mankind and the environment. And also, the concept of health and safety generally refers to the working conditions and contains standards and responsibilities (Glavic & Lukman, 2007).

Boudreau and Ramstad (2005) stated that human resources have a very important place for sustainability. Social sustainability will focus more on the welfare of people and quality of life, the ability to maintain oneself and all dependents based on one's salary, access to paid labor for anyone who wishes, and social security when there is no paid work, but still working for the public good (Omann & Spangenberg, 2002).

To ensure sustainability in all disciplines, it is believed that the social dimension of sustainability must be ensured first. Because human, which is the most important factor in ensuring sustainability, has an important role in realizing economic and environmental sustainability factors. Therefore, more emphasis has been placed on social sustainability among disciplines. Social sustainability focuses on social relationships, interactions and meeting human needs that affect sustainable development. For this reason, it is important that business administrations increase the level of life, ensure social integration and value employee and Human Rights (Kesen, 2016).

OVERVIEW OF MARITIME TRANSPORTATION IN THE COVID-19 PANDEMIC

The effects of the pandemic have started to be felt in a wide area in a very short time. By the end of 2020, according to the OECD International Transport Forum, it is predicted that global transport will decrease by 36% (URL-1). According to the data of the United Nations Conference on Trade and Development (UNCTAD, 2020), since more than 80% of the global trade volume is carried out by maritime transport, the commercial losses experienced throughout the world economy due to the pandemic in question have also negatively affected the maritime sector. With its crucial role in ensuring the persistence of global trade and supply chain during and after the pandemic, maritime transportation has become more prominent. The fact that numerous global businesses around the world have taken measures to protect port employees and seafarers, but have made recommendations that ports remain open for vessels and concerned operations, has shown this. According to UNCTAD (2020), the increase in adverse economic conditions with the pandemic in 2020 caused a 4.1% decrease in international maritime trade. In 2019 and 2020, a year in which growth momentum slowed, severe pressure continued on international shipping (URL-2).

In the first periods of 2021, the world fleet reached 99,800 ships of 100 grt and above, equivalent to a capacity of 2,134,639,907 dwt. The global maritime merchant fleet grew by +3% in the year before January 2021 (UNCTAD, 2021). Although, when the contract activities of the ships are examined by BIMCO, in the first quarter of 2020, tankers decreased by 17.8% (806.500 DWT), dry cargo ships decreased from 6.9 million DWT to 1.6 million DWT, and oil tankers decreased by -53% compared to the first 2 months of 2019 (URL-3).

With these developments, the supply capacity of container transportation is still increasing and the fact that ships are growing is also an ongoing concern for the sector. Experience with ships and ports shows that container ship sizes have probably peaked. On the other hand, the carriers, not the ports, benefit from the economies of scale due to the growing ships. According to the data, an increase of 1% in the average ship size means a 0.52% decrease in the time the ship spends at the port per container. This situation creates great pressure on the ports (URL-2).

During the pandemic period, container trade fell just 1.1 percent. Global container port throughput has fallen at a similar rate as shown in Figure 1, reaching a total of 815.6 million twenty-foot equivalent units (TEU) in 2020.

Figure 1. Median time in port, maximum vessel sizes, and number of port calls, container ships, 2020.
Source: UNCTAD, (2021).

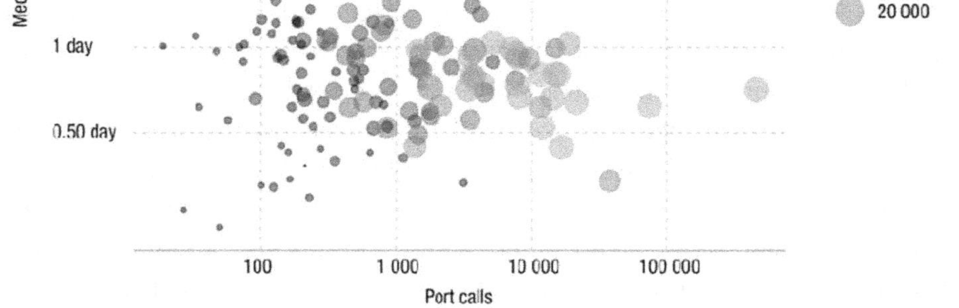

Looking at Figure 2, worldwide economic output fell by 3.5 percent and trade in commodities by 5.4 percent in 2020, while maritime shipments fell by 3.8 percent to 10.65 billion tons (UNCTAD, 2021).

Figure 2. International Seaborne Trade in 2020.
Source: UNCTAD, (2021).

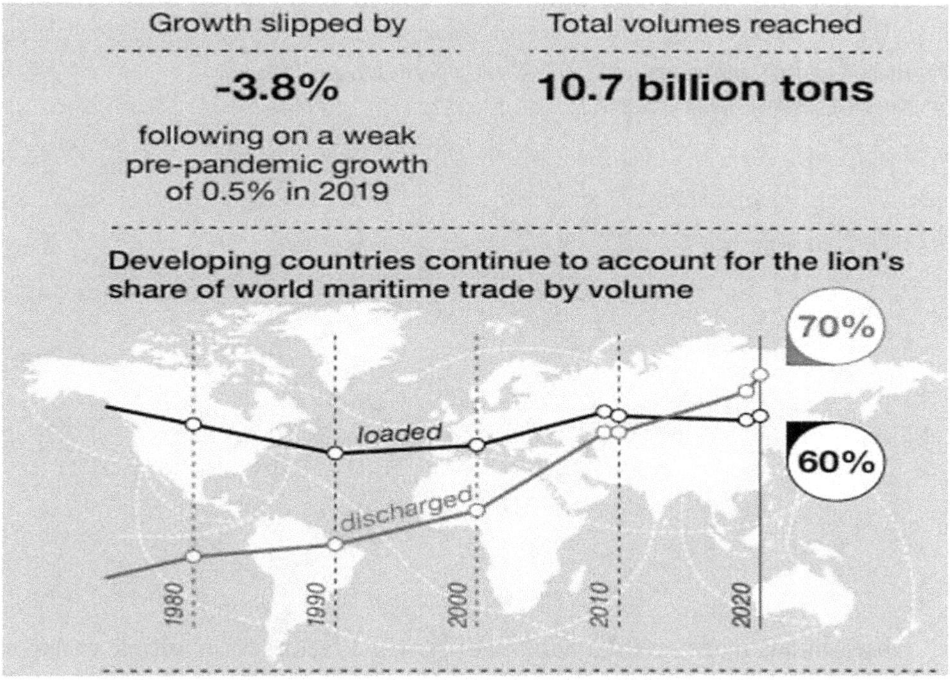

The war between Russia and Ukraine has a negative impact on the trade and logistics of the Black Sea region, and thus on maritime transport. The search for alternative trade routes for the transport of goods in the region accelerated. Because of the war, many commodities have to be procured from further away. This has increased the global demand for ships and the cost of shipping worldwide. Rising grain prices and shipping costs since 2020 have exacerbated this situation due to the war. Between February and May 2022, the freight rates paid for the transport of dry bulk cargoes, primarily grain, increased by approximately 60% (UNCTAD, 2022).

The measures taken due to the pandemic have caused a decrease in speed at almost every point of maritime trade, from loading at the port to on-board operation. These delays at the port and during loading/unloading cause delays of up to one week not only at the departure and destination but also at all intermediate ports.

This, in turn, creates chain delays, such as congestion in ports and sometimes ships waiting for other ships to leave.

In 2020, the new corana virus had a important influence on ports worldwide. In addition to posing health risks for seafarers and port workers in everywhere, it also significantly reduced the capacity of trade. In Figure 3, between 2016 and 2018 cargoes had been rising at a median value of five percent and revenues of six percent per year. In 2020, but, volumes fell by four percent and revenues by nine percent.

Figure 3. Cargo and revenue, 2016–2020 (percentage change).
Source: UNCTAD, (2021).

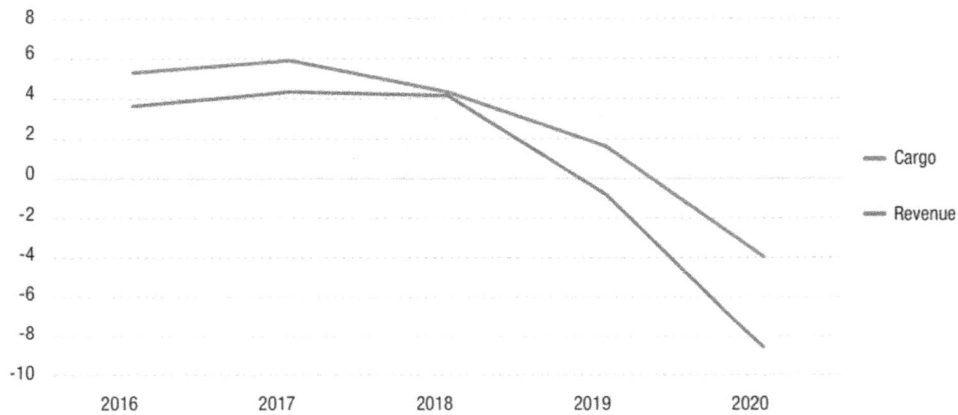

Observations made reveal a number of strategic factors for maritime transport and trade, summarized below (URL-2).

- A paradigm shift that prioritizes risk management and resilience,
- Accelerated change in globalization models and supply chain designs,
- New consumer spending and behavior,
- Strengthening of digitalization and dematerialization,
- A significant increase in the use of electronic commerce documents,
- Interoperability becomes more important with standards,
- The importance of cyber security, increasing cyber-attacks,
- Regulations in maritime transport to adapt to the new business environment brought by the epidemic
- Greater need for systematic and coordinated policy responses at the global level.

KEY WORKERS FOR THE SUSTAINABILITY OF WORLD TRADE: "SEAFARERS"

Ships need manpower to carry out their activities. Seafarer is the general name of those who work on that ship in order to make a direct or indirect contribution to the operation and management of the ship. In the MLC (2006), a seafarer is defined as any person employed on board a ship which the convention applies (ILO, 2012). The main factors in maritime transport are the ship and the crew. No matter how simple or complex the physical sea assets, the real assets of the company are the crew, who are liable for the navigation and operation of the ship. Without them, the company's commercial survival is extremely vulnerable (Leggate et al., 2005). Since the seafarer is one of the most important elements of maritime transportation, the knowledge and experience of the crew on the ships is of great importance for the competitiveness and continuity of the shipping companies.

The new Seafarer Workforce Report for 2021 by BIMCO and the International Chamber of Shipping highlights the need for the sector to crucial rise recruitment and training levels to avoid a severe shortage in the overall supply of officers by 2026. It is emphasized in the report that an extra 89510 officers will be needed by 2026. In addition, the report predict that 1.89 million seafarers work the world fleet, which currently operates more than 74,000 ships worldwide (BIMCO/ICS, 2021). There is a shortage of officers with the competence of the management level, especially on offshore and tanker ships (BIMCO, 2021).

In addition to basic seafaring activities such as daily maintenance-attitude work on ships, berthing-departure maneuvers, seafarers are also faced with constant life safety risks (Fei & Lu, 2015). Maritime is characterized as a line of business that does not accept mistakes with its injury and fatal accident rates (AMSA, 2010). In addition to situations that concern the whole ship such as collision, grounding and fire in the ship explain why the maritime profession is one of the dangerous business lines. The maritime profession is one of the professions that requires hierarchy, with a lifestyle that is relatively different to those working on land due to its working style, level of responsibility, pace and nature (Guo et al., 2006).

Until decades ago, working on a ship to become an officer was seen as an appealing profession, an opportunity to see the world, then move to a settled job on land. This is no longer the case today. The shortage of skilled seafarers, especially deck and engine officers, in the shipping industry has been a growing concern (McLaughlin, 2015; Caesar, 2013). Due to their long stay away from home and lower levels of competence among the crew, as well as increased responsibilities, working at sea today has decimated its attractiveness. In addition, the increasing supply of seafarers with inadequate training and questionable qualifications, and communication problems between crews and officers increase the risk of human error, hindering safe ship operation (Leggate et al., 2005).

Recovery from the effects of the pandemic is particularly important and highlights the necessity to address true worries that could lead seafarers away from their maritime careers. To ensure that the supply of STCW-certified seafarers keeps up with the demand, trends in seafarer retention must be analyzed, responsive to seafarers' needs, and the global seafarer workforce must be regularly monitored (BIMCO, 2021).

Considering all these difficulties, the importance of work-life balance, flexible and short deployment, quality of life on board, and communication opportunities for the crew so that they do not stay away from their social life and their families become important for seafarers. For shipping to be sustainable, skilled seafarers and officers must be retention and the attraction to seafaring must continue to be the main focus in the future (Cahoon et al., 2010).

Today, rapid progress in information technologies and automation has become an important factor for the efficient operation of the vessel. The impact of technological developments has made the role of human labor even more important in terms of control and monitoring. All of this leads to the deduction that employee policy has to goal at personnel retention more than personnel rapid turnover (Leggate et al., 2005).

In addition, in accordance with the developing trends, structural differentiation is being made on ships according to the load. Today, there are ships specially produced for the loads they will carry, and it has become a prerequisite for the companies to be equipped and experienced for the seafarers who will work on such ships. Therefore, qualified workforce is needed more than ever (Pourzanjanı et al., 2002).

Despite the fact that a pandemic that shook the world, such as Covid-19, also negatively affected the maritime sector, approximately 80 percent of world trade is still carried out by ships. Maritime transportation is the most advantageous type of transportation per ton-mile load when evaluated in terms of economies of scale. For example, 4000 trucks are needed to transport 150 thousand tons of iron to be carried by a bulk carrier (Demirci, 2019). Given the importance of shipping, the ILO has encouraged states to recognize seafarers as "key workers" who provide the global trade flow and carrying of medical supplies, food, safety materials and other critical goods vital during the Covid-19 (ILO, 2021). The IMO Secretary-General has called on all Member States to recognize seafarers as "key workers", lift entire barriers to their documentation and lift trip restrictions so they can return home (IMO, 2020b). In order to ensure that supply chains are not disrupted, states must make team changes safely. About 150,000 seafarers need to be changed over each month in accordance with international maritime legislations for the health and well-being of the crew (IMO, 2020a). In June 2020, approximately 300,000 seafarers required international flights for crew changes. In addition, the 70,000 seafarers who were on passenger ships at that time remained on board (Doumbia-Henry, 2020).

THE DIFFICULTIES EXPERIENCED BY THE SEAFARERS DURING THE PANDEMIC

The maritime profession is recognized in the literature as a highly dangerous, difficult and stressful job, with a range of potential adverse effects on physical and mental health (Slišković, 2020). Factors such as busy work pace, workplace noise, stress, insomnia, withdrawal from social life, time pressure, physiological needs, lack of recreation affect not only the mental health of seafarers, but also on turnover intentions (Gu et al., 2020). When looking at the sources of occupational stress in maritime, the most common ones among seafarers are high workload, long working hours, being away from home and family for a long time (Slišković, 2020). Lack of physical recreation, social activities and internet access also creates a source of stress for seafarers. The high workload of seafarers and overtime hours cause more fatigue for seafarers. Fatigue is recognized as a great threat to maritime safety and mental health among crew; reported being under extreme stress, particularly owing to fatigue and lack of good social relations and control on ship (Lucas et al., 2021). Poor working conditions not only reason work accidents, illness, tension, fatigue and dissatisfaction, but they are also the sources of rapid seafarer turnover and reduced productivity (Hafez, 1999). In addition, the overall well-being of seafarers is greatly impacted by increased job complexity and reduced crew numbers due to technological advances.

Seafarers who provide a key service to the community have faced greater health and safety risks during the pandemic. Seafarers are unable to return home or join their ships due to the measures taken to prevent the spread of the corona virus. Crew changes have been disrupted due to travel bans, border closures and quarantine measures. Due to these problems in changing crews, some seafarers have had to work on ships beyond the maximum 11-month duty period based on the provisions of the MLC 2006. With the pandemic, seafarers in an isolated and limited working environment have experienced increasing physical and mental exhaustion. Given its multicultural and hierarchical nature, negative relationships can present themselves as a particular source of stress on board. Continuing to work on board despite the end of the employment contract and the uncertainty of the leave date add to fatigue and stress and can affect the performance of safe shipboard operations (Slišković, 2020). Such difficulties are unsustainable for the safety of the crew and the safe functioning of maritime transport.

In the literature, studies have been carried out on the problems experienced by seafarers during the pandemic period. Of these, Pauksztat et al. (2020) provide an overview of the preliminary findings of a study of seafarers' experiences during the Covid-19 pandemic. They aimed to examine the impact of the pandemic on the mental and physical health as well as the lives of seafarers on board, and identify factors that could reduce the negative influence of the Covid-19. Some key findings from the study are summarized below (Pauksztat et al., 2020):

- Most seafarers have reported the severe effects of the pandemic on crew changes and interactions between ship and shore. It has emerged that the pandemic differs according to the extent to which it affects the employment of seafarers, their working and social life on board.
- Almost half of those surveyed reported a rise in their workload during the pandemic compared to previous periods.
- The main challenges reported by seafarers were fatigue, tensions, ship-shore interactions such as crew changeover, inability to leave shore and hardships in obtaining supplies.
- More More than 40 percent of seafarers said they experienced symptoms of depression several times a week, while more than half reported symptoms of anxiety. They also experienced symptoms of fatigue and exhaustion.

Another study on the difficulties experienced by seafarers during the pandemic was conducted by Sliskovic (2020). Sliskovic aimed to explain how the COVID-19 pandemic is reflected in the well-being of seafarers. The study is based on the personal experiences of seafarers on ship and at home during the pandemic period. Emerging themes included physical, mental, social and economic well-being. Most of the seafarers' responses on board were about the threatened physical, mental, and social well-being, while most of the seafarers at home reported their trouble towards their economic well-being (Sliskovic, 2020).

The Covid-19 pandemic caused port operations to slow down. In the new working order, port employees were divided into certain shifts, which led to a slowdown in active operations. Many countries have imposed national restrictions on ports, including (ICS, 2021):

- Delayed port clearance;
- Preventing crew changes and shore leave;
- Prevention of handling of cargo or supplies; and
- Rejection of harbour entry of ships

In addition to the strict measures implemented in the ports, the inability of the seafarers to go out in the ports has already caused morale problems for the crew who stayed on the ship for a long time. The precautions and restrictions taken by the local governments caused the planned and usual supply times to be extended. The inability to make supplies such as fresh water and provisions, which are very important for the welfare of the seafarers, also created difficulties for the seafarers.

Because in an environment where socialization is limited, it is one of the biggest expectations of seafarers that the food is sufficient and of high quality, and that even a multicultural menu structure is offered.

The cruise industry was also severely affected by the epidemic. Unlike other types of commercial vessels, it had to stop operations around the world. Most countries have banned cruise ships from entering their territorial waters. Many seafarers working on these ships remained on board because they were not allowed to disembark in the ports. Most of the crew were not paid. The seafarers experienced great anxiety and stress that led to suicide (Doumbia-Henry, 2020).

The pandemic has affected port and landside operations and has left seafarers in a precarious position with an unprecedented global crew change crisis. These people, who provide key services to society, faced health and safety risks. During the epidemic, they were left in a state of increasing physical and mental exhaustion, as they could not return to their homes or join their ships due to the measures taken to prevent the spread of the virus.

MARITIME LABOUR CONVENTION (MLC, 2006)

Seafarers' rights are complex as they are governed by both national and international conventions. Owing to the global nature of sea transportation, the protection of seafarers at the universal level is a very important issue. For this reason, efforts have been made to review international maritime labor standards and form a new convention under one roof that is applicable, consistent and adapted to today's conditions. In this context, within the framework of the studies carried out in the meetings held between 2001-2005, the Maritime Labour Convention (MLC) was created as a result of updating and merging 69 official documents, including 37 ILO Conventions, 29 Recommendations and 3 amendments not included in ILO Conventions. The Maritime Labor Convention was adopted at the International Labor Organization Conference held in Geneva in February 2006 with the participation of 106 countries. The convention entered into force on 20th August, 2013 for Member States meeting this requirement, 12 months after the ratification of 30 countries holding 33% of the total ship tonnage (MLC, 2006). The Maritime Labor Convention, also known as the Seafarers' Bill of Rights, determines the minimum rights of crews onboard. Maritime labour certificate must be on ships over 500 gross tons operating in international waters or between harbor of distinct countries (URL-4).

The purpose of the MLC is to compose a sole and consistent tool that sets the minimum international standard and brings together more than 68 international working standards for crew on ships. MLC's aim is to preserve crews' social rights and employment on the ship (Barnett & Pekcan, 2017). In the MLC, regulations and code are regulated below five headings: minimum requirements for crew to work onboard; food, recreational places, health protection, employment conditions, medical care, accommodation, social security protection and seafarer welfare (MLC, 2006).

Although MLC 2006 is a convention that defines seafarers' rights on ships and their living and working conditions, these rights could not every time be guaranteed in the Covid-19 pandemic. The inability to change personnel due to the pandemic has caused difficulties in the implementation of MLC standards. According to MLC 2006, seafarers are entitled to annual leave of at least 2.5 calendar days per month, especially in terms of working hours. According to the contract, seafarers have the right to repatriation, while the maximum service period of seafarers on board should be less than 12 months. In addition, the importance of the principles regarding the facilitation of shore authorization, transit, transfer or repatriation of seafarers in the Seafarers' Identity Documents Convention, 1958, (Revised), 2003, as amended (No. 185) becomes evident (ILO, 2003).

SOLUTIONS AND RECOMMENDATIONS

The coronavirus global epidemic has caused a global crisis that has affected all aspects of life and dealt a heavy blow to working life. For the maritime sector, it has also severely disrupted the functioning of maritime, affecting the jobs of approximately 2 million seafarers around the world.

The Covid-19 global pandemic has highlighted the importance of seafarers being recognized as key workers by all governments. In order for seafarers to continue to perform their critical duties, they must be provided with adequate protection from the epidemic and have access to medical care and the ability to return to their ships and homes. If shipping is to fulfill its vital role in keeping the global supply chain running, it must be ensured that teams can be changed at the required intervals. In this sense, personnel change can be accelerated by opening the borders of foreign countries especially for seafarers and increasing the number of airline flights. ICS 2021 has published the coronavirus guidance for ship operators for the health of seafarers. In this published guide, management of covid-19 cases on board, shipboard measures to address risks associated with Covid-19, seafarers' access to medical care at harbours and covid-19 guide has been created regarding other health issues. By implementing the principles in this guide, seafarers' health will be more assured. In addition, access to welfare services should be provided in ports whenever possible during epidemics such as Covid-19. Providing necessary medical care and health services to seafarers, which is one of the main principles of MLC 2006, is an important issue. Seafarers should be provided with rapid access to necessary medicines and medical facilities for treatment. Protecting seafarers with personal protective equipment stipulated by the WHO, especially in their contacts with pilots, ship agency personnel, port workers and port state control officers who may join the ship from outside, is one of the important steps taken to prevent the spread of the Covid-19 virus inside the ship.

Due to the fact that there is a global epidemic, measures are first taken by the states. However, it is very important for the sustainability of the maritime labour force to take measures to increase the welfare of the seafarers both in the pandemic period and in other periods in the shipping companies where seafarers work. Pauksztat, B., et al., 2020, provided recommendations for shipping companies in their study. These recommendations (Pauksztat, B., et al., 2020):

- Effective preventive measures and providing of medical care
- Repatriation organizing
- Provide free internet on ship for crew
- Providing seafarers with access to basic supplies, including medical care and mental health support
- Have a fatigue risk management system in place.

In this sensitive period, ensuring the flow of goods through maritime transport is important for the exit from the crisis. The actions taken at UNCTAD (2020) for the post-Covid-19 period are of strategic importance. Among these strategic actions, it stands out especially in terms of making transportation networks durable, using ship and port traffic data effectively, ensuring the sustainability of maritime transportation by creating plans and protocols for business continuity. Because in order to provide these factors, the maritime labour force must be sustainable. The cooperation between the private sector and governments is of great importance in order to ensure the rights of seafarers, which is the most important factor in maritime transport, which has an important role in the global economic recovery, to ensure health conditions and to implement policies regarding personnel exchange.

FUTURE RESEARCH DIRECTIONS

This study inspires some potential future research areas. For example, studies can be conducted on the role of seafarers in terms of continuity of the supply chain. In addition, the study may inspire studies on how the semi-autonomous and autonomous ships in the future, together with technological developments, will affect the sustainability of the maritime labour force. In addition, since the current study focuses only on the literature review on how seafarers were affected during the Covid-19 period, further contributions to the literature can be made by empirical studies that will be conducted in the future.

CONCLUSION

Covid-19 has caused a great impact on ports and other stakeholders, especially maritime transport, and therefore on world trade and travel. The impact of the pandemic on seafarers has been devastating mentally and physically. The measures taken by governments to prevent the spread of the pandemic have shown the limits of cooperation. With the outbreak of the pandemic, countries have closed their maritime areas to maritime transport, which has led to safety and health concerns for seafarers.

As a result, rapid action by changing both the sensitive points and the policies necessary for the continuation of business during and after Covid-19 is of great importance for the sustainability of the global maritime sector. In this period, where being resilient comes to the fore, maritime transport, therefore, seafarers play a key role. Because, it should not be forgotten that the human factor is at the center of sustainability, which is a popular concept today. From this point of view, the recognition of seafarers as "key workers" in terms of the continuity of global trade and the provision of amenities by all countries is a requirement for the sustainability of the maritime labour force. The need for greater recognition of seafarers who are far from their families, eyes and minds, but who work selflessly to transport the goods needed every day and make global trade possible has emerged more sharply during the pandemic. Despite everything, seafarers are the nameless heroes of the pandemic.

REFERENCES

Akçacı, T. & Çınaroğlu, M. S. (2020). Yeni Koronavirüs (Covid-19) Salgınının Lojistik ve Ticarete Etkisi [The Effect of the New Coronavirus (covid-19) Epidemic on Logistics and Trade]. *Gaziantep University Journal of Social Sciences*, *19*, 447-456. doi:10.21547/jss.766159

Akkoyun, A. (2016). *Analysis of Factors That Affect Sustainable Production by Using Fuzzy QFD Method* [Master Thesis]. Yıldız Technical University.

Australian Maritime Safety Authority (AMSA). (2010). *Fact finding report into the reported collision involving the New Zealand registered craft Ady Gil and the Japan registered whaling ship Shonan Maru No.2 in the Southern Ocean on 6 January 2010*. AMSA.

Baltic and International Maritime Council & International Chamber of Shipping (BIMCO/ICS). (2015). *Manpower Report. The global supply and demand for seafarers*. Retrieved from https://www.ics-shipping.org/wp-content/uploads/2020/08/manpower-report-2015-executive-summary.pdf

Baltic and International Maritime Council & International Chamber of Shipping (BIMCO/ICS). (2021). *Seafarer Workforce Report. The global supply and demand for seafarers*. Retrieved from https://www.bimco.org/news/priority-news/20210728---bimco-ics-seafarer-workforce-report

Barnett, M. L., & Pekcan, C. H. (2017). The Human Element in Shipping. Encyclopedia of Maritime and Offshore Engineering, 1974, 1–10. doi:10.1002/9781118476406.emoe033

Boudreau, J. W., & Ramstad, P. M. (2005). Talentship talent segmentation, and sustainability: A new hr decision science paradigm for a new strategy definition. *Human Resource Management*, *44*(2), 129–136. doi:10.1002/hrm.20054

Caesar, L. (2013). Sustaining the Supply of Ship Officers: Making a Case for Succession Planning in Seafarer Recruitment. *Universal Journal of Management*, *1*(1), 6–12. doi:10.13189/ujm.2013.010102

Cahoon, S., Haugstetter, H., & Bhaskar, P. (2010). *Overcoming seafarer shortages: Human resource management and marketing strategies for a sustainable future*. International Association of Maritime Economists Conference, Lisbon, Portugal.

Caradonna, J. L. (2014). Sustainability: A History. Oxford University Press.

Çatuk, C., & Aydın, K. (2021). Covid-19 dünya ve türkiye tedarik zinciri üzerine etkileri [Impacts of Covid-19 on the World and Turkey Supply Chain]. *Adıyaman Üniversitesi Sosyal Bilimler Enstitüsü Dergisi*, (37), 427–449. doi:10.14520/adyusbd.753939

Demirci, E. (2019). Lojistik ilkeleri, İstanbul Üniversitesi [Logistics Principles, Istanbul University]. *Açık ve Uzaktan Eğitim Fakültesi, 332*. http://auzefkitap.istanbul.edu.tr/kitap/uluslararasitvlojistikyonetimi_ao/lojistikilkeleri.pdf

Doumbia-Henry, C. (2020). Shipping and COVID-19: protecting seafarers as frontline workers. *WMU J Marit Affairs, 19*, 279–293. doi:10.1007/s13437-020-00217-9

Fei, J., & Lu, J. (2015). Analysis of students' perceptions of seafaring career in china based on artificial neural network and genetic programming. *Maritime Policy & Management*, *42*(2), 111–126. doi:10.1080/03088839.2013.873545

Glavic, P., & Lukman, R. (2007). *Review of sustainability terms and their definitions*. doi:10.1016/j.jclepro.2006.12.006

Gu, Y., Liu, D., Zheng, G., Yang, C., Dong, Z., & Tee, E. Y. J. (2020). The Effects of Chinese Seafarers' Job Demands on Turnover Intention: The Role of Fun at Work. *International Journal of Environmental Research and Public Health*, *17*(14), 5247. doi:10.3390/ijerph17145247 PMID:32708123

Guo, J. L., Liang, G. S., & Ye, K. D. (2006). An ınfluence model in seafering choice for taiwan navigation students. *Maritime Policy & Management*, *33*(4), 403–421. doi:10.1080/03088830600895725

Hafez, A. A. E. N. (1999). Seafarers' social life and its effect on maritime safety with respect to Egyptian seafarers. *World Maritime University Dissertations*. 46. https://commons.wmu.se/all_dissertations/46

Harris, J. M. (2000). *Basic Principles of Sustainable Development*. Global Development and Environment Institute, Working Paper: 00-04, Tufts University.

ICS. (2021). *Coronavirus (COVID-19)*. Guidance for Ship Operators for the Protection of the Health of Seafarers.

ILO. (2003). *Seafarers' Identity Documents Convention (Revised), 2003, as amended (No. 185)*. https://www.ilo.org/dyn/normlex/en/f?p=NORMLEXPUB:12100:0:NO:P12100_INSTRUMENT_ID:312330

ILO. (2012). *Handbook: Guidance on implementing the Maritime Labour Convention, 2006 and Social Security for Seafarers*. International Labour Office. Retrieved from https://www.ilo.org/wcmsp5/groups/public/---ed_norm/---normes/documents/publication/wcms_170388.pdf

ILO. (2021). *Information note on maritime labour issues and coronavirus (COVID-19)*. Retrieved from https://www.ilo.org/global/standards/maritime-labour-convention/WCMS_741024/lang--en/index.htm

IMO. (2020a). *Circular Letter No. 4204/Add. 14, "Coronavirus (COVID-19)– Recommended framework ofprotocols for ensuring safe ship crew changes and travel during the coronavirus (COVID-19) pandemic"*. IMO.

IMO. (2020b). *Personal message from IMO Secretary-General Kitack Lim to seafarers*. IMO.

Katunian, A. (2019). Sustainability as a new approach for the human resource development in tourism sector. *Public Policy and Administration, 18*(4), 405–417. doi:10.13165/VPA-19-18-4-03

Kaya, D. G. (2020). Koronavirüs pandemisinin küresel ekonomideki izleri: Kamu finansman dengesi, ticaret hacmi, enflasyon, işsizlik ve ekonomik büyüme [Traces of the Coronavirus Panddemic in the Global Economy: Public Finance, balance, trade, volume, inflation, unemployment and economic growth]. *Avrasya Sosyal ve Ekonomi Araştırmaları Dergisi, 7*(5), 221–237.

Kesen, M. (2016). The Role and Importance of Sustainable Human Resource Management in Business Administration. *İnsan ve Toplum Bilimleri Araştırmaları Dergisi, 5*(3), 554-573.

Leggate, H., McConville, J., & Morvillo, A. (2005). International Maritime Transport: Perspectives. Routledge.

Lucas, D., Jego, C., Jensen, O. C., Loddé, B., Pougnet, R., Dewitte, J.-D., Sauvage, T., & Jegaden, D. (2021). Seafarers' mental health in the COVID-19 era: Lost at sea? *International Maritime Health, 72*(2), 138–141. doi:10.5603/IMH.2021.0023 PMID:34212354

Maritime Labour Convention (MLC). (2006). Retrieved December 15, 2020, from http://www.ilo.org›documents›wcms_090250

McLaughlin, H. (2015). Seafarers in the spotlight. *Maritime Policy & Management, 42*(2), 95–96. doi:10.1080/03088839.2015.1006351

Omann, I., & Spangenberg, J. H. (2002). Assessing Social Sustainability: The Social Dimension of Sustainability in a Socio-Economic Scenario. *7th Biennial Conference of the International Society for Ecological Economics*, 1–20. http://seri.at/wp-content/uploads/2010/05/Assessing_social_sustainability.pdf

Pal, T., & Hazra, M. K. (2015). *Sustainable Development*. Yadava Publication.

Pauksztat, B., Grech, M., Kitada, M., & Jensen, R. B. (2020). *Seafarers' experiences during the COVID-19 pandemic: Report*. doi:10.21677/wmu20201213

Pourzanjanı, M., & Schröder, J. U., & Zade, G. (2002). Maritime Education and training (MET) in the european union: How can maritime administrations support MET. *International Association of Maritime Universities (IAMU) Journal, 2*(2), 50–56.

Roca-Puig, V. (2019). The circular path of social sustainability: An empirical analysis. *Journal of Cleaner Production, 212*, 916–924. doi:10.1016/j.jclepro.2018.12.078

Şanlı, O. (2020). Keynesyen model bağlamında Covid-19 pandemisinin küresel ekonomiye muhtemel etkileri: ABD ve Çin ekonomileri üzerine bir araştırma [The Possible Effects of the Covid-19 Pandemic on the Global Economy in the context of the Keynesian Model: A Study on the US and Chinese Economics]. *Avrasya Sosyal ve Ekonomi Araştırmaları Dergisi, 7*(5), 597-634.

Slišković, A. (2020). 'Seafarers' Well-being in the Context of the COVID-19 Pandemic: A Qualitative Study'. *Work (Reading, Mass.), 67*(4), 799–809. doi:10.3233/WOR-203333 PMID:33325430

Tosunoğlu, Ş., & Kasal, S. (2020). Yeni koronavirüs (covid-19) salgını ve sağlıklı küresel ekonomi için politika uygulamaları: IMF'nin rolü [The Novel Coronavirus (covid-19) Epidemic and Policy Implications for a Healthy Global Economy: The Role of the IMF]. *Anadolu Üniversitesi İktisat Fakültesi Dergisi, 2*(1), 35–49.

United Nations Conference on Trade and Development (UNCTAD). (2020). *Review of Maritime Transport*. UNCTAD.

United Nations Conference on Trade and Development (UNCTAD). (2021). *Review of Maritime Transport*. UNCTAD.

United Nations Conference on Trade and Development (UNCTAD). (2022). *Maritime Trade Disrupted: The war in Ukraine and its effects on maritime trade logistics*. https://unctad.org/system/files/official-document/osginf2022d2_en.pdf

Wiersum, K. F. (1995). 200 Years of Sustainability in Forestry: Lessons from History. *Environmental Management, 19*(3), 321–329.

Wilson, M. E. (2020). Travellers give wings to novel coronavirüs (2019-nCov). *Journal of Travel Medicine*, 1–3.

World Commission on Environment and Development (WCED). (1987). *Our Common Future report*. Retrieved January 19, 2020, from https://sustainabledevelopment.un.org/content/documents/5987our-common-future.pdf

KEY TERMS AND DEFINITIONS

COVID-19: The new type of corona virus declared as a pandemic by the World Health Organization.

Difficulties Experienced by the Seafarers: The inability of seafarers to go home or join the ship due to the quarantine practices applied by countries or closing their borders during the pandemic period. In addition, the lack of permissions to land at the ports, the delay or inability of the supplies to be given to the ship.

Key Workers: Recognition of seafarers as "key workers" because of the role they play in maintaining the flow of global trade.

Maritime Transportation: The process of transporting goods by cargo ships at sea.

Seafarer: They are all officers, cadets, crew and auxiliary service personnel working on board.

Seafarer Shortage: The shortage in the supply of seafarers due to the difficulties of the maritime profession.

Strategic Factors: Actions that need to be taken by governments and companies to have a sustainable maritime labour force during special periods such as the Covid-19 pandemic.

Sustainability: It is to ensure the continuity of production and diversity, in short, humanity by using resources effectively.

Chapter 8
Economic Measures for Mitigation of the Consequences of COVID-19:
Evidence From Serbia

Darko Marjanović
Institute of Economic Sciences, Serbia

Ivana Domazet
https://orcid.org/0000-0002-3493-4616
Institute of Economic Sciences, Serbia

ABSTRACT

The outbreak of global health and, consequently, the economic crisis caused by the COVID-19 pandemic interrupted five years of positive economic trends in Serbia. To preserve economic stability, the government of Serbia took appropriate measures and provided support to micro, small, and medium enterprises. The chapter aims to evaluate the packages of economic measures introduced to reduce the negative consequences caused by the pandemic. The research covers the period from 2015 to 2022 (i.e., before and during the crisis and after the adopted economic measures). The analysis is based on officially adopted economic measures with a combination of macroeconomic statistical data and forecasts from the Ministry of Finance of the Republic of Serbia and the Fiscal Council of the Republic of Serbia. The results of the research indicate that the crisis caused by the COVID-19 virus did not cause a significant drop in economic activity in the Republic of Serbia, primarily due to the extensive package of aid to the economy, which amounted to 12.5% of GDP.

DOI: 10.4018/978-1-6684-5950-8.ch008

INTRODUCTION

Covid-19 was first registered in December 2019 in Wuhan (China), caused by the SARS-CoV-2 virus. As almost the whole world was affected faster than anyone could have expected, on March 11, 2020, a pandemic was declared (WHO). As a result, there has been a significant blockade and closure of the economies. This caused a global recession, one of the biggest since the Great Depression of 1928. With the crisis, there is an increase in unemployment, so it is necessary to start the investment cycle, increase employment and thus restore the level of economic activity as before the crisis. The logic is completely justified, considering that with the strengthening of economic activity, one can expect higher tax collection, but also return the debts that were invested through state intervention. According to IMF forecasts, the pandemic of the COVID-19 virus will cause the greatest damage to developed countries, which will contribute to their slower economic growth compared to developing countries and countries in transition.

In early April 2020, when the COVID-19 pandemic was already in full swing, economists predicted that the overall situation that befell all world economies would lead to a major recession. The great decline in economic activity has led to a deepening of economic problems, an increase in the number of unemployed, a decline in living standards, but also a potential increase in poverty and inequality. Concerns have also been raised about the expectation that galloping inflation could force the central banks of many countries to cut aid packages. The decline of the world economy in 2020 was half as weak as in the 1930s, when the economy was down 10 percent. If we recall the global financial crisis that occurred in early 2009, when the global economic decline was 0.1 percent, it can be clearly seen that in its strength, and partly due to rapid geographical expansion, this crisis is significantly larger.

One of the questions that arises is what the new crisis means for globalization. Things will have to change, because companies and people have realized how much they have risked so far. The essence of a large part of globalization is not only in the transport of manufactured goods around the world, but also in the fluctuation of people, ideas and information. The idea that the essence of globalization is in moving production or supply chains to cheaper Asian countries is too simplistic. Of the 100 largest multinational companies in the world, as many as 42 companies said they faced the problem of maintaining business profitability. The uncertainty caused by this crisis has also had a negative impact on global investment. The application of restrictive measures in order to prevent and slow down the spread of the virus has strongly affected the economies of all countries, negatively affecting all economic indicators.

In order to mitigate the negative effects of the crisis, the Government of the Republic of Serbia has adopted the Program of Economic Measures. These measures aimed to help business entities in the country continue their business operations, but also to minimize the other effects caused by the COVID-19 virus pandemic. In this way, two objectives were to be met: (a) supporting the economy, especially the private sector, and (b) helping citizens to retain jobs and wages. The plan was for the economy, after the end of the pandemic, to continue where it left off and to develop even faster. Although the crisis caused by the virus, and which the economy is facing, is of a global character, the Republic of Serbia has pursued a responsible fiscal policy in recent years, which is why it has the opportunity to take on most of the burden of the crisis.

BACKGROUND

COVID-19 is not only an emergency situation that has affected all world economies, but it has become an international economic crisis that surpassed the global financial crisis of 2008. The crisis first disrupted China's economy and continued to expand globally. All world economies have faced a number of challenges that prevent simple comparisons and the application of hitherto known solutions (Guerrieri et al., 2020). According to the World Bank (2020), it is very difficult to estimate which course the pandemic will take and what economic impact it will have on countries' economies. It is precisely for this reason that it is very difficult for the creators of economic policy to define an adequate strategy that will give results, whether it is fiscal or monetary policy. The effect that the virus may have on financial systems depends (a) on how the virus will continue to spread around the world and what its impact will be on economic activity, (b) on the response of fiscal and monetary policy to shock and (c) from the regulatory response to the possible collapse of banks and the banking system (Beck, 2020). Brodeur et al. (2020) examined the literature dealing with the economic consequences of COVID-19 and the government's response to the new situation and concluded that in the first three months after the crisis, there was a significant increase in the number of documents aimed at analysis and discussion on the COVID-19 pandemic.

Countries around the world have reacted differently to the new situation caused by the COVID-19 pandemic, which has contributed to the implementation of appropriate economic measures needed to suppress the crisis and mitigate the new consequences (Chen et al., 2021; Ceylan et al., 2020). Governments around the world have generally responded to the emerging crisis by aggressively pursuing fiscal policy, which was both expected and realistic at the time (Malkin & Layton, 2021; Marjanović et al., 2022; Loayza & Pennings, 2020; Wang et al., 2022). In order to mitigate the negative effects of COVID-19, most countries implemented a series of monetary, fiscal, and financial measures, so that the consequences on the economy were as small as possible (Gourinchas, 2020; Domazet et al., 2018). Eurozone countries have largely relied on fiscal policy to reduce the negative impact of the COVID-19 pandemic on the economy (Haroutunian et al., 2021). Most countries have responded to the crisis caused by the COVID-19 virus with an adequate fiscal policy with the support of monetary policy. This was led by advanced economies that applied a much larger fiscal response (Alberola et al., 2021). Chudik et al. (2021) concluded that fiscal policy plays a key role in mitigating the effects of the pandemic and that countries that have adopted more adequate fiscal support programs will experience less economic contractions. Azad et al. (2021) addressed the impact of the COVID-19 pandemic on the Canadian economy and concluded that fiscal policy was more active than monetary policy and that deficit spending helped boost economic activity in the short term. Therefore, it is very important that the state pursues an adequate tax policy, and through approved tax incentives manages to enable investors to reduce investment risk and make higher profits (Marjanović & Domazet, 2021). In addition, the negative consequences of the COVID-19 pandemic are reflected in the restriction of foreign investments, which implies significantly lower placements compared to previous years. It is very important for the Republic of Serbia to pursue an active fiscal policy in the coming period (Marjanović & Domazet, 2021a; Padhan & Prabheesh, 2021), which can significantly contribute to the growth of the Serbian economy.

Western Balkans countries have introduced measures to help the economy and the population as part of reducing the consequences caused by the COVID-19 crisis. In addition, fiscal packages ranging from 1 to 7 percent of GDP (without guarantees) were provided, which ensured the stability and security of all economic entities to a significant extent (Warwick & Roshen, 2020). In their survey of a sample of 166 countries, Elgin et al. (2020) analyzed the economic policies applied by these countries in order to reduce the negative effects of the COVID-19 crisis and then presented monetary and fiscal measures through a comprehensive database. The results of the research showed that the average age of the population, GDP per capita and the number of total cases are significantly related to the scope of economic policy pursued by a particular country. In order to mitigate the crisis caused by the COVID-19 virus and minimize the negative effects, a well-conducted fiscal policy was of utmost importance. In order to mitigate the consequences of the COVID-19 crisis, in April 2020, the Government of the Republic of Serbia adopted a Decree that regulated all benefits and reliefs intended for economic entities in the private sector. Also, the Decree defines financial assistance, i.e. the payment of a one-time compensation for all adult citizens (Ministry of Finance Republic of Serbia, 2020a).

RESEARCH METHODOLOGY AND OBJECTIVES

In the situation when the COVID-19 pandemic affected the whole world, it became clear that the problems will escalate, especially when it comes to reducing the demand for goods and services, as well as reducing investments. In a very short time, the economic crisis affected both aggregate supply and aggregate demand. There is a huge degree of interdependence of the global economy, which, due to the effect of spilling negative economic and social consequences from one country to another, as well as the complete isolation of over three billion people, leads to consequences of unprecedented proportions. All this forced the countries to adopt appropriate measures in a very short period of time, in order to preserve the health of citizens, preserve jobs, but also provide appropriate assistance and support to economic entities. In general, the countries have mainly focused on several types of support for entrepreneurs: postponement of deadlines for payment of taxes and contributions, easier access to credit, direct assistance to small and medium enterprises. That is why it is not surprising that the Republic of Serbia reacted quickly, and immediately after the outbreak of the crisis, it adopted economic measures aimed at alleviating the recession and stabilizing the economy. These are four groups of economic measures: (a) tax policy measures, (b) direct assistance to the private sector, (c) liquidity conservation measures, and (d) direct assistance to all adult citizens.

Desk research was applied on the basis of officially adopted economic measures, combining macroeconomic statistical data and forecasts of the Ministry of Finance of the Republic of Serbia and the Fiscal Council of the Republic of Serbia. The research covered the period from 2015 to 2022, i.e. the period before the crisis caused by the COVID-19 virus and the period during the crisis but after the adopted economic measures.

The chapter is segmented into three interconnected units:

1. Analysis of the state of the Serbian economy before the outbreak of the pandemic (2015-2019).
2. Analysis of economic measures adopted by the Republic of Serbia in order to alleviate the consequences caused by the pandemic.
3. Analysis of the state of the Serbian economy after the adopted economic measures (2021-2022).

Based on the defined methodology and clearly set goals, the focus of the work will be on the state of the Serbian economy before the pandemic, as well as the importance of the economic measures adopted by the Republic of Serbia, which had an impact on the entire economy during the crisis.

MAIN FOCUS OF THE CHAPTER

Serbian Economy Before the COVID-19 Pandemic (2015-2019)

The Serbian economy in 2015-2019 made significant progress, which was reflected in the improvement of its economic performance, primarily in reducing the public debt and fiscal deficit. In that period, fiscal consolidation began in Serbia. The primary goal was to reduce the share of public debt in GDP and reduce the fiscal deficit, which amounted to about 67.5% of GDP at that time. The period of fiscal consolidation lasted until 2017 when a surplus was achieved, while the share of public debt in GDP was reduced to 53% at the end of 2019. In the analyzed period (2015-2019) the cumulative GDP growth was 18%, while the highest annual GDP growth was 4,5% at the end of 2018. The processing industry, wholesale and retail trade, transport and construction are the most deserving of such economic growth.

In 2018, compared to the previous year, the GDP was nominally higher by 6.6%, while real GDP growth in the same period amounted to 4.4%. Observed by activities, in 2018 the most significant participation in the formation of GDP was: the processing industry sector (14.5%) and the wholesale and retail trade and motor vehicle repair sector (11.5%), while all other sectors had less than 7%. In 2019 Serbia's GDP was nominally higher by around 6.8%, and in real terms by 4.2%, compared to 2018. The manufacturing sector (13.7%) and the wholesale and retail trade and motor vehicle repair sector (11.4%) had the most significant participation in GDP formation, while all other sectors had significantly smaller participation.

Total economic activity in the Republic of Serbia in 2019, measured by real GDP growth, increased by 4.0% compared to 2018. Compared to the previous year, gross investments in fixed assets in 2019 achieved real growth of 14.2%. Industrial production in 2019 had a growth of 0.3% physical volume compared to the previous year. Agricultural production in 2019 compared to 2018 saw a decline in the physical volume of 0.1%.

If the labor market were to be observed in the analyzed period, the unemployment rate decreased from 18.2% (2015) to 10.9% (2019). However, the problem that dates back to a more extended period and is related to the unemployment rate between women and men (11.5% compared to 10.4%) has not been solved. On the other hand, we should not ignore that women are still less present in the labor market, which is reflected in the inactivity rate of 38%, which is 13% higher than the inactivity rate of men. With the improvement of the situation in the labor market, there was also an increase in wages, which had an increasing trend since the end of 2015. However, this growth trend was not uniform, given that average wages continuously grew faster in the public sector (6%) than in the private sector (4%). The average salary in Serbia was the highest in 2019 when it amounted to around 460 euros. Although the economic growth was the result of the progress of the processing industry and wholesale and retail trade, the highest salaries were not recorded in these sectors. Still, they were significantly higher for employees in the finance and insurance sectors. According to official data from the Statistical Office of the Republic of Serbia, the average net salary in these sectors was around 810 euros. In comparison, the processing industry sector had an average salary of around 410 euros.

The primary sources of growth in 2019 were higher investment spending, especially in terms of infrastructure works and personal consumption, stimulated by the growth of wages and pensions, but also the stability of the national currency. Year-on-year inflation did not change significantly in 2019 and amounted to 1.5% in November, which is at the lower limit of the NBS target (3.0% ± 1.5 p.p.). In the period January-October 2019, Serbia attracted 3.1 billion euros in net foreign direct investments, which represents an increase of 37.5% compared to the same period in 2018, whereby this volume of FDI entirely covered the deficit of the current balance of payments.

Economic Measures to Mitigate the Consequences of the COVID-19 Crisis in the Republic of Serbia

When it became clear that COVID-19 would cause certain consequences, even the largest international financial institutions did not realize that the coronavirus would cause a global recession. Initially, it was thought that the economy would move in the shape of the letter V, where first there would be a sharp decline in economic activity, and then a rapid recovery of the world economy. Such optimistic forecasts and plans were quickly replaced by more realistic ones, given that there was a rapid increase in the number of people infected with coronavirus, which caused the collapse of the health systems of most countries. Even then, it was possible to talk about the economic consequences of the pandemic. At the beginning of the pandemic (March 2020), the "hardest" scenarios that could hit the world economy were considered. In the next 2-3 months, the leading economic institutions constantly revised the rates of decline of the world economy and, in the end, concluded that the scenarios set at the beginning of the pandemic actually became very realistic.

At the beginning of April 2020, the Republic of Serbia presented four sets of economic measures, with the main goal of mitigating the consequences of the COVID-19 virus pandemic. The plan of the Serbian authorities was that such economic measures, on the one hand, ensure the economic stability of the state and, on the other hand, help micro, small and medium enterprises in the private sector to cope with the recession.

Table 1. Program of economic measures to mitigate the negative consequences of the pandemic.

Naziv Mera	In Billion RSD	In Billion EUR	% BDP
Tax policy measures	**161**	**1.4**	**2,9**
Postponement of the payment of income tax and payable contributions for the private sector, during the state of emergency, with the subsequent repayment of liabilities incurred in installments starting in 2021 at the earliest	140	1.2	2,5
Postponement of advance payment of profit tax in the second quarter	21	0.2	0,4
Exemption of donors from VAT obligations	-	-	.
Direct assistance to employees	**97,3**	**0.83**	**1,8**
Direct assistance to entrepreneurs (both flat-rate taxpayers and those who pay real income tax), micro, small and medium-sized enterprises in the private sector - payment of aid in the amount of minimum income (during the state of emergency - 3 minimum wages)	92,8	0.79	1,7
Direct assistance to large companies in the private sector - payment of assistance in the amount of 50% of the net minimum wage (during the state of emergency) for employees whose employment has been terminated.	4,5	0.04	0,1
Measures for liquidity of the economy	**264**	**2.24**	**4,8**
Support to the economy through the Fund for Development of the Republic of Serbia	24	0.2	0,4
Guarantee scheme to support the economy through banks	240	2.04	4,4
Other measures	**86**	**0.73**	**1,6**
Moratorium on the payment of dividends until the end of the year	16	0.14	0,3
Payment of 100 euros to all adult citizens	70	0.59	1,3
Total (1,2,3,4)	**608,3**	**5.1**	**11,0**

Source: Fiscal Council of the Republic of Serbia (2020)

Business entities could not count on financial assistance: (a) if they reduced the number of employees by more than 10% during the state of emergency. Exceptions are employees who were engaged for a certain period and whose contract expired during the period of the state of emergency, as well as employees who temporarily suspended work before March 15, 2020.

The total value of economic support measures amounted to 608.3 billion dinars, or 5.1 billion euros, which is about 11% of GDP.

The First Package of Economic Measures

One of the major problems faced by businesses during the pandemic was the inability to pay taxes regularly. Therefore, the first package of economic measures was directly related to tax policy, so the action is focused on tax relief, in practice on delaying the payment of due tax liabilities. With these measures, all entities were given the opportunity to postpone the payment of their due tax liabilities. Tax liabilities could be paid in installments, with repayment scheduled to begin no earlier than January 2021. This package of economic measures envisages that the payment of taxes and contributions will be postponed for 3 (three) months, with the postponement of the advance payment of profit tax for Q2 2020, the exemption from profit tax for donations and the postponement of income tax for all entrepreneurs.

Table 2. Fiscal benefits and direct payments to economic entities in order to mitigate the economic consequences of the COVID-19 pandemic.

Type of Incentive	Duration	Period	Amount
Deferment of income tax and payable contributions	3 months	April, May, June until January 4, 2021, ie in 24 installments	Personal income tax and contributions for compulsory social insurance
Deferment of advance payment of profit tax	3 months	March, April and May 2020 (until the submission of the final tax return)	Advance payment of profit tax for 3 months
Direct benefits (financial incentives)	3 months	May, June and July 2020	Minimalna zarada za mesec mart 30.367,04 RSD (258 EUR)

Source: Authors, based on the Ministry of Finance of the Republic of Serbia (2020-2021)

Business entities have been given the opportunity to postpone the payment of taxes and contributions on salaries and wage compensations until January 4, 2021. In addition, they were given the opportunity to postpone the advance payment of income tax for March, April and May 2020 until the submission of the final corporate income tax return for the current year. After the expiration of this deadline, an additional option was given to regulate these liabilities in 24 equal monthly installments without interest. When it comes to the payment of non-refundable funds from the budget, they were entitled to: entrepreneur, flat rate entrepreneur, agricultural workers, entrepreneur another person, legal entities classified as micro, small and medium. All economic entities could use the benefits of this regulation if they did not lay off more than 10% of workers as of March 15, 2020. According to the Decree (Ministry of Finance of the Republic of Serbia, 2020), the conditions that need to be met in order for this measure to be applicable are clearly defined. In case of violation of the conditions, the business entity was obliged to pay all obligations that were deferred together with interest, which runs from the due date of each individual obligation, within 5 days from the date of loss of rights (dividend payments and / or reduction of the number of employees by more than 10%). Additionally, there was an obligation to return the received funds together with interest, which flows from the payment of funds within 5 days from the date of loss of rights (dividend payments and / or reduction of the number of employees by more than 10%).

Table 3. Obligations of business entities on the basis of fiscal and direct benefits.

<table>
<tr><th>Type of Incentive</th><th>Deadline</th><th>Administrative Obligation</th><th colspan="2">Prohibited</th></tr>
<tr><td>Postponement of payment of taxes and contributions on salaries and compensations</td><td>04/30/2020</td><td>Submit PPP-PD form</td><td rowspan="3">Reduce the number of employees by more than 10% within 3 months from the last payment, ie by October 31, 2020 (Excluding termination of fixed-term employment concluded before March 15, 2020)</td><td rowspan="3">Payment of profits by the end of 2020</td></tr>
<tr><td>Deferment of advance payment of profit tax</td><td>-</td><td>-</td></tr>
<tr><td>Direct benefits</td><td>04/25/2020</td><td>Inform TA which bank will make the payment</td></tr>
</table>

Source: Authors, based on the Ministry of Finance of the Republic of Serbia (2020-2021)

The main goal of the adopted measures was to increase the liquidity of all business entities in the economic sector. It is very important to mention that employers are given the opportunity to extend their obligations regarding the payment of taxes and contributions after January 2021 for a maximum of 24 months, with a state guarantee that they will not pay interest on outstanding obligations during that period. When it comes to donations directed to institutions that actively participate in preventing the spread of the virus and treating citizens from COVID-19 disease, a decision was made that these donors are exempt from VAT.

The total amount of funds intended for economic entities within the first package of economic measures was 161 billion Serbian dinars, or 1.4 billion euros.

The Second Package of Economic Measures

Given that the COVID-19 pandemic greatly affected the liquidity of business entities, the second set of economic measures aimed to support companies through the form of direct benefits, which were reflected in the payment of three minimum wages. The first payment of the minimum wage in the amount calculated from the number of full-time employees for whose wages the employer submitted the PPP-PD Form (Individual Income Tax Return) for the accounting period, and the amount of the basic minimum net salary for that month, was made successively: in May, June, and the beginning of July 2020. This assistance is intended for entrepreneurs and small and medium enterprises in the private sector. It is also intended for large companies through a subsidy of 50 percent of the minimum wage, for those employees who are on forced leave due to the reduction in the volume of work. Also, to all entrepreneurs, flat-rate enterpreneurs and small and medium businesses, the state paid three minimum wages for each employee.

Looking at the second package of economic measures, the state has drawn a clear line between small and medium-sized enterprises, on the one hand, and large enterprises, on the other. This was done mostly due to differences in the economic strength of taxpayers, given that the assumption is that economic entities classified as large companies have greater economic strength compared to entrepreneurs, micro, small and medium-sized legal entities. It is for this reason that these entities received financial compensation in the amount of the net minimum wage for each employee.

When it comes to large economic entities, the state has undertaken the obligation to pay part of the salary for employees who are still employed by the employer, but are not actively employed during the crisis due to reduced workload. In this way, the state intended to encourage large employers not to lay off workers, while in the case of other economic entities (entrepreneurs, micro, small and medium enterprises) the state sought to aid them in maintaining liquidity and continue to perform their business activities smoothly. The aim of the state was to stimulate large economic entities with these measures to maintain the existing level of employment.

The total amount of funds intended for economic entities within the second package of economic measures was 97.3 billion Serbian dinars or 0.83 billion euros.

The Third Package of Economic Measures

In order to preserve the liquidity of economic entities in a situation when the economic crisis is in full swing, without any clear indications when it could end, the state has adopted another package of economic measures. Due to the impact of the spread of the coronavirus, the third package of economic measures was primarily aimed at reducing external influences, which are reflected in the interruption of the supply chain and their consequences (reduction of employment and illiquidity of economic entities).

In April 2020, the Government of the Republic of Serbia adopted another Decree, all to reduce the negative effects of the COVID-19 crisis. This Decree provided how financial support for business entities would be provided, given that it was necessary to provide working capital and maintain their liquidity (Ministry of Finance of the Republic of Serbia, 2020).

Within this package of economic measures, the state gave the opportunity to entrepreneurs, micro, small and medium business entities, agricultural farms and cooperatives, which are registered in the relevant register through the Development Fund of the Republic of Serbia, to get more favorable loans with one percent interest rate annually. All this was done in order to maintain their liquidity. It should be noted that this type of assistance was contracted with commercial banks and that the state was the guarantor of the approved funds.

The total amount of funds intended for economic entities within the third package of economic measures was 264 billion Serbian dinars or 2.24 billion euros.

The Fourth Package of Economic Measures

In order to mitigate the consequences caused by the COVID-19 virus, which affected both the economy and the population, a decision was made to pay a one-time financial aid of EUR 100 in RSD equivalent to all adult citizens of the Republic of Serbia. The goal of this package was to, in addition to direct financial assistance to citizens, influence the increase in consumption and thus the liquidity of companies. Citizens could apply for financial assistance by phone or online, via the application. The payment of financial aid began on May 25, 2020, and about 4.2 million citizens of the Republic of Serbia who applied in one of the provided ways were entitled to it.

The total amount of funds intended for citizens within the fourth package of economic measures was 70 billion Serbian dinars, or 0.59 billion euros.

The State of the Serbian Economy After the Adopted Package of Economic Measures (2021-2022)

Despite the pandemic and unprecedented global reduction in economic activity, the Republic of Serbia managed to avoid serious consequences for the economy and to preserve full macroeconomic and financial stability in 2021-2022 by timely adoption and effective implementation of monetary and fiscal measures.

Without the package of economic measures that was adopted, the fiscal part of which had to be partly financed by an increase in public debt, the drop in Serbia's GDP in 2020 would have been over 6%, and full recovery due to the loss of production and human capacities would have lasted from three to five years. Instead, in 2020 the Republic of Serbia recorded a decrease in GDP of only 1.1% and was one of the few countries that already in 2021 overtook the pre-crisis level of economic activity. GDP growth in Q1 2021 was 1.8%, with which the domestic economy exceeded the level of economic activity from the pre-pandemic period. At the end of December 2021, the share of public debt in GDP was 56.9%, which represents decrease of 0.1 p.p. compared to the 2020 level.

How important the adopted economic measures were can be seen in the example of the labor market. In the period Q1-Q3 2021 the average number of employees was higher by 3.3% compared to the same period of the previous year, which was primarily the result of employment growth in the private sector (4.4%), while in the public sector the growth was 0.5%. In Q2 2021 the rate of the population outside the labor force was significantly reduced by as much as 4.1 p.p. and amounted to 45.7%. This is an indicator of recovery in the labor market, due to the return to the level before the crisis caused by the pandemic. The average net salary in the period January-December 2021 was around 560 euros, which is 5.4% more compared to the same period of the previous (2020) year.

With an adequate and timely fiscal policy, the state provided a package of economic measures, which, on the one hand, had a positive impact on economic entities and the population, and on the other hand, significantly influenced the main macro indicators in 2022. How significant the packages of economic measures adopted by the state were, can be seen through the absence of negative effects of the COVID-19 pandemic. The best example is the labor market, where there has been no decrease in wages and no increase in unemployment, regardless of whether the private or public sector is observed. Based on all of the facts, it can be concluded that all four packages of economic measures contributed to the maintenance of stability and economic growth of Serbia.

SOLUTIONS AND RECOMMENDATIONS

When formulating economic measures, the Republic of Serbia consulted the practices and experiences of developed economies, but also countries from its immediate surroundings. The fiscal space for providing support to the economy and the population is partly a consequence of the restrictive fiscal policy which stopped the trend of accelerated borrowing of the country. In order to preserve the financial system, the NBS (National Bank of Serbia) has adopted appropriate interim measures. They were reflected in the delay in repayment (moratorium) of loans and liabilities based on financial leasing, which cannot be shorter than 90 days, or until a state of emergency. During this period, banks did not charge default interest on overdue and unsettled receivables from customers, nor did they initiate enforcement proceedings and forced collection against debtors.

It is very important to note that all adopted measures (fiscal and direct benefits) could be used by economic entities in the private sector, provided that starting from March 15, 2020 until the entry into force of the Regulation did not reduce the number of employees by more than 10%. It is clearly stated that fiscal and direct benefits can be used only by those economic entities that were established and registered with the competent authority before March 15, 2020, ie if they became VAT payers in the specified period. With the measures defined in this way, the creators of economic policy wanted to prevent the increase in unemployment, which is a logical consequence of the decline in economic activity, but also to discourage manipulation during the allocation of funds (Ministry of Finance of the Republic of Serbia, 2020).

There are several key challenges that economic policymakers in the Republic of Serbia must face in the coming period. First, the Serbian economy is not isolated and largely depends on economic flows in the EU and neighboring countries. By far the largest part of the foreign trade of the Republic of Serbia is with these countries, and the possible deterioration of the economic situation will affect its economic activity. The largest percentage of investments come from EU countries, which are a significant factor in the development of the Serbian economy. Therefore, it is very important to use EU financial support in the most efficient way possible and improve cooperation with European institutions and jointly seek answers to emerging economic issues.

Second, the crisis as a consequence of the pandemic does not have an equal impact on all economic sectors. While, for example, the telecommunications and construction sectors are relatively little affected, the hospitality and tourism sectors face serious challenges. A scenario in which restricting the movement of people continues to impede recovery in these sectors and creates strong pressure on employment is very possible. In that case, it will be necessary to define measures that would mitigate the decline in economic activity in the sectors most affected. Despite the fact that the fiscal space of the state is not completely exhausted, the capacities of the state, after several months of financial support to the economy, are relatively limited.

Third, the share of public debt in GDP is slowly returning to the level of approximately 60%, which requires special attention, given that the Republic of Serbia in this parameter can not be compared with more developed countries whose reputation allows a significantly higher level of indebtedness. Otherwise, it is possible to easily get into the "vicious circle of indebtedness" from which it is very difficult to get out. In addition, the issue of financial sustainability can be directly reflected in the quality of the provision of other types of public sector services. Financial allocations that amortize the impact of the pandemic may cause certain health and social care services to be postponed or abolished, which may increase inequality. At the same time, the countries in which the degree of economic inequality is already pronounced are most affected. It is very important to define alternative economic policies in the coming period, in case the global crisis caused by the pandemic lasts and there is an increase in unemployment, accelerated closure of companies and a sharp decline in economic activity.

The response of the Republic of Serbia to the economic crisis caused by the coronavirus was a strong state intervention. The idea behind such an intervention is to help as much of the private sector as possible to survive, ie that the current decline in business activity does not lead to permanent and excessive job losses and huge damage to citizens, the economy and, ultimately, for public finances in general.

FUTURE RESEARCH DIRECTIONS

The global crisis caused by the COVID-19 virus, with a wide range of consequences for almost all aspects of life - economic, social and political pointed to the critical need for readiness to respond adequately in emergencies/crises. which carry a great health risk for a part of the population and pose a great challenge to the complete health infrastructure as well as many other resources of the society. The crisis has severely jeopardized all-important business segments - investment plans, demand for products and services, as well as liquidity and supply chains.

The emphasis in this chapter is on the analysis of the adopted economic measures that were supposed to minimize the negative effects caused by the COVID-19 virus pandemic. Given that the analysis is focused on one transition economy (Republic of Serbia), future research could be extended to the most developed or developing countries. The analysis done in this way would show how some developed countries fought the pandemic of the COVID-19 virus, ie what economic measures they applied to stop the decline of their economy. It would also be important to conduct parallel research involving two or more economies. In that way, we could determine the effects of economic measures, which were adopted by each state. In addition, the analysis would show the current position when it comes to the competitiveness of the analyzed countries, which can largely reflect the attractiveness of the country in attracting foreign direct investment. On the other hand, expanding the analysis would indicate possible limitations or omissions in some countries in the selection of economic measures, which could be regulated through active fiscal and monetary policy in the future. In each of these cases, the analysis would be based on the available secondary data of the reference institutions from each country involved in the survey. However, in order to obtain information from economic entities and the population, future research could also be based on the collection of primary data. It is recommended that future researchers conduct research directly (focus groups) or indirectly (online questionnaire), in order to obtain primary data, which are very important for future analysis and making recommendations for government officials in each of the analyzed economies. The results obtained in such research would significantly help economic policymakers to set goals and implement tasks based on available analyzes that would enable economic growth in the economy over a longer period of time.

CONCLUSION

The Republic of Serbia has taken adequate measures in the past ten years, which have largely ensured fiscal stability. This enabled the adoption of a comprehensive package of economic measures immediately after the outbreak of the COVID-19 virus pandemic. During 2020 an adequate economic policy was pursued, with the aim of minimizing the recession caused by the pandemic. Since the beginning of the pandemic, the Republic of Serbia has managed to successfully cope with economic and health challenges and implement strong measures to support the economy and the population. These were mainly fiscal and monetary measures. The result was favorable, and this was reflected in a lower decline in GDP compared to most world economies. On the other hand, such measures have significantly affected the increase in fiscal costs. As the economy is in recession and public debt is rising sharply, space for future incentives is limited.

Despite the fact that the pandemic caused a global decline in economic activity, the Republic of Serbia managed to avoid more serious consequences for the economy, but also preserve macroeconomic and financial stability. The reason for that is the timely adoption and effective implementation of monetary and fiscal measures. These measures contributed to the recovery of key indicators of economic activity (retail trade, industry and exports) in Q3 2020. An even more significant result of these measures is that the Republic of Serbia preserved existing production capacities and continued to develop new ones. Thus, it provided the basis for stable economic growth both in 2021 and in the following years.

One of the reasons why it ended 2020 with a minimal decline in economic activity is that the economy of the Republic of Serbia has continuously increased its profitability from 2015 to 2019. Adopting a comprehensive aid package as soon as possible and maintaining confidence during the most difficult months of the pandemic, were key to the rapid recovery of fundamental sectors of the economy. Despite the package of economic measures, all economic indicators remained within sustainable limits, which contributed to maintaining stable economic growth in the medium term. Thanks to the responsible economic policy pursued during the pandemic, as well as full coordination of monetary and fiscal policy, the cost of government borrowing has been significantly reduced, with an increase in the share of debt in Serbian dinars, thus reducing currency risk.

The importance of the adopted package of economic measures is clearly seen in the fact that the decline in a gross domestic product of Serbia in 2020, if it were not for these measures, would be over 6%, while the recovery would take three to five years, mostly due to loss of production and workforce capacities. The result of the adopted measures is a reduction of gross domestic product of only 1.1% in 2020, which contributed to exceeding the pre-crisis level of economic activity in 2021. If we compare this crisis with the one in 2009, we can see that the decline in gross domestic product was 2.7%, which contributed to GDP reaching pre-crisis levels only in 2013, mostly due to loss of production capacity and labor. The measures taken to mitigate the consequences of the crisis caused by COVID-19 are aimed at economic entities registered in the Republic of Serbia and which are not part of the financial sector, ie beneficiaries of public funds. When conceiving the measures, the Government did what was possible, adjusting this package of measures to the current budget capacities of the country. A quick package of measures for economic recovery was made, and it was clear that these measures were going in the right direction, both in size and typology, in line with those taken by other European countries. At the beginning of the pandemic, the European Union provided financial assistance to both its members and countries outside the EU zone. The Republic of Serbia received about 15 million euros for health needs and about 78 million euros for economic recovery, with the addition of funds intended for support at the regional level. The EU has allocated around 700 million euros for the region of the Western Balkans, with the largest part going to the Republic of Serbia.

The package of economic measures adopted by the Government so far has not endangered the macroeconomic and fiscal stability of the country. Compared to other European countries, the Republic of Serbia has solid economic parameters, while adequately adopted measures have helped it not to fall into a deeper recession. In accordance with the situation at the global level, when it comes to the COVID-19 virus pandemic, the Republic of Serbia should take into account all important indicators and accordingly adopt economic measures in the coming period, in order to cope with the crisis. In this context, it is very important to take into account the risks of a longer pandemic and its very strong impact on certain economic sectors. Economic policymakers should develop several economic policy alternatives and crisis mitigation measures in line with different scenarios at the global level.

ACKNOWLEDGMENT

This chapter is financed by the Ministry of Education, Science, and Technological Development of the Republic of Serbia.

REFERENCES

Alberola, E., Arslan, Y., Cheng, G., & Moessner, R. (2021). Fiscal response to the COVID-19 crisis in advanced and emerging market economies. *Pacific Economic Review, 26*(4), 459–468. Advance online publication. doi:10.1111/1468-0106.12370

Azad, N. F., Serletis, A., & Xu, L. (2021). Covid-19 and monetary–fiscal policy interactions in Canada. *The Quarterly Review of Economics and Finance, 82*, 376–384. doi:10.1016/j.qref.2021.06.009

Beck, T. (2020). Finance in the times of coronavirus. In Economics in the Time of COVID-19. London: Centre for Economic Policy Research.

Brodeur, A., Gray, D., Islam, A. & Bhuiyan, S.J. (2020). *A literature review of the Economics of COVID-19*. Institute of Labor Economics, IZA DP No. 13411.

Ceylan, R. F., Ozkan, B., & Mulazimogullari, E. (2020). Historical evidence for economic effects of COVID-19. *The European Journal of Health Economics, 21*(6), 817–823. doi:10.100710198-020-01206-8 PMID:32500243

Chen, C., Shi, Y., Zhang, P., & Ding, C. (2021). A Cross-Country Comparison of Fiscal Policy Responses to the COVID-19 Global Pandemic. *Journal of Comparative Policy Analysis, 23*(2), 262–273. doi:10.1080/13876988.2021.1878885

Chudik, A., Mohaddes, K., & Raissi, M. (2021). Covid-19 fiscal support and its effectiveness. *Economics Letters, 205*, 109939. Advance online publication. doi:10.1016/j.econlet.2021.109939

Domazet, I., Marjanović, D., & Stošić, I. (2018). The attractiveness of the domicile economy through tax incentives. *Ekonomika preduzeća, 7/8*, 434-445.

Elgin, C., Basbug, G., & Yalaman, A. (2020). Economic policy responses to a pandemic: Developing the Covid-19 economic stimulus index. In COVID Economics: Vetted and real-time papers. London: Centre for Economic Policy Research.

Fiscal Council of the Republic of Serbia. (2020). *Evaluation of the anti-crisis program of economic measures*. Author.

Gourinchas, P. O. (2020). Flattening the pandemic and recession curves. In Mitigating the COVID Economic Crisis: Act Fast and Do Whatever. London: Centre for Economic Policy Research.

Guerrieri, V., Lorenzoni, G., Straub, L., & Werning, I. (2020). *Macroeconomic Implications of COVID-19: Can Negative Supply Shocks Cause Demand Shortages?* NBER Working Paper No. 26918.

Haroutunian, S., Osterloh, S., & Sławińska, K. (2021). *The initial fiscal policy responses of euro area countries to the COVID-19 crisis. Economic Bulletin Articles* (Vol. 1). European Central Bank.

Loayza, N. & Pennings, S. (2020). *Macroeconomic Policy in the Time of COVID-19: A Primer for Developing Countries.* World Bank Group.

Malkin, A. J., & Layton, A. (2021). The global fiscal response to COVID-19: Risks and repercussions. *Economic Analysis and Policy*, *69*, 340–349. doi:10.1016/j.eap.2020.12.016

Marjanović, D., & Domazet, I. (2021). Tax competitiveness as a significant factor in attracting foreign investment – the case of Serbia. *Argumenta Oeconomica*, *2*(47), 63–80. doi:10.15611/aoe.2021.2.04

Marjanović, D., & Domazet, I. (2021). Foreign Direct Investments: A Key Factor for Business Globalization. In Y. Bayar (Ed.), *Institutional, Economic, and Social Impacts of Globalization and Liberalization* (pp. 96–116). IGI Global. doi:10.4018/978-1-7998-4459-4.ch006

Marjanović, D., Domazet, I., & Vukmirović, I. (2022). Social Environment as a Factor of Capital Investment in Serbia. *Eastern European Economics*, *60*(3), 247–264. Advance online publication. doi:10.1080/00128775.2022.2048181

Ministry of Finance of the Republic of Serbia. (2020). *Decree on fiscal benefits and direct benefits to economic entities in the private sector and financial assistance to citizens and the goal of mitigating the economic consequences caused by the COVID-19 disease.* Official Gazette of RS, no. 54/2020 and 60/2020.

Ministry of Finance of the Republic of Serbia (2020a). *Decree on establishing the Program of financial support to economic entities for maintaining liquidity and working capital in difficult economic conditions due to the COVID-19 pandemic caused by the SARS-CoV-2 virus.* Official Gazette of RS, no. 54/2020.

Padhan, R., & Prabheesh, K. P. (2021). The economics of COVID-19 pandemic: A survey. *Economic Analysis and Policy*, *70*, 220–237. doi:10.1016/j.eap.2021.02.012 PMID:33658744

Wang, T., Gao, K., Wen, C., Xiao, Y., & Bingzheng, Y. (2022). Assessing the nexus between fiscal policy, COVID-19, and economic growth. *Environmental Science and Pollution Research International*, *29*(43), 1–15. doi:10.100711356-022-20358-z PMID:35484459

Warwick, J. M., & Roshen, F. (2020). *The Global Macroeconomic Impacts of COVID-19: Seven Scenarios.* CAMA Working Paper No. 19/2020. Available at SSRN: https://ssrn.com/abstract=3547729

World Bank Group. (2020). *Economic and social impact of COVID-19.* REF No. 17. Author.

KEY TERMS AND DEFINITIONS

Budget: The budget is a document that contains a list of planned revenues and expenditures of the state for one year. The revenue plan shows how much money and from what sources the state plans to collect it, while expenditures show what the state intends to spend the collected money on. The state budget is prepared by the Ministry of Finance in cooperation with other ministries and budget users, according to a precisely determined procedure defined by the Law on the Budget System of the Republic of Serbia.

COVID-19: The name of the illness caused by the coronavirus SARS-CoV-2. COVID-19 stands for "coronavirus disease 2019." A mild to severe respiratory illness that is caused by a coronavirus (severe acute respiratory syndrome coronavirus 2 of the genus Betacoronavirus).

Economic Policy: Economic policy refers to the actions that governments take in the economic field. It covers the systems for setting interest rates and government budget as well as the labor market, national ownership, and many other areas of government interventions into the economy.

Fiscal Policy: Fiscal policy refers to the use of government spending and tax policies to influence economic conditions, especially macroeconomic conditions, including aggregate demand for goods and services, employment, inflation, and economic growth.

Pandemic: An outbreak of a disease that occurs over a wide geographic area (such as multiple countries or continents) and typically affects a significant proportion of the population.

Tax Incentives: A tax incentive is an aspect of a country's tax code designed to incentivize or encourage a particular economic activity by reducing tax payments for a company in the said country. Tax incentives have traditionally been used by governments as tools to promote a particular economic goal. They are preferential tax treatments that are offered to a selected group of taxpayers and take the form of exemptions, tax holidays, credits, investment allowances, preferential tax rates and import tariffs (or customs duties), and deferral of tax liability.

Chapter 9
The Transformation of Global Trade in a New World:
Deglobalization and Its Risk in International Trade Post COVID-19

Reenu Kumari
Meerut Institute of Engineering and Technology, India

Ashwani Sharma
Meerut Institute of Engineering and Technology, India

ABSTRACT

COVID-19 has reduced international joint ventures. However, most of the organizations across the world have adopted deglobalization, and it has aided in facing the problems of natural disasters and other challenges. Thus, with globalization and internationalization reduced, organizations are focused on the domestic markets for the investment and manufacturing process. This chapter highlights deglobalization. International trade is also one of the expected survivor tools of the current pandemic situation, but due to COVID-19, it has depreciated, and people have started to believe in deglobalization, which has increased the value of domestic markets. Further, this chapter discusses the risk of deglobalization in the world economy and the consequences of deglobalization on international trade post COVID-19.

DOI: 10.4018/978-1-6684-5950-8.ch009

INTRODUCTION

International trading meaning is to trading of resources (goods and services) worldwide. The exchange of trade among countries shows a massive contribution to economic growth. The world is globalized due to raising its importance in recent centuries economically, politically, and socially. However, globalization is a complex idea; it incorporates significantly more than exchange transparency and development of capital. It shows in residents of various nations exchanging thoughts and government cooperation to handle political issues worldwide. The exchange of goods and services is an important part of economic growth. It helps to reduce poverty, generate employment, and create long-term relationships between two different kinds of nations. Trade also helps to minimize the barriers between progressed and emerging nations; these barriers include the approach to the global market, ambiguous regulatory and administrative environment, political situations, etc. (Kumari & Sharma, 2021).

But the worldwide economy is confronting new difficulties, including defeating the sluggish economy in the world and limits risk due to a down world economy. Also, nations should oversee worldwide business and exchange under the developing deglobalization situation (Kim, Li, P., & Lee, 2020). Suddenly, from the end of 2019, world economy is facing new challenges i.e., covid 19, that will be included minimizing the risk (social, health, environmental, physiological etc), overcoming the slow economy and reduce the depressed GDP across the world. Moreover, whole World must manage import and export and trade under the growing deglobalization (Kim et al., 2020). As World aware deglobalization is inverse concept of globalization and it is reduced interdependence and integration towards the across the country. Deglobalization has increased post covid 19 so it has created trade imbalance, high unemployment, and downfall in trade between countries.

Deglobalization term is the result of significant changes in many developed countries, where trade contribution to total economic activity is low from the 1910s until the 1970s.This turn down implies that their economies become less coordinated with the other world economies regardless of the extending extent of economies globalization (NYUDS, 2013). Basically, the deglobalization was only considered in two longer periods, specifically during the 1930s during the great depression and the 2010s, while following the great trade collapse the time of the world trade slowdown set in (Hoekman & Bernhard, 2015).

In the year 2020, the world economy has shrunk due to reducing the exchange the goods & services from one place to another place. Thus, it will take time to improve the GDP growth rate, increase exchange of goods and services, and enhance international trade, because due the covid 19 high risks are spread and all the kind of business into a depression in all over the world. However, Covid 19 hit is not new but still world required taking lots of steps and a history demonstration that shows the cyclic phenomenon of how countries overcome the effects of the recession. These affect different regions however, some areas have been especially affected by the shocks and some of them are impacted excessively less (Van Bergeijk, 2017).

The huge drop in business and output volume has been marked in the year 2020 since World War II. The drop in both world industrial production and merchandise exchanges the primary portion of 2020 were of comparable profundity to those at the box of the Global Financial Crisis (GFC). In any case, they emerged and vanished all the more rapidly, working with a V-formed recovery in 2020. International trade starts grow strongly in 2021 and trade continued to grow strongly in 2021 and has balance some, however not all, of the cumulative losses from the precarious decays seen before (Arriola, Kowalski & Tongeren, 2021).

Beginning pandemic-period assumptions for a two-digit decrease in global business exchange 2020 did not emerge. The business volume of international business has recovered to the pre-pandemic level at an uncommonly high speed from around mid-2020 (Figure 1).

Figure 1. Volume of International Business and Industrial production.
Source: OECD calculations based on CPB World Trade Monitor

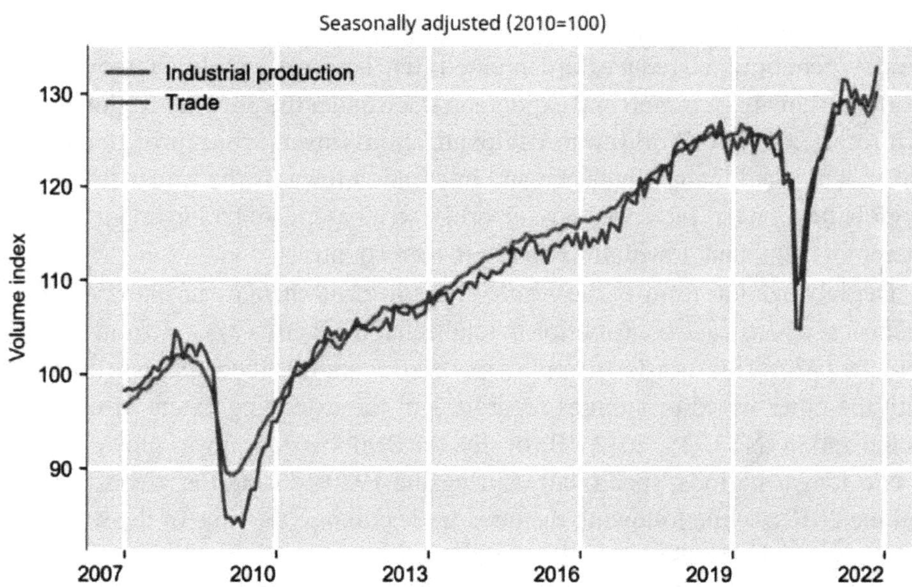

The above figure 1 shows that the result was the global impact of covid 19 and the global world was started converting into deglobalization. After that world knew that interdependency is beneficial for economics, politics, and administration but it may impact very fast if something will happen in any country that's why deglobalization represents the process of weakening interdependence among nations. Therefore, our chapter has tried to find out how the deglobalization scenario is different from the time period between 1930 and 2008. Due to covid 19, deglobalization makes the world economy more defensive and creates job opportunities pf the manufacturer, and give us a chance to sell our goods and services within our country.

Therefore, this chapter ha attempt to construct four distinct contributions to existing literature: firstly, to discuss deglobalization in depth against globalization; Secondly, to analyze the risk of deglobalization in the World Economy; Thirdly, the consequences of globalization including import tariffs and non-tariff barriers to trade, reshoring policy and decrease in exports, GVC reconfiguration and Covid 19; fourthly, discussed the forthcoming policies and necessary actions; lastly, concluded our chapter.

DEGLOBALIZATION AND ITS FACTS

History of Deglobalization Against the Globalization

Globalization work with international economies but in contrast, deglobalization is not integrated with the worldwide economies. Globalization has provided new opportunities for both countries host and home. For the support of working globalization, international bodies are involved like World Trade Organization (WTO), International Monetary Fund (IMF), and United Nations Conference on Trade and Development (UNCTAD) (Kim et al., 2020). These three government bodies work together and encourage international trade enhance economic growth. Although, some criticism came out against globalization, may be due to the unfairness and not equalization among the trading countries. Therefore, some countries followed regionalism which has resulted in Regional Corporation for example free trade agreements (FTAs), the US state currently has 14 FTAs with 20 countries and these countries are supported by the deviation from multinationalism and globalism.

Figure 2 shows globalization and deglobalization 1880-2022. Globalization and deglobalization have contradictory competition throughout history in 2022. During 1929-1979 first deglobalization has come due to I world war and the depression. Further, during the II world war, most of the western countries became WTO members and tried to eliminate trade barriers. They have successes till 2007 but in 2008 again globalization converse into deglobalization. At that time disturb the financial system and international trade caused nations to worry about income divide and inequality. Although, international trade helps to grow economic growth due to financial crisis created a new pattern of deglobalization. After 2010 situation of deglobalization changed and convert into globalization.

Figure 2. Globalization and Deglobalization 1880-2020. (Openness of the World Economy index numbers 2008=100).
Source: KOF globalization index

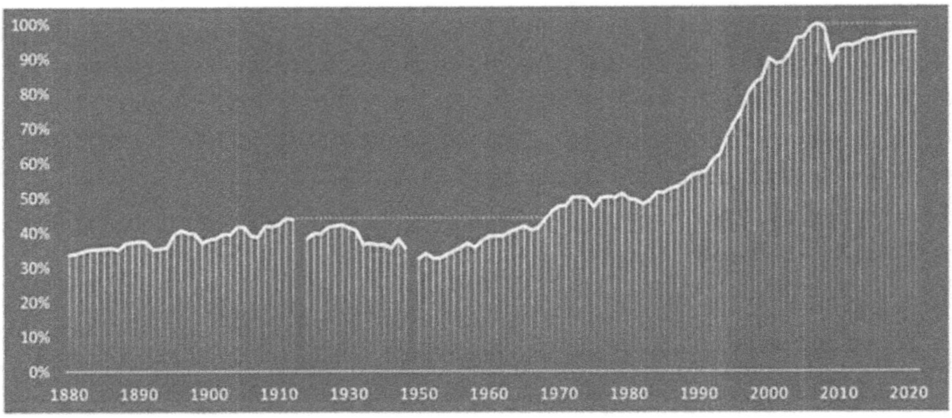

KOF Globalization Index

For the measurement of deglobalization inverse of globalization index and this index work as show opposite association between globalization and deglobalization. Basically, the KOF index comprises three items like social, economic, and political dimensions. Table 1 shows the basic structure of the KOF globalization index. KOF globalization index shows that the USA and developed countries implemented trade barriers on imported products. If the KOF globalization index will increase then economic growth also increased. Economic globalization includes financial and trade globalization. Although, Figge and Martesns (2014) have suggested two more dimensions like technological and ecological globalization in the Maastricht Globalization index. Technological globalization includes measuring the assess ability of communication technology and ecological globalization is distinct features. As culture globalization is the most problematic dimension to adopt by Saich (2000) and Rosendorf (2000).

Based on the KOF globalization index, we can easily analyze the current scenario of globalization on basis of various aspects so based globalization index interprets deglobalization as the slowness or declining pattern of globalization across the border (e.g., since 2008 economic globalization has not been clear). The trade disputes between US and China are not easy to calculate. Social globalization is not shown an increase during the situation of financial crisis and covid-19 because personal interactions (including tourism and immigration) are decreasing but high-tech product & technical data transfer has increased. Since 2014, the world has experienced a downward trend in trade. Therefore, KOF globalization index shows different dimension and reveal that birth of deglobalization.

Table 1. Basic framework of the KOF globalization index.

Economic Globalization: **Trade globalization** • *Trade in goods & services* **Financial Globalization** • *Foreign direct investment (FDI)* • *Portfolio investment*	**Social Globalization:** **Interpersonal Globalization** • *International voice traffic* • *Transfers* **Information Globalization** • *Patent applications* • *International students* **Cultural Globalization:** • *Trade in cultural goods* • *Trademark applications*	**Political Globalization:** • *Embassies* • *UN peace keeping missions*

Source: Gygli et al., (2018)

Why Import Reduced and Its Share of the GDP

From the period of 1880 -2000, shows that positive trend of world trade excluding 12% negative trend of trade in 2013. Similarly, growth rate found negative less than 7% in 1958, 1972, 1980 and 1982 (Van Bergeijk, 2011). The global economic growth rates were showing a slow trend after 2008 (financial crisis) and world trade in G7 also fall due to deglobalization. This shows that just opposite pattern of globalization and trend of imports can judge the deglobalization at the country level. Higher deglobalization shows that home country import is not increasing. There are many reasons to expand the deglobalization like continuously provide the jobs. The unemployment is major problem in the world but with the help of deglobalization creates new job opportunities which will resolve the job protection issues country by country. Due to the deglobalization countries promote reshoring policies and companies return to their home county may contribute to create new job opportunities. Other reasons of the deglobalization are inequalities in income distribution situation deglobalization is the income divide problem because high correlation between income gap and economies entities which involve in international trade. For the overcome of inequality in various countries implement high tariff and non-tariff barrier (NTBs) for the imported goods and services. This concept was not a new but it protecting international trade. If any nation applies the protective policy receives political and social support, then these policies will strengthen deglobalization.

Figure 3. Volume growth rates of Merchandise imports in World economy (Quarterly). Source: UNCTAD, 2021

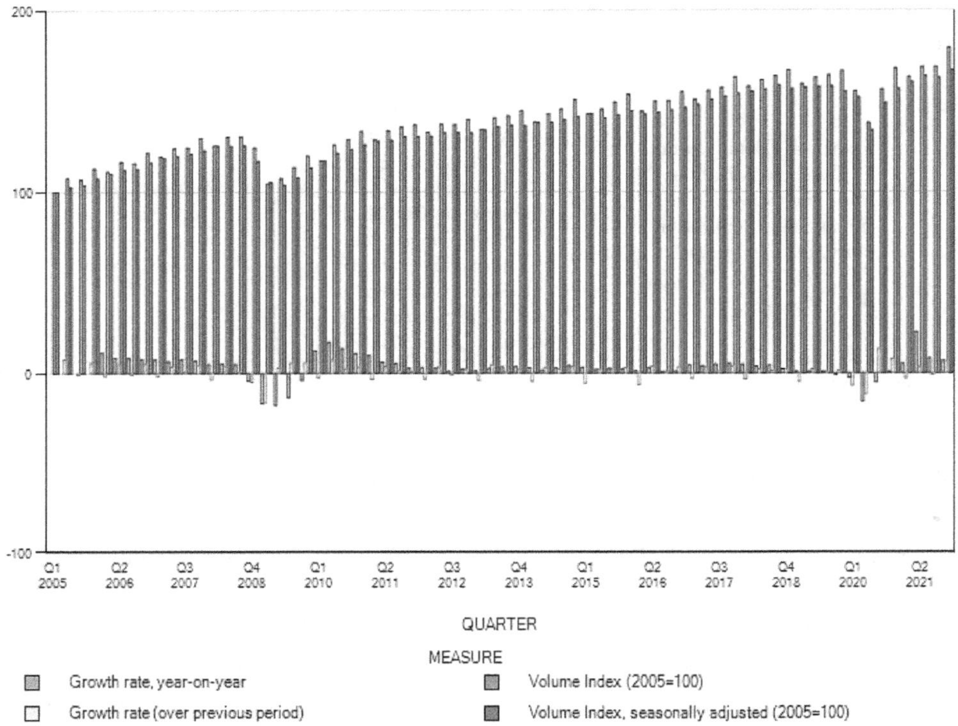

For example, G 7 imports of goods and services trend not changed in positive manner since 2008 due to the financial crisis and then encourage deglobalization. Imports of goods and services include the value of goods and other market services received from the rest of the worlds. They include the value of merchandise, freight, insurance, royalties, travel, etc. but exclude compensation of employees, transfer payment and investment incomes. Figure 3 shows that the trend of growth rate year on year and growth rate where growth rate fall then countries emphasis on the deglobalization (Van Bergeijk, 2019).

RISK OF DEGLOBALIZATION IN WORLD ECONOMY

The covid-19 pandemic exposes the reality of threats and it spreads across the world but governments must work on the basic requirement, not only contain the borders. State run administrations from Europe to the US went to free and clumsy lengths solutions to contain transmission of covid-19. Furthermore, more as of late immunization protectionism has prompted lacking endeavors to inoculate in developing nations. There is big mismatch between global threats and deglobalization during the pandemic and crises

A similar standard applies to different regions. Crime on the level globally can't be actually countered without more coordinated policing and acknowledged norms of equity, Health issues and diseases is never diversified and constrained according to border (Sharma, Kumari & Goel, 2022) and similarly, the environment emergency cannot be met by states laying out their own autonomous objectives without reference to others' exercises. What's more, digital attacks can't be forestalled without all inclusive guidelines of digital cleanliness and worldwide shows to restrict the production of hostile digital weapons.

Regularly a decrease of the degree of global coordination of economies and the world economy at large are supposed to apply second round impacts connected with four input systems: (Peter & Edward Elgar, 2010).

- A decrease in (the rate of growth) worldwide trade will take care adversely into long-run growth.
- Deficiency of association among different economies and co-development of economies.
- Policy of trade assessment in the sense that decreases the global communication and lower development will arouse safeguards and non-economic regions where diminished collaboration among nations and, surprisingly, a rising risk of worldwide clash can be anticipated (Murshed & Mansoob, 2018).

The world economy appears to be a shrink globally after the pandemic, the state administrative and people of nations refuses the barrier free trade in a manner unlike anything seen since the tariff wars and competitive devaluations of the 1930s. Moreover, the result will be more slow development of nations, however a huge fall in public livelihoods for everything except maybe the biggest and most differentiated economies in the world.

Consequences of Deglobalization

There are following consequences of deglobalization: a) tariffs and non- tariff barriers on trade; b) Reshoring policy and decrease in exports; c) GVC reconfiguration and Covid 19; d) Shrinking of foreign investment.

Tariffs and Non-Tariff Barriers on Trade

Due the increase the pandemic situation all the local government wants to encourage locally produced goods and services because of price advantages, guard to local producers and encouraged their services. During the corona virus increase unemployment so government was decided if our manufacture and producer sell our good to the local market then they found the more jobs and fulfill the requirement of local people. During the pandemic situation tariff and non-tariff barrier (quota, licenses, embargoes and sanctions, voluntary export restraints, import deposits etc.) are increased and affect to the international trade. At the time most of the countries start new business and they were expertise in our area and produce goods and services according the local requirements. Therefore, they did not want to trade with other countries which was increased the deglobalization. The appearance of deglobalization such as the appearance protecting the trade led by the USA, the Brexit implementation in the UK and global crisis caused by the coronavirus disease and undetermined risk of the current international order is increasing. In this condition, the different state institutional environments can weaken or reinforce the role of globalization and deglobalization.

Reshoring Policy and Decrease in Exports

All the economies of the globe intermingle economically, socially & politically to form of systematic structure. Deglobalization can be assumed that deter the economic growth of all the economies, increase uncertainty & conflict, and expand the protectionism. But, due to the coronavirus disease, most countries have not fulfilled the demand of exporters and they have produced only for their own country. Handling the division of developing and developed countries and the resulting deglobalization, economies should be pursued policies through international connection and cooperation, based on the various kinds of economies strategies.

GVC Reconfiguration and Covid 19

All the economies are closely related with Global Value Chain (GVC) activities, mainly SMEs & MNEs. The GVC of MNEs is greatly influenced by uncertainty in worldwide business. When coronavirus affect to the economies then GVCs requires rearrangement, which includes huge transaction costs. Most of the businesses are affect by the corporate social responsibility (CSR) and in the case of SMEs, they have required institutional care and fortification which have noteworthy impact. Thus, by the conservation of global & political aspect, through the maintenance of the political and global aspects, the nation can respond to deglobalization for the support of MNEs.

Shrinking of Foreign Investment

As per the UNCTAD, (2020), during 2016- 2019, the inflows of foreign capital were decline as comparison of international trade. In 1990s, FDI inflows experienced the fastest growth in all the developing counties because of the industrial policy and more trade openness polices. FDI inflows increased at the 20% per year but since the 2001 recession was affected to the developed countries due to the Global Financial Crisis (GFC), average growth of FDI was 8% but after recession or GFC only 1% growth. Based on the annual report of UNCTAD (2018, 2019) in various regions FDI records a very low level. In 2017, FDI decreased by 23% and moreover 13% in 2018, in terms of the amount it was falling to less than $ 1300 billion, which was recorded lowest level after the GFC. Due to reduction of FDI flows increase unemployment, disconnection among the countries, fall in international trade, increase transportation cost etc. Thus, tried to find deeper cause of FDI fall and starting to analyses who were the highest contributor in FDI inflows. From the developed countries FDI inflows was high to the development of developing counties but after the GFC it was less. Although some countries recorded negative FDI inflows as a result of the withdrawal of investment funds in MNCs because they believed that in deglobalization is better than globalization.

PRINCIPLES OF DEGLOBALIZATION

According to Walden Bello (2018)

- In domestic market production should be centralized either not used export of the production.
- If domestic market provides proper subsidiarity facilities, then domestic production should be enhanced.
- In terms of the industrial policy like tariff, trade and subsidies should be used to revitalize and the reinforce manufacture sectors.

- Economic activity must be emphasis on the growth of economy and upgrade the living standard, encourage the suitable environment and encouraging procreative nation.
- In the property complex should be include all the mixed economy that would be includes the cooperatives, private enterprises, state enterprises and common corporations.
- The local success of the nation should be shown in different field of works. Highest contribution of the government budget to devote into the agriculture then other filed (manufacturing and services)
- Society must be regularly watched to the working of private sector and process of working must be institutionalized.

CONCLUSION

Globalization has its own benefits as the increased flow of capital, better production facilities and prices, sharing of technology and limited resources, exchange between culture and values, increase per capita income, advancement in process and technology, and opening the barriers. But, on the other side, there is the threat of impact of one nation to another nation due to any miss happening and then whole world economy may be in difficulties that's why many nations think that globalization is the inverse concept of globalization. And, deglobalization will help to protect against upcoming difficulties and reduce interdependence but in the future, it will create trade imbalance, high unemployment, and a downfall in trade between countries. Covid-19 is a great and present example that directly tries to implement deglobalization and this situation was very different from 1930 and 2008.

The deglobalization word was heard so many times during the pandemic to make the local economy more defensive and free dependency but it was directly impacting the world economy. Overall deglobalization is not a regular term, it always comes to mind of nations during hard situations, debates between developed and developing countries, and resource allocation; otherwise, globalization is a need of the world for economic, political, and socially development. But still, the world has required taking lots of steps for planning to make a balance between globalization and deglobalization debate. That will demonstrate to need work on basic problem difficulties and suggest and create a new model of solution to overcoming these difficulties to maintain imbalance among the nations. This study will benefits the future researchers to provide needed material in doing research, and will guide them in understanding the risk of deglobalisation on international trade and also help to understanding the basic difference on deglobalisation and globalization on world economy.

REFERENCES

Arriola, C., Kowalski, P., & van Tongeren, F. (2021). *The impact of COVID-19 on directions and structure of international trade*. Academic Press.

BelloW. (2018). https://systemicalternatives.org/2014/05/09/what-is-to-be-done-the-six-pillars-of-deglobalization/

Figge, L., & Martens, P. (2014). Globalisation Continues: The Maastricht Globalisation Index Revisited and Updated. *Globalizations*, *7731*(April), 1–19. doi:10.1080/14747731.2014.887389

Hoekman, B. (2015). The Global Trade Slowdown: A New Normal? European University Institute.

Jones, G. (2005). *Multinationals and Global Capitalism: From the Nineteenth to the Twenty First Century*. Oxford University Press.

Kim, H. M., Li, P., & Lee, Y. R. (2020). *Observations of deglobalization against globalization and impacts on global business*. International Trade, Politics and Development. doi:10.1108/ITPD-05-2020-0067

Kumari, R., & Sharma, A. (2021). Impact of COVID-19 on International Trade: New Evidence from Economic Sectors. In Impact of Global Issues on International Trade (pp. 233-248). IGI Global.

Murshed, S. M. (2018). *Challenges to the liberal peace*. BLISS.

New York University Department of Sociology. (2013). *The Sociology Project*. Pearson.

Rosendorf, N. M. (2000). *Governance in a Globalizing World, Social and Cultural Globalization: Concepts, History, and Americas Role*. Brookings Institution Press.

Saich, T. (2000). Globalization, Governance, and the Authoritarian Westphalian State: The Case of China. *Global Governance*, 208–228.

Sharma, A., Kumari, R., & Goel, N. (2022). Universal Health Coverage (UHC): Case Study on World's Health Emerging Strategy After the COVID-19 Pandemic. In Handbook of Research on Global Networking Post COVID-19 (pp. 328-341). IGI Global.

The KOF Globalisation Index – Revisited - ETH Z. (n.d.) https://ethz.ch/content/dam/ethz/special-interest/dual/kof dam/documents/Globalization/2018/KOF_Globalisation%20Index_Revisited.pdf

UNCTAD. (2018). *World Investment Report, Investment and New Industrial Policies*. United nations.

UNCTAD. (2019). *World Investment Report, Beyond Uncertainty*. United nations.

UNCTAD. (2020). *World Investment Report, Reducing inequality*. United nations.

UNCTAD. (2020). *World Investment Report, Road to Recovery*. United nations.

Van Bergeijk, G. (2011). On the brink of deglobalization: An alternative perspective on the causes of the world trade collapse. *Journal of Economic Literature*, *49*(3), 747–749.

Chapter 10
Impacts on Economic Foundations During Globalization:
A Cross-Country Empirical Study (1996-2015)

Debasish Roy
https://orcid.org/0000-0002-0706-9743
Sikkim University, India

ABSTRACT

After three decades of disintegration of the former Union of Soviet Socialist Republics (USSR) and former socialist nations from the Eastern Bloc, the burning issue related to apparent success or failure of globalization and economic transition still persists. This chapter is aimed at formulation of Index of Economic Foundation (IEF) that would help to assess the impact of globalization on a country and how far it has been successful in adapting the model of market economy. In order to serve the purpose, a time series study has been conducted on 10 sample countries spread across Central and Eastern Europe and the independent nation-states that evolved from the disintegration of erstwhile USSR for the time period of 20 years (1996 – 2015) (Base Year = 1995: IEF = 100). The final estimations based on the estimated Present Values (PV) of IEFs' discounted by the values of Gini Coefficient (GIC) on a year-to-year basis for all the sample countries yielded interesting results and findings. The issues of deglobalization and reglobalization were also discussed in reference to year 2020.

DOI: 10.4018/978-1-6684-5950-8.ch010

INTRODUCTION

Globalization has been regarded as an indispensable medium of transition from planned to market economy. However, it has been subjected to a mixed bag of reactions among the scholars. Scholars like Nobel laureate economist Joseph Stiglitz (2008), Brown (2008), and De Soto (2008) had been critical of globalization on the grounds of disastrous outcomes of market liberalization in South America and Sub-Saharan Africa, abject failure in improving the conditions of the poor accompanied by an increase in the quantum of absolute poverty across the world in the aftermath of globalization, and lack of both adequate infrastructural framework and governmental effectiveness required for 'mitigating' the adverse effects of transition respectively.

Collier's (2008) work pointed to the fact that 5 billion people's income had increased in the developing countries due to globalization; however, at the same time about 1 billion people in the poorest parts of Africa and some other "land-locked" countries suffered the worst as the fallout of globalization.

Bhagwati's (2008) support for globalization came with a caution that the fruits of globalization may be achieved if the glaring issues of gender discrimination, poverty alleviation and exploitation of children as laborers were handled as top priorities.

The focal point of this research is centered around the formulation of an index, formally termed as Index of Economic Foundation (IEF); based on *six* independent variables (regressors) which would help to provide us a *normative* view about how a country that has adopted economic transition has been able to perform on the major economic grounds in a holistic sense. The choice of variables and the rational reasons for choices are as follows:

1. **Change in GDP** – A high level of growth in the level of GDP (in current US$) on an annual basis would imply that globalization has helped to boost the economic growth of the country in transition *per se*;
2. **Ratio of Trade to GDP** – The ratio of Trade to GDP acts as a major indicator (variable) in deriving the IEF of a country as a greater share of trade in GDP for the said country indicates that it is becoming more 'globalized' and transitioning towards market economy;
3. **Ratio of FDI to Gross Domestic Product** – The FDI to GDP ratio (FDIGDP) acts an indicator of the given economy's strength in terms of a *preferred destination* for attracting foreign investments to foster economic growth;
4. **Ratio of Gross Capital Formation to GDP** – Since private (physical) capital formation is essential for the growth of *gross* investment of a given economy, hence the ratio of gross capital formation to GDP plays the role of a major indicator in determining the strength of the economic foundation of an economy in transition;

5. **Product Concentration Index** – The Product Concentration Index (PCI) which is also referred to as 'The Herfindahl - Hirschmann Index (Product HHI)' is used to measure the level of 'concentration' of products that are generally produced by a country. The values of normalized HHI ranges between 0 and 1;
6. **Product Diversification Index** – The Product Diversification Index (PDI) is computed by measuring the absolute deviation of the trade structure of a country from world structure. The diversification index ranges between 0 and 1. A value closer to 1 indicates greater divergence from the world pattern; and
7. **Gini coefficient** – The Gini coefficient (GIC) measures the extent of deviation between the existing and perfectly equal distributions of income among the individuals or households within an economy. It ranges between 0 to 100 where 0 refers to perfect equality and 100 refers to perfect inequality.

The PCI and PDI are used to formulate the Index of Economic Foundation (IEF) in order to analyze the effects of globalization on the levels of creativity and innovation for the economies in transition. For instance, a country characterized by a combination of lower value of PCI and higher value of PDI could be cited as an ideal example of the success story of economic transition. The inclusion of Gini coefficient is associated with a specific objective. A country in the transitional phase of globalization may experience high growth rates of economy, however, it is also necessary to peruse whether the effects of economic growth percolates to the most underprivileged and vulnerable sections of the society from the viewpoint of a development economist. Hence first, the IEF is estimated as the sum (difference) of *Weighted Arithmetic Mean* of the *Relative Changes (RC)* of *six* variables with reference to the Base Year IEF = 100 (**Base Year = 1995**) and (from) 100, i.e., the sum of the relative changes in Gross Domestic Product, Trade to GDP, Ratio of FDI to Gross Domestic Product, Formation of Gross Capital as a percentage of GDP, PCI, and PDI respectively. They are termed as Gross Domestic Product Relative Change (GDPRC), Trade to GDP Relative Change (TGDPRC), Relative Change in the Ratio of FDI to Gross Domestic Product (FDIGDPRC), Relative Change in the Formation of Gross Capital as a percentage of GDP (GCFRC), Relative Change in PCI (PCIRC), and Relative Change in PDI (PDIRC) respectively. The estimated IEFs' are then *discounted* by the Gini Coefficient (GIC) on a year-to-year basis to derive the Index of Economic Foundation Present Value (s) (IEFPV) of each sample country respectively to judge the *actual* scenario related to the countries' performances over the time period of 20 years (1996 – 2015).

LITERATURE REVIEW

Although the transitional phase of planned to liberalized economy has been characterized by phases of short and long-run turbulences like stagflation and economic recession, a group of scholars have expressed their support in favor of globalization subject to given conditions, e.g., Dollar *et al.* (2008) have opined that a country's investment climate is positively correlated to trade liberalization by virtue of an empirical study; Schultz's (2008) cross – country study showed that trade liberalization was strongly correlated to the upliftment of women's socio-economic status; Fan Gang's (2008) research work pointed out that China's success story of transition was completely reliant on internal institutional reforms and it specifically emphasized on the effectiveness of government policies that must be country-specific and *not* universally replicable.

De Melo *et al.* (2001) in their research work have suggested that the success of transition is primarily dependent on the pre-transition conditions, clusters of economies (homogenous or heterogenous), and other related factors. The study by Hoskisson *et al.* (2000) has projected that the progress rates of the economies in transition were divergent in manner; under these circumstances, the major onus was on the respective policymakers to formulate and implement productive market-based strategies.

The research by Lin *et al.* (2014) exhibited a *positive weak* correlation between Trade to GDP ratio and Government Expenditure to GDP (G ¤ Y) ratio (ranging between 0.1 to 0.2) for the Small Developing Countries (SDC).

By using quintile regression method, Perugini and Selezneva (2015) showed that the labor deregulation policy had helped in appreciating the level of inequality in the allocation of salaries at the middle and top levels of management while reducing the level of inequality at the bottom level of corporate sectors for a sample of ten sample countries under transition dating back to pre-2007 era till 2009.

Babecky and Havranek's (2014) study for a sample of twenty-six countries in the Central Asian and East European regions illustrated that despite their short-run externalities, the structural reforms had a positive effect on economic growths in the long run.

Trends in labor share, capital intensity in production and Total Factor Productivity (TFP) for the economies in transition during the time period 1990 – 2010 exhibited contrasting results in comparison to the countries that belonged to EU – 15, the OECD, and the Rest of the World respectively (Refer to Figures: 1 – 3) (Rincon-Aznar *et al.*, 2015) as below:

Figure 1. Labor share dynamics in transition economies (1990 – 2010)
[Sources: Penn World Tables; Rincon-Aznar et al., 2015; p. 60]

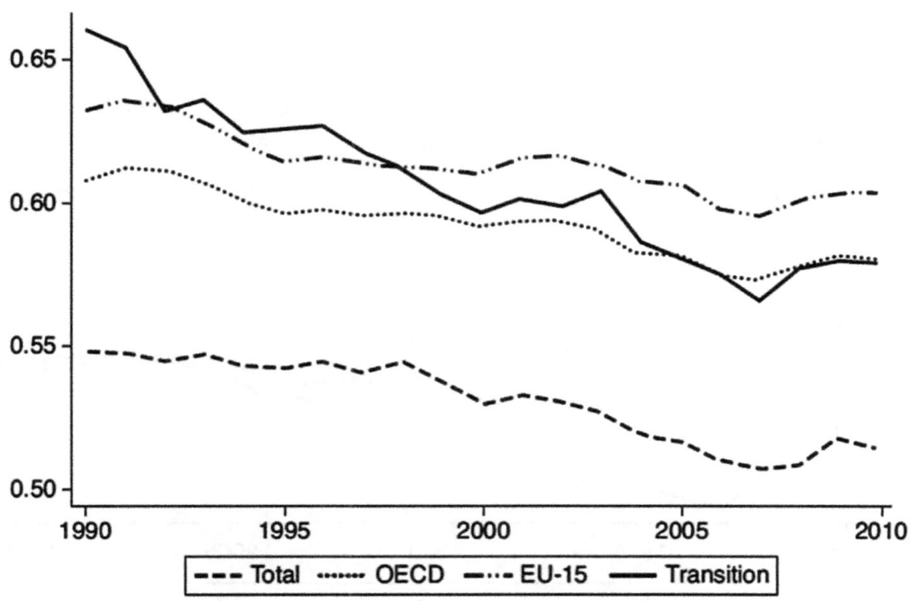

Figure 2. Real Capital to GDP ratio (1990 – 2010)
[Sources: Penn World Tables; Rincon-Aznar et al., 2015; p. 67]

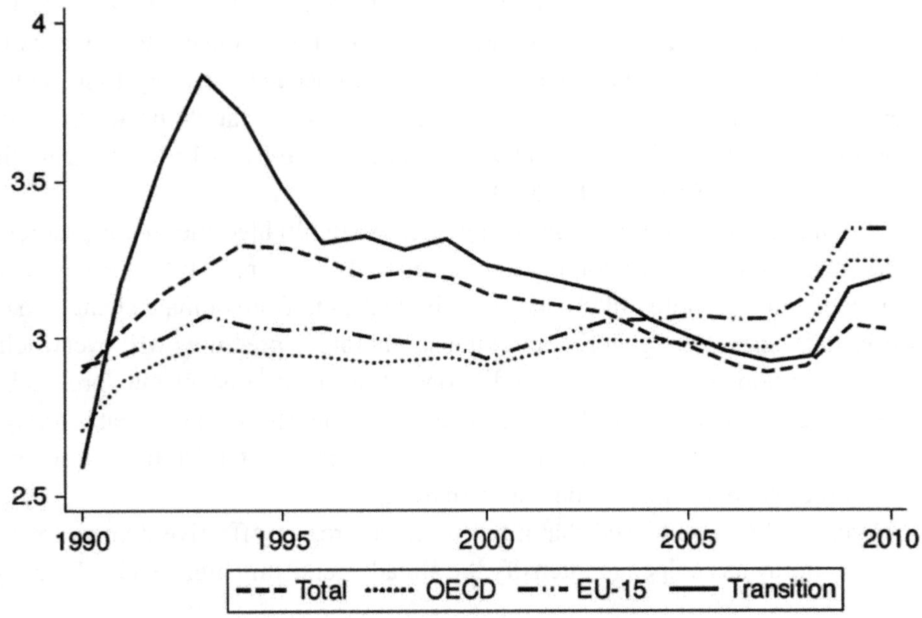

Figure 3. Relative Total Factor Productivity (TFP) (1990 – 2010)
[Sources: Penn World Tables; Rincon-Aznar et al., 2015; p. 68]

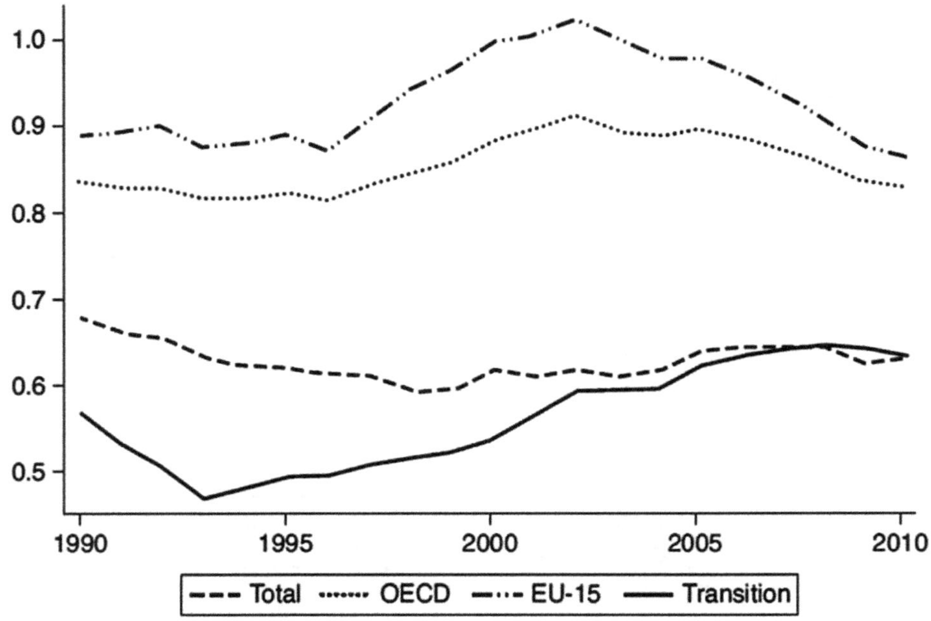

The share of labor to output (GDP) ratio declined steadily in the transition phase as compared to EU – 15 countries within the time period 1990 – 2010 due to capital-deepening of the production processes. On the other hand, the share of real capital to GDP ratio for the economies in transition rose sharply during the period 1990 – 1993, however; it fell at a rapid pace during the reconstruction phase and stabilized below 3 percent per annum during the last decade of twenty-first century whereas the relative Total Factor Productivity (TFP) level caught up with the rest of the world during 2000 – 2010 but was well below the EU – 15 level during the entire tenure of 20 years (1990 – 2010).

Hirst and Thompson (2019) have specifically highlighted the major problems of globalization in the forthcoming days as quoted (2019, p. 21): "This may seem pessimistic but it is highly likely that a crisis stemming from climate change, mass poverty in the developing world, and intense migratory pressures will overwhelm global institutions of governance and cooperation in the distant but foreseeable future, sometime in the second half of this century". They have opined that in today's turbulent times, nation states might become more salient to stand as barriers against global forces beyond supranational governance.

Akyüz (2018) has showed that a fall in the aggregate effective demand of the global economy has helped to intensify the already persisting high levels of income inequality where the surplus economies are unwilling to expand and the deficit economies are characterized by sporadic credit booms.

Perraton (2019) has pointed out that the current global scenario; although quite bleak in nature, is unlikely to experience a collapse of global integration as well as a reversal of the structural changes of the world as quoted (2019, p. 72): "Nevertheless, the inequalities generated by 'actually existing globalisation' should be addressed, as recent interventions including Michie (2017) and UNCTAD (2016) do. Moving on from the 'crisis of globalisation' is likely to require a shift towards a more multi-polar architecture for the global economy, reflecting the shifts in global economic activity".

According to Jean (2020), COVID-19 pandemic has helped to highlight two important strategic domains of health and infrastructure. Elliott *et al.* (2020) have emphasized on three major areas of globalization and cooperation, the green transition and pricing carbon externalities, and the issues related to uncertainty and timing respectively in order to become well-prepared to face future global crises. The pandemic caused a rupture in the global supply chain and the lockdowns across the world proved to be a strategic measure full of uncertainties in policy-making (Elliott *et al.*, 2020; p. 1209). Finally, Bonadio *et al.* (2021) in their empirical study consisting of 64 countries across the globe have suggested that one-fourth of the model-implied real GDP fall is due to disruptions of the global supply chains. The "renationalization" policy of global supply policy did not help to mitigate the problem and become resilient in terms of domestic contraction of labor force.

Hence a comprehensive analysis of the relevant research works helps us to realize that economic transition supported by globalization possesses the quality of a 'double-edged sword' which should be implemented with extreme care and caution depending on country–specific, internal frameworks for its successful implementation.

Descriptions and Definitions of Data (Variables)

In order to formulate the Index of Economic Foundation (IEF) and the Index of Economic Foundation Present Value (IEFPV) respectively, the descriptions of relevant data (variables) are given below:

1. Trade

"International merchandise trade measures the value of goods which add or subtract from the stock of material resources of an economy by entering or leaving its territory (United Nations, 2011). Unless otherwise stated in country notes, the value of exports is recorded as the free-on-board value (FOB), whereas the value of imports includes the cross-border insurance and freight costs from the exporting to the importing economy (so-called CIF value)" [United Nations Conference on Trade and Development (UNCTAD, n. d.)];

2. Gross Domestic Product (GDP) (Current US$)

"GDP at purchaser's prices is the sum of gross value added by all resident producers in the economy plus any product taxes and minus any subsidies not included in the value of the products. It is calculated without making deductions for depreciation of fabricated assets or for depletion and degradation of natural resources. Data are in current U.S. dollars. Dollar figures for GDP are converted from domestic currencies using single year official exchange rates. For a few countries where the official exchange rate does not reflect the rate effectively applied to actual foreign exchange transactions, an alternative conversion factor is used" (The World Bank, n. d.);

3. Foreign Direct Investment (FDI)

"Foreign direct investment refers to direct investment equity flows in the reporting economy. It is the sum of equity capital, reinvestment of earnings, and other capital. Direct investment is a category of cross-border investment associated with a resident in one economy having control or a significant degree of influence on the management of an enterprise that is resident in another economy. Ownership of 10 percent or more of the ordinary shares of voting stock is the criterion for determining the existence of a direct investment relationship. Data are in current U.S. dollars" (The World Bank, n. d.);

4. Trade to GDP Ratio (TGDP)

"Trade is the sum of exports and imports of goods and services measured as a share of gross domestic product" (The World Bank, n. d.);

5. Gross Capital Formation (GCF)

The Gross Capital Formation as per the World Bank definition is the "Annual growth rate of gross capital formation based on constant local currency. Aggregates are based on constant 2010 U.S. dollars. Gross capital formation (formerly gross domestic investment) consists of outlays on additions to the fixed assets of the economy plus net changes in the level of inventories. Fixed assets include land improvements (fences, ditches, drains, and so on); plant, machinery, and equipment purchases; and the construction of roads, railways, and the like, including schools, offices, hospitals, private residential dwellings, and commercial and industrial buildings.

Inventories are stocks of goods held by firms to meet temporary or unexpected fluctuations in production or sales, and 'work in progress.' According to the 1993 SNA, net acquisitions of valuables are also considered capital formation." (The World Bank, n. d.);

6. Product Concentration Index (PCI)

As per the definition of UNCTAD, the Product Concentration Index or Herfindahl - Hirschmann Index (Product HHI) may be defined as a measure of the degree of product concentration. The values of normalized HHI fall between the range of 0 to 1.

It may be estimated by using the formula below:

$$H_j = \sqrt{\sum_{i=1}^{n} (x_{ij} / X)^2}$$

where H_j= Country or Country Group Index j,

x_{ij}= Value of export for country j and product i,
X = Gross value of trade for Country or Country Group Index j, and
n = Number of exportable products produced by the country (SITC Revision 3) respectively.

When the index values are closer to 1, they indicate that a country's trade pattern (exports or imports or both) is heavily skewed towards a few products. On the other hand, when the index value gets closer to 0; it implies that the country's trade pattern (exports or imports or both) is more secular in nature and uniformly distributed among a series of products" [United Nations Conference on Trade and Development (UNCTAD, n. d.)];

7. Product Diversification Index (PDI)

As per the definition of UNCTAD, the Product Diversification Index may be defined as: "The diversification index is computed by measuring the absolute deviation of the trade structure of a country from world structure:

$$DX_j = \sum_i | h_{ij} - h_j | / 2$$

where h_{ij}= The share of trade (exports or imports or both) for product i in case of a country or country group j,

h_i = The share of trade (exports or imports or both) for product i out of total global trade (exports or imports or both).

The range of values of PDI is between 0 and 1. When the value of PDI of a country gets closer to 1, it contemplates that country's greater diversification in production compared to the world pattern.

PDI is a modified version of Finger and Kreinin's (1979) measure of similarity in trade" [United Nations Conference on Trade and Development (UNCTAD, n. d.)]; and

8. Gini Coefficient (GIC)

The standard definition of the Gini Coefficient (GIC) is as follows: "The Gini coefficient is based on the comparison of cumulative proportions of the population against cumulative proportions of income they receive, and it ranges between 0 in the case of perfect equality and 1 in the case of perfect inequality" [Organisation for Economic Co – Operation and Development (OECD, n. d.)]. According to another definition (Abridged and truncated): "Gini index measures the extent or proportion to which the distribution of income among individuals or households within an economy deviates from a perfectly equal distribution" (The World Bank, n. d.).

METHODICAL PROCEDURES

The 'methodical procedures' section is primarily divided into *four* steps as follows:

1. To start off, the *first* step consists of calculation of the Foreign Direct Investment to GDP ratio (FDIGDP) for 10 sample countries that had undergone transition from planned to market economy (1995 – 2015),
2. The *second* part consists of estimations of Gross Domestic Product Relative Change (GDPRC), Trade to GDP Relative Change (TGDPRC), FDI to GDP Relative Change (FDIGDPRC), GCF Relative Change (GCFRC), PCI Relative Change (PCIRC), and PDI Relative Change (PDIRC) respectively for the time period 1996 – 2015 (**Fixed Base Year = 1995**).

For example, in case of *positive* values for both the *base* and *current* years, the traditional procedure has been applied:

$$TGDPRC_1 = [(TGDPR_{1996} - TGDPR_{1995}) / TGDPR_{1995}] \times 100$$
$$TGDPRC_2 = [(TGDPR_{1997} - TGDPR_{1995}) / TGDPR_{1995}] \times 100$$
, ..., and so on;

$$FDIGDPRC_1 = [(FDIGDP_{1996} - FDIGDP_{1995}) / FDIGDP_{1995}] \times 100$$
$$FDIGDPRC_2 = [(FDIGDP_{1997} - FDIGDP_{1995}) / FDIGDP_{1995}] \times 100$$
, ..., and so on; (Das, 2008);

3. 3. The *third* part comprises of estimation of Relative Changes (RC) in IEF (IEFRC) for each sample country on a year-to-year basis for the time period (1996 – 2015). The IEFRC is computed as the '*Weighted Arithmetic Mean* (WAM) (Roy, 2020)' of the relative changes of the six variables by allotting 16.7 percent (approximately) weightage to each of them. Formally,

IEFRC = 0.167(*GDPRC* + *TGDPRC* + *FDIGDPRC* + *GCFRC* + *PCIRC* + *PDIRC*)

Once the IEFRCs' are enumerated on a yearly basis for the sample countries, the annual IEFs' are computed by simply adding (subtracting) the values of IEFRCs' to (from) 100 (Since IEF for the **Base Year: 1995 = 100**).

Formally, *IEF* = 100 ± *IEFRC*; (Roy, 2020)

Table 1. Estimation of missing observations of Gini Coefficients (Country: Armenia)

Year	GIC (y)	x	x * y	x * x
1999	36.2	-10	-362	100
2001	35.4	-8	-283.2	64
2002	34.8	-7	-243.6	49
2003	33	-6	-198	36
2004	37.5	-5	-187.5	25
2005	36	-4	-144	16
2006	29.7	-3	-89.1	9
2007	31.2	-2	-62.4	4
2008	29.2	-1	-29.2	1
2009	28	0	0	0
2010	30	1	30	1
2011	29.4	2	58.8	4
2012	29.6	3	88.8	9
2013	30.6	4	122.4	16
2014	31.5	5	157.5	25
2015	32.4	6	194.4	36
2016	32.5	7	227.5	49
2017	33.6	8	268.8	64
2018	34.4	9	309.6	81
	615	**-1**	**-141.2**	**589**
	x = (Year - 2009)			
	GIC (y) = 32.36 - 0.185x			
	GIC for the year 1996 = 34.8			
	GIC for the year 1997 = 34.6			
	GIC for the year 1998 = 34.4			
	GIC for the year 2000 = 34			

Table 2. Estimation of missing observations of Gini Coefficients (Country: Belarus)

Year	GIC (y)	x	x * y	x * x
1998	32	-10	-320	100
1999	31.7	-9	-285.3	81
2000	31.2	-8	-249.6	64
2001	30.6	-7	-214.2	49
2002	30.3	-6	-181.8	36
2003	28.8	-5	-144	25
2004	26.5	-4	-106	16
2005	27.6	-3	-82.8	9
2006	28.3	-2	-56.6	4
2007	29.6	-1	-29.6	1
2008	27.8	0	0	0
2009	27.7	1	27.7	1
2010	28.6	2	57.2	4
2011	27.2	3	81.6	9
2012	26.5	4	106	16
2013	26.6	5	133	25
2014	27.2	6	163.2	36
2015	25.6	7	179.2	49
2016	25.3	8	202.4	64
2017	25.4	9	228.6	81
2018	25.2	10	252	100
	589.7	**0**	**-239**	**770**
	x = (Year - 2008)			
	GIC (y) = 28 + 0.31x			
	GIC for the year 1996 = 24.3			
	GIC for the year 1997 = 24.6			

Table 3. Estimation of missing observations of Gini Coefficients (Country: Bulgaria)

Year	GIC (y)	x	x * y	x * x
1992	30.7	-19	-583.3	361
2006	35.7	-5	-178.5	25
2007	36.1	-4	-144.4	16
2008	33.6	-3	-100.8	9
2009	33.8	-2	-67.6	4
2010	35.7	-1	-35.7	1
2011	34.3	0	0	0
2012	36	1	36	1
2013	36.6	2	73.2	4
2014	37.4	3	112.2	9
2015	38.6	4	154.4	16
2016	40.6	5	203	25
2017	40.4	6	242.4	36
	469.5	**-13**	**-289.1**	**507**
	x = (Year - 2011)			
	GIC (y) = 36.48 + 0.365x			
	GIC for the year 1996 = 31			
	GIC for the year 1997 = 31.4			
	GIC for the year 1998 = 31.7			
	GIC for the year 1999 = 32.1			
	GIC for the year 2000 = 32.4			
	GIC for the year 2001 = 32.8			
	GIC for the year 2002 = 33.2			
	GIC for the year 2003 = 33.6			
	GIC for the year 2004 = 34			
	GIC for the year 2005 = 34.3			

Table 4. Estimation of missing observations of Gini Coefficients (Country: Czech Republic)

Year	GIC (y)	x	x * y	x * x
1992	20.7	-33	-683.1	1089
1993	26.6	-31	-824.6	961
1996	25.8	-25	-645	625
2002	26.6	-13	-345.8	169
2004	27.5	-9	-247.5	81
2005	26.9	-7	-188.3	49
2006	26.7	-5	-133.5	25
2007	26	-3	-78	9
2008	26.3	-1	-26.3	1
2009	26.2	1	26.2	1
2010	26.6	3	79.8	9
2011	26.4	5	132	25
2012	26.1	7	182.7	49
2013	26.5	9	238.5	81
2014	25.9	11	284.9	121
2015	25.9	13	336.7	169
2016	25.4	15	381	225
2017	24.9	17	423.3	289
	467	**-46**	**-1087**	**3978**
	x = 2 × (Year - 2008.5)			
	GIC (y) = 26.016 + 0.028 (x + 0.5)			
	GIC for the year 1997 = 26.6			
	GIC for the year 1998 = 25.4			
	GIC for the year 1999 = 25.5			
	GIC for the year 2000 = 25.5			
	GIC for the year 2001 = 25.6			
	GIC for the year 2003 = 25.7			

Table 5. Estimation of missing observations of Gini Coefficients (Country: Estonia)

Year	GIC (y)	x	x * y	x * x
1993	39.5	-33	-1303.5	1089
2003	37.2	-13	-483.6	169
2004	33.6	-11	-369.6	121
2005	33.4	-9	-300.6	81
2006	33.7	-7	-235.9	49
2007	31.2	-5	-156	25
2008	31.9	-3	-95.7	9
2009	31.4	-1	-31.4	1
2010	32	1	32	1
2011	32.5	3	97.5	9
2012	32.9	5	164.5	25
2013	35.1	7	245.7	49
2014	34.6	9	311.4	81
2015	32.7	11	359.7	121
2016	31.2	13	405.6	169
2017	30.4	15	456	225
	533.3	**-18**	**-903.9**	**2224**
	x = 2 × (Year - 2009.5)			
	GIC (y) = 34.1 + 0.682 (x + 0.5)			
	GIC for the year 1996 = 16			
	GIC for the year 1997 = 17.4			
	GIC for the year 1998 = 18.8			
	GIC fro the year 1999 = 20.1			
	GIC for the year 2000 = 21.1			
	GIC for the year 2001 = 22.8			
	GIC for the year 2002 = 24.2			

Table 6. Estimation of missing observations of Gini Coefficients (Country: Kazakhstan)

Year	GIC (y)	x	x * y	x * x
1996	35.4	-25	-885	625
2001	36	-15	-540	225
2002	34.8	-13	-452.4	169
2003	33.7	-11	-370.7	121
2004	31.8	-9	-286.2	81
2005	39.8	-7	-278.6	49
2006	30.2	-5	-151	25
2007	30.1	-3	-90.3	9
2008	28.5	-1	-28.5	1
2009	28.2	1	28.2	1
2010	28	3	84	9
2011	28	5	140	25
2012	28.2	7	197.4	49
2013	27.1	9	243.9	81
2014	27	11	297	121
2015	26.8	13	348.4	169
2016	27.2	15	408	225
2017	27.5	17	467.5	289
	548.3	**-8**	**-868.3**	**2274**

x = 2 × (Year - 2008.5)

GIC (y) = 30.34 - 0.275 (x + 0.5)

GIC for the year 1997 = 36.5

GIC for the year 1998 = 36

GIC for the year 1999 = 35.4

GIC for the year 2000 = 35

Table 7. Estimation of missing observations of Gini Coefficients (Country: Kyrgyz Republic)

Year	GIC (y)	x	x * y	x * x
1998	46.4	-21	-974.4	441
2000	31	-17	-527	289
2001	30.2	-15	-453	225
2002	30.3	-13	-393.9	169
2003	28.7	-11	-315.7	121
2004	34.8	-9	-313.2	81
2005	32.6	-7	-228.2	49
2006	37.4	-5	-187	25
2007	33.9	-3	-101.7	9
2008	31.5	-1	-31.5	1
2009	29.9	1	29.9	1
2010	30.1	3	90.3	9
2011	27.8	5	139	25
2012	27.4	7	191.8	49
2013	28.8	9	259.2	81
2014	26.8	11	294.8	121
2015	29	13	377	169
2016	26.8	15	402	225
2017	27.3	17	464.1	289
2018	27.7	19	526.3	361
	618.4	**-2**	**-751.2**	**2740**

x = 2 × (Year - 2008.5)

GIC (y) = 30.9 - 0.252 (x + 0.5)

GIC for the year 1996 = 37
GIC for the year 1997 = 36.6
GIC for the year 1999 = 35.6

Table 8. Estimation of missing observations of Gini Coefficients (Country: Slovenia)

Year	GIC (y)	x	x * y	x * x
1987	23.6	-43	-1014.8	1849
1993	29.2	-31	-905.2	961
1997	24.1	-23	-554.3	529
1999	24	-19	-456	361
2004	24.8	-9	-223.2	81
2005	24.6	-7	-172.2	49
2006	24.4	-5	-122	25
2007	24.4	-3	-73.2	9
2008	23.7	-1	-23.7	1
2009	24.8	1	24.8	1
2010	24.9	3	74.7	9
2011	24.9	5	124.5	25
2012	25.6	7	179.2	49
2013	26.2	9	235.8	81
2014	25.7	11	282.7	121
2015	25.4	13	330.2	169
2016	24.8	15	372	225
2017	24.2	17	411.4	289
	449.3	**-60**	**-1509.3**	**4834**

x = 2 × (Year - 2008.5)

GIC (y) = 24.96 - 0.0025 (x + 0.5)

GIC for the year 1997 = 25
GIC for the year 1998 = 25
GIC for the year 2000 = 25
GIC for the year 2001 = 25
GIC for the year 2002 = 25
GIC for the year 2003 = 25

Table 9. Estimation of missing observations of Gini Coefficients (Country: Ukraine)

Year	GIC (y)	x	x * y	x * x
1992	29.7	-16	-475.2	256
1993	28.9	-15	-433.5	225
1995	39.3	-13	-510.9	169
1996	35.2	-12	-422.4	144
2002	29	-6	-174	36
2003	28.7	-5	-143.5	25
2004	28.9	-4	-115.6	16
2005	29	-3	-87	9
2006	29.8	-2	-59.6	4
2007	27	-1	-27	1
2008	26.6	0	0	0
2009	25.3	1	25.3	1
2010	24.8	2	49.6	4
2011	24.6	3	73.8	9
2012	24.7	4	98.8	16
2013	24.6	5	123	25
2014	24	6	144	36
2015	25.5	7	178.5	49
2016	25	8	200	64
2017	26	9	234	81
2018	26.1	10	261	100
	582.7	**-22**	**-1060.7**	**1270**

x = (Year - 2008)

GIC (y) = 27.37 - 0.361x

GIC for the year 1997 = 31.3
GIC for the year 1998 = 31
GIC for the year 1999 = 30.6
GIC for the year 2000 = 30.2
GIC for the year 2001 = 29.9

4. The *fourth* and final step is divided into *two* sections: first, estimation of *missing observations* for Gini Coefficients (GIC) for 9 out of 10 sample countries (except Russian Federation) with the help of Least Squares method (Das, 2008; Roy, 2022)

(Refer to Tables: 1 – 9), and second; *discounting* of the yearly IEFs' by their respective GICs' in order to enumerate the annual Index of Economic Foundation Present Values (IEFPV) and simultaneously review the sample countries' positions in the era of globalization. Formally,

$$IEFPV_{1996} = \frac{IEF_{1996}}{1+\left(\frac{GIC_{1996}}{100}\right)},\ IEFPV_{1997} = \frac{IEF_{1997}}{1+\left(\frac{GIC_{1997}}{100}\right)},\ \ldots..$$ (Refer to Tables: 10 – 19)

Table 10. Estimation of Index of Economic Foundation (IEF) and Index of Economic Foundation Present Value (IEFPV) (1996–2015) (1996–2015) (Country: Armenia)

Year	GDP	FDI	TGDP	GCF	FDIGDP	PCI	PDI	GDPRC	TGDPRC	FDIGDPRC	GCFRC	PCIRC	PDIRC	IEFRC	IEF	GIC	IEFPV
1995	1.468E+09	25320000	86.1149	20.8086	1.724423	0.128452	0.59708										
1996	1.597E+09	17570000	79.2296	21.0954	1.196608	0.134713	0.59519	8.761836	-7.9954809	-30.608215	1.37865	4.87452	-0.3167	-3.9842	96.0158	34.8	71.2283
1997	1.639E+09	51940000	78.5477	23.2657	3.537382	0.233132	0.65231	11.65791	-8.7872317	105.134281	11.8082	81.4937	9.25087	35.0929	135.093	34.6	100.366
1998	1.894E+09	2.32E+08	71.8425	22.6864	15.82594	0.245654	0.68789	28.97256	-16.573685	817.752765	9.02408	91.2422	15.209	157.604	257.604	34.4	191.67
1999	1.845E+09	1.22E+08	70.5605	20.7689	8.311146	0.345795	0.71164	25.68687	-18.062363	381.966825	-0.1907	169.203	19.1868	96.2983	196.298	36.2	144.125
2000	1.912E+09	1.04E+08	72.2333	21.9223	7.095775	0.299884	0.7214	30.18736	-16.119782	311.486967	5.35242	133.461	20.8226	80.8651	180.865	34	134.974
2001	2.118E+09	69868500	69.8643	22.9044	4.758406	0.224611	0.71421	44.27861	-18.870833	175.941943	10.0717	74.8608	19.6174	50.9833	150.983	35.4	111.509
2002	2.376E+09	1.11E+08	73.9845	25.4183	7.540967	0.363914	0.74681	61.8407	-14.086251	337.303814	22.153	183.308	25.0775	102.6	202.6	34.8	150.296
2003	2.807E+09	1.23E+08	80.0514	28.3479	8.366924	0.391471	0.7755	91.17536	-7.0411653	385.201393	36.2321	204.762	29.882	123.369	223.369	33	167.946
2004	3.577E+09	2.47E+08	73.0706	29.1226	16.83155	0.30614	0.75802	143.586	-15.147471	876.068754	39.9546	138.331	26.9545	201.625	301.625	37.5	219.363
2005	4.9E+09	2.92E+08	70.1397	35.7654	19.8917	0.354888	0.77828	233.7473	-18.550944	1053.52773	71.8784	176.281	30.3488	257.872	357.872	36	263.141
2006	6.384E+09	4.67E+08	61.0301	42.2255	31.77324	0.266182	0.76158	334.8142	-29.129374	1742.54341	102.923	107.223	27.5518	380.988	480.988	29.7	370.846
2007	9.206E+09	6.68E+08	56.975	44.3516	45.47188	0.214486	0.69969	526.9967	-33.838307	2536.9335	113.141	66.9779	17.1863	537.9	637.9	31.2	486.204
2008	1.166E+10	9.44E+08	54.5423	47.9428	64.2731	0.247663	0.70658	694.2452	-36.663278	3627.22377	130.399	92.8065	18.3393	754.392	854.392	29.2	661.294
2009	8.648E+09	7.6E+08	57.2742	41.1451	51.7627	0.217834	0.72033	488.9692	-33.490878	2901.7407	97.7313	69.5844	20.6428	590.863	690.863	28	539.737
2010	9.26E+09	5.29E+08	64.643	38.8148	36.04952	0.225389	0.7394	530.6733	-24.934003	1990.52682	86.5325	75.4662	23.8372	447.017	547.017	30	420.782
2011	1.014E+10	6.53E+08	69.4356	31.9218	44.48764	0.202251	0.7312	590.7302	-19.368648	2479.85686	53.407	57.453	22.4629	530.757	630.757	29.4	487.447
2012	1.062E+10	4.97E+08	75.9667	24.681	33.82353	0.18605	0.69496	623.2306	-11.784394	72.1528546	18.6096	44.8405	16.3938	127.24	227.24	29.6	175.34
2013	1.112E+10	3.46E+08	76.5562	22.1525	23.57068	0.21828	0.74217	657.4293	-11.099898	1266.8736	6.4585	69.9321	24.301	335.649	435.649	30.6	333.575
2014	1.161E+10	4.07E+08	75.6117	21.283	27.69009	0.225091	0.75698	690.6678	-12.196702	1505.7599	2.28017	75.234	26.781	381.421	481.421	31.5	366.1
2015	1.055E+10	1.84E+08	71.5933	20.7305	12.54007	0.251719	0.78449	618.7368	-16.86305	627.203737	-0.375	95.9639	31.3878	226.009	326.009	32.4	246.23

Table 11. Estimation of Index of Economic Foundation (IEF) and Index of Economic Foundation Present Value (IEFPV) (1996 – 2015) (Country: Belarus)

Year	GDP	FDI	TGDP	GCF	FDIGDP	PCI	PDI	GDPRC	TGDPRC	FDIGDPRC	GCFRC	PCIRC	PDIRC	IEFRC	IEF	GIC	IEFPV
1995	1.4E+10	1.5E+07	103.718	24.7498	0.10521	0.49098	0.6984										
1996	1.5E+10	1E+08	96.7749	23.5192	0.74789	0.09506	0.47715	5.612162	-6.69438	610.884354	-4.9722	-80.638	-31.68	82.0853	182.085	24.3	146.489
1997	1.4E+10	3.5E+08	125.516	26.837	2.51634	0.09506	0.47841	1.114545	21.01655	2291.83674	8.43301	-80.638	-31.499	368.377	468.377	24.6	375.905
1998	1.5E+10	2E+08	122.958	26.712	1.45427	0.09538	0.47741	8.941278	18.54979	1282.31293	7.928	-80.573	-31.643	200.919	300.919	32	227.969
1999	1.2E+10	4.4E+08	120.835	23.7068	3.17763	0.11256	0.5036	-13.127	16.5033	2920.40816	-4.2143	-77.074	-27.892	469.101	569.101	31.7	432.119
2000	1.3E+10	1.2E+08	141.609	25.3987	0.85023	0.16996	0.5468	-8.84455	36.53262	708.163265	2.62173	-65.384	-21.707	108.564	208.564	31.2	158.966
2001	1.2E+10	9.6E+07	137.045	23.7609	0.68562	0.14968	0.54329	-11.5787	32.13201	551.70068	-3.9958	-69.514	-22.21	79.4224	179.422	30.6	137.383
2002	1.5E+10	2.5E+08	131.002	22.1769	1.76845	0.16594	0.5232	4.448483	26.30576	1580.95238	-10.396	-66.202	-25.087	251.67	351.67	30.3	269.893
2003	1.8E+10	1.7E+08	134.142	24.9543	1.22954	0.17486	0.5237	27.59038	29.333	1068.70748	0.82638	-64.385	-25.015	172.843	272.843	28.8	211.834
2004	2.3E+10	1.6E+08	142.137	28.6673	1.17229	0.21372	0.5418	65.64007	37.04106	1014.28571	15.8284	-56.471	-22.423	175.65	275.65	26.5	217.905
2005	3E+10	3.1E+08	118.884	28.4605	2.19428	0.2764	0.5701	116.1903	14.62247	1985.71429	14.9927	-43.705	-18.37	344.907	444.907	27.6	348.674
2006	3.7E+10	3.6E+08	124.295	32.1841	2.5557	0.31082	0.58045	164.4755	19.83925	2329.2517	30.038	-36.694	-16.889	415.004	515.004	28.3	401.406
2007	4.5E+10	1.8E+09	128.154	34.0919	12.9345	0.28649	0.57839	224.0424	23.55969	12194.5578	37.7462	-41.65	-17.183	2070.18	2170.18	29.6	1674.52
2008	6.1E+10	2.2E+09	129.599	37.6417	15.6584	0.30877	0.58394	334.8736	24.95347	14783.6735	52.0887	-37.111	-16.389	2523.68	2623.68	27.8	2052.96
2009	5.1E+10	1.9E+09	108.636	36.864	13.4298	0.30226	0.58251	264.0969	4.741164	12665.3061	48.9468	-38.438	-16.594	2154.68	2254.68	27.7	1765.6
2010	5.7E+10	1.4E+09	115.918	40.6564	9.97232	0.24671	0.54296	309.5313	11.76243	9378.91157	64.2695	-49.751	-22.257	1615.41	1715.41	28.6	1333.91
2011	6.2E+10	4E+09	157.974	37.2176	28.6445	0.28973	0.57268	341.9897	52.31103	27127.2109	50.3753	-40.99	-18.001	4585.48	4685.48	27.2	3683.56
2012	6.6E+10	1.5E+09	153.085	35.0943	10.4747	0.29319	0.58527	370.0968	47.59731	9856.46259	41.7962	-40.284	-16.198	1709.91	1809.91	26.5	1430.76
2013	7.6E+10	2.2E+09	119.816	38.798	16.0749	0.24775	0.52304	440.5405	15.52068	15179.5918	56.761	-49.54	-25.11	2602.96	2702.96	26.6	2135.04
2014	7.9E+10	1.9E+09	110.651	34.841	13.326	0.25047	0.53702	464.0568	6.68468	12566.6667	40.773	-48.985	-23.107	2167.68	2267.68	27.2	1782.77
2015	5.6E+10	1.7E+09	115.915	29.0347	11.8252	0.24492	0.55245	304.0366	11.75939	11140.1361	17.3128	-50.115	-20.899	1900.37	2000.37	25.6	1592.65

Table 12. Estimation of Index of Economic Foundation (IEF) and Index of Economic Foundation Present Value (IEFPV) (1996 – 2015) (Country: Bulgaria)

Year	GDP	FDI	TGDP	GCF	FDIGDP	PCI	PDI	GDPRC	TGDPRC	FDIGDPRC	GCFRC	PCIRC	PDIRC	IEFRC	IEF	GIC	IEFPV
1995	1.9E+10	9E+07	55.2627	17.7288	0.47621	0.08762	0.48432										
1996	1.2E+10	1.1E+08	85.8207	1.15736	0.8866	0.08812	0.50839	-35.2367	55.29586	86.1782002	-93.472	0.58127	4.9685	3.05255	103.053	31	78.6661
1997	1.1E+10	5E+08	86.4637	9.72739	4.46095	0.09611	0.49969	-40.3898	56.45951	836.76424	-45.132	9.69596	3.17351	136.762	236.762	31.4	180.184
1998	1.5E+10	5.4E+08	77.0452	18.7086	3.5748	0.08332	0.5028	-20.8215	39.41632	650.680405	5.52685	-4.9073	3.81379	112.285	212.285	31.7	161.188
1999	1.4E+10	8.2E+08	90.075	19.8437	6.00843	0.09581	0.52382	-28.2142	62.99419	1161.72397	11.9294	9.3549	8.15485	204.324	304.324	32.1	230.374
2000	1.3E+10	1E+09	77.7457	19.0461	7.5609	0.12745	0.53228	-30.2238	40.68389	1487.7301	7.43072	45.4696	9.90211	260.165	360.165	32.4	272.028
2001	1.4E+10	8.1E+08	79.0814	21.3511	5.73161	0.11786	0.51383	-25.2844	43.10083	1103.59308	20.4318	34.5168	6.093	197.075	297.075	32.8	223.701
2002	1.6E+10	9E+08	75.2696	20.529	5.51526	0.10508	0.50492	-13.5933	36.2033	1058.16232	15.795	19.9275	4.25311	186.791	286.791	33.2	215.309
2003	2.1E+10	2.1E+09	79.0139	22.0742	9.91625	0.10171	0.48934	11.38727	42.97871	1982.33538	24.5105	16.0885	1.03498	346.389	446.389	33.6	334.124
2004	2.6E+10	3.1E+09	93.0639	23.4334	11.7462	0.10908	0.48712	37.79422	68.40275	2366.60535	32.177	24.4952	0.57668	421.675	521.675	34	389.31
2005	3E+10	4.1E+09	99.7142	27.7397	13.7202	0.12042	0.48555	57.34502	80.43677	2781.13455	56.467	37.4429	0.25397	502.18	602.18	34.3	448.384
2006	3.4E+10	7.9E+09	111.047	32.0563	22.9044	0.15252	0.48494	81.10551	100.9447	4709.73979	80.8154	74.0835	0.12751	841.136	941.136	35.7	693.542
2007	4.4E+10	1.4E+10	123.61	33.6272	31.247	0.13047	0.50344	133.9166	123.6765	6461.63325	89.6759	48.9102	3.9465	1143.63	1243.63	36.1	913.759
2008	5.4E+10	1E+10	124.786	36.9533	18.9142	0.13636	0.48805	186.7729	125.8049	3871.84618	108.437	55.6374	0.76938	724.878	824.878	33.6	617.424
2009	5.2E+10	3.9E+09	92.736	28.5382	7.4937	0.1062	0.45045	173.9206	67.80943	1473.62005	60.9713	21.2066	-6.9949	298.422	398.422	33.8	297.774
2010	5E+10	1.8E+09	103.713	22.521	3.65921	0.11568	0.44545	165.303	87.67279	668.406637	27.0306	32.0295	-8.0262	162.069	262.069	35.7	193.124
2011	5.7E+10	2.1E+09	117.874	21.3587	3.6675	0.12539	0.43264	202.1793	113.2984	670.146596	20.4747	43.1183	-10.672	173.091	273.091	34.3	203.344
2012	5.4E+10	1.8E+09	124.535	21.8863	3.31047	0.13964	0.44411	184.5333	125.351	595.17279	23.4506	59.3753	-8.3028	163.263	263.263	36	193.576
2013	5.6E+10	2E+09	130.118	21.009	3.57797	0.13372	0.48307	192.8433	135.4529	651.345624	18.5022	52.6168	-0.2588	175.084	275.084	36.6	201.379
2014	5.7E+10	1.1E+09	130.632	21.5072	1.92254	0.10527	0.44184	199.6484	136.3846	303.717944	21.3122	20.1496	-8.7723	112.073	212.073	37.4	154.347
2015	5.1E+10	2.2E+09	127.025	20.9933	4.3047	0.09306	0.46537	166.7118	129.8572	803.953874	18.4136	6.21841	-3.9133	186.874	286.874	38.6	206.98

Table 13. Estimation of Index of Economic Foundation (IEF) and Index of Economic Foundation Present Value (IEFPV) (1996 – 2015) (Country: Czech Republic)

Year	GDP	FDI	TGDP	GCF	FDIGDP	PCI	PDI	GDPRC	TGDPRC	FDIGDPRC	GCFRC	PCIRC	PDIRC	IEFRC	IEF	GIC	IEFPV
1995	5.98E+10	2.6E+09	83.895	34.1705	4.29533	0.04459	0.36746										
1996	6.7E+10	1.4E+09	81.4933	36.1061	2.14266	0.04786	0.37439	12.06187	-2.86275	-50.116478	5.66438	7.32269	1.88399	-4.341	95.659	25.8	76.0405
1997	6.18E+10	1.3E+09	85.0742	32.9779	2.08197	0.05776	0.37354	3.373385	1.405583	-51.529526	-3.4901	29.5415	1.65404	-3.1742	96.8258	26.6	76.4817
1998	6.65E+10	3.7E+09	84.6886	30.9406	5.56497	0.0707	0.38144	11.23312	0.94601	29.5585579	-9.4523	58.564	3.80436	15.7756	115.776	25.4	92.3251
1999	6.49E+10	6.3E+09	86.2613	29.826	9.73153	0.07907	0.38604	8.518154	2.820548	126.560533	-12.714	77.3133	5.05429	34.5921	134.592	25.5	107.245
2000	6.16E+10	5E+09	98.2331	31.9463	8.08941	0.08419	0.40691	3.134712	55.14679	88.3302201	-6.5092	88.7987	10.734	39.9392	139.939	25.5	111.505
2001	6.75E+10	5.6E+09	99.31	32.1208	8.35368	0.08745	0.38916	12.9617	18.37419	94.4826942	-5.9985	96.1095	5.90471	36.9724	136.972	25.6	109.054
2002	8.19E+10	8.5E+09	91.526	30.617	10.373	0.1098	0.39269	37.03022	9.09593	141.494853	-10.399	146.239	6.86518	55.0543	155.054	26.6	122.476
2003	9.96E+10	2E+09	95.0152	29.6936	2.02884	0.08987	0.37917	66.6683	13.25496	-52.766387	-13.102	101.554	3.18545	19.7992	119.799	25.7	95.3056
2004	1.19E+11	6.4E+09	113.868	30.0251	5.39052	0.09015	0.40225	99.34886	35.72727	25.4972539	-12.132	102.169	9.46574	43.346	143.346	27.5	112.428
2005	1.36E+11	1.4E+10	122.015	29.5512	10.0749	0.09316	0.3975	127.9868	45.43814	134.554995	-13.518	108.921	8.17337	68.5926	168.593	26.9	132.855
2006	1.55E+11	7.1E+09	127.633	30.3827	4.58756	0.09972	0.40488	160.0786	52.1337	6.80349023	-11.085	123.632	10.1829	56.9575	156.958	26.7	123.881
2007	1.89E+11	1.4E+10	130.373	32.3943	7.3011	0.09665	0.41272	216.5618	55.40017	69.9775454	-5.1981	116.74	12.3172	77.6331	177.633	26	140.979
2008	2.36E+11	8.8E+09	124.289	31.3311	3.7398	0.09216	0.39888	294.3385	48.14816	-12.933495	-8.3095	106.685	8.55036	72.7465	172.747	26.3	136.775
2009	2.06E+11	5.3E+09	113.493	26.8008	2.5568	0.10092	0.40747	244.9228	35.27961	-40.474871	-21.568	126.324	10.8875	59.2285	159.229	26.2	126.172
2010	2.07E+11	1E+10	128.967	27.3599	4.90068	0.10522	0.41185	247.094	53.72447	14.0932551	-19.931	135.959	12.0802	73.8367	173.837	26.6	137.312
2011	2.28E+11	4.2E+09	138.785	27.1909	1.83758	0.10572	0.43627	281.3395	65.42708	-57.219106	-20.426	137.095	18.7252	70.8236	170.824	26.4	135.145
2012	2.07E+11	9.4E+09	147.537	26.3598	4.54883	0.10686	0.43521	246.9243	75.85975	5.90169439	-22.858	139.65	18.4364	77.319	177.319	26.1	140.618
2013	2.09E+11	7.4E+09	147.978	25.0132	3.51361	0.10579	0.43496	250.3137	76.38507	-18.199412	-26.799	137.25	18.3683	72.8864	172.886	26.5	136.669
2014	2.08E+11	8.1E+09	158.727	26.0101	3.89218	0.11292	0.42942	247.6636	89.19726	-9.3858345	-23.881	153.228	16.8608	78.947	178.947	25.9	142.134
2015	1.87E+11	1.7E+09	156.1	27.9832	0.90987	0.11842	0.40617	212.5517	86.06585	-78.817174	-18.107	165.579	10.5333	62.9675	162.968	25.9	129.442

Table 14. Estimation of Index of Economic Foundation (IEF) and Index of Economic Foundation Present Value (IEFPV) (1996 – 2015) (Country: Estonia)

Year	GDP	FDI	TGDP	GCF	FDIGDP	PCI	PDI	GDPRC	TGDPRC	FDIGDPRC	GCFRC	PCIRC	PDIRC	IEFRC	IEF	GIC	IEFPV
1995	4.5E+09	2.1E+08	139.247	26.4111	4.59795	0.08132	0.50519										
1996	4.8E+09	1.7E+08	133.14	27.483	3.46956	0.07403	0.50102	6.27739	-4.38536	-24.541135	4.05848	-8.9674	-0.8269	-4.7308	95.2692	16	82.1286
1997	5.1E+09	2.7E+08	151.248	30.7233	5.32372	0.09327	0.49703	14.44893	8.618946	15.784713	16.3269	14.6938	-1.6165	11.3761	111.376	17.4	94.8689
1998	5.7E+09	6E+08	157.064	31.6245	10.5118	0.11255	0.52065	25.97019	12.7957	128.618768	19.7393	38.3922	3.05904	38.0959	138.096	18.8	116.242
1999	5.8E+09	3.3E+08	143.988	25.9038	5.65585	0.12441	0.55843	28.10746	3.405018	23.0082042	-1.9209	52.9759	10.5374	19.3522	119.352	20.1	99.3773
2000	5.7E+09	4.2E+08	126.329	28.4761	7.30961	0.21792	0.57885	26.5961	-9.27664	58.9755741	7.81856	167.959	14.5798	44.4421	144.442	21.1	119.275
2001	6.3E+09	5.9E+08	126.364	29.5817	9.4722	0.18138	0.55409	39.16192	-9.25175	106.009456	12.0045	123.037	9.67948	46.7734	146.773	22.8	119.522
2002	7.4E+09	3.4E+08	123.243	32.9403	4.58781	0.12161	0.54312	63.91165	-11.4928	-0.2204492	24.7214	49.5349	7.5075	22.327	122.327	24.2	98.492
2003	9.9E+09	1E+09	122.732	35.1972	10.5111	0.12062	0.52922	119.6092	-11.8601	128.6035	33.2667	48.3156	4.75658	53.7819	153.782	37.2	112.086
2004	1.2E+10	1.1E+09	129.994	34.6565	8.94975	0.14025	0.47163	170.0061	-6.64448	94.6467692	31.2193	72.4545	-6.6431	59.1732	159.173	33.6	119.142
2005	1.4E+10	3.1E+09	136.02	33.3572	21.6874	0.14352	0.44565	213.4477	-2.3169	371.6756	26.2999	76.4753	-11.786	112.299	212.299	33.4	159.145
2006	1.7E+10	1.8E+09	136.728	39.8322	10.3347	0.15956	0.48831	278.2345	-1.80879	124.767182	50.8161	96.2078	-3.342	90.8125	190.812	33.7	142.717
2007	2.2E+10	3E+09	134.009	40.0079	13.5133	0.10649	0.45567	399.0321	-3.76157	193.899348	51.4813	30.9461	-9.8019	110.299	210.299	31.2	160.289
2008	2.4E+10	2E+09	136.523	31.635	8.11309	0.09834	0.43932	441.8465	-1.95604	76.4502602	19.7792	20.9285	-13.039	90.6682	190.668	31.9	144.555
2009	2E+10	1.9E+09	116.108	21.0098	9.45242	0.13094	0.41428	338.9703	-16.6171	105.5793	-20.451	61.0097	-17.995	75.0826	175.083	31.4	133.244
2010	2E+10	2.6E+09	142.522	21.6914	13.1629	0.12017	0.42743	337.8475	2.352142	186.278441	-17.87	47.7715	-15.392	90.1645	190.165	32	144.064
2011	2.3E+10	1.1E+09	165.904	25.6781	4.78442	0.14459	0.48361	420.0633	19.14409	4.0555456	-2.7756	77.7906	-4.2723	85.6676	185.668	32.5	140.126
2012	2.3E+10	1.8E+09	169.492	29.3615	7.70648	0.1374	0.47175	415.6429	21.72055	67.6070455	11.1711	68.9592	-6.6203	96.4134	196.413	32.9	147.79
2013	2.5E+10	1.1E+09	165.381	27.1977	4.3446	0.10674	0.45466	461.8585	18.76811	-5.5099187	2.9783	31.2565	-10.003	83.2248	183.225	35.1	135.622
2014	2.7E+10	1.8E+09	159.195	27.0987	6.65453	0.1176	0.45691	495.2539	14.32606	44.7283257	2.60333	44.6075	-9.558	98.6602	198.66	34.6	147.593
2015	2.3E+10	-7E+08	149.842	25.001	-3.1041	0.11586	0.4696	412.4448	7.60876	-167.51109	-5.3393	42.4728	-7.0447	47.1052	147.105	32.7	110.855

Table 15. Estimation of Index of Economic Foundation (IEF) and Index of Economic Foundation Present Value (IEFPV) (1996 – 2015) (Country: Kazakhstan)

Year	GDP	FDI	TGDP	GCF	FDIGDP	PCI	PDI	GDPRC	TGDPRC	FDIGDPRC	GCFRC	PCIRC	PDIRC	IEFRC	IEF	GIC	IEFPV
1995	2E+10	9.6E+08	82.5224	23.3193	4.73243	0.20359	0.73137										
1996	2.1E+10	1.1E+09	71.2736	16.1466	5.40518	0.23026	0.72508	3.244531	-13.6312	14.2158248	-30.758	13.1009	-0.8595	-2.448	97.552	35.4	72.0473
1997	2.2E+10	1.3E+09	72.3596	15.5983	5.9614	0.2708	0.76697	8.793551	-12.3153	25.9690994	-33.11	33.0142	4.8681	4.53661	104.537	36.5	76.5836
1998	2.2E+10	1.2E+09	65.2042	15.8046	5.20166	0.29386	0.81684	8.642936	-20.9861	9.91516177	-32.225	44.3374	11.6867	3.56181	103.562	36	76.1484
1999	1.7E+10	1.6E+09	82.5792	17.7762	9.40678	0.38286	0.82333	-17.1956	0.068762	98.7726045	-23.77	88.0514	12.5737	26.4167	126.417	35.4	93.3654
2000	1.8E+10	1.4E+09	105.7	18.139	7.49247	0.62998	0.57189	-10.2203	28.08605	58.3217229	-22.214	209.432	-21.806	40.2666	140.267	35	103.901
2001	2.2E+10	2.8E+09	92.8491	26.8764	12.7155	0.48288	0.80841	8.728577	12.51377	168.688287	15.2542	137.18	10.5347	58.8166	158.817	36	116.777
2002	2.5E+10	2.6E+09	94.0317	27.2877	10.5067	0.50221	0.80945	20.91991	13.94685	122.014703	17.018	146.674	10.676	55.2082	155.208	34.8	115.14
2003	3.1E+10	2.5E+09	91.4633	25.7039	8.0537	0.52227	0.79283	51.33619	10.83454	70.1810075	10.2261	156.527	8.40338	51.2514	151.251	33.7	113.127
2004	4.3E+10	5.6E+09	96.4092	26.3111	13.0129	0.54827	0.78046	111.7944	16.82791	174.97198	12.8299	169.302	6.71213	82.073	182.073	31.8	138.143
2005	5.7E+10	2.5E+09	97.7625	30.9698	4.45711	0.60536	0.75414	180.3711	18.46783	-5.8177172	32.8077	197.34	3.11434	71.0472	171.047	39.8	122.351
2006	8.1E+10	7.6E+09	91.4535	33.9008	9.39605	0.59877	0.74463	297.5786	10.82266	98.54603	45.3768	194.104	1.81317	108.04	208.04	30.2	159.785
2007	1E+11	1.2E+10	92.1616	35.5267	11.419	0.56861	0.74335	414.6182	11.68074	141.293177	52.3492	179.291	1.63876	133.479	233.479	30.1	179.461
2008	1.3E+11	1.7E+10	94.2948	27.5065	12.6039	0.5911	0.73775	554.9504	14.2657	166.331041	17.9561	190.336	0.87247	157.452	257.452	28.5	200.352
2009	1.2E+11	1.4E+10	75.7661	29.4146	12.3806	0.58642	0.77513	465.9513	-8.18728	161.611559	26.1385	188.036	5.98315	139.922	239.922	28.2	187.147
2010	1.5E+11	7.5E+09	74.1383	25.3735	5.03631	0.62761	0.76599	626.6375	-10.1598	6.42112694	8.80941	208.269	4.73375	140.785	240.785	28	188.113
2011	1.9E+11	1.4E+10	73.1179	22.9981	7.14351	0.60728	0.74889	845.4383	-11.3964	50.9479791	-1.377	198.286	2.39656	180.716	280.716	28	219.309
2012	2.1E+11	1.4E+10	73.7237	25.2297	6.56165	0.59234	0.73763	920.8866	-10.6622	38.6528058	8.19237	190.948	0.85688	191.479	291.479	28.2	227.363
2013	2.4E+11	1E+10	65.4076	24.5696	4.2307	0.65832	0.74659	1061.436	-20.7396	-10.602012	5.36186	223.353	2.08134	210.148	310.148	27.1	244.019
2014	2.2E+11	7.3E+09	64.972	25.7902	3.30063	0.65667	0.74903	986.7392	-21.2674	-30.255046	10.5963	222.544	2.41504	195.129	295.129	27	232.385
2015	1.8E+11	6.6E+09	53.0497	27.9079	3.56737	0.56276	0.79036	805.0047	-35.7148	-24.618582	19.6775	176.416	8.06603	158.138	258.138	26.8	203.579

Table 16. Estimation of Index of Economic Foundation (IEF) and Index of Economic Foundation Present Value (IEFPV) (1996 – 2015) (Country: Kyrgyz Republic)

Year	GDP	FDI	TGDP	GCF	FDIGDP	PCI	PDI	GDPRC	TGDPRC	FDIGDPRC	GCFRC	PCIRC	PDIRC	IEFRC	IEF	GIC	IEFPV
1995	1.66E+09	9.6E+07	71.8243	18.3405	5.785	0.13707	0.69036										
1996	1.83E+09	4.7E+07	87.2958	25.1973	2.58474	0.16641	0.7055	10.0271	21.54078	-55.319953	-55.32	21.406	2.19357	-9.2454	90.7546	35.4	67.027
1997	1.77E+09	8.4E+07	84.4771	21.6801	4.74131	0.19563	0.68594	6.43253	17.61642	-18.041297	-18.041	42.7208	-0.6397	5.00792	105.008	36.5	76.9289
1998	1.65E+09	1.1E+08	94.5093	15.4441	6.63614	0.34448	0.73922	-0.90636	31.58407	14.712812	14.7128	151.317	7.07741	36.4163	136.416	36	100.306
1999	1.25E+09	4.4E+07	99.1995	18.0262	3.55569	0.2583	0.73733	-24.8015	38.11417	-38.536029	-38.536	88.4442	6.80345	5.24805	105.248	35.4	77.7312
2000	1.37E+09	-2360125	89.4309	20.01	-0.1723	0.32743	0.75721	-17.5392	24.51353	-102.97858	-102.98	138.882	9.68392	-8.4029	91.5971	35	67.8497
2001	1.53E+09	5006733	73.7469	17.9993	0.32829	0.34617	0.72691	-8.18186	2.676872	-94.325237	-94.325	152.553	5.29414	-6.0514	93.9486	36	69.0799
2002	1.61E+09	4661964	82.9207	17.6067	0.29035	0.2356	0.69487	-3.33382	15.44946	-94.981012	-94.981	71.8846	0.65341	-17.551	82.4486	34.8	61.1637
2003	1.92E+09	4.6E+07	83.9328	11.83	2.37334	0.26925	0.72738	15.53201	16.85853	-58.97424	-58.974	96.4353	5.36326	2.70677	102.707	33.7	76.8188
2004	2.21E+09	1.8E+08	93.8157	14.4884	7.9338	0.22072	0.70038	33.14328	30.61843	37.144288	37.1443	61.03	1.45243	33.4221	133.422	31.8	101.231
2005	2.46E+09	4.3E+07	95.084	16.4182	1.73012	0.18482	0.70863	48.11683	32.38423	-70.09302	-70.093	34.8388	2.64643	-3.7	96.3	39.8	68.8842
2006	2.83E+09	1.8E+08	120.75	24.1958	6.42244	0.1666	0.70724	70.62837	68.11864	11.018816	11.0188	21.5478	2.44556	30.7963	130.796	30.2	100.458
2007	3.8E+09	2.1E+08	137.058	26.643	5.46787	0.17923	0.70228	128.9298	90.82462	-5.4819668	-5.482	30.7627	1.72699	40.2134	140.213	30.1	107.774
2008	5.14E+09	3.8E+08	146.106	28.949	7.33454	0.2434	0.74557	209.4461	103.4216	26.78534	26.7853	77.5761	7.99726	75.3353	175.335	28.5	136.448
2009	4.69E+09	1.9E+08	133.379	27.2704	4.03784	0.27444	0.7469	182.3606	85.70207	-30.201543	-30.202	100.223	8.1904	52.6789	152.679	28.2	119.094
2010	4.79E+09	4.7E+08	133.233	27.4016	9.86093	0.28525	0.73214	188.6396	85.49837	70.456744	70.4567	108.11	6.05187	88.2022	188.202	28	147.033
2011	6.2E+09	6.9E+08	136.18	25.473	11.0646	0.2901	0.68486	273.1305	89.60143	91.264229	91.2642	111.645	-0.7964	109.351	209.351	28	163.556
2012	6.61E+09	2.6E+08	139.676	34.9611	3.95037	0.28602	0.61697	297.656	94.469	-31.713617	-31.714	108.668	-10.631	71.1226	171.123	28.2	133.481
2013	7.34E+09	6.1E+08	134.027	33.8988	8.34376	0.38666	0.65729	341.5982	86.60376	44.230777	44.2308	182.093	-4.7897	115.661	215.661	27.1	169.678
2014	7.47E+09	3.4E+08	125.126	36.7567	4.59301	0.36779	0.70357	349.6095	74.21156	-20.604841	-20.605	168.325	1.9142	92.1417	192.142	27	151.293
2015	6.68E+09	1.1E+09	110.962	34.6715	17.1312	0.45482	0.67252	302.0532	54.49036	196.13163	196.132	231.816	-2.5836	163.007	263.007	26.8	207.418

Table 17. Estimation of Index of Economic Foundation (IEF) and Index of Economic Foundation Present Value (IEFPV) (1996 – 2015) (Country: Russian Federation)

Year	GDP	FDI	TGDP	GCF	FDIGDP	PCI	PDI	GDPRC	TGDPRC	FDIGDPRC	GCFRC	PCIRC	PDIRC	IEFRC	IEF	GIC	IEFPV
1995	4E+11	2.1E+09	55.1829	25.4389	0.522257	0.25593	0.67308										
1996	3.9E+11	2.6E+09	47.9225	23.6674	0.658454	0.25593	0.67038	-0.96383	-13.157	26.0786663	-6.9637	3.63E-05	-0.4023	0.765328	100.765	46.1	68.9701
1997	4E+11	4.9E+09	47.2569	21.9764	1.201359	0.26195	0.67287	2.374434	-14.3631	130.0322	-13.611	2.350209	-0.0323	17.79174	117.792	38.4	85.1096
1998	2.7E+11	2.8E+09	55.7723	14.9641	1.019119	0.22224	0.67596	-31.4968	1.06799	95.1375934	-41.176	-13.1661	0.42751	1.799003	101.799	38.1	73.714
1999	2E+11	3.3E+09	69.3933	14.8303	1.662283	0.25595	0.6823	-50.4706	25.75141	218.288326	-41.702	0.007802	1.36913	25.54064	125.541	37.4	91.3687
2000	2.6E+11	2.7E+09	68.0939	18.6938	1.031161	0.28131	0.65479	-34.3399	23.39674	97.4432962	-26.515	9.915598	-2.7178	11.19716	111.197	37.1	81.1066
2001	3.1E+11	2.8E+09	61.1109	21.9498	0.928663	0.29323	0.6561	-22.4846	10.74237	77.8172991	-13.715	14.57156	-2.523	10.73469	110.735	36.9	80.8873
2002	3.5E+11	3.5E+09	59.6454	20.0295	1.005536	0.29678	0.66573	-12.6579	8.086816	92.5366738	-21.264	15.9608	-1.092	13.59505	113.595	37.3	82.7349
2003	4.3E+11	7.9E+09	59.1283	20.859	1.842377	0.3098	0.67215	8.800838	7.149612	252.772285	-18.004	21.04535	-0.1382	45.27105	145.271	40	103.765
2004	5.9E+11	1.5E+10	56.5819	20.9013	2.606185	0.32075	0.66157	49.42127	2.535109	399.023678	-17.837	25.32438	-1.7109	76.12604	176.126	40.3	125.535
2005	7.6E+11	1.6E+10	56.7132	20.0775	2.029804	0.35205	0.65372	93.15936	2.773219	288.660114	-21.076	37.5543	-2.8772	66.36571	166.366	41.3	117.739
2006	9.9E+11	3.8E+10	54.7334	21.1716	3.797718	0.35173	0.64169	150.275	-0.81457	627.174387	-16.775	37.43183	-4.6643	132.1046	232.105	41	164.613
2007	1.3E+12	5.6E+10	51.7061	24.1645	4.298948	0.34838	0.63846	228.5926	-6.30047	723.148319	-5.0095	36.12019	-5.1435	161.9013	261.901	42.3	184.049
2008	1.7E+12	7.5E+10	53.3825	25.5012	4.502699	0.36325	0.62289	319.8964	-3.26268	762.161766	0.24506	41.93065	-7.4572	185.5857	285.586	41.6	201.685
2009	1.2E+12	3.7E+10	48.4351	18.9264	2.992129	0.34749	0.6463	209.1098	-12.2281	472.922988	-25.601	35.77222	-3.9787	112.6663	212.666	39.8	152.122
2010	1.5E+12	4.3E+10	50.3555	22.6151	2.830827	0.36626	0.65725	285.5307	-8.748	442.037383	-11.1	43.1086	-2.3525	124.746	224.746	39.5	161.108
2011	2E+12	5.5E+10	48.0354	24.2607	2.692357	0.37653	0.63987	417.2524	-12.9524	415.523633	-4.6313	47.12109	-4.9349	142.8964	242.896	39.7	173.87
2012	2.2E+12	5.1E+10	47.1514	24.5537	2.290796	0.3824	0.61048	458.3029	-14.5544	338.634065	-3.4797	49.41447	-9.3008	136.5028	236.503	40.7	168.09
2013	2.3E+12	6.9E+10	46.2871	23.2717	3.019398	0.37743	0.60836	479.5848	-16.1205	478.144262	-8.5192	47.47293	-9.6159	161.8244	261.824	40.9	185.823
2014	2.1E+12	2.2E+10	47.8013	22.3909	1.069876	0.3696	0.62243	420.6191	-13.3765	104.856335	-11.982	44.41098	-7.5259	89.50038	189.5	39.9	135.454
2015	1.4E+12	6.9E+09	49.3593	22.1487	0.502608	0.31623	0.64492	244.7163	-10.5532	-3.7622225	-12.934	23.55737	-4.1843	39.47339	139.473	37.7	101.288

Table 18. Estimation of Index of Economic Foundation (IEF) and Index of Economic Foundation Present Value (IEFPV) (1996–2015) (1996–2015) (Country: Slovenia)

Year	GDP	FDI	TGDP	GCF	FDIGDP	PCI	PDI	GDPRC	TGDPRC	FDIGDPRC	GCFRC	PCIRC	PDIRC	IEFRC	IEF	GIC	IEFPV
1995	2.1E+10	1.5E+08	93.1168	25.4657	0.70438	0.09444	0.45979										
1996	2.2E+10	1.7E+08	93.5093	25.1069	0.80578	0.10108	0.44201	0.725963	0.421592	14.3955945	-1.4092	7.03419	-3.8673	2.88349	102.883	25	82.3068
1997	2.1E+10	3.3E+08	96.2613	26.1973	1.61103	0.10217	0.46896	-2.75907	3.376997	128.717381	2.87274	8.18623	1.99388	23.7314	123.731	24.1	99.703
1998	2.2E+10	2.2E+08	96.6841	27.1957	0.97398	0.11316	0.45679	3.718621	3.831079	38.2756073	6.79339	19.8217	-0.652	11.9647	111.965	25	89.5718
1999	2.3E+10	1.1E+08	92.5419	29.1186	0.46937	0.10873	0.44307	6.365425	-0.61739	-33.364005	14.3443	15.1267	-3.6356	-0.2968	99.7032	24	80.4058
2000	2E+10	1.4E+08	103.948	28.9023	0.66931	0.10424	0.45385	-4.97651	11.63164	-4.9786995	13.495	10.3715	-1.2921	4.04179	104.042	24	83.9047
2001	2.1E+10	5E+08	104.534	26.6744	2.40081	0.10237	0.46919	-2.22887	12.26128	240.841612	4.7463	8.39185	2.04437	44.3428	144.343	25	115.474
2002	2.3E+10	1.8E+09	103.651	25.4446	7.87488	0.10792	0.46641	10.01145	11.31323	1017.99296	-0.0831	14.2735	1.44062	175.825	275.825	25	220.66
2003	3E+10	5.4E+08	102.325	26.562	1.80734	0.10762	0.46948	38.78982	9.888511	156.587278	4.30489	13.9603	2.10797	37.6065	137.606	25	110.085
2004	3.4E+10	7.6E+08	111.557	28.7976	2.21736	0.11114	0.4827	61.17658	19.80285	214.797791	13.0837	17.6791	4.98389	55.254	155.254	24.8	124.402
2005	3.6E+10	9.7E+08	120.263	28.461	2.68129	0.1188	0.49656	69.56733	29.15249	280.662191	11.7618	25.7926	7.99768	70.8223	170.822	24.6	137.097
2006	3.9E+10	6.9E+08	129.788	30.2916	1.75279	0.10778	0.49717	84.90367	39.38242	148.843476	18.9503	14.1228	8.13035	52.3888	152.389	24.4	122.499
2007	4.8E+10	1.9E+09	137.127	33.0466	3.92553	0.14086	0.44041	124.8308	47.26365	457.306349	29.7688	49.1565	-4.2151	117.352	217.352	24.4	174.72
2008	5.6E+10	1.1E+09	134.732	32.8857	1.94544	0.14892	0.47923	160.172	44.69094	176.193559	29.1371	57.6909	4.22709	78.6853	178.685	23.7	144.451
2009	5E+10	-3E+08	113.122	23.4513	-0.6889	0.15932	0.44321	135.8914	21.4839	-197.79885	-7.9104	68.7022	-3.6067	2.79358	102.794	24.8	82.3667
2010	4.8E+10	3.2E+08	127.491	22.3616	0.66266	0.16607	0.45345	125.5561	36.91571	-5.9228591	-12.189	75.8505	-1.3795	36.4718	136.472	24.9	109.265
2011	5.2E+10	8.8E+08	139.278	21.6901	1.70033	0.16167	0.49286	141.2693	49.57339	141.394598	-14.827	71.1873	7.1924	65.9651	165.965	24.9	132.878
2012	4.7E+10	3.4E+07	142.384	18.7593	0.072	0.15625	0.49011	118.1527	52.90956	-89.778203	-26.335	65.4468	6.59369	21.1649	121.165	25.6	96.4689
2013	4.8E+10	1E+08	143.756	19.5866	0.21491	0.15842	0.48859	126.6832	54.38289	-69.488673	-23.086	67.7445	6.26377	27.0832	127.083	26.2	100.7
2014	5E+10	1E+09	145.55	19.374	2.04159	0.15559	0.47415	133.843	56.30886	189.843872	-23.921	64.7453	3.12255	70.6571	170.657	25.7	135.765
2015	4.3E+10	1.7E+09	146.296	19.1637	4.01518	0.16619	0.43796	101.8065	57.11012	470.033091	-24.747	75.9721	-4.7486	112.571	212.571	25.4	169.514

Table 19. Estimation of Index of Economic Foundation (IEF) and Index of Economic Foundation Present Value (IEFPV) (1996–2015) (1996–2015) (Country: Ukraine)

Year	GDP	FDI	TGDP	GCF	FDIGDP	PCI	PDI	GDPRC	TGDPRC	FDIGDPRC	GCFRC	PCIRC	PDIRC	IEFRC	IEF	GIC	IEFPV
1995	4.8E+10	2.7E+08	97.2297	26.6832	0.553783	0.10588	0.57145										
1996	4.5E+10	5.2E+08	93.8566	22.6708	1.16926	0.10612	0.57146	-7.58245	-3.46916	111.140716	-15.037	0.23392	0.0029	14.2148	114.215	35.2	84.4784
1997	5E+10	6.2E+08	84.2414	21.4459	1.242263	0.12556	0.59709	4.016545	-13.3583	124.323288	-19.628	18.5907	4.48657	19.7385	119.739	31.3	91.1946
1998	4.2E+10	7.4E+08	86.0497	20.8172	1.773979	0.12319	0.60525	-13.1303	-11.4985	220.338578	-21.984	16.3489	5.91565	32.6651	132.665	31	101.271
1999	3.2E+10	5E+08	101.952	17.513	1.570583	0.13001	0.60851	-34.4988	4.856551	183.609959	-34.367	22.7927	6.48513	24.8131	124.813	30.6	95.569
2000	3.1E+10	6E+08	119.858	19.8038	1.903298	0.13114	0.60606	-35.1607	23.27334	243.690468	-25.782	23.8571	6.05736	39.3226	139.323	30.2	107.007
2001	3.8E+10	7.9E+08	104.001	21.8132	2.085731	0.12019	0.58532	-21.242	6.964396	276.633527	-18.251	13.5228	2.42822	43.3426	143.343	29.9	110.348
2002	4.2E+10	6.9E+08	100.657	20.1907	1.636302	0.12455	0.60562	-12.1589	3.524443	195.477346	-24.332	17.6396	5.98063	31.0219	131.022	29	101.567
2003	5E+10	1.4E+09	107.459	21.9426	2.843212	0.12224	0.56995	3.879235	10.52046	413.416693	-17.766	15.4539	-0.2623	70.8736	170.874	28.7	132.769
2004	6.5E+10	1.7E+09	113.772	21.0959	2.6458	0.1341	0.58036	34.44203	17.01347	377.768819	-20.94	26.6577	1.55982	72.7504	172.75	28.9	134.019
2005	8.6E+10	7.8E+09	97.1768	22.5065	9.07296	0.14373	0.609	78.49204	-0.05442	1538.36136	-15.653	35.7561	6.57194	273.912	373.912	29	289.855
2006	1.1E+11	5.6E+09	91.4617	24.5428	5.20586	0.14257	0.59235	123.2717	-5.93232	840.054852	-8.0217	34.6586	3.65712	164.615	264.615	29.8	203.863
2007	1.4E+11	1E+10	90.8135	27.7812	7.148989	0.13822	0.58868	195.7232	-6.59897	1190.93785	4.11479	30.5492	3.01576	236.29	336.29	27	264.796
2008	1.8E+11	1.1E+10	96.9473	27.3926	5.950501	0.14927	0.61011	272.9566	-0.29043	974.519373	2.65854	40.9863	6.76552	216.266	316.266	26.6	249.815
2009	1.2E+11	4.8E+09	89.8663	17.0684	4.072121	0.1155	0.59963	142.904	-7.57316	635.32852	-36.033	9.09298	4.93222	124.775	224.775	25.3	179.39
2010	1.4E+11	6.5E+09	98.1401	18.3724	4.742924	0.1297	0.56867	182.1038	0.936321	756.459516	-31.146	22.4995	-0.4853	155.061	255.061	24.8	204.376
2011	1.6E+11	7.2E+09	106.242	20.444	4.417145	0.13239	0.57331	238.4082	9.268894	697.631716	-23.383	25.0394	0.32515	157.882	257.882	24.6	206.968
2012	1.8E+11	8.2E+09	104.093	19.6147	4.650663	0.12147	0.59742	264.5868	7.058922	739.799494	-26.491	14.7311	4.54517	167.372	267.372	24.7	214.412
2013	1.8E+11	4.5E+09	95.1497	16.4258	2.459766	0.11994	0.61212	280.2021	-2.13929	344.175343	-38.442	13.2789	7.11829	100.699	200.699	24.6	161.075
2014	1.3E+11	8.5E+08	100.692	13.3965	0.634441	0.12716	0.66843	176.8984	3.56073	14.5649479	-49.794	20.103	16.9714	30.384	130.384	24	105.148
2015	9.1E+10	-4E+08	107.807	15.9333	-0.40536	0.13492	0.68249	88.80659	10.87828	-173.19779	-40.287	27.4295	19.4321	-11.156	88.8436	25.5	70.7917

The major reason for deriving IEFPV for the sample countries is to ensure how well the countries under transition have managed to mitigate the adverse effects of globalization, *per se*, since countries that opted for transition to market economy are most vulnerable in regards to their structural and socio-economic transformations.

RESULTS OF THE STUDY AND RELATED FINDINGS

The list of observations based on the test results are noted as follows (Refer to Tables: 20 – 29).

Table 20. Regression results of Index of Economic Foundation (IEF) on Gross Domestic Product (GDP), Trade to GDP ratio (TGDP), Gross Capital Formation ratio (GCF), Foreign Direct Investments to GDP ratio (FDIGDP), Product Concentration Index (PCI), and Product Diversification Index (PDI) (1996 – 2015) (Country: Armenia)

Model 1: OLS, using observations 1996-2015 (T = 20) Dependent variable: IEF HAC standard errors, bandwidth 2 (Bartlett kernel)					
	Coefficient	**Std. Error**	**t-Ratio**	**p-Value**	
const	118.814	224.770	0.5286	0.6060	
GDP	8.56206e-09	5.56923e-09	1.537	0.1482	
TGDP	−4.76037	2.72191	−1.749	0.1039	
GCF	2.32625	1.67461	1.389	0.1881	
FDIGDP	7.15258	1.53123	4.671	0.0004***	***
PCI	15.7335	262.204	0.06000	0.9531	
PDI	406.607	526.194	0.7727	0.4535	

Mean dependent var	370.7280	S.D. dependent var	214.1293
Sum squared resid	61345.85	S.E. of regression	68.69433
R-squared	0.929583	Adjusted R-squared	0.897082
F(6, 13)	35.78614	P-value(F)	2.38e-07
Log-likelihood	−108.6643	Akaike criterion	231.3286
Schwarz criterion	238.2987	Hannan-Quinn	232.6892
rho	−0.300195	Durbin-Watson	2.575414

Table 21. Regression results of Index of Economic Foundation (IEF) on Gross Domestic Product (GDP), Trade to GDP ratio (TGDP), Gross Capital Formation ratio (GCF), Foreign Direct Investments to GDP ratio (FDIGDP), Product Concentration Index (PCI), and Product Diversification Index (PDI) (1996 – 2015) (Country: Belarus)

Model 1: OLS, using observations 1996-2015 (T = 20) Dependent variable: IEF HAC standard errors, bandwidth 2 (Bartlett kernel)					
	Coefficient	**Std. Error**	**t-Ratio**	**p-Value**	
const	8.28879e-07	2.76268e-06	0.3000	0.7689	
GDP	1.19280e-09	0.00000	1.757e+008	<0.0001	***
TGDP	0.160692	4.77175e-09	3.368e+007	<0.0001	***
GCF	0.673406	2.36037e-08	2.853e+007	<0.0001	***
FDIGDP	158.420	1.47191e-08	1.076e+010	<0.0001	***
PCI	33.9457	3.75754e-06	9.034e+006	<0.0001	***
PDI	23.8640	6.29342e-06	3.792e+006	<0.0001	***

Mean dependent var	1299.945	S.D. dependent var	1235.053
Sum squared resid	7.81e-13	S.E. of regression	2.45e-07
R-squared	1.000000	Adjusted R-squared	1.000000
F(6, 13)	0.000000	P-value(F)	1.000000
Log-likelihood	280.3603	Akaike criterion	−546.7207
Schwarz criterion	−539.7506	Hannan-Quinn	−545.3600
rho	0.058723	Durbin-Watson	1.600589

Table 22. Regression results of Index of Economic Foundation (IEF) on Gross Domestic Product (GDP), Trade to GDP ratio (TGDP), Gross Capital Formation ratio (GCF), Foreign Direct Investments to GDP ratio (FDIGDP), Product Concentration Index (PCI), and Product Diversification Index (PDI) (1996 – 2015) (Country: Bulgaria)

Model 1: OLS, using observations 1996-2015 (T = 20) Dependent variable: IEF HAC standard errors, bandwidth 2 (Bartlett kernel)					
	Coefficient	**Std. Error**	**t-Ratio**	**p-Value**	
const	−5.24555e-09	2.35966e-09	−2.223	0.0446	**
GDP	8.77965e-010	0.00000	3.724e+010	<0.0001	***
TGDP	0.301590	8.91197e-012	3.384e+010	<0.0001	***
GCF	0.940092	1.56133e-011	6.021e+010	<0.0001	***
FDIGDP	34.9987	1.42999e-011	2.447e+012	<0.0001	***
PCI	190.225	5.80973e-09	3.274e+010	<0.0001	***
PDI	34.4122	4.85090e-09	7.094e+009	<0.0001	***

Mean dependent var	417.5608	S.D. dependent var	284.5570
Sum squared resid	2.38e-18	S.E. of regression	4.28e-10
R-squared	1.000000	Adjusted R-squared	1.000000
F(6, 13)	0.000000	P-value(F)	1.000000
Log-likelihood	407.3633	Akaike criterion	−800.7266
Schwarz criterion	−793.7565	Hannan-Quinn	−799.3659

Table 23. Regression results of Index of Economic Foundation (IEF) on Gross Domestic Product (GDP), Trade to GDP ratio (TGDP), Gross Capital Formation ratio (GCF), Foreign Direct Investments to GDP ratio (FDIGDP), Product Concentration Index (PCI), and Product Diversification Index (PDI) (1996 – 2015) (Country: Czech Republic)

Model 1: OLS, using observations 1996-2015 (T = 20) Dependent variable: IEF HAC standard errors, bandwidth 2 (Bartlett kernel)					
	Coefficient	**Std. Error**	**t-Ratio**	**p-Value**	
const	−38.0118	24.4629	−1.554	0.1442	
GDP	2.62695e-010	8.86662e-012	29.63	<0.0001	***
TGDP	0.175762	0.0201127	8.739	<0.0001	***
GCF	0.753395	0.178769	4.214	0.0010	***
FDIGDP	3.81889	0.0737681	51.77	<0.0001	***
PCI	396.220	24.6660	16.06	<0.0001	***
PDI	128.810	54.6402	2.357	0.0347	**

Mean dependent var	150.4951	S.D. dependent var	26.63136
Sum squared resid	23.84561	S.E. of regression	1.354355
R-squared	0.998230	Adjusted R-squared	0.997414
F(6, 13)	1649.535	P-value(F)	5.87e-18
Log-likelihood	−30.13745	Akaike criterion	74.27490
Schwarz criterion	81.24502	Hannan-Quinn	75.63554
rho	−0.161936	Durbin-Watson	2.271017

Table 24. Regression results of Index of Economic Foundation (IEF) on Gross Domestic Product (GDP), Trade to GDP ratio (TGDP), Gross Capital Formation ratio (GCF), Foreign Direct Investments to GDP ratio (FDIGDP), Product Concentration Index (PCI), and Product Diversification Index (PDI) (1996 – 2015) (Country: Estonia)

Model 1: OLS, using observations 1996-2015 (T = 20) Dependent variable: IEF HAC standard errors, bandwidth 2 (Bartlett kernel)					
	Coefficient	**Std. Error**	**t-Ratio**	**p-Value**	
const	−2.02817e-07	2.81997e-07	−0.7192	0.4847	
GDP	3.70550e-09	0.00000	1.185e+009	<0.0001	***
TGDP	0.119692	9.03381e-010	1.325e+008	<0.0001	***
GCF	0.631047	2.74285e-09	2.301e+008	<0.0001	***
FDIGDP	3.62481	3.50990e-09	1.033e+009	<0.0001	***
PCI	204.941	5.33143e-07	3.844e+008	<0.0001	***
PDI	32.9907	6.30173e-07	5.235e+007	<0.0001	***

Mean dependent var	163.5494	S.D. dependent var	34.63161
Sum squared resid	3.20e-14	S.E. of regression	4.96e-08
R-squared	1.000000	Adjusted R-squared	1.000000
F(6, 13)	0.000000	P-value(F)	1.000000
Log-likelihood	312.3078	Akaike criterion	−610.6157
Schwarz criterion	−603.6456	Hannan-Quinn	−609.2550
rho	0.344286	Durbin-Watson	1.232376

Table 25. Regression results of Index of Economic Foundation (IEF) on Gross Domestic Product (GDP), Trade to GDP ratio (TGDP), Gross Capital Formation ratio (GCF), Foreign Direct Investments to GDP ratio (FDIGDP), Product Concentration Index (PCI), and Product Diversification Index (PDI) (1996–2015) (Country: Kazakhstan)

Model 1: OLS, using observations 1996-2015 (T = 20)
Dependent variable: IEF
HAC standard errors, bandwidth 2 (Bartlett kernel)

	Coefficient	**Std. Error**	**t-Ratio**	**p-Value**	
const	2.67400e-08	3.25798e-08	0.8208	0.4266	
GDP	8.18024e-010	0.00000	1.975e+010	<0.0001	***
TGDP	0.201965	2.57780e-010	7.835e+008	<0.0001	***
GCF	0.714717	4.45408e-010	1.605e+009	<0.0001	***
FDIGDP	3.52180	1.04656e-09	3.365e+009	<0.0001	***
PCI	81.8635	2.46901e-08	3.316e+009	<0.0001	***
PDI	22.7884	3.26886e-08	6.971e+008	<0.0001	***

Mean dependent var	200.3009	S.D. dependent var	69.70520
Sum squared resid	6.43e-16	S.E. of regression	7.03e-09
R-squared	1.000000	Adjusted R-squared	1.000000
F(6, 13)	0.000000	P-value(F)	1.000000
Log-likelihood	351.3792	Akaike criterion	−688.7585
Schwarz criterion	−681.7883	Hannan-Quinn	−687.3978
rho	−0.317174	Durbin-Watson	2.609603

Table 26. Regression results of Index of Economic Foundation (IEF) on Gross Domestic Product (GDP), Trade to GDP ratio (TGDP), Gross Capital Formation ratio (GCF), Foreign Direct Investments to GDP ratio (FDIGDP), Product Concentration Index (PCI), and Product Diversification Index (PDI) (1996 – 2015) (Country: Kyrgyz Republic)

Model 1: OLS, using observations 1996-2015 (T = 20) Dependent variable: IEF HAC standard errors, bandwidth 2 (Bartlett kernel)					
	Coefficient	**Std. Error**	**t-Ratio**	**p-Value**	
const	−1.26347e-08	1.45580e-08	−0.8679	0.4012	
GDP	1.00340e-08	0.00000	6.804e+009	<0.0001	***
TGDP	0.232048	4.76955e-011	4.865e+009	<0.0001	***
GCF	−5.60599e-010	3.32653e-010	−1.685	0.1158	
FDIGDP	5.76202	1.43518e-010	4.015e+010	<0.0001	***
PCI	121.593	1.35523e-08	8.972e+009	<0.0001	***
PDI	24.1421	1.81082e-08	1.333e+009	<0.0001	***

Mean dependent var	143.8180	S.D. dependent var	50.71479
Sum squared resid	2.19e-16	S.E. of regression	4.11e-09
R-squared	1.000000	Adjusted R-squared	1.000000
F(6, 13)	0.000000	P-value(F)	1.000000
Log-likelihood	362.1416	Akaike criterion	−710.2831
Schwarz criterion	−703.3130	Hannan-Quinn	−708.9225

Table 27. Regression results of Index of Economic Foundation (IEF) on Gross Domestic Product (GDP), Trade to GDP ratio (TGDP), Gross Capital Formation ratio (GCF), Foreign Direct Investments to GDP ratio (FDIGDP), Product Concentration Index (PCI), and Product Diversification Index (PDI) (1996 – 2015) (Country: Russian Federation)

Model 1: OLS, using observations 1996-2015 (T = 20) Dependent variable: IEF HAC standard errors, bandwidth 2 (Bartlett kernel)					
	Coefficient	**Std. Error**	**t-Ratio**	**p-Value**	
const	2.09682e-07	1.80659e-07	1.161	0.2667	
GDP	4.21368e-011	0.00000	5.417e+009	<0.0001	***
TGDP	0.302026	3.32206e-010	9.092e+008	<0.0001	***
GCF	0.655165	8.72677e-010	7.508e+008	<0.0001	***
FDIGDP	31.9128	1.64350e-09	1.942e+010	<0.0001	***
PCI	65.1209	8.59100e-08	7.580e+008	<0.0001	***
PDI	24.7617	2.26938e-07	1.091e+008	<0.0001	***

Mean dependent var	177.8194	S.D. dependent var	62.28077
Sum squared resid	2.02e-15	S.E. of regression	1.25e-08
R-squared	1.000000	Adjusted R-squared	1.000000
F(6, 13)	0.000000	P-value(F)	1.000000
Log-likelihood	339.9389	Akaike criterion	−665.8778
Schwarz criterion	−658.9077	Hannan-Quinn	−664.5172
rho	−0.523506	Durbin-Watson	2.897936

Table 28. Regression results of Index of Economic Foundation (IEF) on Gross Domestic Product (GDP), Trade to GDP ratio (TGDP), Gross Capital Formation ratio (GCF), Foreign Direct Investments to GDP ratio (FDIGDP), Product Concentration Index (PCI), and Product Diversification Index (PDI) (1996 – 2015) (Country: Slovenia)

Model 1: OLS, using observations 1996-2015 (T = 20) Dependent variable: IEF HAC standard errors, bandwidth 2 (Bartlett kernel)					
	Coefficient	**Std. Error**	**t-Ratio**	**p-Value**	
const	−1.06984e-07	1.20241e-07	−0.8898	0.3898	
GDP	7.80559e-010	0.00000	4.310e+008	<0.0001	***
TGDP	0.178987	3.46653e-010	5.163e+008	<0.0001	***
GCF	0.654474	8.36179e-010	7.827e+008	<0.0001	***
FDIGDP	23.6616	2.45673e-09	9.631e+009	<0.0001	***
PCI	176.478	3.09042e-07	5.711e+008	<0.0001	***
PDI	36.2485	2.14005e-07	1.694e+008	<0.0001	***

Mean dependent var	150.5654	S.D. dependent var	45.42230
Sum squared resid	2.79e-15	S.E. of regression	1.47e-08
R-squared	1.000000	Adjusted R-squared	1.000000
F(6, 13)	0.000000	P-value(F)	1.000000
Log-likelihood	336.6995	Akaike criterion	−659.3989
Schwarz criterion	−652.4288	Hannan-Quinn	−658.0383
rho	−0.135427	Durbin-Watson	2.143278

Table 29. Regression results of Index of Economic Foundation (IEF) on Gross Domestic Product (GDP), Trade to GDP ratio (TGDP), Gross Capital Formation ratio (GCF), Foreign Direct Investments to GDP ratio (FDIGDP), Product Concentration Index (PCI), and Product Diversification Index (PDI) (1996 – 2015) (Country: Slovenia)

Model 1: OLS, using observations 1996-2015 (T = 20) Dependent variable: IEF HAC standard errors, bandwidth 2 (Bartlett kernel)					
	Coefficient	**Std. Error**	**t-Ratio**	**p-Value**	
const	−9.16461e-08	1.10132e-07	−0.8321	0.4204	
GDP	3.45682e-010	0.00000	3.747e+009	<0.0001	***
TGDP	0.171415	1.81034e-010	9.469e+008	<0.0001	***
GCF	0.624613	2.46463e-09	2.534e+008	<0.0001	***
FDIGDP	30.0960	4.09605e-09	7.348e+009	<0.0001	***
PCI	157.415	6.12209e-07	2.571e+008	<0.0001	***
PDI	29.1657	1.69590e-07	1.720e+008	<0.0001	***

Mean dependent var	198.2421	S.D. dependent var	83.48267
Sum squared resid	6.73e-15	S.E. of regression	2.28e-08
R-squared	1.000000	Adjusted R-squared	1.000000
F(6, 13)	0.000000	P-value(F)	1.000000
Log-likelihood	327.9006	Akaike criterion	−641.8012
Schwarz criterion	−634.8311	Hannan-Quinn	−640.4405
rho	−0.357390	Durbin-Watson	2.646310

The regression equations are summarized as shown in Table 30.

Table 30. Regression equations of Index of Economic Foundation (IEF) on Gross Domestic Product (GDP), Ratio of Trade to GDP (TGDP), Ratio of Gross Capital Formation to GDP (GCF), Ratio of FDI to Gross Domestic Product (FDIGDP), Product Concentration Index (PCI), and Product Diversification Index (PDI) respectively for 10 sample countries (1996 – 2015)

Country	Regression Equation	Reference
Armenia	$IEF = 7.153FDIGDP$	Table 20
Belarus	$IEF = 0.16TGDP + 0.67GCF + 158FDIGDP + 34PCI + 24PDI$	Table 21
Bulgaria	$IEF = 0.3TGDP + 0.94GCF + 35FDIGDP + 190\,PCI + 34PDI$	Table 22
Czech Republic	$IEF = 0.18TGDP + 0.75GCF + 4FDIGDP + 396PCI + 129PDI$	Table 23
Estonia	$IEF = 0.12TGDP + 0.63GCF + 3.62FDIGDP + 205PCI + 33PDI$	Table 24
Kazakh-stan	$IEF = 0.2TGDP + 0.71GCF + 3.52FDIGDP + 82PCI + 23PDI$	Table 25
Kyrgyz Republic	$IEF = 0.23TGDP + 6FDIGDP + 122PCI + 24PDI$	Table 26
Russian Federation	$IEF = 0.3TGDP + 0.66GCF + 32FDIGDP + 65PCI + 25PDI$	Table 27
Slovenia	$IEF = 0.18TGDP + 0.65GCF + 24FDIGDP + 176PCI + 36PDI$	Table 28
Ukraine	$IEF = 0.17TGDP + 0.62GCF + 30FDIGDP + 157PCI + 29PDI$	Table 29

It should be noted that in case of 9 sample countries, the coefficients of the regressor GDP showed statistical significance at 99 percent Confidence Interval (CI) or better; however, the values of the coefficients were extremely small and hence they were *not* included in the final regression equations.

By taking help from Table 30 as a resource, it may be statistically inferred that the IEF for 9 sample countries is *most* sensitive in case of Product Concentration Index (PCI). In other words, the countries in transition to market economy have completely *specialized* themselves in production of a selective group of commodities rather than emphasizing on *diversification* in order to achieve *gains from specialization* from trade;

- Apart from PCI; both FDIGDP and PDI are the two *key* factors which affect the IEFs' of the sample countries in a significant manner. In case of Belarus, FDI to GDP ratio plays extremely significant role. Hence it may be safely inferred that Belarus as a nation is heavily dependent on FDI for economic growth. However, the infusion of FDI in the economy of Belarus is not emphatically translated into formation of gross capital since the coefficient of GCF for Belarus is 0.7 contemplating an inelastic effect of GCF on IEF;
- 8 out of 10 sample countries have displayed *positive* effects of GCF on IEF. Thus, it may be inferred that majority of the countries under transition follow

the 'basic' rule of creation of gross capital allowing for growth of public investment essential for growth of GDP, although *none* of the 10 sample countries showed an *elastic* relationship in reference to *marginal rate of change* in IEF with respect GCF, i.e., $\frac{\partial IEF}{\partial GCF} > 1$;

- The Trade to GDP Ratio (TGDP) proved to be a statistically significant variable among the 5 independent variables to affect the IEF for 9 out of 10 sample countries. However, the impact of TGDP on IEF proved to be quite weak as the *marginal rate of change* of IEF with respect to TGDP or $\left(\frac{\partial IEF}{\partial TGDP}\right)$ ranges between 0.12 and 0.3;
- The *marginal rate* of change of IEF with respect to FDIGDP, i.e., $\left(\frac{\partial IEF}{\partial FDIGDP}\right)$ has proved to be extremely *sensitive* for all the sample countries ranging from 3.52 to as high as 158 – reiterating the fact that the countries under transition are explicitly dependent on FDI for economic growth. This particular factor gives rise to a serious concern related to globalization of transitional economies when the foreign investments start drying up - particularly in the times of global recession and pandemics like COVID – 19;
- The major 'influence' of globalization may be highlighted by virtue of greater product diversification as it acts as one of the major indicators of rapid technological innovation for the home country. Thus, the estimation of Product concentration elasticity of diversification (ξ) for each sample country gets the top priority in assessing the impact of globalization. It is expressed as the ratio of proportionate change of Product Diversification Index (PDI) to the proportionate change of Product Concentration Index (PCI) of a country. Formally,

$$\xi = \frac{PCI}{PDI} \times \left(\frac{\frac{\partial IEF}{\partial PCI}}{\frac{\partial IEF}{\partial PDI}}\right) = \frac{PCI}{PDI} \times \frac{\partial PDI}{\partial PCI}$$

where ξ = Product concentration elasticity of diversification.

For example, in case of Belarus; $\frac{\partial IEF}{\partial PCI} = 34$ and $\frac{\partial IEF}{\partial PDI} = 24$.

Hence for Belarus, ξ for the years 2016 and 2017 could be estimated as:

$$\xi_{2016} = \left(\frac{0.167937}{0.516257}\right) \times \left(\frac{34}{24}\right) \approx 0.46,$$

$$\xi_{2017} = \left(\frac{0.170316}{0.520702}\right) \times \left(\frac{34}{24}\right) \approx 0.463, \ldots\text{, and so on.}$$

Thus, a tabular representation of the Product concentration elasticities of diversification for the sample countries would help us to interpret the impacts of globalization on technological innovation on trade and export – oriented commodity markets as below (Refer to Table 41):

Table 31. Product concentration elasticities of diversification for 10 sample countries (1996 – 2015)

Country	Product Concentration Elasticity of Diversification (ξ)
Armenia	Not Applicable
Belarus	$\xi = 1.42 \times \left(\frac{PCI}{PDI}\right)$
Bulgaria	$\xi = 5.6 \times \left(\frac{PCI}{PDI}\right)$
Czech Republic	$\xi = 3.07 \times \left(\frac{PCI}{PDI}\right)$
Estonia	$\xi = 6.21 \times \left(\frac{PCI}{PDI}\right)$
Kazakhstan	$\xi = 3.6 \times \left(\frac{PCI}{PDI}\right)$
Kyrgyz Republic	$\xi = 5.04 \times \left(\frac{PCI}{PDI}\right)$
Russian Federation	$\xi = 2.6 \times \left(\frac{PCI}{PDI}\right)$
Slovenia	$\xi = 4.9 \times \left(\frac{PCI}{PDI}\right)$
Ukraine	$\xi = 5.4 \times \left(\frac{PCI}{PDI}\right)$

By the help of Table 31, it may be statistically inferred that PDIs' for 9 countries are highly sensitive in terms of changes in their respective PCIs'. An interesting fact which emerges from the statistical data is that the countries in transition are initially involved in producing a specialized group of products for export which in turn strongly triggers the need for diversification; and finally, a clearer picture emerges when the regression equations of IEFIPV on IEF for the 10 sample countries are enumerated for further analysis (Refer to Tables 32 – 41) as follows:

Table 32. Regression of Index of Economic Foundation Present Value (IEFPV) on Index of Economic Foundation (IEF) (1996 – 2015) (X Variable 1: IEF) (Country: Armenia)

SUMMARY OUTPUT								
Regression Statistics								
Multiple R	0.9997059							
R Square	0.9994119							
Adjusted R Square	0.9993793							
Standard Error	4.1754088							
Observations	20							
ANOVA								
	df	*SS*	*MS*	*F*	*Significance F*			
Regression	1	533330.1895	533330	30591.3	1.56013E-30			
Residual	18	313.812698	17.434					
Total	19	533644.0022						
	Coefficients	*Standard Error*	*t Stat*	*P-value*	*Lower 95%*	*Upper 95%*	*Lower 95.0%*	*Upper 95.0%*
Intercept	-7.9597903	1.903194239	-4.1823	0.00056	-11.958253	-3.9613275	-11.958253	-3.9613275
X Variable 1	0.7824296	0.004473487	174.904	1.6E-30	0.77303114	0.79182804	0.77303114	0.79182804

Table 33. Regression of Index of Economic Foundation Present Value (IEFPV) on Index of Economic Foundation (IEF) (1996 – 2015) (X Variable 1: IEF) (Country: Belarus)

SUMMARY OUTPUT								
Regression Statistics								
Multiple R	0.999938							
R Square	0.999876							
Adjusted R Square	0.9998691							
Standard Error	11.115903							
Observations	20							
ANOVA								
	df	*SS*	*MS*	*F*	*Significance F*			
Regression	1	17927613.47	17927613	145088	1.28994E-36			
Residual	18	2224.139394	123.5633					
Total	19	17929837.61						
	Coefficients	*Standard Error*	*t Stat*	*P-value*	*Lower 95%*	*Upper 95%*	*Lower 95.0%*	*Upper 95.0%*
Intercept	-3.391315	3.658257173	-0.92703	0.36618	-11.0770277	4.29439855	-11.0770277	4.29439855
X Variable 1	0.7865003	0.002064821	380.90484	1.3E-36	0.782162267	0.79083832	0.78216227	0.79083832

Table 34. Regression of Index of Economic Foundation Present Value (IEFPV) on Index of Economic Foundation (IEF) (1996 – 2015) (X Variable 1: IEF) (Country: Bulgaria)

SUMMARY OUTPUT								
Regression Statistics								
Multiple R	0.9998492							
R Square	0.9996985							
Adjusted R Square	0.9996818							
Standard Error	3.7380996							
Observations	20							
ANOVA								
	df	*SS*	*MS*	*F*	*Significance F*			
Regression	1	833993.5108	833994	59684.4	3.81821E-33			
Residual	18	251.5209942	13.9734					
Total	19	834245.0318						
	Coefficients	*Standard Error*	*t Stat*	*P-value*	*Lower 95%*	*Upper 95%*	*Lower 95.0%*	*Upper 95.0%*
Intercept	2.9896802	1.510722437	1.97897	0.06333	-0.18422983	6.1635903	-0.18422983	6.1635903
X Variable 1	0.7362668	0.003013733	244.304	3.8E-33	0.729935203	0.74259844	0.729935203	0.74259844

Table 35. Regression of Index of Economic Foundation Present Value (IEFPV) on Index of Economic Foundation (IEF) (1996 – 2015) (X Variable 1: IEF) (Country: Czech Republic)

SUMMARY OUTPUT								
Regression Statistics								
Multiple R	0.9997503							
R Square	0.9995007							
Adjusted R Square	0.999473							
Standard Error	0.4815445							
Observations	20							
ANOVA								
	df	*SS*	*MS*	*F*	*Significance F*			
Regression	1	8355.450756	8355.45	36032.7	3.57766E-31			
Residual	18	4.173931315	0.23189					
Total	19	8359.624687						
	Coefficients	*Standard Error*	*t Stat*	*P-value*	*Lower 95%*	*Upper 95%*	*Lower 95.0%*	*Upper 95.0%*
Intercept	0.7370071	0.633510981	1.16337	0.25987	-0.593950099	2.06796427	-0.593950099	2.06796427
X Variable 1	0.787435	0.004148262	189.823	3.6E-31	0.778719839	0.79615019	0.778719839	0.79615019

Table 36. Regression of Index of Economic Foundation Present Value (IEFPV) on Index of Economic Foundation (IEF) (1996 – 2015) (X Variable 1: IEF) (Country: Estonia)

SUMMARY OUTPUT								
Regression Statistics								
Multiple R	0.9878292							
R Square	0.9758066							
Adjusted R Square	0.9744625							
Standard Error	3.5769496							
Observations	20							
ANOVA								
	df	*SS*	*MS*	*F*	*Significance F*			
Regression	1	9288.910372	9288.91	726.004	5.32513E-16			
Residual	18	230.3022306	12.7946					
Total	19	9519.212603						
	Coefficients	*Standard Error*	*t Stat*	*P-value*	*Lower 95%*	*Upper 95%*	*Lower 95.0%*	*Upper 95.0%*
Intercept	21.937164	3.957040361	5.54383	2.9E-05	13.62373078	30.2505974	13.62373078	30.2505974
X Variable 1	0.6384589	0.023695364	26.9445	5.3E-16	0.58867679	0.68824101	0.58867679	0.68824101

Table 37. Regression of Index of Economic Foundation Present Value (IEFPV) on Index of Economic Foundation (IEF) (1996 – 2015) (X Variable 1: IEF) (Country: Kazakhstan)

SUMMARY OUTPUT								
Regression Statistics								
Multiple R	0.99928							
R Square	0.9985604							
Adjusted R Square	0.9984805							
Standard Error	2.2306497							
Observations	20							
ANOVA								
	df	*SS*	*MS*	*F*	*Significance F*			
Regression	1	62126.46408	62126.5	12485.7	4.9278E-27			
Residual	18	89.5643671	4.9758					
Total	19	62216.02845						
	Coefficients	*Standard Error*	*t Stat*	*P-value*	*Lower 95%*	*Upper 95%*	*Lower 95.0%*	*Upper 95.0%*
Intercept	-10.860906	1.55281467	-6.9943	1.6E-06	-14.1232484	-7.59856327	-14.1232484	-7.59856327
X Variable 1	0.8203446	0.007341577	111.74	4.9E-27	0.804920512	0.83576868	0.80492051	0.83576868

Table 38. Regression of Index of Economic Foundation Present Value (IEFPV) on Index of Economic Foundation (IEF) (1996 – 2015) (X Variable 1: IEF) (Country: Kyrgyz Republic)

SUMMARY OUTPUT								
Regression Statistics								
Multiple R	0.9995124							
R Square	0.9990251							
Adjusted R Square	0.998971							
Standard Error	1.3410423							
Observations	20							
ANOVA								
	df	*SS*	*MS*	*F*	*Significance F*			
Regression	1	33173.37952	33173.4	18446.1	1.47558E-28			
Residual	18	32.37109911	1.79839					
Total	19	33205.75062						
	Coefficients	*Standard Error*	*t Stat*	*P-value*	*Lower 95%*	*Upper 95%*	*Lower 95.0%*	*Upper 95.0%*
Intercept	-8.3314318	0.922551746	-9.0309	4.2E-08	-10.26964112	-6.3932225	-10.26964112	-6.3932225
X Variable 1	0.823917	0.0060664	135.816	1.5E-28	0.811171928	0.836662	0.811171928	0.836662

Table 39. Regression of Index of Economic Foundation Present Value (IEFPV) on Index of Economic Foundation (IEF) (1996 – 2015) (X Variable 1: IEF) (Country: Russian Federation)

SUMMARY OUTPUT								
Regression Statistics								
Multiple R	0.9995796							
R Square	0.9991593							
Adjusted R Square	0.9991126							
Standard Error	1.2997192							
Observations	20							
ANOVA								
	df	*SS*	*MS*	*F*	*Significance F*			
Regression	1	36140.06125	36140.1	21393.9	3.89042E-29			
Residual	18	30.40686063	1.68927					
Total	19	36170.46811						
	Coefficients	*Standard Error*	*t Stat*	*P-value*	*Lower 95%*	*Upper 95%*	*Lower 95.0%*	*Upper 95.0%*
Intercept	2.4305874	0.899569894	2.70194	0.01459	0.540661211	4.32051364	0.540661211	4.32051364
X Variable 1	0.700267	0.00478761	146.267	3.9E-29	0.690208625	0.71032542	0.690208625	0.71032542

Table 40. Regression of Index of Economic Foundation Present Value (IEFPV) on Index of Economic Foundation (IEF) (1996 – 2015) (X Variable 1: IEF) (Country: Slovenia)

SUMMARY OUTPUT

Regression Statistics	
Multiple R	0.9998713
R Square	0.9997425
Adjusted R Square	0.9997282
Standard Error	0.5992755
Observations	20

ANOVA

	df	*SS*	*MS*	*F*	*Significance F*
Regression	1	25100.26009	25100.3	69891.6	9.22453E-34
Residual	18	6.464359335	0.35913		
Total	19	25106.72445			

	Coefficients	*Standard Error*	*t Stat*	*P-value*	*Lower 95%*	*Upper 95%*	*Lower 95.0%*	*Upper 95.0%*
Intercept	0.1309762	0.475020553	0.27573	0.7859	-0.867004903	1.1289574	-0.867004903	1.1289574
X Variable 1	0.8001901	0.003026778	264.37	9.2E-34	0.793831096	0.80654914	0.793831096	0.80654914

Table 41. Regression of Index of Economic Foundation Present Value (IEFPV) on Index of Economic Foundation (IEF) (1996 – 2015) (X Variable 1: IEF) (Country: Ukraine)

SUMMARY OUTPUT

Regression Statistics	
Multiple R	0.998997
R Square	0.997996
Adjusted R Square	0.997885
Standard Error	3.058877
Observations	20

ANOVA

	df	*SS*	*MS*	*F*	*Significance F*
Regression	1	83872.40933	83872.4	8963.86	9.67881E-26
Residual	18	168.4210674	9.35673		
Total	19	84040.83039			

	Coefficients	*Standard Error*	*t Stat*	*P-value*	*Lower 95%*	*Upper 95%*	*Lower 95.0%*	*Upper 95.0%*
Intercept	-2.33728	1.801331614	-1.2975	0.21083	-6.12173779	1.44717679	-6.12173779	1.44717679
X Variable 1	0.79586	0.008405989	94.6777	9.7E-26	0.778199174	0.81351983	0.77819917	0.81351983

The regression results are documented below (Refer to Table 42):

Table 42. Regression equations of Index of Economic Foundation Present Value (IEFPV) on Index of Economic Foundation (IEF) for 10 sample countries (1996 – 2015)

Country	Regression Equation of TIIPV on TII	Reference
Armenia	$IEFPV = -8 + 0.78IEF$	Table 30
Belarus	$IEFPV = 0.79IEF$	Table 31
Bulgaria	$IEFPV = 0.74IEF$	Table 32
Czech Republic	$IEFPV = 0.79IEF$	Table 33
Estonia	$IEFPV = 22 + 0.64IEF$	Table 34
Kazakhstan	$IEFPV = -11 + 0.82IEF$	Table 35
Kyrgyz Republic	$IEFPV = -8 + 0.82IEF$	Table 36
Russian Federation	$IEFPV = 2.43 + 0.7IEF$	Table 37
Slovenia	$IEFPV = 0.8IEF$	Table 38
Ukraine	$IEFPV = 0.8IEF$	Table 39

From Table: 42 above, it may be clearly inferred that all the sample countries have displayed a *positive* regressionary relationship between their IEFPVs' and IEFs'. In other words, the effect of Gini Coefficient (GIC) as a *discount factor* has proved to be *positive* for deflating the IEFs' for each of the countries contemplating the fact that these countries have somehow partly managed to mitigate the *adverse effects* stemmed from inequalities in distribution of wealth and income respectively. One more interesting fact which emerges from the findings (Refer to Table 42) is that the *marginal rate of change* of IEFPV to IEF, i.e., $\left(\frac{dIEFPV}{dIEF}\right)$ is *inelastic* and varies between the range from 0.64 to 0.82.

Note

Ordinary Least Squares (OLS) method was used to derive the regression results of IEF on GDP, TGDP, GCF, FDIGDP, PCI, and PDI respectively. The final results were found to be statistically significant at 5 percent level of significance or better and they successfully passed the Granger and Newbold's (1974) *Thumb rule test of Econometric Regression*. The software GRETL v.1.9.4 was used for the analytics.

THE BURNING ISSUES OF INCOME INEQUALITY, DEGLOBALIZATION AND REGLOBALIZATION

The global pandemic outbreak due to COVID – 19 caused a worldwide havoc both in terms of financial meltdown and immense loss of lives and livelihoods. This pandemic has exposed the utter vulnerability of existing global socio-economic systems and simultaneously stirred up the ongoing issue regarding the efficacy and legitimacy of globalization. A broad section of scholars and policymakers are candidly advocating about the *reverse* procedures of globalization, namely, Deglobalization and Reglobalization. Before approaching those said topics, a prelude containing the issue of transitional impact of globalization for the 10 sample countries in the *pandemic year* of 2020 needs to be discussed as follows:

- For Armenia, the regression equation of IEF may be expressed as (Refer to Table 20):

$$IEF = 7.153FDIGDP \qquad (1)$$

Now by plugging the value of FDIGDP (Armenia) for the year 2020, we have:

$$IEF_{2020} = (7.153 \times 2.955) = 21.137115 \cong 21$$

The regression equation of TIIPV on TII for Armenia is written as (Refer to Table 30):

$$IEF = \text{-}8 + 0.78IEF \qquad (2)$$

Hence the value of IEFPV in case of Armenia for the year 2020 could be derived as:

$$IEFPV_{2020} = \text{-}8 + 0.78IEF_{2020} = \text{-}8 + (0.78 \times 21) = 8.38 \cong 8$$

A quick comparison between the values of IEF for the years 2015 and 2020 (326 and 21 respectively) would help us to clearly identify the level of huge fall in the level of economic foundation accompanied by a massive reduction in the value of IEFPV between 2015 and 2020 (246 and 8 respectively) for Armenia (Refer to Table: 10 for comparison);

- In case of Belarus, the regression equation of IEF is stated as follows (See Table 21):

$$IEF = 0.16TGDP + 0.67GCF + 158FDIGDP + 34PCI + 24PDI \quad (3)$$

Hence the value of IEF for 2020 may be estimated as:

$$IEF_{2020} = (0.16 \times 102.2848) + (0.67 \times 26.272) + (158 \times 9.4302) + (34 \times 0.118) + (24 \times 0.5) = 1539.951408 \cong 1540$$

Similarly, the value of IEFPV for 2020 may be estimated by using the regression equation below (Refer to Table 31):

$$IEFPV = 0.79IEF \quad (4)$$

Hence

$$IEFPV_{2020} = 0.79IEF_{2020} = (0.79 \times 1540) = 1216.6 \cong 1217$$

By comparing the values of IEF for 2015 and 2020 (Refer to Table: 11 for comparison), it may be seen that there has been a reduction in the value from 2000 to 1540 followed by a fall in the value of IEFPV from 1593 to 1217 between 2015 and 2020;

- For Bulgaria, the regression equation of IEF is stated as follows (Insert Table 22):

$$IEF = 0.3TGDP + 0.94GCF + 35FDIGDP + 190PCI + 34PDI \quad (5)$$

Thus, the value of IEF for 2020 would be:

$$IEF_{2020} = (0.3 \times 95.79) + (0.94 \times 18.75) + (35 \times 3.87) + (190 \times 0.085) + (34 \times 0.447) = 213.166 \cong 213$$

The regression equation of IEFPV on IEF for Bulgaria may be expressed as below (Refer to Table 32):

$$IEFPV = 0.74IEF \quad (6)$$

Hence IEFPV for 2020 would be:

$$IEFPV_{2020} = 0.74IEF_{2020} = (0.74 \times 213) = 157.62 \cong 158$$

For Bulgaria, the value of IEF has decreased from 287 to 213 between 2015 and 2020 accompanied by a fall in the value of IEFPV from 207 to 158 between 2015 and 2020 (Refer to Table: 12 for comparison);

- The regression equation of IEF for Czech Republic is stated as follows (Insert Table 23):

$$IEF = 0.18TGDP + 0.75GCF + 4FDIGDP + 396PCI + 129PDI \quad (7)$$

Thus, IEF for the year 2020 may be estimated as follows:

$IEF_{2020} = (0.18 \times 147.812) + (0.75 \times 26) + (4 \times 2.62) + (396 \times 0.128) + (129 \times 0.418) = 161.19616 \cong 161$

The regression equation of IEFPV on IEF for Czech Republic may be expressed as follows (Refer to Table 33):

$$IEFPV = 0.79IEF \quad (8)$$

Hence the value of IEFPV in 2020 would be:

$IEFPV_{2020} = 0.79IEF_{2020} = (0.79 \times 161) = 127.19 \cong 127$

A quick comparison of values of IEF between 2015 and 2020 shows a marginal decrease from 163 to 161 and in a similar manner, the value of IEFPV has decreased from 129 to 127 during the same time period for Czech Republic (Refer to Table 13 for comparison);

- The regression equation of IEF for Estonia is stated as follows (Insert Table 24):

$$IEF = 0.12TGDP + 0.63GCF + 3.62FDIGDP + 205PCI + 33PDI \quad (9)$$

The value of IEF for Estonia for the year 2020 is estimated as:

$IEF_{2020} = (0.12 \times 110) + (0.63 \times 30.24) + (3.62 \times 11.54) + (205 \times 0.086) + (33 \times 0.433) = 105.945 \cong 106$

The regression equation of IEFPV on IEF for Estonia may be written as (Refer to Table 34):

$$IEFPV = 22 + 0.64IEF \quad (10)$$

Hence the estimated value of IEFPV for the year 2020 would be:

$$IEFPV_{2020} = 22 + (0.64 \times 106) = 89.84 \cong 90$$

The values of IEF and IEFPV for Estonia in 2015 were 147 and 111 respectively (Refer to Table 14 for comparison). However, in 2020; the values of IEF and IEFPV declined to 106 and 90 respectively;

- The regression equation of TII for Kazakhstan is stated as follows (Insert Table 25):

$$IEF = 0.2TGDP + 0.71GCF + 3.52FDIGDP + 82PCI + 23PDI \quad (11)$$

The estimated value of IEF for the year 2020 will be:

$$IEF_{2020} = (0.2 \times 48.91) + (0.71 \times 28.52) + (3.52 \times 4.33) + (82 \times 0.51) + (23 \times 0.77) = 104.8028 \cong 105$$

The regression equation of IEFPV on IEF for Kazakhstan may be written as (Refer to Table 35):

$$IEFPV = -11 + 0.82IEF \quad (12)$$

The estimated value of IEFPV in case of Kazakhstan for the year 2020 would be (Refer to Table 35):

$$IEFPV_{2020} = -11 + (0.82 \times 105) = 75.1 \cong 75$$

The estimated values of IEF and IEFPV for Kazakhstan in 2015 were 258 and 204 respectively (Refer to Table 15 for comparison). However, in 2020; the estimated values for IEF and IEFPV showed a *major* dip in values and settled for 105 and 75 respectively;

- The regression equation of IEF for Kyrgyz Republic is stated as follows (Insert Table 26):

$$IEF = 0.23TGDP + 6FDIGDP + 122PCI + 24PDI \quad (13)$$

The estimated value of IEF for the year 2020 would be:

$IEF_{2020} = (0.23 \times 73.6) + (6 \times -5.19) + (122 \times 0.48) + (24 \times 0.75) = 62.348 \cong 62$

The regression equation of IEFPV on IEF for Kyrgyz Republic may be expressed as below (Refer to Table 36):

$$IEFPV = -8 + 0.82IEF \quad (14)$$

The estimated value of IEFPV for Kyrgyz Republic for 2020 would be:

$IEFPV_{2020} = -8 + (0.82 \times 62) = 42.48 \cong 43$

There has been a significant reduction in the values of both IEF and IEFPV for Kyrgyz Republic in 2020 as compared to 2015 (Refer to Table 16 for comparison). The values of IEF and IEFPV in 2015 were 263 and 207 respectively that declined to 62 and 43 respectively in 2020 contemplating the fact that Kyrgyz Republic was not successful in mitigating the adverse effects of the pandemic;

- The regression equation of IEF for Russian Federation is stated as follows (Insert Table 27):

$$IEF = 0.3TGDP + 0.66GCF + 32FDIGDP + 65PCI + 25PDI \quad (15)$$

By plugging the values of the regressors for the year 2020 in equation: (15), we have the estimated value of IEF for Russian Federation as below:

$IEF_{2020} = (0.3 \times 38.6) + (0.66 \times 24) + (32 \times 0.64) + (65 \times 0.26) + (25 \times 0.61) = 80.05 \cong 80$

The regression equation of IEFPV on IEF for Russian Federation may be expressed as below (Refer to Table 37):

$$IEFPV = 2.43 + 0.7TII \qquad (16)$$

The estimated value of IEFPV for Russian Federation for the year 2020 would be:

$$IEFPV_{2020} = 2.43 + (0.7 \times 80) = 58.43 \cong 58$$

By comparing the IEF and IEFPV values for the years 2015 and 2020 in case of Russian Federation (Refer to Table 17 for comparison), it may be found that there has been a moderate reduction in the value of IEF from 139 to 80 accompanied by an equally moderate fall in the value of IEFPV from 101 to 58 respectively. Hence for Russian Federation, the impact of the pandemic on its economic foundation was *moderate*;

- The regression equation of IEF for Slovenia is stated as follows (Insert Table 28):

$$IEF = 0.18TGDP + 0.65GCF + 24FDIGDP + 176PCI + 36PDI \qquad (17)$$

The estimated value of IEF for Slovenia for the year 2020 would be:

$$IEF_{2020} = (0.18 \times 162.19) + (0.65 \times 20) + (24 \times 0.91) + (176 \times 0.2) + (36 \times 0.47) = 116.1542 \cong 116$$

The regression equation of IEFPV on IEF for Slovenia may be expressed as below (Refer to Table 38):

$$IEFPV = 0.81IEF \qquad (18)$$

Hence the estimated value of IEFPV for the year 2020 would be:

$$IEFPV_{2020} = (0.81 \times 116) = 93.96 \cong 94$$

By comparing the IEF and IEFPV values for the years 2015 and 2020 in case of Slovenia (Refer to Table 18 for comparison), it may be found that there had been significant reductions in the values of IEF (from 213 to 116) and IEFPV (from 169 to 94) respectively.

This proves that Slovenia, as a nation; failed to mitigate the economic disaster originated from the pandemic; and

- Finally, the regression equation of IEF for Ukraine is stated as follows (Insert Table 29):

$$IEF = 0.17TGDP + 0.62GCF + 30FDIGDP + 157PCI + 29PDI \tag{19}$$

Now the estimated value of Ukraine's IEF for the year 2020 would be:

$IEF_{2020} = (0.17 \times 66.33) + (0.62 \times 7.51) + (30 \times 0.195) + (157 \times 0.16) + (29 \times 0.69) = 66.9123 \cong 67$

The regression equation of IEFPV on IEF for Ukraine is expressed as below (Refer to Table 39):

$$IEFPV = 0.81IEF \tag{20}$$

Hence the estimated value of IEFPV for Ukraine in 2020 would be:

$IEFPV_{2020} = (0.81 \times 67) = 54.27 \cong 54$

In comparison to the estimated values of IEF and IEFPV in 2015 (89 and 71 respectively), the estimated values of IEF and IEFPV for Ukraine reduced to 67 and 54 respectively (Refer to Table 19 for comparison). Hence it shows that Ukraine was more or less successful in mitigating the adverse effects on its economic foundation due to COVID - 19 pandemic. Hence a summarized view of the results and findings projects the holistic picture that 9 out of 10 sample countries that embraced transition from planned to market economy failed to mitigate the adverse effects of globalization, especially in the *benchmark* year of 2020; mainly due to inequal distribution of income and wealth among the poor. The only exceptional country was Czech Republic which did not bear the brunt of the pandemic and it *almost* nullified the adverse impacts on its economic foundation during the trying times.

A significant research work by Aristei and Perugini (2015, pp. 44 - 47) based on the European Bank for Reconstruction and Development's (EBRD) (2010, 2012) transition indicators for *nine* sectors, namely, Large Scale Privatization (LSP), Small Scale Privatization (SSP), Governance and Enterprise Restructuring (GER), Price Liberalization (PL), Trade and Foreign Exchange System (TFE), Competition Policy (CP), Banking Reform and Interest Rate Liberalization (BR), Securities Markets and Non-bank Financial Institutions (SFI), and Infrastructure (I) respectively and by simultaneously segregating the countries in transition into 7 clusters helped to establish some interesting facts as follows:

1. Cluster 1 countries comprising of Czech Republic, Hungary, Poland and Slovak Republic, and Cluster 3 countries consisting of Bulgaria and Romania were at the lowest levels of inequality at the early phase of transition; however, by the turn of second decade of 21st century, Bulgaria and Romania had achieved the highest levels of income inequality (in terms of Gini coefficient);
2. Cluster 2 countries comprising of Estonia, Latvia, and Lithuania experienced a very high degree of inequality in income distribution (an average Gini Index of 35) at the beginning of transition period and the trend continued by the end of the first 10 years of twenty first century;
3. Cluster 4 countries consisting of Croatia, FYR Macedonia, and Slovenia showed signs of high disparities in income distribution by the late 1980s', but gradually converged to a moderate Gini Index of 30 points by the by the turn of second decade of 21st century;
4. Cluster 5 countries comprising of Kazakhstan, Moldova, Russian Federation, and Ukraine and Cluster 6 countries consisting of Albania, Armenia, Georgia, and Kyrgyz Republic which were created from the disintegration of erstwhile USSR exhibited one of the highest income inequalities in the world at the initial phase of transition to the market economy and barring the exception of Russian Federation, the remaining nations managed to curb the Gini Index to around 35 points by the by the turn of second decade of 21st century; and
5. Finally, Cluster 7 comprising of Azerbaijan, Belarus, Tajikistan, Turkmenistan, and Uzbekistan displayed mild level of income inequality at the beginning phase of economic transition – most probably due to their low progress towards transition. This although helped in mitigating the adverse effects of economic transition, however; failed to usher in the major structural changes in the fields of LSP, GER, PL, and TFE respectively.

The results and findings of my research work consisting of 10 sample countries spread over the 7 clusters showed conformity to the findings of Aristei and Perugini (2015) as well.

The primary common reason which has surfaced for a surge in the level of inequality (within reasonable ranges) among the countries in transition was the coordinated and balanced form of migration from planned to market economy. Apart from that, a sustained high level of income inequality (for example, in case of Russian Federation) should be primarily attributed to extreme crony capitalism coupled with the adopted policy of unrestricted neoliberalism. To quote Aristei and Perugini (2015, p. 55): "To sum up, the transition patterns that were more coordinated and balanced (but not necessarily quicker) were able to keep the rise in income inequality within reasonable ranges. In contrast, transition was relatively more pro-inequality when price liberalisation and privatisation were not accompanied by progress in competition policy and development of financial markets, which lagged behind or were implemented in later stages of transition". In this context, the concept of globalization has been mired in the discourse of its apparent success in the 'polished' form of neoliberalism. To quote Bishop and Payne (2021, p. 4): "...At its heart, the term connotes only a spatial expansion of the terrain on which political economy functions. It was the neoliberal project that coloured globalization, propelling it forward to become the 'actually existing' variant within which we live at the start of the 2020s". In order to save the basic essence of globalization, they have suggested that the new globalization model should be 'improved' on its positive aspects and simultaneously minimize its negative aspects. They have classified the fast-emerging alternative model of neoliberal globalization into two categories, namely, *Deglobalization 'from the right'* and *Deglobalization 'from the left'*. The concept of deglobalization 'from the right' initiated from the aftermath of 2008 subprime crisis which ultimately led to acute global recession since 'The Great Depression' of 1929. According to Bishop and Payne (2021, p. 5), the victory of Donald Trump in the 2016 US Presidential Elections established the advent of Deglobalization 'from the right' which Blyth (2016) had termed as the era of 'Neonationalism'. The political ideologies of Deglobalization 'from the right' are based on protectionist trade practices, and pro-business policies favoring the large corporates. Its quintessential pillars are essentially based on the policies that may be summed up as quoted (Bishop and Payne, 2021; p. 7): "pro-marketization, pro-rich, and likely to do little economically for those who voted for him (Trump) having lost their jobs in the de-industrialized parts of the US. He is, in essence, a hyper-neoliberal at home and a neo-nationalist abroad".

On the other hand, Deglobalization 'from the left' mainly suffers the social distinctions stemmed from the categorization of 'deserving' and undeserving' sections of the society in regards to access to social welfare and related services. To quote Bishop and Payne (2021, p. 10): "Such 'nativist socialism', as John Narayan (2019) calls it, largely equates the 'working class', on which Brexit supposedly depends, and for which it supposedly must be delivered, with the white working class. This xenophobia serves to elide the agency of non-white populations in their struggles against domestic legacies of colonialism and undermines collective anti-racist and anti-imperialist action by shattering national and global solidarity (Bhambra, 2017; Bhambra & Holmwood, 2018)".

Since both the doctrines of Deglobalization 'from the left' and Deglobalization 'from the right' have their own limitations, a new concept of 'Reglobalization' has emerged among the scholars and political commentators. Helleiner (2014, p. 22) has coined the term 'cooperative decentralization' based on functioning of the future global financial governance which falls between 'strengthened liberal multilateralism' and 'fragmentation and conflict' (Helleiner, 2014; pp. 168 – 176).

The idea of 'cooperative decentralization' acts on the idea of managing the global financial governance by the states within certain minimum international standards through the Financial Stability Bureau in order to control the unrestrained flow of funds in highly precarious and sensitive sectors so that the extremely adverse effects of neoliberal globalization could be minimized. However, he reminded of a caveat that "rather than detailed one-size-fits-all rules, those standards could be based around broad principles that allowed significant national or regional policy space" (Helleiner, 2014; p. 176).

Thus, to sum up, in order to make globalization work, the process of 'reglobalization' is necessary by keeping the merits of globalization in place and simultaneously mitigating its adverse effects.

THE LIMITATIONS OF STUDY

The limitations of this research are as follows:

Since a panel data study is usually more preferred to a time series analysis by the researchers, this research work is falling short on that aspect. Also, this research paper does not take into account the impacts of globalization on the respective labor markets, work environments, and employment opportunities of the sample countries in question. An additional inclusion of the effects on socio - political system (style of governance and the nature of democracy) in the post-transitional phase could have made the article more interesting in nature.

FINAL DISCUSSION AND CONCLUSION

The primary objective of this research work was to formulate and implement the concept of Index of Economic Foundation (IEF) in the real-world scenario with the help of a time series study (1996 – 2015) with the Base Year of 1995 and consisting of 10 sample countries which went through the phase of economic transition. The application of IEF is not limited to the selective countries for study but it may be used for other countries that went through the transitional phase as well in order to make a holistic evaluation of economic transition as an *obvious* outcome of globalization. Needless to state that the prime 'benchmarks' of this evaluation procedure would be sustainable economic growth and egalitarian distribution of income and wealth respectively. From the cross – country econometrical and statistical analyses, the major findings point to the fact that Product Concentration Index (PCI), Ratio of FDI to Gross Domestic Product (FDIGDP), and PDI are the three major parameters which dictate the outputs of IEF for the economies in transition in contrary to the popular belief that the Trade share to GDP plays the pivotal role for effective transition.

The issue of successful economic transition as a result of globalization rests on two major factors, i.e., positive growth of gross capital formation leading to an incremental effect on Net Fixed Assets (NFA) for the said economy and simultaneous egalitarian distribution of the fruits of economic growth among the underprivileged sections of the society. This study on 10 sample countries has failed to find any significant impact of globalization as the estimated Index of Economic Foundation Present Values (IEFPV) of none of those countries failed to exhibit strong *elastic* correlation to Index of Economic Foundation (IEF). Keeping these important factors in mind, this paper could help to open new vistas of research for a major topic related to transitional economies and open new vistas for further research.

DATA DECLARATIONS AND RESOURCES

1. http://unctadstat.unctad.org/;
2. https://databank.worldbank.org/
3. https://stats.oecd.org/

DECLARATION OF CONFLICTS OF INTERESTS

The author declares no conflicts of interests.

REFERENCES

Akyüz, Y. (2018). Inequality, financialisation and stagnation. *Economic and Labour Relations Review*, *29*(4), 428–445. doi:10.1177/1035304618812572

Aristei, D., & Perugini, C. (2015). The Drivers of Personal Income Inequality in Transition, and the Role of Reform Approaches. In C. Perugini & F. Pompei (Eds.), *Inequalities During and After Transition in Central and Eastern Europe* (pp. 41–58). The Palgrave Macmillan. doi:10.1057/9781137460981_3

Babecky, J., & Havranek, T. (2014). Structural reforms and growth in transition: A meta – analysis. *Economics of Transition and Institutional Change*, *22*(1), 13–42. doi:10.1111/ecot.12029

Bhagwati, J. (2008). Globalization with a human face. In E. Zedillo (Ed.), *The Future of Globalization: Explorations in light of recent turbulence* (pp. 34–39). Routledge.

Bhambra, G. K. (2017). Brexit, Trump, and 'methodological whiteness': On the misrecognition of race and class. *The British Journal of Sociology*, *68*(S1), S214–S232. doi:10.1111/1468-4446.12317 PMID:29114873

Bhambra, G. K., & Holmwood, J. (2018). Colonialism, Postcolonialism and the Liberal Welfare State. *New Political Economy*, *23*(5), 574–587. doi:10.1080/13563467.2017.1417369

Bishop, M. L., & Payne, A. (2021). The political economies of different globalizations: Theorizing reglobalization. *Globalizations*, *18*(1), 1–21. doi:10.1080/14747731.2020.1779963

Blyth, M. (November 15, 2016). Global Trumpism. Why Trump's Victory Was 30 Years in the Making and Why It Won't Stop Here. *Foreign Affairs*. Retrieved from https://www.foreignaffairs.com/articles/2016-11-15/global-trumpism

Bonadio, B., Huo, Z., Levchenko, A. A., & Pandalai-Nayar, N. (2021). Global supply chains in the pandemic. *Journal of International Economics, 133*, 1 – 23. doi:10.1016/j.jinteco.2021.103534

Brown, M. M. (2008). Building partnerships for an inclusive globalization. In E. Zedillo (Ed.), *The Future of Globalization: Explorations in light of recent turbulence* (pp. 58–61). Routledge.

Collier, P. (2008). Africa and globalization. In E. Zedillo (Ed.), *The Future of Globalization: Explorations in light of recent turbulence* (pp. 40–57). Routledge.

Das, N. G. (2008). Statistical Methods: Vol. I & II. *New Delhi: McGraw Hill Education* Private Limited.

De Melo, M., Denizer, C., Gelb, A., & Tenev, S. (2001). Circumstance and Choice: The Role of Initial Conditions and Policies in Transition Economies. *The World Bank Economic Review*, *15*(1), 1–31. doi:10.1093/wber/15.1.1

De Soto, H. (2008). Missing ingredients of globalization. In E. Zedillo (Ed.), *The Future of Globalization: Explorations in light of recent turbulence* (pp. 19–33). Routledge.

Dollar, D., Hallward-Driemeir, M., & Mengistae, T. (2008). Investment climate and international integration in Asian developing countries. In E. Zedillo (Ed.), The Future of Globalization: Explorations in light of recent turbulence (pp. 85 – 104). Oxford, UK: Routledge.

EBRD. (2010). *Transition Report 2010: Integration across borders*. https://www.ebrd.com/downloads/research/transition/tr10.pdf

EBRD. (2012). *Transition Report 2010: Recovery and Reform.* www.ebrd.com/transitionreport

Elliott, R. J. R., Schumacher, I., & Withagen, C. (2020). Suggestions for a Covid-19 Post-Pandemic Research Agenda in Environmental Economics. *Environmental and Resource Economics, 76*(4), 1187–1213. doi:10.100710640-020-00478-1 PMID:32836846

Finger, J. M., & Kreinin, M. E. (1979). A Measure of 'Export Similarity' and Its Possible Uses. *Economic Journal (London), 89*(356), 905–912. doi:10.2307/2231506

Gang, F. (2008). Combining policies to benefit from globalization: the case of China. In E. Zedillo (Ed.), *The Future of Globalization: Explorations in light of recent turbulence* (pp. 270–283). Routledge.

Granger, C. W. J., & Newbold, P. (1974). Spurious regressions in econometrics. *Journal of Econometrics, 2*(2), 111–120. doi:10.1016/0304-4076(74)90034-7

Gujarati, D. N. (2003). *Basic Econometrics* (4th ed.). McGraw – Hill, Inc.

Helleiner, E. (2014). *The Status Quo Crisis: Global Financial Governance After the 2008 Meltdown.* Oxford University Press. doi:10.1093/acprof:oso/9780199973637.001.0001

Herfindahl, O. C. (1959). *Copper Costs and Prices: 1870 – 1957.* The Johns Hopkins University Press.

Hirschman, A. O. (1964). The Paternity of an Index. *The American Economic Review, 54*(5), 761–762.

Hirst, P., & Thompson, G. (2019). The future of globalisation. In J. Michie (Ed.), *The Handbook of Globalisation* (3rd ed., pp. 16–31). Edward Elgar Publishing.

Hoskisson, R. E., Eden, L., Lau, C. M., & Wright, M. (2000). Strategy in Emerging Economies. *Academy of Management Journal, 43*(3), 249–267. doi:10.5465/1556394

Jean, S. (2020). How the COVID-19 Pandemic Is Reshaping the Trade Landscape and What to Do About It. *Inter Economics, 55*(3), 135–139. doi:10.100710272-020-0890-4 PMID:32536707

Lin, F., Li, B., & Sim, N. C. S. (2014). Trade openness and government size of small developing countries: An instrumental approach. *Economics of Transition and Institutional Change, 22*(4), 783–808. doi:10.1111/ecot.12053

Michie, J. (2017). *Advanced Introduction to Globalisation.* Edward Elgar.

Misch, F., Gemmell, N., & Kneller, R. (2014). Using surveys of business perceptions as a guide to growth – enhancing financial reforms. *Economics of Transition and Institutional Change*, *22*(4), 683–725. doi:10.1111/ecot.12049

Narayan, J. (2019). British Black Power: The anti-imperialism of political blackness and the problem of nativist socialism. *The Sociological Review*, *67*(5), 945–967. doi:10.1177/0038026119845550

Perraton, J. (2019). The scope and implications of globalisation. In J. Michie (Ed.), *The Handbook of Globalisation* (3rd ed., pp. 50–76). Edward Elgar Publishing.

Perugini, C., & Selezneva, E. (2015). Labour market institutions, crisis and gender earnings gap in Eastern Europe. *Economics of Transition and Institutional Change*, *23*(3), 517–564. doi:10.1111/ecot.12072

Rincon-Aznar, A., Vecchi, M., & Venturini, F. (2015). Functional Income Distribution in European Transition Countries. In C. Perugini & F. Pompei (Eds.), *Inequalities During and After Transition in Central and Eastern Europe* (pp. 59–92). Palgrave Macmillan. doi:10.1057/9781137460981_4

Roy, D. (2020). Formulation of Governance and Democracy Index (GDI) and Governance, Democracy, and Emancipation Index (GDEI): A Cross-country Empirical Study (1998 – 2017). *Open Political Science*, *4*(1), 15–26. doi:10.1515/openps-2021-0002

Roy, D. (2022). Formulation of Digitization Impact Index (DII): A Cross-Country Empirical Study (2009–2018). *International Journal of Innovation in the Digital Economy*, *13*(1), 1–34. doi:10.4018/IJIDE.292628

Stiglitz, J. (2008). The future of globalization: lessons from Cancún and recent financial crises. In E. Zedillo (Ed.), *The Future of Globalization: Explorations in light of recent turbulence* (pp. 70–82). Routledge.

UNCTAD. (2016). *Trade and Development Report 2016: Structural Transformation for Inclusive and Sustained Growth*. United Nations.

APPENDIX 1: ACRONYMS

GDP: Gross Domestic Product (In Current US Dollar)
FDI: Foreign Direct Investment (In Current US Dollar)
TGDP: Trade to GDP Ratio (In percentage)
GCF: Gross Capital Formation (As a percentage of GDP)
FDIGDP: Foreign Direct Investment to GDP Ratio (In percentage)
PCI: Product Concentration Index
PDI: Product Diversification Index
GDPRC: Gross Domestic Product Relative Change
TGDPRC: Trade to GDP Relative Change
FDIGDPRC: FDI to GDP Relative Change
GCFRC: Gross Capital Formation Relative Change
PCIRC: Product Concentration Index Relative Change
PDIRC: Product Diversification Index Relative Change
IEFRC: Index of Economic Foundation Relative Change
IEF: Index of Economic Foundation
GIC: Gini Coefficient
IEFPV: Index of Economic Foundation Present Value

Compilation of References

Abdin, M. J. (2015). Foreign Direct Investment (FDI) in SAARC Countries. *Global Journal of Management and Business Research. C Finance*, *15*(8), 13–20. doi:10.2139srn.2660625

Abi-Rached, J. M. (2021). The Covid-19 caesura and the post-pandemic future. *Biosocieties*, *16*(1), 142–156. doi:10.105741292-020-00212-6

Acemoglu, D., Johnson, S., Robinson, J. A., & Thaicharoen, Y. (2003). Institutional causes, macroeconomics symptoms: Volatility, crises, and growth. *Journal of Monetary Economics*, *50*(1), 49–122. doi:10.1016/S0304-3932(02)00208-8

AFI. (2020). *Importancia económica y social del sector vitivinícola en España* [Economic and Social Importance of the Wine Sector in Spain]. Available at: https://www.interprofesionaldelvino.es/publicaciones/informes-importancia-sector/nacional/

AFI. (2020). *Importancia económica y social del sector vitivinícola en España* [Economical and Social Importance of the Wine Sector in Spain]. Available at: https://www.interprofesionaldelvino.es/publicaciones/informes-importancia-sector/nacional/

Agostino, M., & Trivieri, F. (2016). European wines exports towards emerging markets. The role of geographical identity. *Journal of Industry, Competition and Trade*, *16*(2), 233–256. doi:10.100710842-015-0210-z

Akçacı, T. & Çınaroğlu, M. S. (2020). Yeni Koronavirüs (Covid-19) Salgınının Lojistik ve Ticarete Etkisi [The Effect of the New Coronavirus (covid-19) Epidemic on Logistics and Trade]. *Gaziantep University Journal of Social Sciences*, *19*, 447-456. doi:10.21547/jss.766159

Akkoyun, A. (2016). *Analysis of Factors That Affect Sustainable Production by Using Fuzzy QFD Method* [Master Thesis]. Yıldız Technical University.

Akyüz, Y. (2018). Inequality, financialisation and stagnation. *Economic and Labour Relations Review*, *29*(4), 428–445. doi:10.1177/1035304618812572

Alberola, E., Arslan, Y., Cheng, G., & Moessner, R. (2021). Fiscal response to the COVID-19 crisis in advanced and emerging market economies. *Pacific Economic Review*, *26*(4), 459–468. Advance online publication. doi:10.1111/1468-0106.12370

Al-Najjar, B., & Belghitar, Y. (2011). Corporate cash holdings and dividend payments: Evidence from simultaneous analysis. *Managerial and Decision Economics*, *32*(4), 231–241. doi:10.1002/mde.1529

Al-Swidi, A., Huque, S. M. R., Hafeez, M. H., & Shariff, M. N. M. (2014). The role of subjective norms in theory of planned behavior in the context of organic food consumption. *British Food Journal*, *116*(10), 1561–1580. doi:10.1108/BFJ-05-2013-0105

Alves, P. (2018). Cash holdings around the world: Financial crisis, culture and shareholder rights. *MPRA Paper*, 100159.

Amadieu, P., Maurel, C., & Viviani, J. L. (2013). Intangibles, export intensity, and company performance in the French wine industry. *Journal of Wine Economics*, *8*(2), 198–224. doi:10.1017/jwe.2013.27

Anderson, J. E., & Marcouiller, D. (2002). Insecurity and the pattern of trade: An empirical investigation. *The Review of Economics and Statistics*, *84*(2), 342–352. doi:10.1162/003465302317411587

Andrews, L., Higgins, A., Andrews, M., & Lalor, J. (2012). Classic grounded theory to analyse secondary data: Reality and reflections. *The Grounded Theory Review*, *11*(1), 12–26.

Anita, S. S., Tasnova, N., & Nawar, N. (2022). Are non-performing loans sensitive to macroeconomic determinants? an empirical evidence from banking sector of SAARC countries. *Future Business Journal*, *8*(1), 1–16. doi:10.118643093-022-00117-9

Anon, L. (2015a). Wines exports in the ascendancy. *Alimentaria*, *463*, 34–36.

Anon, L. (2015b). Export of bulk and bottled wines. Should Spain follow the Italian example? *Enologos*, *17*(96), 80–81.

Anon, L. (2020). The sky's the limit for Australian Tempranillo. *The Australian & New Zealand Grapegrower & Winemaker*, *676*, 44–48.

Aristei, D., & Perugini, C. (2015). The Drivers of Personal Income Inequality in Transition, and the Role of Reform Approaches. In C. Perugini & F. Pompei (Eds.), *Inequalities During and After Transition in Central and Eastern Europe* (pp. 41–58). The Palgrave Macmillan. doi:10.1057/9781137460981_3

Arriola, C., Kowalski, P., & van Tongeren, F. (2021). *The impact of COVID-19 on directions and structure of international trade*. Academic Press.

Australian Maritime Safety Authority (AMSA). (2010). *Fact finding report into the reported collision involving the New Zealand registered craft Ady Gil and the Japan registered whaling ship Shonan Maru No.2 in the Southern Ocean on 6 January 2010*. AMSA.

Aylward, D. (2005). What makes a successful SME exporter within the Australian wine industry. *The Australian & New Zealand Grapegrower & Winemaker*, *497*, 122–127.

Aysan, A. F., Ozturk, H., Polat, A. Y., & Saltoğlu, B. (2016). Macroeconomic drivers of loan quality in Turkey. *Emerging Markets Finance & Trade*, *52*(1), 98–109. doi:10.1080/1540496X.2016.1105688

Aysan, A. F., Polat, A. Y., Tekin, H., & Tunalı, A. S. (2022). The ascent of geopolitics: Scientometric analysis and ramifications of geopolitical risk. *Defence and Peace Economics*, 1–19. doi:10.1080/10242694.2022.2062981

Ayuda, M., Esteban, E., Martín-Retortillo, M., & Pinilla, V. (2020). The blue water footprint of the Spanish wine industry: 1935–2015. *Water (Basel)*, *12*(7), 1872. doi:10.3390/w12071872

Azad, N. F., Serletis, A., & Xu, L. (2021). Covid-19 and monetary–fiscal policy interactions in Canada. *The Quarterly Review of Economics and Finance*, *82*, 376–384. doi:10.1016/j.qref.2021.06.009

Azolibe, C. B. (2020). Banking Sector Intermediation Development and Growth of a Developing Economy: An Empirical Investigation of Nigeria. Research Square, 1–18. doi:10.21203/rs.3.rs-95127/v1

Babecky, J., & Havranek, T. (2014). Structural reforms and growth in transition: A meta – analysis. *Economics of Transition and Institutional Change*, *22*(1), 13–42. doi:10.1111/ecot.12029

Baltic and International Maritime Council & International Chamber of Shipping (BIMCO/ICS). (2015). *Manpower Report. The global supply and demand for seafarers.* Retrieved from https://www.ics-shipping.org/wp-content/uploads/2020/08/manpower-report-2015-executive-summary.pdf

Baltic and International Maritime Council & International Chamber of Shipping (BIMCO/ICS). (2021). *Seafarer Workforce Report. The global supply and demand for seafarers.* Retrieved from https://www.bimco.org/news/priority-news/20210728---bimco-ics-seafarer-workforce-report

Barnett, M. L., & Pekcan, C. H. (2017). The Human Element in Shipping. Encyclopedia of Maritime and Offshore Engineering, 1974, 1–10. doi:10.1002/9781118476406.emoe033

Bates, T. W., Chang, C. H., & Chi, J. D. (2018). Why has the value of cash increased over time? *Journal of Financial and Quantitative Analysis*, *53*(2), 749–787. doi:10.1017/S002210901700117X

Beck, T. (2020). Finance in the times of coronavirus. In Economics in the Time of COVID-19. London: Centre for Economic Policy Research.

Behmiri, N. B., Rebelo, J. F., Gouveia, S., & António, P. (2019). Firm characteristics and export performance in Portuguese wine firms. *International Journal of Wine Business Research*, *31*(3), 419–440. doi:10.1108/IJWBR-07-2018-0032

BelloW. (2018). https://systemicalternatives.org/2014/05/09/what-is-to-be-done-the-six-pillars-of-deglobalization/

Bhagwati, J. (2008). Globalization with a human face. In E. Zedillo (Ed.), *The Future of Globalization: Explorations in light of recent turbulence* (pp. 34–39). Routledge.

Bhambra, G. K. (2017). Brexit, Trump, and ‘methodological whiteness’: On the misrecognition of race and class. *The British Journal of Sociology, 68*(S1), S214–S232. doi:10.1111/1468-4446.12317 PMID:29114873

Bhambra, G. K., & Holmwood, J. (2018). Colonialism, Postcolonialism and the Liberal Welfare State. *New Political Economy, 23*(5), 574–587. doi:10.1080/13563467.2017.1417369

Bhandari, V., & Mohite, V. (2022). Entrepreneurship Ecosystem: An Appraisal for Sultanate of Oman Using the Ease of Doing Business Index. Research Square, 1–16. doi:10.21203/rs.3.rs-1203598/v1

Bishop, M. L., & Payne, A. (2021). The political economies of different globalizations: Theorizing reglobalization. *Globalizations, 18*(1), 1–21. doi:10.1080/14747731.2020.1779963

Blyth, M. (November 15, 2016). Global Trumpism. Why Trump’s Victory Was 30 Years in the Making and Why It Won’t Stop Here. *Foreign Affairs*. Retrieved from https://www.foreignaffairs.com/articles/2016-11-15/global-trumpism

Bonadio, B., Huo, Z., Levchenko, A. A., & Pandalai-Nayar, N. (2021). Global supply chains in the pandemic. *Journal of International Economics, 133*, 1 – 23. doi:10.1016/j.jinteco.2021.103534

Boudreau, J. W., & Ramstad, P. M. (2005). Talentship talent segmentation, and sustainability: A new hr decision science paradigm for a new strategy definition. *Human Resource Management, 44*(2), 129–136. doi:10.1002/hrm.20054

Brodeur, A., Gray, D., Islam, A. & Bhuiyan, S.J. (2020). *A literature review of the Economics of COVID-19*. Institute of Labor Economics, IZA DP No. 13411.

Brown, M. M. (2008). Building partnerships for an inclusive globalization. In E. Zedillo (Ed.), *The Future of Globalization: Explorations in light of recent turbulence* (pp. 58–61). Routledge.

Caesar, L. (2013). Sustaining the Supply of Ship Officers: Making a Case for Succession Planning in Seafarer Recruitment. *Universal Journal of Management, 1*(1), 6–12. doi:10.13189/ujm.2013.010102

Cahoon, S., Haugstetter, H., & Bhaskar, P. (2010). *Overcoming seafarer shortages: Human resource management and marketing strategies for a sustainable future*. International Association of Maritime Economists Conference, Lisbon, Portugal.

Caldara, D., & Iacoviello, M. (2022). Measuring geopolitical risk. *The American Economic Review, 112*(4), 1194–1225. doi:10.1257/aer.20191823

Caradonna, J. L. (2014). Sustainability: A History. Oxford University Press.

Carrasco, I., Castillo-Valero, J. S., Córcoles, C., & Carchano, M. (2021). Greening Wine Exports? Changes in the Carbon Footprint of Spanish Wine Exports. *International Journal of Environmental Research and Public Health, 18*(17), 9035. doi:10.3390/ijerph18179035 PMID:34501620

Castillo, J., & Garcia-Cortijo, M. (2014). Gravity dynamics of Spanish wine exports, 1986-2012. *Historia Agraria*, *64*, 1–8.

Castillo-Valero, J. S., Carrasco, I., Carchano, M., & Córcoles, C. (2021). What Is the Environmental Impact of Wine Entering Global Value Chains? Studying the Evolution of CO2 Emissions from the Export of Spanish Denomination of Origin Wines. *Foods*, *10*(7), 1664. doi:10.3390/foods10071664 PMID:34359535

Çatuk, C., & Aydın, K. (2021). Covid-19 dünya ve türkiye tedarik zinciri üzerine etkileri [Impacts of Covid-19 on the World and Turkey Supply Chain]. *Adıyaman Üniversitesi Sosyal Bilimler Enstitüsü Dergisi*, (37), 427–449. doi:10.14520/adyusbd.753939

Cervera Ferrer, F. J., & Compés López, R. (2018). The performance of Spanish wine exports in international markets. *Economia Agraria y Recursos Naturales, 18*, 23-48.

Ceylan, R. F., Ozkan, B., & Mulazimogullari, E. (2020). Historical evidence for economic effects of COVID-19. *The European Journal of Health Economics*, *21*(6), 817–823. doi:10.100710198-020-01206-8 PMID:32500243

Chakraborty, C., & Jana, A. (2021). Economic Growth and Trade-related Variables: An Empirical Study Using Indian Data. In Global Tariff War: Economic, Political and Social Implications (pp. 141–152). Emerald Publishing Limited. doi:10.1108/978-1-80071-314-720211011

Chang, Y., Benson, K., & Faff, R. (2017). Are excess cash holdings more valuable to firms in times of crisis? Financial constraints and governance matters. *Pacific-Basin Finance Journal*, *45*, 157–173. doi:10.1016/j.pacfin.2016.05.007

Chen, C., Shi, Y., Zhang, P., & Ding, C. (2021). A Cross-Country Comparison of Fiscal Policy Responses to the COVID-19 Global Pandemic. *Journal of Comparative Policy Analysis*, *23*(2), 262–273. doi:10.1080/13876988.2021.1878885

Chen, H. C., Chou, R. K., & Lu, C. L. (2018). Saving for a rainy day: Evidence from the 2000 dot-com crash and the 2008 credit crisis. *Journal of Corporate Finance*, *48*, 680–699. doi:10.1016/j.jcorpfin.2017.12.025

Chudik, A., Mohaddes, K., & Raissi, M. (2021). Covid-19 fiscal support and its effectiveness. *Economics Letters*, *205*, 109939. Advance online publication. doi:10.1016/j.econlet.2021.109939

Claessens, S., Djankov, S., & Xu, L. C. (2000). Corporate performance in the East Asian financial crisis. *The World Bank Research Observer*, *15*(1), 23–46. doi:10.1093/wbro/15.1.23

Collier, P. (2008). Africa and globalization. In E. Zedillo (Ed.), *The Future of Globalization: Explorations in light of recent turbulence* (pp. 40–57). Routledge.

Crick, J., & Crick, D. (2021). Internationalizing the coopetition construct: Quadratic effects on financial performance under different degrees of export intensity and an export geographical scope. *Journal of International Marketing*, *29*(2), 62–80. doi:10.1177/1069031X20988260

Crick, J., & Crick, D. (2022). Coopetition and international entrepreneurship: The influence of a competitor orientation. *International Journal of Entrepreneurial Behaviour & Research*, *28*(3), 801–828. doi:10.1108/IJEBR-06-2021-0519

D'Mello, R., Krishnaswami, S., & Larkin, P. J. (2008). Determinants of corporate cash holdings: Evidence from spin-offs. *Journal of Banking & Finance*, *32*(7), 1209–1220. doi:10.1016/j.jbankfin.2007.10.005

Das, N. G. (2008). Statistical Methods: Vol. I & II. *New Delhi: McGraw Hill Education* Private Limited.

De Melo, M., Denizer, C., Gelb, A., & Tenev, S. (2001). Circumstance and Choice: The Role of Initial Conditions and Policies in Transition Economies. *The World Bank Economic Review*, *15*(1), 1–31. doi:10.1093/wber/15.1.1

De Soto, H. (2008). Missing ingredients of globalization. In E. Zedillo (Ed.), *The Future of Globalization: Explorations in light of recent turbulence* (pp. 19–33). Routledge.

Demiralay, S., & Kilincarslan, E. (2019). The impact of geopolitical risks on travel and leisure stocks. *Tourism Management*, *75*, 460–476. doi:10.1016/j.tourman.2019.06.013

Demirci, E. (2019). Lojistik ilkeleri, İstanbul Üniversitesi [Logistics Principles, Istanbul University]. *Açık ve Uzaktan Eğitim Fakültesi, 332.* http://auzefkitap.istanbul.edu.tr/kitap/uluslararasitvlojistikyonetimi_ao/lojistikilkeleri.pdf

Demir, E., Díez-Esteban, J. M., & García-Gómez, C. D. (2019). The impact of geopolitical risks on cash holdings of hospitality companies: Evidence from emerging countries. *Journal of Hospitality and Tourism Management*, *39*, 166–174. doi:10.1016/j.jhtm.2019.04.004

Demirguc-Kunt, A., Peria, M. S. M., & Tressel, T. (2020). The global financial crisis and the capital structure of firms: Was the impact more severe among SMEs and non-listed firms? *Journal of Corporate Finance*, *60*, 101514. doi:10.1016/j.jcorpfin.2019.101514

Deyoung, R., Gron, A., Torna, G., & Winton, A. (2015). Risk overhang and loan portfolio decisions: Small business loan supply before and during the financial crisis. *The Journal of Finance*, *70*(6), 2451–2488. doi:10.1111/jofi.12356

Dickey, D. A., & Fuller, W. A. (1979). Distribution of the Estimators for Autoregressive Time Series with a Unit Root. *Journal of the American Statistical Association*, *74*(366a), 427–431. do i:10.1080/01621459.1979.10482531

Dittmar, A., Mahrt-Smith, J., & Servaes, H. (2003). International Corporate Governance and Corporate Cash Holdings. *Journal of Financial and Quantitative Analysis*, *38*(1), 111. doi:10.2307/4126766

Dollar, D., Hallward-Driemeir, M., & Mengistae, T. (2008). Investment climate and international integration in Asian developing countries. In E. Zedillo (Ed.), The Future of Globalization: Explorations in light of recent turbulence (pp. 85 – 104). Oxford, UK: Routledge.

Domazet, I., Marjanović, D., & Stošić, I. (2018). The attractiveness of the domicile economy through tax incentives. *Ekonomika preduzeća, 7/8*, 434-445.

Doshi, R., Kelley, J. G., & Simmons, B. A. (2019). The Power of Ranking: The Ease of Doing Business Indicator and Global Regulatory Behavior. *International Organization*, *73*(3), 611–643. doi:10.1017/S0020818319000158

Doumbia-Henry, C. (2020). Shipping and COVID-19: protecting seafarers as frontline workers. *WMU J Marit Affairs, 19*, 279–293. doi:10.1007/s13437-020-00217-9

Duchin, R., Ozbas, O., & Sensoy, B. A. (2010). Costly external finance, corporate investment, and the subprime mortgage credit crisis. *Journal of Financial Economics*, *97*(3), 418–435. doi:10.1016/j.jfineco.2009.12.008

EBRD. (2010). *Transition Report 2010: Integration across borders.* https://www.ebrd.com/downloads/research/transition/tr10.pdf

EBRD. (2012). *Transition Report 2010: Recovery and Reform.* www.ebrd.com/transitionreport

Echeverría, R., & Gopinath, M. (2008). Export behaviour in the Chilean agribusiness and food processing industry. *Chilean Journal of Agricultural Research*, *68*(4), 368–379. doi:10.4067/S0718-58392008000400007

Elgin, C., Basbug, G., & Yalaman, A. (2020). Economic policy responses to a pandemic: Developing the Covid-19 economic stimulus index. In COVID Economics: Vetted and real-time papers. London: Centre for Economic Policy Research.

Elliott, R. J. R., Schumacher, I., & Withagen, C. (2020). Suggestions for a Covid-19 Post-Pandemic Research Agenda in Environmental Economics. *Environmental and Resource Economics*, *76*(4), 1187–1213. doi:10.100710640-020-00478-1 PMID:32836846

Engle, R., & Granger, C. (1991). *Long-run economic relationships: Readings in cointegration.* Oxford University Press. https://econpapers.repec.org/bookchap/oxpobooks/9780198283393.htm

Erum, N., Hussain, S., & Yousaf, A. (2016). Foreign Direct Investment and Economic Growth in SAARC Countries. *The Journal of Asian Finance. Economics and Business*, *3*(4), 57–66. doi:10.13106/jafeb.2016.vol3.no4.57

Eurostat. (2022a). *All data/ Population and social conditions/ Demography, population stock and balance/ Population (national level).* Retrieved from: https://ec.europa.eu/eurostat/databrowser/view/demo_pjan/default/table?lang=en

Eurostat. (2022b). *National accounts/Data/Main tables.* Retrieved from: https://ec.europa.eu/eurostat/web/national-accounts/data/main-tables

Eviews. (2022). *Innovative Solutions for econometric analysis, forecasting & simulation.* Retrieved from: https://www.eviews.com/home.html

Fei, J., & Lu, J. (2015). Analysis of students' perceptions of seafaring career in china based on artificial neural network and genetic programming. *Maritime Policy & Management*, *42*(2), 111–126. doi:10.1080/03088839.2013.873545

Fernandez, E. (2012). Specialising in low quality: Spain and the international market of wine, 1950-1990. *Historia Agraria*, *56*, 41–57.

Fernández-Olmos, M., Gargallo-Castel, A., & Malorgio, G. (2021). Do institutional networks affect winery survival? *British Food Journal*, *123*(7), 2478–2491. doi:10.1108/BFJ-09-2020-0836

Ferreira, M. A., & Vilela, A. S. (2004). Why do firms hold cash? Evidence from EMU countries. *European Financial Management*, *10*(2), 295–319. doi:10.1111/j.1354-7798.2004.00251.x

Ferrer, J. R. (2021). Managerial capabilities and generic business strategies in the wineries of the'Cava'protected designation of origin. *Spanish Journal of Agricultural Research*, *19*(3), 108–121. doi:10.5424jar/2021193-18018

Figge, L., & Martens, P. (2014). Globalisation Continues: The Maastricht Globalisation Index Revisited and Updated. *Globalizations*, *7731*(April), 1–19. doi:10.1080/14747731.2014.887389

Finger, J. M., & Kreinin, M. E. (1979). A Measure of 'Export Similarity' and Its Possible Uses. *Economic Journal (London)*, *89*(356), 905–912. doi:10.2307/2231506

Fiscal Council of the Republic of Serbia. (2020). *Evaluation of the anti-crisis program of economic measures*. Author.

Fischer, C., & Gil-Alana, L. (2009). The nature of the relationship between international tourism and international trade: The case of German imports of Spanish wine. *Applied Economics*, *41*(11), 1345–1359. doi:10.1080/00036840601019349

Foley, C. F., & Manova, K. (2015). *International trade, multinational activity, and corporate finance*. NBER Working Paper Series, No: 20634.

Francois, J., & Manchin, M. (2006). *Institutional quality, infrastructure, and the propensity to export*. Working Paper.

Francois, J., & Manchin, M. (2013). Institutions, infrastructure, and trade. *World Development*, *46*, 165–175. doi:10.1016/j.worlddev.2013.02.009

Frank, M. Z., & Goyal, V. K. (2009). Capital structure decisions: Which factors are reliably important? *Financial Management*, *38*(1), 1–37. doi:10.1111/j.1755-053X.2009.01026.x

Fuensanta, M., Sancho, F., & Marco, V. (2015). In vino veritas: Factores competitivos en distritos industriales productores de vino. *Journal of Regional Research*, (32), 149–164.

Galán, M., Moral-Agúndez, A., & Casquet, C. (2014). Valuation and importance of the extrinsic attributes of the product from the firms perspective in a Spanish wine protected designation of origin. *Spanish Journal of Agricultural Research*, *3*(3), 568–579. doi:10.5424jar/2014123-6036

Galati, A., Crescimanno, M., Rossi, M., Farruggia, D., & Tinervia, S. (2014). The determinants affecting the internationalisation of the Italian SMEs producing sparkling wines: An empirical study on the RBV of the firms. *International Journal of Globalisation and Small Business*, *6*(2), 100–118. doi:10.1504/IJGSB.2014.066463

Gang, F. (2008). Combining policies to benefit from globalization: the case of China. In E. Zedillo (Ed.), *The Future of Globalization: Explorations in light of recent turbulence* (pp. 270–283). Routledge.

García, F., Cosano-Carrillo, A., & Sánchez-Cañizares, S. (2015). Exploratory analysis of foreign markets for Spanish organic wines. *Ciencia e Investigación Agraria: Revista Latinoamericana de Ciencias de la Agricultura*, *42*(2), 139–152.

Garcia-Fernandez, F., & Cordero-Borjas, A. (2010). Proceso de gestion del conocimiento en Carabobo (Venezuela) y Tamaulipas (Mexico). *Pensamiento & Gestión*, *28*, 132–154.

Gil-Alana, L., & Fischer, C. (2010). International travelling and trade: Further evidence for the case of Spanish wine based on fractional vector autoregressive specifications. *Applied Economics*, *42*(19), 2417–2434. doi:10.1080/00036840701858083

Glavic, P., & Lukman, R. (2007). *Review of sustainability terms and their definitions*. doi:10.1016/j.jclepro.2006.12.006

González, P., & Dans, E. (2018). The'terroirist'social movement: The reawakening of wine culture in Spain. *Journal of Rural Studies*, *61*, 184–196. doi:10.1016/j.jrurstud.2018.04.014

Gourinchas, P. O. (2020). Flattening the pandemic and recession curves. In Mitigating the COVID Economic Crisis: Act Fast and Do Whatever. London: Centre for Economic Policy Research.

Granger, C. W. J., & Newbold, P. (1974). Spurious regressions in econometrics. *Journal of Econometrics*, *2*(2), 111–120. doi:10.1016/0304-4076(74)90034-7

Guerrieri, V., Lorenzoni, G., Straub, L., & Werning, I. (2020). *Macroeconomic Implications of COVID-19: Can Negative Supply Shocks Cause Demand Shortages?* NBER Working Paper No. 26918.

Gujarati, D. N. (2003). *Basic Econometrics* (4th ed.). McGraw – Hill, Inc.

Gunawardhana, C. S., & Damayanthi, N. M. M. (2020). Determinants of Foreign Direct Investment and its impact on Economic Growth: Evidence from South Asian Association for Regional Corporation (SAARC) Countries. *Kelaniya Journal of Management*, *8*(2), 91. doi:10.4038/kjm.v8i2.7605

Gundlach, A. (2015). Brand often more important than región. *Wein+Markt, 10*, 34-37.

Guo, J. L., Liang, G. S., & Ye, K. D. (2006). An ınfluence model in seafering choice for taiwan navigation students. *Maritime Policy & Management*, *33*(4), 403–421. doi:10.1080/03088830600895725

Gürler, M. (2016). *Rekabetçiliğin Orta Gelir Tuzağından Çıkıştaki Etkisi: Türkiye Analizi* [The Effect of Competitiveness on Getting Out of the Middle Income Trap: Analysis of Turkey] [PhD Thesis]. Marmara University Institute of Social Sciences. Retrieved from https://tez.yok.gov.tr/UlusalTezMerkezi/TezGoster?key=Br_XTptK8CZ70f0JGX9xElMxSRn6vvzfG2ieGoPn1cC86ezAG3-IOuIswc7Uvmww

Gürler, M. (2021). The effect of the researchers, research and development expenditure as innovation inputs on patent grants and high-tech exports as innovation outputs in OECD and emerging countries especially in BRIICS. *European Journal of Science and Technology*, (32), 1140–1149. doi:10.31590/ejosat.1051899

Gu, Y., Liu, D., Zheng, G., Yang, C., Dong, Z., & Tee, E. Y. J. (2020). The Effects of Chinese Seafarers' Job Demands on Turnover Intention: The Role of Fun at Work. *International Journal of Environmental Research and Public Health*, *17*(14), 5247. doi:10.3390/ijerph17145247 PMID:32708123

Hafez, A. A. E. N. (1999). Seafarers' social life and its effect on maritime safety with respect to Egyptian seafarers. *World Maritime University Dissertations*. 46. https://commons.wmu.se/all_dissertations/46

Hakim, C. (1982). *Secondary analysis in social research: A guide to data sources and methods with examples*. Allen and Unwin/Unwin Hyman.

Haroutunian, S., Osterloh, S., & Sławińska, K. (2021). *The initial fiscal policy responses of euro area countries to the COVID-19 crisis. Economic Bulletin Articles* (Vol. 1). European Central Bank.

Harris, J. M. (2000). *Basic Principles of Sustainable Development.* Global Development and Environment Institute, Working Paper: 00-04, Tufts University.

Helleiner, E. (2014). *The Status Quo Crisis: Global Financial Governance After the 2008 Meltdown*. Oxford University Press. doi:10.1093/acprof:oso/9780199973637.001.0001

Herfindahl, O. C. (1959). *Copper Costs and Prices: 1870 – 1957.* The Johns Hopkins University Press.

Hirschman, A. O. (1964). The Paternity of an Index. *The American Economic Review*, *54*(5), 761–762.

Hirst, P., & Thompson, G. (2019). The future of globalisation. In J. Michie (Ed.), *The Handbook of Globalisation* (3rd ed., pp. 16–31). Edward Elgar Publishing.

Hoekman, B. (2015). The Global Trade Slowdown: A New Normal? European University Institute.

Hoskisson, R. E., Eden, L., Lau, C. M., & Wright, M. (2000). Strategy in Emerging Economies. *Academy of Management Journal*, *43*(3), 249–267. doi:10.5465/1556394

Hossain, M. T., Hassan, Z., Shafiq, S., & Basit, A. (2018). Ease of doing business and its impact on inward FDI. *Indonesian Journal of Management and Business Economics*, *1*(1), 52–65. doi:10.32455/ijmbe.v1i1.52

Huang, X., & Liu, X. (2017). How do firms finance their exports?–evidence from China. *The Journal of International Trade & Economic Development*, *26*(2), 154–173. doi:10.1080/09638199.2016.1227869

IBM-SPSS. (2022). *IBM SPSS Statistics*. https://www.ibm.com/products/spss-statistics

ICEX. (2021). *Directorios de exportadores españoles*. Available at: https://www.icex.es/icex/es/navegacion-principal/nuevos-exportadores/empresas-asociaciones-organismos/directorios-de-exportadores-espanyoles/index.html?idSector=120

ICS. (2021). *Coronavirus (COVID-19)*. Guidance for Ship Operators for the Protection of the Health of Seafarers.

ILO. (2003). *Seafarers' Identity Documents Convention (Revised), 2003, as amended (No. 185)*. https://www.ilo.org/dyn/normlex/en/f?p=NORMLEXPUB:12100:0:NO:P12100_INSTRUMENT_ID:312330

ILO. (2012). *Handbook: Guidance on implementing the Maritime Labour Convention, 2006 and Social Security for Seafarers*. International Labour Office. Retrieved from https://www.ilo.org/wcmsp5/groups/public/---ed_norm/---normes/documents/publication/wcms_170388.pdf

ILO. (2021). *Information note on maritime labour issues and coronavirus (COVID-19)*. Retrieved from https://www.ilo.org/global/standards/maritime-labour-convention/WCMS_741024/lang--en/index.htm

IMO. (2020a). *Circular Letter No. 4204/Add. 14, "Coronavirus (COVID-19)–Recommended framework ofprotocols for ensuring safe ship crew changes and travel during the coronavirus (COVID-19) pandemic"*. IMO.

IMO. (2020b). *Personal message from IMO Secretary-General Kitack Lim to seafarers*. IMO.

International Labour Organization (ILO). (2022a). *ILOSTAT explorer: Unemployment rate by sex and age*. Retrieved from: https://www.ilo.org/shinyapps/bulkexplorer49/?lang=en&segment=indicator&id=UNE_2EAP_SEX_AGE_RT_A

International Labour Organization (ILO). (2022b). *ILOSTAT explorer: Working hours lost due to the COVID-19 crisis, by sex*. Retrieved from: https://www.ilo.org/shinyapps/bulkexplorer6/?lang=en&segment=indicator&id=HOW_2LSS_SEX_RT_A

Jain, R., & Singh, J. B. (2009). Trade Pattern in SAARC Countries: Emerging Trends and Issues. *Reserve Banks of India Occasional Papers, 30*(3), 72–116.

Jean, S. (2020). How the COVID-19 Pandemic Is Reshaping the Trade Landscape and What to Do About It. *Inter Economics*, *55*(3), 135–139. doi:10.100710272-020-0890-4 PMID:32536707

Jensen, M. C. (1986). Agency cost of free cash flow, corporate finance and takeovers. *The American Economic Review*, *76*(2), 323–329.

Jiang, Y., Tian, G., Wu, Y., & Mo, B. (2020). Impacts of geopolitical risks and economic policy uncertainty on Chinese tourism-listed company stock. *International Journal of Finance & Economics*, *27*(1), 320–333. doi:10.1002/ijfe.2155

Jones, G. (2005). *Multinationals and Global Capitalism: From the Nineteenth to the Twenty First Century*. Oxford University Press.

Kappa, K. (2022). Do the vegetable exports lead to economic growth? An empirical evidence in selected SAARC economies. *Journal of Public Affairs*, *22*(2), 1–11. doi:10.1002/pa.2484

Katunian, A. (2019). Sustainability as a new approach for the human resource development in tourism sector. *Public Policy and Administration*, *18*(4), 405–417. doi:10.13165/VPA-19-18-4-03

Kaufmann, D., Kraay, A., & Mastruzzi, M. (2011). The worldwide governance indicators: Methodology and analytical issues. *Hague Journal on the Rule of Law*, *3*(2), 220–246. doi:10.1017/S1876404511200046

Kaya, D. G. (2020). Koronavirüs pandemisinin küresel ekonomideki izleri: Kamu finansman dengesi, ticaret hacmi, enflasyon, işsizlik ve ekonomik büyüme [Traces of the Coronavirus Panddemic in the Global Economy: Public Finance, balance, trade, volume, inflation, unemployment and economic growth]. *Avrasya Sosyal ve Ekonomi Araştırmaları Dergisi*, *7*(5), 221–237.

Kesen, M. (2016). The Role and Importance of Sustainable Human Resource Management in Business Administration. *İnsan ve Toplum Bilimleri Araştırmaları Dergisi*, *5*(3), 554-573.

Kim, H. M., Li, P., & Lee, Y. R. (2020). *Observations of deglobalization against globalization and impacts on global business*. International Trade, Politics and Development. doi:10.1108/ITPD-05-2020-0067

Köhr, C. K., Malorgio, G., & Aragrande, M. (2017). Exploring determinants of internationalisation: The case of late starters. *International Journal of Wine Business Research*, *29*(2), 159–177. doi:10.1108/IJWBR-05-2016-0015

Kotcharin, S., & Maneenop, S. (2020). Geopolitical risk and corporate cash holdings in the shipping industry. *Transportation Research Part E, Logistics and Transportation Review*, *136*(January), 101862. doi:10.1016/j.tre.2020.101862

Kotcharin, S., & Maneenop, S. (2020). Geopolitical risk and shipping firms' capital structure decisions in belt and road initiative countries. *International Journal of Logistics Research and Applications*, *23*(6), 544–560. doi:10.1080/13675567.2020.1766003

Kumari, R., & Sharma, A. (2021). Impact of COVID-19 on International Trade: New Evidence from Economic Sectors. In Impact of Global Issues on International Trade (pp. 233-248). IGI Global.

La Porta, R., Lopez-de-Silanes, F., Shleifer, A., & Vishny, R. W. (2000). Agency problems and dividend policies around the world. *The Journal of Finance*, *55*(1), 1–33. doi:10.1111/0022-1082.00199

Le, A. T., & Tran, T. P. (2021). Does geopolitical risk matter for corporate investment? Evidence from emerging countries in Asia. *Journal of Multinational Financial Management, 62*, 100703. doi:10.1016/j.mulfin.2021.100703

Leamer, E. E. (1985). Sensitivity analyses would help. *The American Economic Review, 75*(3), 308–313. https://www.jstor.org/stable/1814801

Lee, B. S., & Suh, J. (2011). Cash holdings and share repurchases: International evidence. *Journal of Corporate Finance, 17*(5), 1306–1329. doi:10.1016/j.jcorpfin.2011.06.006

Lee, C. C., & Wang, C. W. (2021). Firms' cash reserve, financial constraint, and geopolitical risk. *Pacific-Basin Finance Journal, 65*, 101480. doi:10.1016/j.pacfin.2020.101480

Leggate, H., McConville, J., & Morvillo, A. (2005). International Maritime Transport: Perspectives. Routledge.

Levchenko, A. (2007). Institutional quality and international trade. *The Review of Economic Studies, 74*(3), 791–819. doi:10.1111/j.1467-937X.2007.00435.x

Levi, A., & Folwell, R. (1995). US demand for imported wines. *Journal of International Food & Agribusiness Marketing, 7*(1), 79–91. doi:10.1300/J047v07n01_05

Lin, F., Li, B., & Sim, N. C. S. (2014). Trade openness and government size of small developing countries: An instrumental approach. *Economics of Transition and Institutional Change, 22*(4), 783–808. doi:10.1111/ecot.12053

LiPuma, J. A., Newbert, S. L., & Doh, J. P. (2013). The effect of institutional quality on firm export performance in emerging economies: A contingency model of firm age and size. *Small Business Economics, 40*(4), 817–841. doi:10.100711187-011-9395-7

Loayza, N. & Pennings, S. (2020). *Macroeconomic Policy in the Time of COVID-19: A Primer for Developing Countries.* World Bank Group.

Lucas, D., Jego, C., Jensen, O. C., Loddé, B., Pougnet, R., Dewitte, J.-D., Sauvage, T., & Jegaden, D. (2021). Seafarers' mental health in the COVID-19 era: Lost at sea? *International Maritime Health, 72*(2), 138–141. doi:10.5603/IMH.2021.0023 PMID:34212354

Macedo, A., Rebelo, J., & Gouveia, S. (2019). Export propensity and intensity in the wine industry: A fractional econometric approach. *Bio-Based and Applied Economics, 8*(3), 261–277.

Maiti, S. (2016). Export and Economic Growth in India: An Econometric Analysis. *Look East, 6*(1), 68–78.

Malkin, A. J., & Layton, A. (2021). The global fiscal response to COVID-19: Risks and repercussions. *Economic Analysis and Policy, 69*, 340–349. doi:10.1016/j.eap.2020.12.016

Marco-Lajara, B., Zaragoza-Saez, P., & Martínez-Falcó, J. (2022e). Green Innovation: Balancing Economic Efficiency With Environmental Protection. In Frameworks for Sustainable Development Goals to Manage Economic, Social, and Environmental Shocks and Disasters (pp. 239-254). IGI Global.

Marco-Lajara, B., Zaragoza-Sáez, P., Martínez-Falcó, J., & Millan-Tudela, L. (2022f). Corporate Social Responsibility: A Narrative Literature Review. In Frameworks for Sustainable Development Goals to Manage Economic, Social, and Environmental Shocks and Disasters (pp. 16-34). IGI Global.

Marco-Lajara, B., Zaragoza-Sáez, P., Martínez-Falcó, J., & Sánchez-García, E. (2022a). Green Intellectual Capital in the Spanish Wine Industry. In Innovative Economic, Social, and Environmental Practices for Progressing Future Sustainability (pp. 102-120). IGI Global. doi:10.4018/978-1-7998-9590-9.ch006

Marco-Lajara, B., Zaragoza-Saez, P., Martínez-Falcó, J., & Sánchez-García, E. (2022c). COVID-19 and Wine Tourism: A Story of Heartbreak. In Handbook of Research on SDGs for Economic Development, Social Development, and Environmental Protection (pp. 90-112). IGI Global.

Marco-Lajara, B., Zaragoza-Sáez, P., Martínez-Falcó, J., & Sánchez-García, E. (2022d). El capital intelectual verde como hoja de ruta para la sostenibilidad: el caso de bodegas Luzón. *GeoGraphos: Revista Digital para Estudiantes de Geografía y Ciencias Sociales, 13*(147), 137-146.

Marco-Lajara, B., Martínez-Falcó, J., Ruiz-Fernández, L., & Seva-Larrosa, P. (2022l). Evolución del pensamiento en la disciplina de dirección estratégica: la visión de la empresa basada en las capacidades dinámicas y en el conocimiento. In *Investigación y transferencia de las ciencias sociales frente a un mundo en crisis* (pp. 1801–1826). Dykinson.

Marco-Lajara, B., Seva-Larrosa, P., Martínez-Falcó, J., & García-Lillo, F. (2022i). Wine clusters and Protected Designations of Origin (PDOs) in Spain: An exploratory analysis. *Journal of Wine Research*, 1–22.

Marco-Lajara, B., Seva-Larrosa, P., Martinez-Falco, J., & Sanchez-Garcia, E. (2021a). How Has COVID- 19 Affected The Spanish Wine Industry? An Exploratory Analysis. *Natural Volatiles & Essential Oils Journal, 8*(6), 2722–2731.

Marco-Lajara, B., Seva-Larrosa, P., Ruiz-Fernandez, L., & Martinez-Falco, J. (2021b). The Effect of COVID- 19 on the Spanish Wine Industry. In *Impact of Global Issues on International Trade* (pp. 211–232). IGI Global. doi:10.4018/978-1-7998-8314-2.ch012

Marco-Lajara, B., Zaragoza Sáez, P., & Martínez-Falcó, J. (2022j). Does Green Intellectual Capital Affect Green Performance? The Mediation of Green Innovation. *Telematique, 21*(1), 4594–4602.

Marco-Lajara, B., Zaragoza-Sáez, P. C., Martínez-Falcó, J., & Sánchez-García, E. (2022h). *Does green intellectual capital affect green innovation performance? Evidence from the Spanish wine industry*. British Food Journal, Ahead-of-print.

Marco-Lajara, B., Zaragoza-Sáez, P., Martínez-Falcó, J. M., & Sánchez-García, E. (2022k). Las rutas del vino de España: el impacto económico derivado de las visitas a bodegas y museos. In *Investigación y transferencia de las ciencias sociales frente a un mundo en crisis* (pp. 1774–1800). Dykinson.

Marco-Lajara, B., Zaragoza-Saez, P., Martínez-Falcó, J., & Millan-Tudela, L. A. (2022b). Analysing the Relationship Between Green Intellectual Capital and the Achievement of the Sustainable Development Goals. In *Handbook of Research on Building Inclusive Global Knowledge Societies for Sustainable Development* (pp. 111–129). IGI Global. doi:10.4018/978-1-6684-5109-0.ch005

Marco-Lajara, B., Zaragoza-Sáez, P., Martínez-Falcó, J., & Ruiz-Fernández, L. (2022g). The Effect of Green Intellectual Capital on Green Performance in the Spanish Wine Industry: A Structural Equation Modeling Approach. *Complexity, 2022*, 1–17.

Marco-Lajara, B., Zaragoza-Sáez, P., Martínez-Falcó, J., & Sánchez-García, E. (2022d). El capital intelectual verde como hoja de ruta para la sostenibilidad: El caso de bodegas Luzón. *GeoGraphos: Revista Digital para Estudiantes de Geografía y Ciencias Sociales*, *13*(147), 137–146.

Maritime Labour Convention (MLC). (2006). Retrieved December 15, 2020, from http://www.ilo.org›documents›wcms_090250

Marjanović, D., & Domazet, I. (2021). Foreign Direct Investments: A Key Factor for Business Globalization. In Y. Bayar (Ed.), *Institutional, Economic, and Social Impacts of Globalization and Liberalization* (pp. 96–116). IGI Global. doi:10.4018/978-1-7998-4459-4.ch006

Marjanović, D., & Domazet, I. (2021). Tax competitiveness as a significant factor in attracting foreign investment – the case of Serbia. *Argumenta Oeconomica*, *2*(47), 63–80. doi:10.15611/aoe.2021.2.04

Marjanović, D., Domazet, I., & Vukmirović, I. (2022). Social Environment as a Factor of Capital Investment in Serbia. *Eastern European Economics*, *60*(3), 247–264. Advance online publication. doi:10.1080/00128775.2022.2048181

Martinez-Ruiz, J. (2016). The Spanish wine trade with England in the second half of the seventeenth century: Towards constructing a new annual series and preliminary results. *Historia Agraria*, *70*, 11–24.

Mcinnes, A., Colombage, S., Grose, R., Imam, T., & Grose, R. (2022). Opportunities and Barriers for FinTech in SAARC and ASEAN Countries. *Journal of Risk and Financial Management, 15*(2), 2–37. doi:10.3390/jrfm15020077

McLaughlin, H. (2015). Seafarers in the spotlight. *Maritime Policy & Management*, *42*(2), 95–96. doi:10.1080/03088839.2015.1006351

Michie, J. (2017). *Advanced Introduction to Globalisation*. Edward Elgar.

Ministry of Commerce & Industry. (2019). *Indian global trade share*. https://pib.gov.in/PressReleasePage.aspx?PRID=1593704

Ministry of Finance of the Republic of Serbia (2020a). *Decree on establishing the Program of financial support to economic entities for maintaining liquidity and working capital in difficult economic conditions due to the COVID-19 pandemic caused by the SARS-CoV-2 virus*. Official Gazette of RS, no. 54/2020.

Ministry of Finance of the Republic of Serbia. (2020). *Decree on fiscal benefits and direct benefits to economic entities in the private sector and financial assistance to citizens and the goal of mitigating the economic consequences caused by the COVID-19 disease*. Official Gazette of RS, no. 54/2020 and 60/2020.

Misch, F., Gemmell, N., & Kneller, R. (2014). Using surveys of business perceptions as a guide to growth – enhancing financial reforms. *Economics of Transition and Institutional Change*, *22*(4), 683–725. doi:10.1111/ecot.12049

Modigliani, F., & Miller, M. H. (1958). The cost of capital, corporate finance and theory of investment. *The American Economic Review*, *48*(4), 261–297.

Muğaloğlu, E., Polat, A. Y., Tekin, H., & Dogan, A. (2021a). Oil price shocks during the COVID-19 pandemic: Evidence from United Kingdom energy stocks. *Energy Research Letters*, *2*(1). Advance online publication. doi:10.46557/001c.24253

Muğaloğlu, E., Polat, A. Y., Tekin, H., & Kılıç, E. (2021b). Assessing the impact of Covid-19 pandemic in Turkey with a novel economic uncertainty index. *Journal of Economic Studies (Glasgow, Scotland)*. Advance online publication. doi:10.1108/JES-02-2021-0081

Muhammad, A., Shahid, M., Syed, S. H., Muhammad, F., & Hassan, M. A. (2011). Empirical Analysis of Determinants of Economic Growth: Evidence from SAARC Countries. *Journal of Economics and Behavioral Studies*, *3*(2), 115–121. doi:10.22610/jebs.v3i2.261

Mukherjee, S., Baral, M. M., Venkataiah, C., Pal, S. K., & Nagariya, R. (2021). Service robots are an option for contactless services due to the COVID-19 pandemic in the hotels. *Decision (Washington, D.C.)*, *48*(4), 445–460. doi:10.100740622-021-00300-x

Murshed, S. M. (2018). *Challenges to the liberal peace*. BLISS.

Narayan, J. (2019). British Black Power: The anti-imperialism of political blackness and the problem of nativist socialism. *The Sociological Review*, *67*(5), 945–967. doi:10.1177/0038026119845550

Nasir, A., Arshah, R., & Ab Hamid, M. (2018). The significance of main constructs of theory of planned behavior in recent information security policy compliance behavior study: a comparison among top. *International Journal of Engineering and Technology*, *7*(2), 737–741.

National Institution for Finance and Development (NIFD). (2022). *Data: China's macro leverage ratio*. Retrieved from: http://114.115.232.154:8080/

New York University Department of Sociology. (2013). *The Sociology Project*. Pearson.

North, D. C. (1993). Institutions and credible commitment. *Journal of Institutional and Theoretical Economics*, *149*, 11–23.

OEC World. (2020). *India (IND) and Bangladesh (BGD) Trade*. https://oec.world/en/profile/bilateral-country/ind/partner/bgd

OEMV. (2020). *Perfil de la empresa exportadora de vino* [Profile of the Wine Exporting Company]. Available at https://www.oemv.es/perfil-de-la-empresa-exportadora-de-vino-ano-2020

OEMV. (2021a). *Exportaciones españolas de vino y productos vitivinícolas* [Spanish Exports of Wine and Wine Products]. Available at: https://oemv.es/exportaciones-espanolas-de-vino-ano-2021

OEMV. (2021b). *Importaciones españolas de vino y productos vitivinícolas*. Available at: https://www.oemv.es/importaciones-espanolas-de-vino-ano-2021

OEMV. (2021b). *Perfil de la empresa exportadora de vino* [Profile of the Wine Exporting Company]. Available at https://www.oemv.es/perfil-de-la-empresa-exportadora-de-vino-ano-2021

OEMV. (2021c). *Perfil de la empresa exportadora de vino* [Profile of the Wine Exporting Company]. Available at https://www.oemv.es/perfil-de-la-empresa-exportadora-de-vino-ano-2021

Omann, I., & Spangenberg, J. H. (2002). Assessing Social Sustainability: The Social Dimension of Sustainability in a Socio-Economic Scenario. *7th Biennial Conference of the International Society for Ecological Economics*, 1–20. http://seri.at/wp-content/uploads/2010/05/Assessing_social_sustainability.pdf

Organisation for Economic Co-operation and Development (OECD). (2022a). *Economic Outlook No 111-June 2022*. Retrieved from: https://stats.oecd.org/Index.aspx?DataSetCode=EO

Organisation for Economic Co-operation and Development (OECD). (2022b). *National accounts*. Retrieved from: https://stats.oecd.org/Index.aspx?DataSetCode=SNA_TABLE1

Our World in Data. (2022a). *Dataset: Home/Coronavirus/Vaccinations*. Retrieved from: https://ourworldindata.org/coronavirus

Ozkan, A., & Ozkan, N. (2004). Corporate cash holdings: An empirical investigation of UK companies. *Journal of Banking & Finance*, *28*(9), 2103–2134. doi:10.1016/j.jbankfin.2003.08.003

Özsoy, Ö. (2021). Dilemma in Health during Pandemic in OECD Countries: Increasing Health Expenditures for Preventing against the Pandemic Will Cause a Crowding-out in Increasing the Employment in Nursing Service or not? *European Journal of Science and Technology*, (32), 1094–1102.

Özsoy, Ö., & Gürler, M. (2021a). *Poverty and social exclusion of older people in ageing European Union and Turkey. J Public Health*. doi:10.100710389-021-01525-x

Özsoy, Ö., & Gürler, M. (2021b). The Negative Effects of COVID-19 on the Sustainable Development Goals, Economic Growth, Foreign Trade, and Social Life. *Advances in Human Services and Public Health*, 105–155. doi:10.4018/978-1-7998-8202-2.ch007

Pablo-Valenciano, J., & Roman-Sanchez, I. (2011). Consumption, merchandising and prospects of Spanish wine market. *Agroalimentaria*, *17*(33), 51–61.

Pacheco, L. M. (2017). Internationalization vs family ownership and management: The case of Portuguese wine firms. *International Journal of Wine Business Research*, *29*(2), 195–209. doi:10.1108/IJWBR-10-2016-0034

Padhan, R., & Prabheesh, K. P. (2021). The economics of COVID-19 pandemic: A survey. *Economic Analysis and Policy*, *70*, 220–237. doi:10.1016/j.eap.2021.02.012 PMID:33658744

Pal, T., & Hazra, M. K. (2015). *Sustainable Development*. Yadava Publication.

Pascual, F., & Díaz, M. (2008). An approach to the valuation of Rioja wine. *Journal of Wine Research*, *19*(1), 33–50. doi:10.1080/09571260802164020

Patrick, S. (2018). Correlation coefficients: Appropriate use and interpretation. *Anesthesia and Analgesia*, *126*(5), 1763–1768. doi:10.1213/ANE.0000000000002864 PMID:29481436

Paudel, Y., & Shrestha, S. (2022). Agroforestry Practices Prevailing in SAARC Countries: A Review. *Indonesian Journal of Social and Environmental Issues*, *3*(1), 10–18. doi:10.47540/ijsei.v3i1.390

Pauksztat, B., Grech, M., Kitada, M., & Jensen, R. B. (2020). *Seafarers' experiences during the COVID-19 pandemic: Report*. doi:10.21677/wmu20201213

Perraton, J. (2019). The scope and implications of globalisation. In J. Michie (Ed.), *The Handbook of Globalisation* (3rd ed., pp. 50–76). Edward Elgar Publishing.

Perugini, C., & Selezneva, E. (2015). Labour market institutions, crisis and gender earnings gap in Eastern Europe. *Economics of Transition and Institutional Change*, *23*(3), 517–564. doi:10.1111/ecot.12072

Polat, A. Y. (2020a). Borç vadesi ve finansal kriz: Türkiye örneği. *Journal of Erciyes University Faculty of Economics and Administrative Sciences*, (1), 118-130.

Polat, A. Y. (2020b). Davranışsal iktisat ve kamu politikaları [Behavioral Economics and Public Policy]. In *Ekonomi ve İşletmede Güncel Yaklaşımlar* (pp. 101-133). Gazi Kitabevi.

Polat, A. Y. (2018). Subprime mortgages and lending bubbles. *Bulletin of Monetary Economics and Banking*, *21*(2), 191–216.

Polat, A. Y. (2020a). Borç vadesi ve finansal kriz: Türkiye örneği [Debt Maturity and Financial Crisis: The case of Turkey]. *Erciyes Üniversitesi İktisadi ve İdari Bilimler Fakültesi Dergisi*, (1), 118–130. doi:10.18070/erciyesiibd.846318

Polat, A. Y. (2020b). Davranışsal iktisat ve kamu politikaları. In *Ekonomi ve İşletmede Güncel Yaklaşımlar* [Behavioral economics and public policy. In Economics and Current Approaches in Business] (pp. 101–133). Gazi Kitabevi.

Polat, A. Y. (2021). *Davranışsal finans teorisi ve kripto paralar* [Behavioral Finance Theory and Cryptocurrencies]. Efe Akademi Yayınları.

Polat, A. Y., Aysan, A. F., Tekin, H., & Tunali, A. S. (2021). Bitcoin-specific fear sentiment matters in the COVID-19 outbreak. *Studies in Economics and Finance*, *39*(1), 98–110. doi:10.1108/SEF-02-2021-0080

Pourzanjanı, M., & Schröder, J. U., & Zade, G. (2002). Maritime Education and training (MET) in the european union: How can maritime administrations support MET. *International Association of Maritime Universities (IAMU) Journal*, *2*(2), 50–56.

Quintela, S., Villarán, M., Armentia, I., & Elejalde, E. (2012). Ochratoxin A in Spanish exportation wine market. *Food Control*, *25*(2), 501–504. doi:10.1016/j.foodcont.2011.11.023

Rajan, P., & Lee, J. Y. (2003). *Contract enforcement and the volume of international trade in different types of goods*. Working Paper.

Rajan, R. G., & Zingales, L. (1995). What do we know about capital structure? Some evidence from international data. *The Journal of Finance*, *50*(5), 1421–1460. doi:10.1111/j.1540-6261.1995.tb05184.x

Rebelo, J., Compés, R., Faria, S., Gonçalves, T., Pinilla, V., & Simon-Elorz, K. (2021). Covid-19 lockdown and wine consumption frequency in Portugal and Spain. *Spanish Journal of Agricultural Research*, *19*(2), 105–121.

Rincon-Aznar, A., Vecchi, M., & Venturini, F. (2015). Functional Income Distribution in European Transition Countries. In C. Perugini & F. Pompei (Eds.), *Inequalities During and After Transition in Central and Eastern Europe* (pp. 59–92). Palgrave Macmillan. doi:10.1057/9781137460981_4

Roca-Puig, V. (2019). The circular path of social sustainability: An empirical analysis. *Journal of Cleaner Production*, *212*, 916–924. doi:10.1016/j.jclepro.2018.12.078

Rodrigo-Alarcón, J., Parra-Requena, G., & García-Villaverde, P. M. (2014). Efectividad de la orientación emprendedora: El papel del capital social y las capacidades. *Investigaciones Europeas de Dirección y Economía de la Empresa*, *20*(3), 131–139. doi:10.1016/j.iedee.2013.09.002

Rodríguez García, J., & Vieira Rodríguez, Á. (2017). Análisis del Mercado de los Vinos de Jerez-Xérès-Sherry y Manzanilla de Sanlúcar de Barrameda en el periodo 1982-2012. *Revista de Estudios Andaluces*, *34*(1), 155–200.

Rosendorf, N. M. (2000). *Governance in a Globalizing World, Social and Cultural Globalization: Concepts, History, and Americas Role*. Brookings Institution Press.

Roy, D. (2020). Formulation of Governance and Democracy Index (GDI) and Governance, Democracy, and Emancipation Index (GDEI): A Cross-country Empirical Study (1998 – 2017). *Open Political Science*, *4*(1), 15–26. doi:10.1515/openps-2021-0002

Roy, D. (2022). Formulation of Digitization Impact Index (DII): A Cross-Country Empirical Study (2009–2018). *International Journal of Innovation in the Digital Economy*, *13*(1), 1–34. doi:10.4018/IJIDE.292628

Saich, T. (2000). Globalization, Governance, and the Authoritarian Westphalian State: The Case of China. *Global Governance*, 208–228.

Saleem, R., Nasreen, S., & Azam, S. (2022). Role of financial inclusion and export diversification in determining green growth: Evidence from SAARC economies. *Environmental Science and Pollution Research International*, *29*(40), 1–14. doi:10.100711356-022-20096-2 PMID:35420339

Şanlı, O. (2020). Keynesyen model bağlamında Covid-19 pandemisinin küresel ekonomiye muhtemel etkileri: ABD ve Çin ekonomileri üzerine bir araştırma [The Possible Effects of the Covid-19 Pandemic on the Global Economy in the context of the Keynesian Model: A Study on the US and Chinese Economics]. *Avrasya Sosyal ve Ekonomi Araştırmaları Dergisi*, *7*(5), 597-634.

Seva-Larrosa, P., Martínez-Falcó, J., & Ruiz-Fernández, L. (2022). Analizando las principales variables empresariales en los clusters vinícolas españoles teniendo en cuenta la localización de las empresas y su pertenencia a una marca colectiva. In *Miradas sobre el emprendimiento ante la crisis del coronavirus* (pp. 629–634). Dykinson.

Sharma, A., Kumari, R., & Goel, N. (2022). Universal Health Coverage (UHC): Case Study on World's Health Emerging Strategy After the COVID-19 Pandemic. In Handbook of Research on Global Networking Post COVID-19 (pp. 328-341). IGI Global.

Siriwardana, M. (2007). *Looking beyond SAARC: some trade liberalisation options for Sri Lanka.* doi:10.1080/10357820108713321

Slišković, A. (2020). 'Seafarers' Well-being in the Context of the COVID-19 Pandemic: A Qualitative Study'. *Work (Reading, Mass.)*, *67*(4), 799–809. doi:10.3233/WOR-203333 PMID:33325430

Song, L., & Zhou, Y. (2020). The COVID-19 pandemic and its impact on the global economy: What does it take to turn crisis into opportunity? *China & World Economy*, *28*(4), 1–25. doi:10.1111/cwe.12349

Stiglitz, J. (2008). The future of globalization: lessons from Cancún and recent financial crises. In E. Zedillo (Ed.), *The Future of Globalization: Explorations in light of recent turbulence* (pp. 70–82). Routledge.

Suarez-Ortega, S. (2003). Export barriers: Insights from small and medium-sized firms. *International Small Business Journal*, *21*(4), 403–419. doi:10.1177/02662426030214002

Suay-Matallana, I., & Guillem-Llobat, X. (2018). Poisoned wine: Regulation, chemical analyses, and Spanish-French trade in the 1930s. *Ambix*, *65*(2), 99–121. doi:10.1080/00026980.2018.1452838 PMID:29661062

Sun, Z., & Wang, Y. (2015). Corporate precautionary savings: Evidence from the recent financial crisis. *The Quarterly Review of Economics and Finance*, *56*, 175–186. doi:10.1016/j.qref.2014.09.006

Taneja, N., & Bimal, S. (2020). *Informal Trade in the SAARC Region.* Springer. doi:10.1007/978-981-15-3932-9_14

Tekin, H. (2020b). Firma riski ve COVID-19: *Birleşik Krallıktaki havayolu yolcu taşımacılığı örneği* [Example of Air Passenger Transport in the UK]. 7. Uluslararası Muhasebe ve Finans Araştırmaları Kongresi.

Tekin, H. (2020d). Optimal leverage of travel and leisure firms in Europe. *Marmara Conference on European Studies (MCES) 2020*, 387-394. http://katalog.marmara.edu.tr/muyayinevi/YN875.pdf

Tekin, H. (2021a). Avrupa'da kâr payı dağıtımı, pay geri alımları ve finansal krizler [Dividend distribution, share buybacks and financial crises in Europe]. *5. Uluslararası Ekonomi ve Finans Konferansı Gelisim-UWE 2021*. http://acikerisim.gelisim.edu.tr/xmlui/handle/11363/2893

Tekin, H. (2021a). Avrupa'da kâr payı dağıtımı, pay geri alımları ve finansal krizler [Dividend distribution, share buybacks and financial crises in Europe]. In *5. Uluslararası Ekonomi ve Finans Konferansı Gelisim-UWE 2021*. http://acikerisim.gelisim.edu.tr/xmlui/handle/11363/2893

Tekin, H. (2022b). *Gelişen ekonomilerde sermaye yapısı* [Capital Structure in Emerging Economies]. Genişletilmiş 2. Baskı, Efe Akademi Yayınları.

Tekin, H. (2022b). *Gelişen ekonomilerde sermaye yapısı. Genişletilmiş 2* [Capital Structure in Emergin Economies. Extended 2]. Efe Akademi Yayınları.

Tekin, H. (2020a). Firm size and dividend policy of European firms: Evidence from financial crises. *Marmara Journal of European Studies*, *28*(1), 109–121. doi:10.29228/mjes.11

Tekin, H. (2020c). How optimal cash changed by the global financial crisis? A multi-country analysis. *Economics and Business Letters*, *9*(2), 114–123. doi:10.17811/ebl.9.2.2020.114-123

Tekin, H. (2021b). How the global financial crisis and international trade affected corporate decisions?: International evidence. In *Impact of Global Issues on International Trade* (pp. 137–157). IGI Global. doi:10.4018/978-1-7998-8314-2.ch008

Tekin, H. (2021c). Market differences and adjustment speed of debt, equity, and debt maturity. *Australian Journal of Management*, *46*(4), 629–651. doi:10.1177/0312896220968266

Tekin, H. (2022a). Does corruption matter on corporate payouts in the Covid era? Evidence from Muslim countries. *FICCOMS FEMFEST International Conference on Economics, Management and Business 2022*.

Tekin, H. (2022c). How do financial constraints and financial crises matter in cash management?: Evidence from developing Asian economies. In *Handbook of Research on Current Trends in Asian Economics, Business, and Administration* (pp. 228–248). IGI Global. doi:10.4018/978-1-7998-8486-6.ch012

Tekin, H., & Polat, A. Y. (2020a). Agency theory: A review in finance. *Anemon: Journal of Social Sciences of Mus Alparslan University*, *8*(4), 1323–1329.

Tekin, H., & Polat, A. Y. (2020b). Is saving vital? Evidence from the financial crisis. *Economics and Business Letters*, *9*(2), 124–134. doi:10.17811/ebl.9.2.2020.124-134

Tekin, H., & Polat, A. Y. (2020c). The global financial crisis and capital structure decisions of Turkish SMEs: A review. *International Journal of Management Economics and Business*, *16*(3), 513–535. doi:10.17130/ijmeb.798509

Tekin, H., & Polat, A. Y. (2021a). Adjustment speed of debt maturity: Evidence from financial crises in East Asia. *Bulletin of Monetary Economics and Banking*, *24*(1), 71–92. doi:10.21098/bemp.v24i1.1287

Tekin, H., & Polat, A. Y. (2021b). Do market differences matter on dividend policy? *Borsa Istanbul Review*, *24*(2), 197–208. doi:10.1016/j.bir.2020.10.009

Tekin, H., & Polat, A. Y. (2021c). *Is leverage a substitute or outcome for governance? Evidence from financial crises*. International Journal of Emerging Markets. doi:10.1108/IJOEM-03-2020-0297

Tekin, H., & Polat, A. Y. (2021d). Küresel finansal krizin araştırma-geliştirme harcamaları ayarlama hızı üzerindeki etkisi [The effect of the global financial crisis on the rate of adjustment of research and development expenditures]. *Verimlilik Dergisi*, *21*(4), 119–131. doi:10.51551/verimlilik.829028

Tekin, H., Polat, A. Y., Aysan, A. F., & Muğaloğlu, E. (2021a). Cash management, governance, and the global financial crisis: Evidence from developing Asia. *Asian Economics Letters*, *2*(4), 27135. doi:10.46557/001c.27135

Tekin, H., Polat, A. Y., & Muğaloğlu, E. (2021b). Küresel finansal kriz ve nakit tutma ayarlama hızı [The Global Financial Crisis and the Pace of Cash Holding Adjustment]. *Anemon Muş Alparslan Üniversitesi Sosyal Bilimler Dergisi*, *9*(4), 1099–1110. doi:10.18506/anemon.888504

Thakor, A. (2015). Lending booms, smart bankers, and financial crises. *The American Economic Review*, *105*(5), 305–309. doi:10.1257/aer.p20151090

The British Centre for Economics and Business Research (CEBR). (2021). *World Economic League Table 2022*. Retrieved from: https://cebr.com/wp-content/uploads/2022/01/WELT-2022.pdf

The International Monetary Fund (IMF). (2022a). *World Economic Outlook, April 2022: War Sets Back The Global Recovery*. Retrieved from: https://www.imf.org/external/datamapper/PCPIPCH@WEO/OEMDC/ADVEC/WEOWORLD

The International Monetary Fund (IMF). (2022b). *IMF Datamapper. World Economic Outlook, April 2022 Database: Inflation rate, average consumer prices*. Retrieved from: https://www.imf.org/-/media/Files/Publications/WEO/2022/April/English/text.ashx

The KOF Globalisation Index – Revisited - ETH Z. (n.d.) https://ethz.ch/content/dam/ethz/special-interest/dual/kof dam/documents/Globalization/2018/KOF_Globalisation%20Index_Revisited.pdf

The World Bank. (2022a). *Global Economic Prospects, June 2022*. Retrieved from: https://openknowledge.worldbank.org/bitstream/handle/10986/37224/9781464818431.pdf?sequence=5&isAllowed=y

The World Bank. (2022b). *Data: World Bank Country and Lending Groups/Country Classification.* Retrieved from: https://databank.worldbank.org/data/download/site-content/OGHIST.xlsx

Timini, J. (2020). Staying dry on Spanish wine: The rejection of the 1905 Spanish-Italian trade agreement. *European Journal of Political Economy*, *63*, 101892. doi:10.1016/j.ejpoleco.2020.101892

Tosunoğlu, Ş., & Kasal, S. (2020). Yeni koronavirüs (covid-19) salgını ve sağlıklı küresel ekonomi için politika uygulamaları: IMF' nin rolü [The Novel Coronavirus (covid-19) Epidemic and Policy Implications for a Healthy Global Economy: The Role of the IMF]. *Anadolu Üniversitesi İktisat Fakültesi Dergisi*, *2*(1), 35–49.

Trade Economics. (2022). *India Imports from Bangladesh - 2022 Data 2023 Forecast 1988-2021 Historical.* https://tradingeconomics.com/india/imports/bangladesh

TradeMap. (2022). *Trade statistics for international business development.* Retrieved from: https://www.trademap.org/Product_SelProduct_TS.aspx?nvpm=1%7c%7c%7c%7c%7cTOTAL%7c%7c%7c2%7c1%7c1%7c1%7c2%7c1%7c1%7c1%7c1%7c1

Trujillo-Bolio, M. (2013). Spanish Wine Export to the New Spain Market: Trade networks and circuits, 1790-1810. *America Latina en la Historia Economica*, *20*(2), 121–150.

UN Department of Economic and Social Affairs (UNDESA). (2022a). *Population Dynamics/ World Population Prospects 2019.* Retrieved from: https://population.un.org/wpp/DataQuery/

UNCTAD. (2016). *Trade and Development Report 2016: Structural Transformation for Inclusive and Sustained Growth.* United Nations.

UNCTAD. (2018). *World Investment Report, Investment and New Industrial Policies.* United nations.

UNCTAD. (2019). *World Investment Report, Beyond Uncertainty.* United nations.

UNCTAD. (2020). *World Investment Report, Reducing inequality.* United nations.

UNCTAD. (2020). *World Investment Report, Road to Recovery.* United nations.

UNCTAD. (2022). *UNCTAD Statistics.* Retrieved from: https://unctadstat.unctad.org/wds/ReportFolders/reportFolders.aspx

UNDESA. (2022b). *Statistic Division: Methodology/Standard country or area codes for statistical use.* Retrieved from: https://unstats.un.org/unsd/methodology/m49/overview/

United Nations Conference on Trade and Development (UNCTAD). (2020). *Review of Maritime Transport.* UNCTAD.

United Nations Conference on Trade and Development (UNCTAD). (2021). *Review of Maritime Transport.* UNCTAD.

United Nations Conference on Trade and Development (UNCTAD). (2022). *Maritime Trade Disrupted: The war in Ukraine and its effects on maritime trade logistics*. https://unctad.org/system/files/official-document/osginf2022d2_en.pdf

Upender, M. (2007). Long Run Equilibrium between Indias's Exports and Imports During 1949-50 - 2004-05. *Applied Econometrics and International Development, 7*(1), 186–196. https://papers.ssrn.com/sol3/papers.cfm?abstract_id=1249742

Van Bergeijk, G. (2011). On the brink of deglobalization: An alternative perspective on the causes of the world trade collapse. *Journal of Economic Literature, 49*(3), 747–749.

Van Hoang, T. H., Gurau, C., Lahiani, A., & Seran, T. L. (2018). Do crises impact capital structure? A chapter of French micro-enterprises. *Small Business Economics, 50*(1), 181–199. doi:10.100711187-017-9899-x

Viviani, J. L. (2009). Export implicit financial performance: The case of French wine companies. *International Food and Agribusiness Management Review, 12*, 23-48.

Wang, K. H., Xiong, D. P., Mirza, N., Shao, X. F., & Yue, X. G. (2021). Does geopolitical risk uncertainty strengthen or depress cash holdings of oil enterprises? Evidence from China. *Pacific-Basin Finance Journal, 66*, 101516. doi:10.1016/j.pacfin.2021.101516

Wang, T., Gao, K., Wen, C., Xiao, Y., & Bingzheng, Y. (2022). Assessing the nexus between fiscal policy, COVID-19, and economic growth. *Environmental Science and Pollution Research International, 29*(43), 1–15. doi:10.100711356-022-20358-z PMID:35484459

Warwick, J. M., & Roshen, F. (2020). *The Global Macroeconomic Impacts of COVID-19: Seven Scenarios*. CAMA Working Paper No. 19/2020. Available at SSRN: https://ssrn.com/abstract=3547729

Wei, P., Jin, C., & Xu, C. (2021). The Influence of the COVID-19 Pandemic on the Imports and Exports in China, Japan, and South Korea. *Frontiers in Public Health, 9*, 682693. Advance online publication. doi:10.3389/fpubh.2021.682693 PMID:34368056

Wiersum, K. F. (1995). 200 Years of Sustainability in Forestry: Lessons from History. *Environmental Management, 19*(3), 321–329.

Wilson, M. E. (2020). Travellers give wings to novel coronavirüs (2019-nCov). *Journal of Travel Medicine*, 1–3.

World Bank Group. (2020). *Economic and social impact of COVID-19*. REF No. 17. Author.

World Bank. (2019). *Why# one south asia?* https://www.worldbank.org/en/programs/south-asia-regional-integration/trade

World Commission on Environment and Development (WCED). (1987). *Our Common Future report*. Retrieved January 19, 2020, from https://sustainabledevelopment.un.org/content/documents/5987our-common-future.pdf

World Data Info. (2021). *Country comparison Bangladesh : Bhutan*. https://www.worlddata.info/country-comparison.php?country1=BGD&country2=BTN

World Health Organization (WHO). (2020a). *State of the world's nursing 2020: investing in education, jobs and leadership*. Retrieved from: https://apps.who.int/iris/rest/bitstreams/1274201/retrieve

World Health Organization (WHO). (2020b). *Home/Newsroom/Fact sheets/Detail/Nursing and midwifery/Key facts*. Retrieved from: https://www.who.int/news-room/fact-sheets/detail/nursing-and-midwifery

World Health Organization (WHO). (2022). *World health statistics 2022: monitoring health for the SDGs, sustainable development goals/Country, WHO region and global statistics*. Retrieved from: https://www.who.int/data/gho/publications/world-health-statistics

World Trade Organization (WTO). (2022). *Merchandise exports by product group*. Retrieved from: https://stats.wto.org/

World trade report 2021. (2021). https://www.wto.org/english/res_e/booksp_e/wtr21_e/00_wtr21_e.pdf

Yujia, S. (2019). Analysis of the Chinese wine market and sales of Spanish wine to China: The case of Torres China. *Esic Market Economics and Business Journal*, *50*(3), 561–579.

About the Contributors

Bartolomé Marco-Lajara (PhD) is Professor at the University of Alicante. His research interests are strategic management and tourism management. He is the author of several books, book chapters and international articles related to teaching methodology and the areas above mentioned. He is a member of the Tourism Research Institute at the University of Alicante since its foundation and the main researcher of a European project 'Next Tourism Generation Alliance' and of the public competitive project for the creation of the Tourist Observatory of the Valencian Community (Spain). He has taken part in others public and private projects, such as the development of the strategic plan of the Alicante province for the period 2010-2020. He is the Assistant Dean of the Economics Faculty at the University of Alicante.

Ahu Coşkun Özer was born in Istanbul in 1981, graduated from Marmara University with a bachelor's degree in 2004, graduated from Marmara University with a master's degree in theory of economics in 2007. In 2012, Dr. Özer graduated from Ph.D. in Istanbul University, started to work as a research assistant in 2011, worked as an assistant professor for 7 years and has been working as an associate professor at the Marmara University Vocational School of Social Sciences in Foreign Trade Program. Her research areas are international economics, foreign trade, economics, business, and entrepreneurship.

Javier Martínez-Falcó (PhD) is Assistant Professor in the Department of Management at the University of Alicante. In the field of research, he focuses his interest on issues related to the Strategic Management of the Company, specifically in the areas of Knowledge Management and Corporate Sustainability of wine companies, on which he has written several publications in the form of articles, book chapters and contributions to conferences. He has also participated in several national research projects and teaches Strategic Management on the ADE, TADE and DADE degree courses.

* * *

Osman Arslan received his MS in Maritime Policy from the University of İstanbul in 2015. He received his Ph.D. in Maritime Transportation Management Engineering from the Piri Reis University in 2021. In 2016 he was hired as the Lecturer by the University of Kocaeli. He still continues as a lecturer. He worked for 5 years as 3rd and 4th captain on ships. His main fields of study are maritime labour force, maritime management, maritime transportation, and ship management.

Ivana Domazet is a Principal Research Fellow at the Institute of Economic Sciences and Professor at the Faculty for Banking, Insurance and Finance, Union University. She teaches courses on Marketing Management, Market Research and Competitiveness Enhancement (postgraduate studies). Her scientific interest refers to: Improving Competitiveness, National Branding, Marketing Research and Strategy, CRM and Strategic Management. She published a numerous papers related to foregoing topics. She is President of Scientific Council at the Institute of Economic Sciences, Vice-president of Board member of the Institute of Economics Sciences, Board member of the Institute of Social Science, member of Serbian Scientific Association of Economists and Serbian Marketing Association.

Tanushree Gupta is currently working as an Assistant Professor in the School of Commerce and Management Sciences at Sandip University Nashik in India. She earned her Master's in Business Administration from Rajasthan Technical University, Kota. She later received her Ph.D. from Amity University Rajasthan, Jaipur. Finance, Microfinance, Stock Market, and International Business are some of her primary academic interests. Furthermore, she has served as ICAI's Co-Principal Investigator and is currently working on a number of other projects. She is a lifetime member of the All India Commerce Association. She is also a review member of the International Journal of Research and Analytical Reviews (Peer reviewed, Referred Journal) and also a member of an editorial board in the International Journal in Management and Social Science (international peer-reviewed journal). Last but not least she has in her credit many research papers/ publications of national and international repute and many of her book chapters have been published in international and Scopus-indexed journals.

Hidayet Zahid Gürbüz is Research Assistant and Doctoral Student at Karabuk University, Turkey. His research topics include cash holdings, financial crises, geopolitical risk, qardh al-hasan and Islamic economy. His research has appeared in journals such as International Journal of Financial Economics and Banking Practices.

Metin Gürler has completed his undergraduate study at İhsan Doğramacı Bilkent University, Department of Economics in 1994. He has completed his master education at Marmara University, Department of Economics. He completed his PhD studies in the same department and worked in various manufacturing and service sectors as a professional and entrepreneur at different levels while he has been working as a consultant in many competitiveness, strategy, innovation and cluster projects. He gave undergraduate and graduate level courses at İstinye University in 2016–2017. He is teaching "International Competitiveness Policy", "Current Issues in Foreign Trade" and "International Retail Management" courses at Medipol University since 2018. Competitiveness of sectors, cities, provinces and nations, clusters, middle income trap, growth economy, economic policy, education, health tourism, health economy and human capital are his main study areas.

Saim Kayadibi graduated from Konya Central Imam Hatip High School in 1991-92. In 1997, he completed his Bachelor Degree in Egypt Al-Azhar University, Faculty of Shariah and Law, Department of Islamic Law. In 1998, he started his MA in Islamic Law at Jordan University. He then went to England for Education in 1999. He started his English language education at Newcastle College. In 2007, he completed his Doctoral Study (M.Phil & PhD) at Durham University, England, with his thesis titled "Istihsan (Juristic Preference): The Forgotten Principle of Islamic Law". Between 2008-2010, he worked as an Assistant Professor at the Akademi Pengajian Islam, Syaria Undang Undang (Faculty of Shariah and Law) in University of Malaya (UM). Between 2010-1011, he worked as Assistant Professor at the Department of Economics, Faculty of Economics and Administrative Sciences, in International Islamic University Malaysia (IIUM), and continued working as Associate Professor at the Department of Economics of the same Faculty between 2011-2019. Simultaneously, he worked as an Associate Professor in Global Islamic Finance University (INCEIF) between 2017-2019 in Malaysia. He received the title of Professor in 2019. He is currently working as Professor in Karabuk University (UNIKA), Faculty of Business Administration, Department of Finance and Banking. He, served as the Chairman of the European Union Halal Standards Committee (CEN/TC 425) between 2013-2016. He worked as the Vice President of the International Relations Department (IAD) of the International Islamic University of Malaysia (IIUM) within the Rectorate for 3 years. He has been the Head of the Finance and Banking Department of the Faculty of Business Administration of Karabuk University since 2020 and served as the Director of the Vocational School of Social Sciences in 2021 and currently working as the Dean of the Faculty of Islamic Sciences at Karabuk University (UNIKA) as of March 2022. In various universities, he has been lecturing Islamic Law; Usul al-Fiqh; Islamic Family Law; Theory of Hukm; Islamic (Participation) Banking and Finance; Interest Free Economic System; Fiqh for Economists; Contracts in Islamic Law; Shariah Oriented Public Policy (Siyasah Shar'iyyah); History of Islamic Economics and Thought and Institutions; Shari'ah Standards for Islamic Financial Institutions; Methodological Foundations of Islamic Economics and Finance. He has many international and national books, articles and papers published in English, Turkish and Arabic languages, and continues scientific researches in the same field.

Reenu Kumari is an Assistant Professor in the Department of Business and Management Studies, Meerut Institute of Engineering and Technology, Meerut, Uttar Pradesh, (India). She has received Ph.D. from the Indian Institute of Technology, Roorkee. She has qualified for UGC NET (JRF) in 2011. She has thirteen-year experience in teaching as well as research also. Her area of specialization is Finance & Accounting. Her area of interest is FDI, Education, Economic Growth, Digitalization, and Trade Openness. She has written and published many research papers in national & international journals and Conferences. She has reviewed various journals including Sage, Emerald, Inderscience, and Elsevier. International Journal of Emerging Markets (IJoEM), Management Research Review (MRR), International Journal of Comparative Management (IJoCM), the Third PAN-IIM World Management Conference, Human Development and Capabilities (JoHDC), the social science Journal (SSJ), Transnational Corporations Review (TCR), South Asian Journal of business studies. She has taken various guest lecturers on research methodology in reputed institutions.

Susobhan Maiti is currently working as an Assistant Professor in the Department of Economics, School of Humanities and Social Science at Jain (Deemed-to-be University). He has published many research papers in the area of industry, efficiency, and productivity in both national and international journals. He received an ICSSR Doctoral fellowship for the year 2017-2018 from the Ministry of Human Resource Development (MHRD) presently the Ministry of Education, Government of India.

Darko Marjanovic is a Research Associate at the Institute of Economic Sciences, Belgrade Serbia. Department: Macroeconomics. His scientific interest refers to: Foreign direct investment, Competitiveness and Public finance. He is author or co-authored more than 50 papers, one monograph and participated in numerous national and international scientific conferences. He is a member of the Scientific Society of Economists of Serbia and reviewer in a scientific journal Economic analysis. He is editor-in-chief of an international publication SEE-6 Economic Outlook that shows an overview of economic trends and short-term forecasts for the seven countries of Southeast Europe: Bosnia and Herzegovina, Croatia, Montenegro, North Macedonia, Romania, Serbia and Slovenia. He was engaged in several projects that he funded

Ministry of Education, Science, and Technological Development of the Republic of Serbia and Provincial Secretariat for Science and Technological Development of the Autonomous Province of Vojvodina.

Luis Antonio Millán-Tudela is Assistant Professor in the Department of Management at the University of Alicante. MBA and Bachelor of Mechanical Engineering, his research focuses on business longevity, and more specifically on the factors that influence the survival of companies. He currently teaches strategic management in the Degree of Business Administration.

Özlem Özsoy has completed his undergraduate study Ege University, Nursing Faculty, Department of Nursing in 1999. She has completed her master education at Ege University, Institute of Health Sciences, Department of Public Health Nursing. She completed her PhD studies in the same department and worked as an academic staff and in various hospitals in health sector as a professional at different levels (last one is a nursing director of a hospital). She gave graduate level courses at İstinye University in 2016–2017. Public health, nursing management, geriatrics, intensive care, pandemics, health education, health tourism, health economy and human capital are her main study areas.

Ali Yavuz Polat is an Associate Professor and Vice-Head at the Department of Economics at Abdullah Gül University, Turkey. He is also co-founder of the experimental economics lab at AGU. Dr. Polat received his Ph.D. degree in Economics from University of Leicester, Business School in the UK and his M.A degree from Johns Hopkins University in the USA. He published scholarly articles in renowned economics and finance journals. Dr. Polat's fields of specialization are financial economics, uncertainty, economic theory, behavioral economics and corporate finance. He has led multiple research projects such as "The analysis of the impact of COVID-19 pandemic in Turkey with a novel economic uncertainty index" funded by The Scientific and Technological Research Council of Turkey (TUBITAK).

Debasish Roy is currently a PhD Research Scholar in Marketing Management at Sikkim University, Gangtok, India with backgrounds in Postgraduate Diploma in Transportation and Logistics Management from Indian Institute of Social Welfare and Business Management (IISWBM) - India's one of the premier Business Schools, and Bachelor of Science (Honors) in Economics from University of Calcutta. His works in the fields of Business and Economics had been published in different international journals and reference books.

Eduardo Sánchez García (PhD) is an assistant professor in the Department of Business Organization at the University of Alicante (Spain). His research is in the field of strategic management of the company. Specifically, he focuses on the study of the territorial agglomeration of companies in clusters and the absorptive capacity, and its influence on the innovative performance and entrepreneurial orientation of companies. He is co-author of several papers presented at conferences, both national and international, as well as several articles and book chapters related to his field of research.

Ashwani Sharma is an assistant professor at the department of Business & Management studies, Meerut Institute of Engineering & Technology, India (MIET). He holds a Ph.D. degree from CCS University Meerut, received MBA Degree from AKTU University Lucknow, and is certified in Digital marketing by Google. He has 12 years experience in teaching and research also. His area of Interest is Digitalisation, Cashless Economy, marketing, economics, new technology and strategies adoption and he is a Coordinator of Research and Development committee at the department of Business & Management studies in MIET. He has published national and international research papers and is also active on digital platforms. He has also copyright ownership of the Design Thinking model for start-ups. He has always tried to expand his research areas according to the scenario.

Disha Sharma is a Finance Faculty, Presently working as an Assistant Professor at Amity Business School, Amity University Chhattisgarh. She has done qualified UGC-NET & SET, did master in three subjects, and completed her Ph.D. from Pt. Ravi Shankar Shukla University, Raipur. She has five years of teaching experience. She has published many papers on her credit of national and international repute. She has also written many book chapters in International and Scopus indexed books. She also has experience as Co-Principal Investigator in ICSSR Project and currently working on many other projects. She has presented various research papers at national and international conferences. She is a lifetime member of the All Indian Commerce Association and All India Accounting Association.

Hasan Tekin is Assistant Professor at Karabuk University, Turkey. He received his Ph.D. in Finance from University of Bradford, UK. His research topics include corporate governance, cash holdings, dividends, financial crises, and leverage. His research has appeared in journals such as Australian Journal of Management, Borsa Istanbul Review, Defence and Peace Economics, Economics and Business Letters, International Journal of Emerging Markets, Journal of Economic Studies, Studies in Economics and Finance.

Patrocinio Zaragoza-Sáez (PhD) is Professor at the University of Alicante (Spain). Her research interests are focused on knowledge management, intellectual capital, sustainable intangible capital and tourism management. She has taken part in several public and private research projects and has published research papers in international journals including Journal of Business Research, Personnel Review, Journal of Knowledge Management, Journal of Intellectual Capital, Knowledge Management Research & Practice, Regional Studies, Current Issues in Tourism, Cornell Hospitality Quarterly, Tourism Management, or International Journal of Contemporary Hospitality Management, among others.

Index

H

I

K

L

M

P

R

S

T

U

W

Ensure Quality Research is Introduced to the Academic Community

Become an Evaluator for IGI Global Authored Book Projects

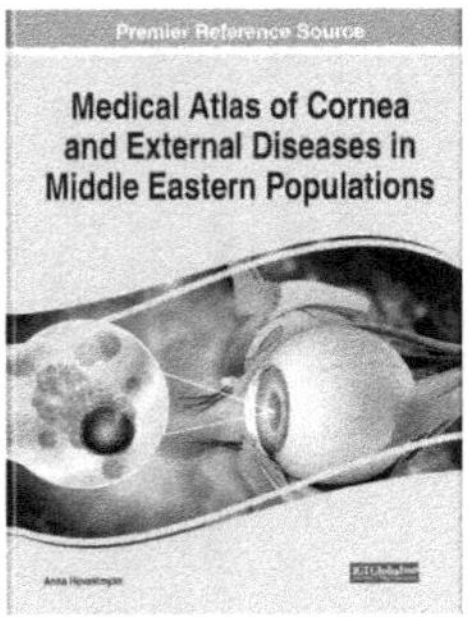

The overall success of an authored book project is dependent on quality and timely manuscript evaluations.

Applications and Inquiries may be sent to:
development@igi-global.com

Applicants must have a doctorate (or equivalent degree) as well as publishing, research, and reviewing experience. Authored Book Evaluators are appointed for one-year terms and are expected to complete at least three evaluations per term. Upon successful completion of this term, evaluators can be considered for an additional term.

If you have a colleague that may be interested in this opportunity, we encourage you to share this information with them.

www.ingramcontent.com/pod-product-compliance
Lightning Source LLC
LaVergne TN
LVHW080642011026
849160LV00014B/1288
* 9 7 8 1 6 6 8 4 5 9 5 4 6 *